The
Antitrust
Revolution

The
Antitrust
Revolution

John E. Kwoka, Jr.
George Washington University

Lawrence J. White
New York University

Scott, Foresman and Company
Glenview, Illinois   Boston   London

To my wife, Anita, and my daughter, Margaret.

J.K.

To the memory of my father, Martin H. White.

L.W.

Acknowledgments

Reprinted by permission of National Petroleum Council, *Petroleum Storage and Transportation Capacities,* 1979.
(pages 29 and 30).

Ad: "Do you need a lawyer?" Reprinted by permission of John Bates (page 136).

Library of Congress Cataloging-in-Publication Data

The Antitrust revolution / (edited by) John E. Kwoka, Jr., Larry J. White.
    p.   cm.
   Includes bibliographies.
   ISBN 0-673-38377-6 : $15.00
    1. Antitrust law—United States.   2.Antitrust law—Economic aspects—United
States. I. Kwoka, John E. II. White, Lawrence J.
KF1652.A53 1989
343.73'072—dc19   88-22067
(347.30372)   CIP

ISBN 0-673-38377-6

123456-MPC-949392919089

Preface

Teaching antitrust economics has always been a fascinating, but frustrating, exercise for students and instructors. The fascination derives from the applicability (if not always the actual application) of microeconomics. The frustration is due to the absence of adequate resource material on antitrust economics. There is, of course, much material on antitrust cases, but almost all of that consists either of casebooks that excerpt from judicial opinions or comprehensive surveys of the history of antitrust. The former provide no economic context or framework, while the latter lack the depth necessary for students to appreciate the economic content of specific cases. Neither focus on recent antitrust, where the role of economics has increased in a remarkable fashion.

This book is the product of that fascination and our frustration with such existing materials. We have asked prominent economists who have been involved in major antitrust proceedings over the past fifteen years to set out the economic analyses that were employed by both sides in these cases. The result of their efforts is a set of case studies, each of which explains how economists think about specific antitrust problems. Moreover, collectively these cases document what may be termed the "antitrust revolution"—the increasingly important role of economics in antitrust since the mid-1970s.

The cases have been carefully selected on the basis of the importance of their economic content, as well as their contribution to the growth of economics in antitrust. We have sought to strike a balance in case selection among the kinds of issues raised and have succeeded, we believe, in covering a very wide range of issues in thirteen cases. It should be noted that the authors complied to an uncommon degree with our requests concerning the focus of their individual case studies and with our requests that they provide a thorough and fair account of the "other" side of the case.

The cases are generally written on the presumption that the reader is familiar with the essentials of basic microeconomics. This permits a reasonably full discussion of the economics of most antitrust issues in these cases. In a number of instances, authors have included more complex material in footnotes or indicated where the reader might go to find more advanced discussion. But it is our belief that the cases can also be understood by a general readership. The book should be useful in undergraduate courses in public policy toward business, in business school courses on public policy, and in law schools, which increasingly provide students with insight into current antitrust policymaking. We also believe that this book can be a valuable supplement in graduate economics courses that cover antitrust. And we have no doubt that antitrust practitioners will be interested in learning how economists go about their analyses of issues in these major cases.

A considerable number of people contributed their comments and suggestions to this undertaking and thereby improved the final product. These include Richard Arnould, William Burnett, Gary Dorman, Thomas Holmes, Patricia Reagan, David Teece, and John Vernon. Special thanks are due to George Lobell and Nancy Siadek of Scott, Foresman and to Eva Skeryjova of George Washington University.

JEK
LJW

Contributors

Gerald W. Brock is Chief of the Common Carrier Bureau of the Federal Communications Commission. He has served as Chief of the Accounting and Audits Division, FCC, and taught economics at Bethel College and the University of Arizona.

Steven R. Cox is Associate Professor of Economics at Arizona State University. He has previously served as Staff Economist at the Federal Trade Commission.

George W. Douglas is President of George W. Douglas and Company, Austin, Texas. He has been Commissioner of the Federal Trade Commission and Associate Professor of Economics at the University of North Carolina at Chapel Hill.

Kenneth G. Elzinga is Professor of Economics at the University of Virginia. He was one of the first Special Economic Assistants in the Antitrust Division of the Department of Justice.

Margaret E. Guerin-Calvert is Senior Economist with Economists, Incorporated. She previously served as Economist and Director of the Analytical Resources Unit, Economic Analysis Group of the Antitrust Division, Department of Justice, and with the Board of Governors of the Federal Reserve System.

George A. Hay is Professor of Law and Economics at Cornell University. He has served as Chief Economist in the Antitrust Division, Department of Justice, and was Associate Professor of Economics at Yale University.

John C. Hilke is a Staff Economist in the Bureau of Economics of the Federal Trade Commission. He previously served as Assistant to the Director of the Bureau of Economics, Federal Trade Commission.

John E. Kwoka, Jr., is Professor of Economics at George Washington University. He has taught at the University of North Carolina at Chapel Hill and at Northwestern University and served as Staff Economist at the Federal Trade Commission and the Antitrust Division, Department of Justice.

Philip B. Nelson is Senior Economist with Economists, Incorporated. He has previously been a Staff Economist and Assistant Director of the Bureau of Economics of the Federal Trade Commission.

Roger G. Noll is Professor of Economics and Director of the Public Policy Program at Stanford University. He has taught at the California Institute of Technology and served as a Senior Fellow at the Brookings Institute.

Bruce M. Owen is President of Economists, Incorporated, and Adjunct Professor of Public Policy Sciences at Duke University. He previously served as the Chief Economist in the Antitrust Division, U.S. Department of Justice.

Lee E. Preston is Professor and Director of the Center for Business and Public Policy at the University of Maryland. He has been Professor in the School of Management at SUNY Buffalo and Professor in the School of Business Administration at the University of California, Berkeley.

F. M. Scherer is Joseph Wharton Professor of Political Economy at Swarthmore College. He has served as the Chief Economist at the Federal Trade Commission and has been Professor of Economics at Northwestern University and the University of Michigan.

Frederick R. Warren-Boulton is Deputy Assistant Attorney General for Economic Analysis. He has been Associate Professor of Economics and a Research Associate in the Center for the Study of American Business at Washington University and is currently Research Associate Professor of Psychology at the American University.

Lawrence J. White is Professor of Economics, Graduate School of Business Administration, New York University, on leave as Board Member of the Federal Home Loan Bank Board. He previously has been Chief Economist in the Antitrust Division, Department of Justice, served as Staff Economist on the Council of Economic Advisers, and taught at Princeton University.

Table of Contents

Introduction

The end of the 1980s marks the one-hundredth anniversary of the Sherman Act and the seventy-fifth anniversary of the Clayton and Federal Trade Commission Acts. Relative to the long history of antitrust under these three fundamental statutes, the current observer is most likely to be impressed by a change of fairly recent vintage. That change consists of the ascendancy of economic analysis in antitrust policy. Economic analysis has come to play a crucial role in determining which kinds of cases are brought by the government, in framing the central issues for adjudication, and in actually establishing the competitive effects of alleged antitrust violations. At the same time, economists themselves have become involved in a major way in antitrust cases, as advisors to companies and the antitrust agencies, as expert witnesses in antitrust cases, and, not infrequently, as critics of judicial opinions.

The reasons for these profound changes are many, but stem from a common theme to which most economists probably subscribe. That theme is the intellectual weakness of the antitrust policy of previous decades. The stringency of merger policy, the antipathy to large companies, the willingness to protect small business came to be known as generally inconsistent with the maximization of economic efficiency. Many economists of earlier times criticized such policies in the usual textbook fashion: they pointed out the inefficiencies that resulted, perhaps offered some quantitative assessment, and concluded that the other objectives being pursued (preservation of fragmented industries, etc.) came at a high cost.

Other economists and antitrust analysts went beyond this "positive" approach and argued strenuously that these other objectives were not meritorious. Rather, they advanced the normative point that economic efficiency should be the principal—some said sole—objective for antitrust policy. Their position led them to careful examination of the microeconomics of various market structures and behavior. They found the received economic wisdom wanting and offered alternative theories and interpretations of economic evidence. They encountered a sympathetic audience, first in much of the business community and subsequently in policy-making agencies and the courts themselves.

In 1965 a leading antitrust scholar with economics training, Donald Turner, was appointed Assistant Attorney General for Antitrust in the Department of Justice. He in turn created the position of Special Assistant for Economics within the Antitrust Division and proceeded to attract outstanding economists from leading universities to help refocus the enforcement agency's attention. Over the next few

1

years, the Economic Policy Office was established within the Antitrust Division with a succession of prominent economists appointed as its head. During the same time, the Federal Trade Commission instituted the practice of selecting leading academic economists as directors of its Bureau of Economics to serve in the capacity of chief economist advising the commissioners on matters of policy.

The institutionalization of economists within the two antitrust agencies signaled the growing importance attributed to economics itself. The ripple effect was substantial. Academic research on questions of policy was assured an interested audience. Antitrust lawyers, both within the agencies and in the private bar, were confronted with the need to provide more of an economically sound basis for their positions, instead of relying exclusively on legal precedents.

The next logical step in this process was the rise of economists themselves to decision-making positions, rather than just advisory, in the antitrust agencies. Economists James Miller and George Douglas served as Commissioners of the FTC, and William Baxter—a lawyer well versed in economics—was the Reagan administration's first Assistant Attorney General for Antitrust in the Department of Justice. The presence of each man acted as milestone events in the revolution of antitrust policy. Ironically, the particular focus to their economics, with its single-minded emphasis on efficiency, elicited as much criticism as had the more populist antitrust policy of the preceding decades. The criticism of both periods reflected the absence of consensus regarding the legislative objectives of antitrust policy.

The dramatic changes in antitrust over this period are exemplified by many comparisons that can be drawn between the 1960s and the 1980s. Most students of antitrust are led at some time through twenty- and thirty-year-old cases that endorsed the populist objective of protecting small business or that prohibited mergers between small companies. By contrast, in this decade, megamergers of petroleum companies have routinely been approved (with only minor modifications) by the Federal Trade Commission, and steel and airline mergers have won Justice Department approval (again with only minor modifications) despite large market shares. All of these recent decisions are said to be based on new economic learning about market structure and competitive effects, although other observers—including a number of economists—disagree.

Similar arguments have been made in the area of firm conduct. Whereas earlier Supreme Court cases held that virtually any tampering with market price was per se illegal, by the late 1970s the Court admitted the possibility of competitive justifications even for price fixing by horizontal competitors. In the area of predatory pricing, the traditional view that price cuts injuring competitors were evidence of predation gave way to the much more permissive view toward dominant firm actions in recent cases. On the other hand, economics has played a more active role in developing novel FTC cases involving brand proliferation as an entry-deterring device and practices that facilitate above-competitive pricing.

Perhaps no areas have undergone more fundamental revision than vertical mergers, vertical pricing practices, and nonprice vertical restraints. In contrast to the hostility toward most vertical arrangements through the mid 1970s, the antitrust agencies hardly ever challenge vertical mergers, and vertical pricing practices are also rarely, if ever, challenged. Recent court decisions have accomplished much the same for nonprice vertical restraints. These new judicial and enforcement attitudes reflect changing economic views of structural and nonstructural relationships between vertically related companies.

Other traditional concerns of antitrust have virtually disappeared from the agenda of the agencies enforcing the law and from the courts. Price discrimination, with its generally ambiguous economic effects, has not been challenged in recent years, though Congress has sought to prevent the Department of Justice and the Federal Trade Commission from ignoring it altogether. Cases in which mergers eliminate potential competitors are now rarely pursued, partly because the judicial standard of proof is so high and partly because of the increasingly common view that potential entrants are numerous. Conglomerate mergers, previously challenged on potential competition grounds or on the grounds of sheer size of the resulting combine, are no longer even the subject of serious debate in the antitrust community.

Whether a Rip Van Winkle of antitrust—who fell asleep in the 1960s and awoke twenty years later—would approve of all these changes depends in part on his perspective. Those who held the view that the antitrust laws were intended to prohibit large companies because of their political and social power, and not only their market power, would be distressed to find that current antitrust ignores these concerns. Those who felt that the rigorous nature—if sometimes excessive zeal—of antitrust policy in the 1950s and 1960s at least provided certainty might find the increasing use of rule-of-reason analysis on balance counterproductive. Some economists have even been concerned over the rapid ascendancy of purely economic objectives in antitrust without explicit legislative approval.

Moreover, and perhaps most importantly, the economics that has gained ascendancy in antitrust in the 1980s—that loosely associated with the Chicago school—by no means represents the unanimous view of economists. Many economists who disapprove of policy of twenty years ago have also dissented from at least some aspects of current policy. Many—perhaps most—economists continue to believe that structure-performance studies can help to reveal real-world effects of concentration and that, properly interpreted, the findings should still play a role in policy formulation. Many economists continue to believe that entry by new firms into markets is generally not as free and easy as others would contend. And some significant fraction of economists continue to believe that predation by dominant firms, or its close cousin, disciplining behavior, by dominant firms does occur.

Nevertheless, most economists undoubtedly find much with which to agree in the newer approach to antitrust. Most would endorse the 1982 Merger Guidelines (or the modest 1984 revision) rather than the original version issued in 1968. Most would applaud the Supreme Court decisions in *General Dynamics* that acknowledged for the first time explicitly that "other pertinent factors" might outweigh the high concentration resulting from an acquisition, or the *GTE Sylvania* decision, which explicitly overturned a previous mistaken ruling on non-price vertical restraints.

Economists are now (perhaps as always) divided on whether to go farther or whether too much distance has already been traversed. Many have noted the decline in government antitrust suits, most markedly those outside of hard-core price-fixing. Whereas some view this with approval, others regard this as proof that economics has led to permissiveness by the antitrust agencies. Some see the growing role for rule of reason as the logical outcome of economic ambiguity about market structure and conduct, while others see this as a device capable of explaining away almost anything. Some point to newer theories of predation or disadvantaging rivals and better empirical studies of market concentration as putting some traditional concerns on sound footing. Others, however, dismiss these as flawed or misinterpreted.

Perhaps most fundamentally, there still is no consensus concerning the purposes of antitrust. It is, indeed, difficult to evaluate the success of new (or old) antitrust without some relatively clear statement of objectives. Moreover, this ambiguity simultaneously implies that at some future time other practitioners of antitrust may be convinced of quite different purposes for antitrust. Indeed, the growth of private antitrust suits, suits by state attorneys general, and the promulgation of separate antitrust guidelines by the states are indicative of dissatisfaction with current federal antitrust enforcement.

Thus, the shape of future antitrust policy and the role of economics in that policy cannot be predicted with certainty. Economics has made some considerable advances in its ability to analyze certain effects of structural changes and behavior patterns in markets, and those advances in understanding cannot be reversed. But to the extent that policy based on those advances requires sympathetic individuals in the enforcement agencies, preservation is not ensured.

Nonetheless, it is probably safe to say that economics has narrowed the bounds of what may be thought of as rational, acceptable antitrust policy. That is, it is altogether unlikely that future administrations or antitrust enforcement chiefs would revert to the policies of the 1950s and 1960s. Any "ratcheting back" from current emphases will almost certainly stop far short of a policy that attacks mergers of small firms, prohibits competitive actions by large firms, or challenges all vertical restraints and mergers. The essence of the revolution in antitrust wrought by economics is likely to be permanent. This book should be seen as a testament and documentation of the economic revolution that has overtaken antitrust policy.

1

Part

Horizontal Structure

The Economic and Legal Context of Horizontal Structure

The economic theory of horizontal structure of firms in a market falls logically into two categories: pure monopoly or a dominant firm with market power, and oligopoly, in which a comparative handful of leading firms may be able explicitly or implicitly to coordinate their behavior and jointly achieve market power. Antitrust concerns about horizontal structure have largely focused on the same two areas. Section 2 of the Sherman Act is concerned with *monopolization,* which is usually given a joint behavioral and structural interpretation. Section 7 of the Clayton Act forbids mergers and acquisitions, the effects of which "may be substantially to lessen competition, or to tend to create a monopoly."

Three of the four cases in this section discuss mergers and antitrust concerns about oligopolistic coordination; the fourth discusses a joint venture among oligopolists. None directly addresses questions of pure monopoly, but the monopoly model is clearly at the heart of any analysis involving market power, and so we first turn our attention to monopoly.

Monopoly

Economic Theory

The microeconomic theory of monopoly is straightforward: a single firm, selling a product for which there are no good substitutes and in which entry by other sellers is not likely, will be able to charge a higher price (at a reduced sales volume) and earn higher profits than would an otherwise similar competitive group of sellers.[1] Most economists would agree that the social loss from this pricing behavior is related to the output reduction: the deadweight loss triangle created by the foregone net value received by consumers because of the reduced output. Some economists, and most politicians, would also count the monopolist's excess profits (above competitive levels) as social loss, while traditional theory considers these excess profits as neutral transfers from consumers to the owners of the monopoly enterprise. Some would claim that at least part of the monopolist's potential excess profits are likely to be dissipated either through socially wasteful efforts to defend the monopoly[2] or through wasteful inefficiency that arises because of the absence of competitive pressures.[3]

Instances of pure monopoly in the U.S. economy can be commonly found, although collectively they account for only a modest fraction of aggregate economic activity. Examples include local telephone, electricity, natural gas, water, and cable television distribution; postal service for first class and bulk mail; the single hardware store, pharmacy, or gasoline station in an isolated crossroads town; and firms producing unique products protected by patents (e.g., those patented pharmaceuticals for which there are no good substitutes).

It is a short leap from the single seller to a dominant firm that has a fringe of smaller competitors. Though technically not a monopoly, this dominant firm is also likely to be able to exercise and enjoy the fruits of market power. The extent of this enjoyment will depend on the elasticity of demand, the elasticity of supply by the fringe, and the ease or difficulty of entry.[4] Many economists would characterize Alcoa in aluminum, IBM in mainframe computers, Xerox in photocopy machines, and Kodak in cameras and film as dominant firms that fit this model, at least for some time periods.

Monopoly can arise in three basic ways. Economies of scale, interacting with the size of the market, may dictate that only one firm can efficiently serve the market. In essence, the technology of production may be such that average costs decline over the entire range that the market demand encompasses, so that lowest costs are achieved when only one seller serves the market. (Note that this is a market-size-dependent concept; for a given technology, small markets may be served by a monopolist, whereas larger markets may be more competitive. Airline city-pair markets appear to be a good example of this.) Thus the local telephone and other services mentioned appear to be instances of technology-driven monopoly, as is the single retailer in the isolated crossroads town. Whether, and the extent to which, market power can be exercised by these structural monopolies is dependent on the elasticity of demand and the ease of potential entry.

The second path to monopoly is through a merger of all the producers to yield a single entity or a dominant entity. Such consolidations were common during the merger wave of 1887–1904, which produced monopolies or dominant firms in petroleum (Standard Oil), steel (U.S.

Steel), tin cans (American Can), cigarettes (American Tobacco), explosives (DuPont), cameras and films (Kodak), and over sixty other major industries.[5]

The third way to monopoly is through government regulation and restriction. Airline routes between some city pairs prior to the late 1970s, taxicab franchises in some cities, intrastate long distance telephone service in some states, and the U.S. Postal Service's monopoly on first class and bulk mailing are examples. Patents are a special case. A government-granted patent in essence creates a property right for an idea, which prevents others from copying the idea and thereby free riding without the permission of the idea's originator. The justification for the patent system is that it encourages invention by allowing investors to exploit their inventions and earn returns on their investments, which free-riding would otherwise prevent or discourage.[6] Most patents probably offer their holders little in the way of monopoly rents, since the inventions frequently have close substitutes. But some inventions (e.g., Polaroid's early patents on self-developing film, Xerox's early patents covering photocopying, pharmaceutical companies' patents on unique drugs) do involve unique products and create true monopolies. Many economists would argue, however, that the social costs of the market power exercised by these infrequent monopolies are probably a worthwhile price to pay for the incentives for invention and innovation created by a patent system.

Antitrust

Government economic regulation (through formal commissions or other bodies) and government ownership have been the most frequent way in which public policy in the United States has tried to deal with monopoly. But antitrust law, from its beginnings in 1890, has also tried to address monopoly problems. Section 2 of the Sherman Act creates a felony offense for "every person who shall monopolize, or attempt to monopolize, or combine or conspire with any other person or persons, to monopolize . . ."

The antitrust approach, however, has not been especially successful. In the *Standard Oil*[7] and *American Tobacco*[8] cases of 1911, the Supreme Court declared that a "rule of reason" should apply to monopolization cases: the courts must look beyond just structural conditions and consider also behavior and intent, as well as the efficiencies of size (economies of scale and scope). As a consequence, government cases alleging monopolization have been infrequent, victories have been rare, and *structural remedies*—i.e., breaking up a monopoly into two or more competitive firms—rarer still.[9] The last major horizontal monopolization case brought by the U.S. Department of Justice was in 1969[10]—the *IBM* case[11]—and the Department dropped the case in 1982. The Federal Trade Commission brought joint monopolization cases against a group of breakfast cereal manufacturers[12] and a group of integrated petroleum companies[13] in the early 1970s, but both actions were dropped by the agency in the early 1980s. Private antitrust suits alleging monopolization are more common, but they almost always involve heavy doses of alleged predatory behavior (see Part II) and intent, and private plaintiffs are not able to obtain structural relief from the courts.[14]

In sum, antitrust has not played a large role in dealing with monopoly market structures through horizontal structural relief. In the absence of major changes in judicial interpretations of Sherman Section 2 and in enforcement policies by the two antitrust enforcement agencies, this characterization will continue to hold true.

Oligopoly

Economic Theory

If we leave the world of monopoly or of the dominant firm, but if we retain the assumption of a relatively small number of sellers in the market, we are in the world of oligopoly. The essence of the oligopoly market structure is that the number of sellers is few enough so that each seller is aware of the identities of its rivals and recognizes that its output and price decision affect their decisions (and that the others probably have similar perceptions). This condition is frequently described as *conjectural interdependence.*

Because of this mutual awareness among oligopolists, there is no definitive solution or outcome to an oligopolistic market structure (unlike the outcomes that can be predicted for monopoly and pure competition). Instead, additional assumptions about the oligopolists' states of mind or behavior must be made before a solution can be predicted. For example, the Cournot assumption—that each firm assumes that its rivals will hold their outputs constant and only adjust their prices in response to any price and quantity changes by that firm—is one that is frequently made by economists, largely because of the mathematical tractability that it provides to oligopoly models and because the results of these models frequently comport with economists' intuitions about outcomes in oligopoly markets. Other assumptions, of course, can and have been made about oligopoly behavior, with differing consequences for model outcomes.

One set of assumptions that is intuitively quite appealing to many economists is that a group of oligopolists will jointly try to coordinate their behavior so as to achieve the monopoly market outcome (which yields the largest aggregate profits), but that they individually may be tempted to "cheat" on any common agreement or understanding (explicit or implicit) for their own extra gain and at the expense of the others.[15] This focuses attention on the structural conditions that would make coordination among oligopolists, and mutual policing of any understanding among them, easier or more difficult. These conditions include the number of sellers and their relative sizes (i.e., seller concentration), since coordination is likely to be easier among a few sellers with large market shares; conditions of entry and of expansion by small firms in the market, since easy entry can eliminate the ability of even a monopolist to exercise market power; the nature of the product, since pricing coordination and policing among oligopolists may be easier for simple products with comparatively few quality dimensions or variations; the number and relative sizes of buyers, since a few large buyers may be able to shop around and induce price cutting by the oligopolists; the sociology and history of the industry; and the legal rules—antitrust—that may make easier or more difficult the formal or informal communications among sellers that aid them in reaching and policing understandings.

Antitrust

Antitrust law has had three approaches to oligopoly market structures. First, as will be discussed in Part 2, practices and arrangements that facilitate coordination among sellers have been attacked. Second, in a handful of cases (e.g., the cereals and petroleum cases mentioned above) oligopolistic market structures have been attacked directly, sometimes under the rubric of *joint monopoly.* And third, under Section 7 of the Clayton Act, mergers that would increase concentration and thereby increase the likelihood of coordinated behavior among oligopolists have been challenged and stopped.

Though the Clayton Act was passed in 1914, Section 7 remained largely a dead letter until 1950, because of an unintended loophole in the original act.[16] In the latter year, however, the Celler-Kefauver Act closed the loophole, and Section 7 gained life. A series of government challenges to mergers in the 1950s and 1960s yielded a set of important Supreme Court decisions, beginning with *Brown Shoe* in 1962,[17] which indicated that the Court was ready to prohibit both horizontal mergers and vertical mergers (i.e., between a customer and a supplier) between firms with even relatively modest market shares and even in industries with relatively easy entry. The Court expressed concern about competition[18] but also opined that Congress had intended to halt mergers so as to preserve market structures with large numbers of firms, even at the sacrifice of some efficiency that might be achieved by a merger. Though the Court backed off somewhat from this quite tough, semi-populist position in a few merger decisions in the 1970s,[19] the body of antitrust law remains basically hostile to mergers between firms with significant market shares, where entry is not obviously easy.

Flushed by the favorable Supreme Court decisions of the 1960s, the Department of Justice's Antitrust Division developed a set of Merger Guidelines in 1968. The Guidelines indicated the circumstances (described primarily in terms of four-seller concentration ratios and the sales shares of the merging firms) in which the DOJ would be likely to challenge mergers, so that the private antitrust bar could provide better guidance to their clients.

These Guidelines were largely scrapped and a new set issued in June 1982.[20] Economists at the DOJ played a large role in the development of the new Guidelines, and the Assistant Attorney General for Antitrust at the time (William Baxter) was well versed in and sympathetic to the teachings of microeconomics. Since the new Merger Guidelines shaped most of the economic arguments that were developed in three of the four cases described in this section, we next turn to a more detailed discussion of those Guidelines.

The DOJ Merger Guidelines

The 1982 Merger Guidelines[21] start from the fundamental premise that the antimerger provisions of the Clayton Act are intended to prevent the exercise or enhancement of market power that might arise as a consequence of a merger.[22] They take as their analytical base the microeconomics monopoly and oligopoly propositions briefly discussed above.

Proceeding from this analytical base, the Guidelines address five crucial issues: the delineation of relevant markets for merger analysis, so as to determine whether the merger partners compete with each other and what their (and other relevant sellers') market shares are; the level of seller concentration in a relevant market that should raise antitrust concern about a merger; the extent and role of entry into the market; other characteristics of market structure that might make coordinated behavior among sellers easier or more difficult; and the extent to which cost savings and efficiencies that arise from the merger should be allowed as a defense to a merger that appears to increase the likelihood of the exercise of market power. Each will be discussed in turn.[23]

Market Definition

Since the prevention or inhibition of the exercise of market power is the goal of merger enforcement, the Guidelines define a market as a product (or clump of products) sold by a group of sellers who, if they acted in concert, could raise their prices by a significant amount for a significant period of time. The Guidelines indicate that a 5-percent increase sustained for one year is the likely value that the DOJ will use in its market definition determinations. The smallest group of sellers who could exercise market power is generally selected as the relevant market for analysis, though larger groups would also satisfy the definition of a market. These principles apply to the determination of product markets as well as geographic markets.

In essence, the Guidelines use a "worst-case scenario" for defining a market: they assume that a merger could cause all the relevant sellers to try to coordinate their behavior; the Guidelines then generally search for the smallest group that might succeed, because its buyers would not switch away to sellers of other products and/or sellers located in other geographic areas in sufficient quantities so as to spoil the profitability of and thus thwart the price increase.

The market definition paradigm largely focuses on groups of sellers (rather than buyers), since it is sellers who might exercise market power. But, if a group of sellers could practice price discrimination and raise prices significantly for a group of customers in a specific geographic area, that group of customers (beyond some de minimus size threshold) should also be treated as a market.

Seller Concentration

With the market boundaries determined (and the presence of the two merger partners in that market ascertained), the focus turns to a post-merger standard of seller concentration that should trigger antitrust concern. The Guidelines use the Herfindahl-Hirschman Index (HHI) for this measurement. The HHI for a market is computed by summing the squared market shares of all of the sellers in the market. Thus, an atomistic market would have an HHI very close to zero; a pure monopoly would have an HHI of 10,000 ($100^2 = 10,000$); and a duopoly consisting of, for example, two firms with 70-percent and 30-percent market shares, respectively, would have an HHI of 5800 ($70^2 + 30^2 = 5800$).

The Guidelines specify DOJ's two decision points: for a market with a post-merger HHI below 1000, the merger will ordinarily not be challenged; for a market with a post-merger HHI above 1800 and the merger itself causing an increase in the HHI of 100 or more, the merger is likely to be challenged (unless entry is easy or other market characteristics make coordinated behavior unlikely). For mergers in between, further analysis of entry conditions and other market characteristics is necessary before a challenge decision is made.[24]

Entry

Since easy entry by new firms could thwart efforts to exercise market power by sellers even in highly concentrated markets, the Merger Guidelines recognize entry as an important component of merger analysis. They indicate that the relevant concept of entry is whether outside firms would be likely to enter a market within two years in response to a significant price increase. But they offer no other quantification of ease or difficulty of entry nor a specific indication of exactly how such a determination should be used in conjunction with the HHI measurement.

Other Market Characteristics

The Guidelines discuss three other market characteristics that oligopoly theory recognizes as important determinants of the ability of sellers to coordinate their behavior: the level of concentration on the buyers' side of the market; the degree of complexity in the quality and service dimensions of the product or products at issue; and the antitrust history of the sellers in the relevant market. Again, the Guidelines offer no quantification and no specific guidance as to what weights these factors should be given.

Cost Savings and Efficiencies

In principle, cost efficiencies achieved by a merger could yield social savings that would more than compensate for the social loss created by the exercise of market power.[25] A continuing dilemma of antitrust policy is whether such savings should be allowed to count as an offset and thus permit an otherwise objectionable merger to be completed.

The 1982 version of the Merger Guidelines took a skeptical view of the promises of cost savings by merger partners.[26] Such efficiencies are easy to promise; they are often difficult to achieve in practice. Also, to the extent that the merger under consideration could lead to coordinated behavior and the exercise of market power over the entire range of sellers, the social loss from this market-wide exercise of market power—not just from the merged entity—would have to be offset by the cost efficiencies created by the merger. The 1984 revision to the Guidelines, however, took a more tolerant view of such promises.

The Cases

The cases in this section all pertain to mergers or joint ventures in industries that could be characterized (at least by some) as concentrated. Hence, they were reviewed by the relevant enforcement agencies, and economic analyses were important in the disputes (or dispute resolutions) that followed.

In the first chapter, F. M. Scherer provides a discussion of Mobil's attempt to acquire Marathon Oil in 1981. Marathon's management resisted and took Mobil to court on antitrust grounds, and the Federal Trade Commission also became involved. As Scherer indicates, the delineation of geographic markets was crucial to the case.

John Kwoka analyzes the 1983 joint venture of General Motors and Toyota and the FTC's decision in this case. Though less of a threat to competition than a complete merger, joint ventures among actual or potential competitors can nevertheless create opportunities for coordinated behavior. Kwoka demonstrates the insightful application of oligopoly theory and the Merger Guidelines to this joint venture.

In early 1986 the Coca-Cola Company tried to acquire the Dr Pepper Company. The FTC's challenge to that merger is described by Lawrence White. As he indicates, the full range of Merger Guidelines propositions were brought to bear in this case.

The deregulation of the airlines has been accompanied by a wave of mergers in that industry. George Douglas discusses the major merger of Eastern and Texas Air and the U.S. Department of Transportation's decision in that case. The role of potential entry and Texas Air's willingness to sell two crucial routes to an entrant in markets where competition might have been diminished were important to this case.

These four studies were written by economists who participated in these important antitrust cases, and show the useful organizational and analytical role that microeconomics played.

Notes

1. A similar argument applies to monopsony: a single buyer in a market, who may be able to buy at a lower price than if competition among buyers prevailed.

2. See Posner (1975).
3. See Leibenstein (1966).
4. See Landes and Posner (1981).
5. See Markham (1955), Nelson (1959), and Scherer (1980, ch. 4).
6. The patent system also encourages public disclosure of the technology to implement the idea.
7. *United States* v. *Standard Oil Co. of New Jersey et al.,* 221 U.S. 1 (1911).
8. *United States* v. *American Tobacco Co.,* 221 U.S. 106 (1911).
9. A survey can be found in Scherer (1980, ch. 20).
10. The AT&T suit discussed by Noll and Owens in a separate chapter in this book was largely a case involving vertical structural relief.
11. *United States* v. *International Business Machines Corporation,* complaint filed January 17, 1969.
12. *In the matter of Kellogg Co. et al.,* docket no. 8883, complaint filed January 24, 1972.
13. *In the matter of Exxon Corporation et al.,* docket no. 8934, complaint filed January 24, 1973.
14. See *International Telephone & Telegraph Corp.* v. *General Telephone & Electronics Corp. et al.,* 518 F. 2d 913 (1975).
15. Theoretical support for these arguments, and the propositions that follow, can be found in Chamberlin (1933), Fellner (1949), Bain (1956), and Stigler (1964). See also Scherer (1980).
16. The 1914 Act forbade mergers that were effected through one company's purchase of the stock of another. Merger candidates quickly realized that they could easily evade this restriction through the one company's purchase of the underlying assets of the other.
17. *Brown Shoe Co.* v. *United States,* 370 U.S. 294 (1962).
18. It is not clear, however, whether the Supreme Court's opinion writers understood the oligopoly market power model outlined above.
19. See *United States* v. *General Dynamics Corp. et al.,* 415 U.S. 486 (1974); and *United States* v. *Marine Bancorporation et al.,* 418 U.S. 602 (1974).
20. The 1982 Guidelines were modified modestly in 1984.
21. Unless otherwise indicated, the discussion below refers to the 1982 Guidelines.
22. The Merger Guidelines thus reject a populist approach that the pure sizes of the merging entities should be a consideration in the evaluation of a merger.
23. More discussion of the specifics of the Merger Guidelines and their application can be found in Fox (1982), Werden (1983), White (1985), and White (1987).
24. There are two ways of translating the HHI decision points of 1000 and 1800 into more familiar terms. An HHI of 1000 would be yielded by a market with 10 equal size firms each having a 10 percent market share; an HHI of 1800 would be yielded by a market with between five and six equal size firms. Alternatively, since most markets do not have equal size firms, the two decision points translate empirically (based on

simple correlations) to four-firm concentration ratios of roughly 50 percent and 70 percent, respectively. See Kwoka (1985).

25. See Williamson (1968).
26. This skeptical approach is also consistent with the Supreme Court's interpretation of Congress's intent in passing Section 7 of the Clayton Act. See *Brown Shoe Co.* v. *United States,* 370 U.S. 294 (1962).

References

Bain, Joe S. *Barriers to New Entry.* Cambridge, Mass.: Harvard University Press, 1956.

Chamberlin, Edward H. *The Theory of Monopolistic Competition.* Cambridge, Mass.: Harvard University Press, 1933.

Fellner, William J. *Competition Among the Few.* New York: Knopf, 1949.

Fox, Eleanor M. "The New Merger Guidelines—A Blueprint for Microeconomic Analysis." *Antitrust Bulletin* 27 (Fall 1982): 519–591.

Kwoka, John E., Jr. "The Herfindahl Index in Theory and Practice." *Antitrust Bulletin* 30 (Winter 1985): 915–947.

Landes, William M., and Richard A. Posner. "Market Power in Antitrust Cases." *Harvard Law Review* 94 (1981): 937–996.

Leibenstein, Harvey. "Allocative Efficiency vs. X-Efficiency." *American Economic Review* 56 (June 1966): 392–415.

Markham, Jesse W. "Summary Evidence and Findings on Mergers." In *Business Concentration and Price Policy,* 141–212. Princeton: Princeton University Press, 1955.

Nelson, Ralph L. *Merger Movements in American Industry, 1895–1956.* Princeton: Princeton University Press, 1959.

Posner, Richard A. "The Social Costs of Monopoly and Regulation." *Journal of Political Economy* 83 (August 1975): 807–827.

Scherer, F. M. *Industrial Market Structure and Economic Performance.* 2d ed. Chicago: Rand McNally, 1980.

Stigler, George J. "A Theory of Oligopoly." *Journal of Political Economy* 72 (February 1964): 55–69.

Werden, Gregory. "Market Delineation and the Justice Department's Merger Guidelines." *Duke Law Journal* (1983): 514–579.

White, Lawrence J. "Antitrust and Video Markets: The Merger of Showtime and the Movie Channel as a Case Study." In *Video Media Competition: Regulation, Economics, and Technology,* edited by Eli M. Noam, 338–363. New York: Columbia University Press, 1985.

White, Lawrence J. "Antitrust and Merger Policy: A Review and Critique." *Journal of Economic Perspectives* 1 (Fall 1987): 13–22.

Williamson, Oliver E. "Economies as an Antitrust Defense: The Welfare Trade-offs." *American Economic Review* 58 (March 1968): 18–36.

Merger in the Petroleum Industry: The *Mobil-Marathon* Case

F. M. Scherer

Introduction

On October 30, 1981, the Mobil Corporation announced a tender offer
to purchase common stock shares sufficient to obtain control of the
Marathon Oil Company. The tender offer was to proceed in two stages.
Up to 40 million of Marathon's 60.1 million shares were to be purchased for $85 each cash, and if at least 30 million shares were obtained,
the remaining shares would be traded for debentures worth $85 each.
At the time of the offer, Mobil had already purchased 178,000 Marathon shares.

Marathon's directors were not eager to see their company acquired,
especially by Mobil. They believed Marathon had performed well; they
saw no why Mobil would manage the company better than it had
been managed, and they concluded that the takeover was not in the interest of Marathon stockholders. They also feared that following a
merger, Mobil would close or cut back sharply Marathon's headquar-
ters operations, which accounted for 10 percent of total employment in
the company's Findlay, Ohio, home. As part of an effort to thwart the
takeover, Marathon filed on November 1 an antitrust suit charging that
the merger would lessen competition in diverse crude oil, refined product, and oil transportation markets.[1]

The Adversaries

Mobil Corporation was at the time the second largest United States industrial corporation in terms of sales. Originally incorporated in 1882
as the Standard Oil Company of New York, it was broken off from the
Standard Oil "trust" following a 1911 antitrust judgment. It expanded
out of its original New York–New England home territory to become

---

F. M. Scherer consulted and testified for Marathon Oil in this case.

the fourth largest refiner of petroleum products in the United States by 1980, originating 6.3 percent of total U.S. motor gasoline sales. It also established a strong international presence, among other things joining the ARAMCO Saudi Arabian crude oil franchise in 1947. With mergers and other changes, its name evolved to Socony-Vacuum (Socony stood for *Standard Oil Co.* of *NY*) in 1931, Socony-Mobil in 1955, and simply Mobil in 1966.

Marathon was also a divested fragment of the Standard Oil trust. It began in 1887 as the Ohio Oil Co., exploiting crude oil discoveries in the Findlay, Ohio, area. After divestiture, it moved into refining and crude oil operations in other parts of the United States and later other nations. Its name was changed to Marathon Oil in 1962. In 1980, it was the 39th-largest U.S. industrial corporation ranked by sales and the ninth-largest domestic petroleum refiner, with a 3.7 percent share of nationwide gasoline sales.

Why Mobil Sought Marathon

Despite its history and size, Mobil had a problem. With sharp increases in the "taxes" levied by Saudi Arabia on the oil ARAMCO members shipped, Mobil had been effectively expropriated from its richest crude oil reserves, receiving little more than a modest per-barrel service fee. And in its home market, Mobil was relatively crude-poor. Its U.S. refineries had a capacity to process 860,000 barrels of oil per day, but its U.S. crude oil reserves were sufficient to cover only 37 percent of that volume. Its proven domestic crude reserves had an expected life of only 6.5 years at 1980 production levels. Mobil was anxious to acquire additional domestic crude oil reserves that would be safe against supply interruptions—for example, a crisis in the Middle East. In 1979 and 1980, it acquired two medium-size domestic crude oil producing companies. During the summer of 1981 it made an $8.8 billion bid for Conoco, Inc., but lost out to the du Pont Company. Marathon was the next step in what came to be called its search for oil "on the floor of the New York Stock Exchange."

Marathon was in a quite different position. Excluding a new Louisiana refinery designed to process imported "sour" (high sulfur) crude, its 168,000 barrels per day of North American crude oil production satisfied (mostly through "swaps" with other crude-holders) half of its refineries' needs. Marathon's "crown jewel" was a 49-percent interest in the Yates field of West Texas, which regularly produced 125,000 barrels per day (for all owners, not merely Marathon) and was believed able to sustain a daily output of 150,000 barrels.[2] Discovered with a 1926 "gusher," Yates was the United States second-largest oil reservoir (after

Prudhoe Bay). Its deposits, located only 2000 feet beneath the earth's surface, had already yielded 900 million barrels, and Marathon's conservatively rated share of the remaining reserves amounted to at least a billion barrels—enough to support 1981 production levels for another 44 years. Marathon also obtained 35,000 barrels of oil daily from deposits in the Big Horn Basin of Wyoming, and 24,000 barrels per day from the Cook Inlet in Alaska, and had additional interests in other parts of the United States and in Canada, the North Sea, Libya, Abu Dabi, and Nigeria.

At the time of Mobil's tender offer for Marathon, crude oil was selling for approximately $35 per (42-gallon) barrel in the United States. An internal study by Mobil's finance staff estimated the value of Marathon's domestic crude oil reserves alone (excluding refineries, pipelines, and other facilities) to be "as high as $180" per share of outstanding Marathon common stock, assuming a continuation of existing world supply and demand conditions.[3] During 1981, before Mobil announced its acquisition offer, Marathon's shares had traded on the New York Stock Exchange in the range of $45 to $80 per share. On the day before Mobil's announcement, Marathon's stock closed at $63.75. Thus, with its $85 per share offer, Mobil sought to augment its crude oil reserves at bargain prices. Marathon's management and employees, however, wanted no part of the bargain, so the company filed suit on antitrust grounds to enjoin Mobil from consummating its offer. A preliminary injunction hearing commenced before the Federal District Court in Cleveland, Ohio, on November 17, 1981, less than three weeks after Mobil's tender offer announcement.

The Market Definition Question

The Celler-Kefauver Act of 1950, which amended the Clayton Antitrust Act of 1914, states that no corporation engaged in commerce shall acquire the stock or assets of another such corporation "where in any line of commerce in any section of the country, the effect of such acquisition may be substantially to lessen competition, or to tend to create a monopoly."

From the statutory language and subsequent Supreme Court interpretations, the typical horizontal merger case turns on two factual points:

1. The boundaries of the relevant market, that is, the line of commerce and section of the country; and
2. Whether the merger sufficiently changes the relevant market's structure so that competition is substantially lessened.

Relevant market questions are in turn divided into two parts: what the product market is, and what geographic bounds that market should encompass. Although other criteria also come into play, Supreme Court decisions interpreting the Celler-Kefauver Act have emphasized the magnitude of the market shares merged in determining whether a merger threatened "substantially to lessen competition." In 1968, the U.S. Department of Justice published a set of Merger Guidelines indicating the concentration changes that would cause the Department under normal circumstances to challenge a merger as anticompetitive.[4] For markets with four-firm concentration ratios below 75 percent—i.e., in which the leading four sellers' combined market shares were less than 75 percent of total industry output—a challenge was said to be likely if the acquiring firm had a market share of 4 percent or more and the acquired firm had a market share of 4 percent or more, or if the acquiring firm had a market share of 10 percent or more and the acquired firm's share was 2 percent or more. Although such guidelines have no legally binding force, they can be, and often are, accorded significant weight by trial courts.

Joining the Issues

In its complaint, Marathon alleged that competition would be lessened in diverse motor gasoline markets and in crude oil transportation, crude oil exploration, product terminal services, and oil shale research and development. However, as is common in preliminary injunction hearings, the November 1981 proceeding in Cleveland was conducted on an expedited basis, considering only the evidence that could be assembled in three weeks' time and scheduling testimony from witnesses for only four days. Given these time constraints, the dispute focused on a narrower question—whether competition would be lessened in the sale of motor gasoline.

Emphasizing the consumers' side of the picture, Marathon's expert economist witness viewed gasoline as a meaningful product market since "the person who pours diesel oil into his or her gas-burning automobile is going to have very serious difficulties." Mobil responded that within certain limits imposed by the flexibility of refining facilities, gasoline and other oil products were substitutable in production, even if not in consumption. But there was no substantial dispute over the appropriateness of gasoline as a product market in the antitrust sense, and the District Court accepted that product market definition.

Much more heatedly contested, and indeed central to the case, was the question of whether the relevant geographic market(s) were national, as alleged by Mobil, or more narrowly constricted to metropolitan areas, states, and regions of the United States, as asserted by Marathon.

If the geographic market for gasoline were the entire United States, or even the area east of the Rocky Mountains—the narrowest definition accepted by Mobil's economist—the impact of the acquisition on the structure of the industry would almost surely be too small to support an antitrust challenge. The combination of Marathon with Mobil would give Mobil a combined national market share of approximately 8.5 percent, propelling it into first place among American gasoline producers. But with a national market definition, as shown in Table 1, the gasoline industry was not highly concentrated before the merger, and the four-seller concentration ratio would rise from 31.4 percent to roughly 34.5 percent. Marathon's 3.1 percent share fell below the 4 percent threshold under the Justice Department's Guidelines for acquired firms in industries with four-firm concentration ratios below 75 percent, while Mobil's 5.4 percent share fell below the 10-percent threshold for acquiring firm market shares. Thus, the merger fell within a "safe harbor" range under the Guidelines.

Market structure and changes in it are analyzed in merger cases because of economic theory and evidence suggesting that the more concentrated a market is, the greater is the likelihood of undetected, undeterred collusion or unaggressive "live and let live" oligopoly pricing. The economist witnesses for Marathon and Mobil agreed that concentration ratios like those in Table 1, if valid, lay on the low side of the point at which oligopoly behavior emerges. Neither was willing to identify a precise numerical point at which competitive structure ends and oligopoly begins. As the Mobil economist testified:

> I would be misrepresenting both my knowledge and the knowledge of the profession if I said there is a critical point measured by one concentration measure or another beyond which thou shalt not tread. . . . But there is a relationship which, beyond a

Table 1
Concentration Ratios in Runs of Petroleum through American Refineries, 1970–80

	Year					
	1970	*1975*	*1977*	*1978*	*1979*	*1980*
Four-firm concentration ratio	34.2%	32.9%	31.8%	32.3%	31.0%	31.4%
Eight-firm concentration ratio	61.0	57.7	55.1	55.8	55.0	54.3
Mobil's share	7.5	6.0	5.4	5.3	5.5	5.4
Marathon's share	1.7	2.3	3.2	3.4	3.2	3.1

Source: Defendant's exhibit 12, *Marathon v. Mobil* hearing.

certain point, causes most economists to worry about competitive behavior, and at a low level, to consider such worries to be redundant and frivolous.[5]

Absent other compelling considerations, the merger was unlikely to be found illegal if the relevant domain of competition were a market of nationwide scope.

Mobil reinforced this conclusion by documenting the generally declining trend in both four-firm and eight-firm concentration ratios between 1970 and 1980. Earlier Supreme Court precedents had placed special emphasis on preventing mergers in industries with a rising concentration trend.[6] Marathon, on the other hand, claimed that the declining national concentration shown by Table 1 stemmed from extensive federal government intervention in petroleum markets. Beginning in 1971, price controls were placed on petroleum products, and in early 1974, the program was modified to include a crude-oil allocation system.[7] "Entitlements" to price-controlled crude oil were given out with a "small refiner bias" sufficiently lucrative to induce considerable investment in refineries too small to be efficient and survive in a competitive market. In 1979, President Carter announced a phaseout of the price controls and entitlements system, and in early 1981 the program ended. Marathon's economist testified that the proliferation of small, independently owned refineries contributed to the observed decline in national concentration ratios. With the elimination of the entitlements system and other developments to be discussed later, he predicted, concentration was likely to increase again in the future.[8]

Marathon's complaint urged that individual states could be viewed as relevant geographic markets. If this contention (disputed by Mobil) were accepted, the measured concentration ratios, shown in Table 2, were considerably higher than those found at the national level. In at least three of the states served by both Marathon and Mobil—Illinois, Michigan, and Wisconsin—the 1968 Department of Justice Guidelines were exceeded. Thus, knowing whether or not the relevant market was national or a series of smaller areas was crucial to how one interpreted the merger's impact on market structure and hence its possible behavioral effects.

The Geographic Structure of Petroleum Distribution

Several approaches have been proposed and used by economists to determine whether relevant markets are local, regional, national, or even international.[9] There are three main variants: assessing the potential

Table 2
Concentration Data for Motor Gasoline Sales in
Seven Midwestern States, 1970

State	Four-Firm Concentration Ratio	Mobil's Share	Marathon's Share	Combined Post-Merger Market Rank
Ohio	53.0%	1.74%	13.92%	2
Illinois	47.0	4.27	12.18	2
Indiana	47.0	2.47	14.53	1
Michigan	44.5	7.68	12.06	1
Wisconsin	44.1	8.14	9.15	1
Florida	41.0	4.52	7.22	1
Tennessee	n.a.	4.49	5.95	2

Source: Marathon complaint; Plaintiff's exhibit E.

for, and magnitude of, product flows across the boundaries of narrowly defined territories; determining the probability that sellers might raise prices at some point in geographic space, taking into account the possibility that such attempts might be undermined if competitive products could flow in from other locations; and assessing the actual price outcomes of competition, or its absence, across varying expanses of geographic space. There was substantial agreement between the economist witnesses for Marathon and Mobil on the criteria to be applied. Although they incorporated facets of all three approaches, both emphasized the analysis of actual price outcomes. Thus, according to Marathon's economist:

> What happens if the price...of gasoline in Cleveland is raised—because of, say, some breakdown of competition? ...Who...might move into this gap to supply more product...until the price has been competed back down to the competitive level?...What you would...look for in trying to encompass all the producers in the relevant geographic market is the question, is there a tendency for prices to become uniform? And if there is such a tendency...one would say that we have a relevant geographic market.[10]

or in the words of Mobil's economist:

> We define the market as the...geographic area within which the price tends to uniformity, allowance being made for trans-

portation costs. . . .[A]nd I have to ask the question: How does that tendency of price to equality get achieved?. . .[S]ince, in general, demanders are not going to move in response to the changing conditions. . .you look for. . .shipments on the supply side.[11]

Rich evidence was presented on the geographic patterns of petroleum refining and marketing and on the opportunities for transporting petroleum products from one part of the United States to another. After closing a small refinery in Buffalo, New York, Mobil had six domestic refineries, with locations and capacities (in barrels of crude oil input per day) as follows:

Location	Capacity
Beaumont, Texas	335,000
Joliet, Illinois	180,000
Torrance, California	123,500
Paulsboro, New Jersey	106,600
Ferndale, Washington	71,500
Augusta, Kansas	50,000

Marathon was a "regional" company with gasoline marketing operations limited to 21 states and with special strength in the Midwest. Its four refineries were as follows:

Location	Capacity
Garyville, Louisiana	255,000
Texas City, Texas	70,000
Robinson, Illinois	195,000
Detroit, Michigan	69,000

Unless the market were viewed as nationwide, Mobil's refineries in California and Washington could be excluded from consideration as competitors to Marathon. Determining the competitive interrelationships of the remaining refineries was more complex. The flow of refined petroleum products in the United States depends upon the location of crude-oil supplies, the means used to transport them, the location of the refineries, and the means used to transport refined products. Crude oil reserves are located preponderantly in the Texas Gulf area and Oklahoma, California, Alaska, and the Rocky Mountains. Around those sources, a distinctive pattern of crude oil and product movements has developed. It can be characterized in terms of Petroleum Allocation

District or PAD groupings developed by the U.S. Department of the Interior. PAD I consists of the East Coast states; PAD II the Midwestern states (from Ohio to North Dakota); PAD III the Gulf Coast States (Texas, Louisiana, Mississippi, Alabama, Arkansas, and New Mexico); PAD IV the Mountain states; and PAD V the West Coast states (plus Nevada). Three of the five have substantial crude oil resources; two do not.

Table 3 shows the pattern of product demand and supply flows in 1980. Gulf states PAD III was largely self-sufficient in meeting its own demands, but also exported extensively to adjacent areas, especially PAD I. PAD II, which was Marathon's principal marketing area, was also fairly self-sufficient, but imported 14 percent of its product needs from PAD III and smaller quantities from PAD I and Canada. Western PADs IV and V were also nearly self-sufficient. The eastern states, on the other hand, did relatively little of their own refining, depending heavily upon imports from PAD III and overseas.

How demand is satisfied depends also upon the cost and availability of transportation media. Crude oil moves to refineries in ocean-going tankers, crude oil pipelines, and (less frequently) river barges. Oil products move from the refinery to market in tankers, product pipelines, barges, rail cars, and tank trucks. There are massive and persistent economies of scale in pipelining and tanker operations. (Tanker operations will not be considered further, since they were infeasible in supplying the interior United States.) The average cost of transporting a barrel of crude oil (or slightly less accurately, petroleum products) one thousand miles by pipelines of diverse design capacities in 1969 was estimated by Pearl and Enos (1975, p. 61) as follows:

Table 3
Pattern of Refined Product Demand and Supply Flows, by Petroleum Allocation District, 1980

Consuming PAD	1980 Consumption (barrels/day)	Percentage of Consumption Obtained from:					
		PAD I	II	III	IV	V	Non-U.S.
I	5,630,000	26	nil	53	nil	nil	21
II	4,505,000	5	77	14	nil	nil	4
III	3,775,000	nil	nil	96	4	nil	nil
IV	507,000	nil	nil	15	85	nil	nil
V	2,570,000	nil	nil	2	3	92	3

Source: Defendant's Exhibit 2, "Regional Oil Dynamics," prepared by the Economics Department of Marathon Oil Company (October 1981).

Pipeline Diameter (inches)	Pipeline Capacity (barrels per day)	1969 Cost per Barrel (cents)
10.75	50,000	40
12.75	80,000	32
16.00	140,000	23
22.00	275,000	16
26.00	400,000	13
32.00	700,000	11
42.00	1,000,000	8
48.00	1,500,000	7

Plainly, supplies obtained through the largest pipelines (i.e., 48-inch diameter pipes with a 1.5-million-barrel daily capacity) were much more economical than those using smaller lines.

In 1981, the "lower 48" U.S. states were richly interconnected with product and (to a lesser degree) crude-oil pipelines, as illustrated in Figures 1 and 2. However, several features were of special relevance to the Marathon-Mobil market definition dispute. For one, product and crude connections between western PADs IV and V and states east of the Rocky Mountains were relatively sparse. Indeed, at the time of the suit, there was no economical means of transporting either crude oil or product from the Pacific states eastward. Second, PAD I was well connected with product pipelines originating in PAD III, including the Colonial (shown in Figure 1 branching at Greensboro, North Carolina), with a 40-inch diameter over much of its length, and the half-million-barrel per day Plantation. It had no comparable crude oil connections. Third and less evident in the figures, the upper midwest was better connected with crude-oil pipelines from the Gulf states than with product pipelines. The largest crude-oil pipeline (the Capline, which heads nearly due north from New Orleans in Figure 2) had a capacity of 1.2 million barrels per day, while the largest product pipeline from the Gulf had a capacity of only 374,000 barrels per day. This meant that it was a half cent or more per gallon in 1981 to ship product than to ship crude oil from the Gulf. This difference helps explain the near self-sufficiency of PAD II in refining products for its own consumption. And more generally, much of the product flow pattern seen in Table 3 becomes explicable in terms of the pipeline interconnections shown by Figures 1 and 2.

Pipelines are not the only transportation medium, but with the exception of foreign-flag tankers, they are the least expensive. The costs of transporting a barrel of petroleum products 1000 miles by various media in 1966 were estimated as follows:[12]

Figure 1
Petroleum Products Pipeline Capacities
(Thousands of Barrels Daily as of December 31, 1978)

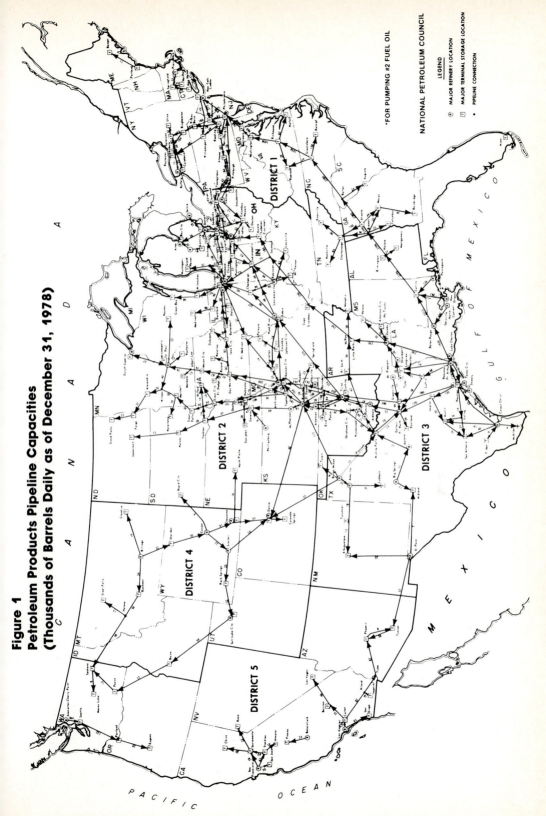

*FOR PUMPING #2 FUEL OIL

NATIONAL PETROLEUM COUNCIL

LEGEND

⊛ MAJOR REFINERY LOCATION

☐ MAJOR TERMINAL STORAGE LOCATION

• PIPELINE CONNECTION

Source: Defendant's Exhibit from the National Petroleum Council, Petroleum Storage and Transportation Capacities, 1979.

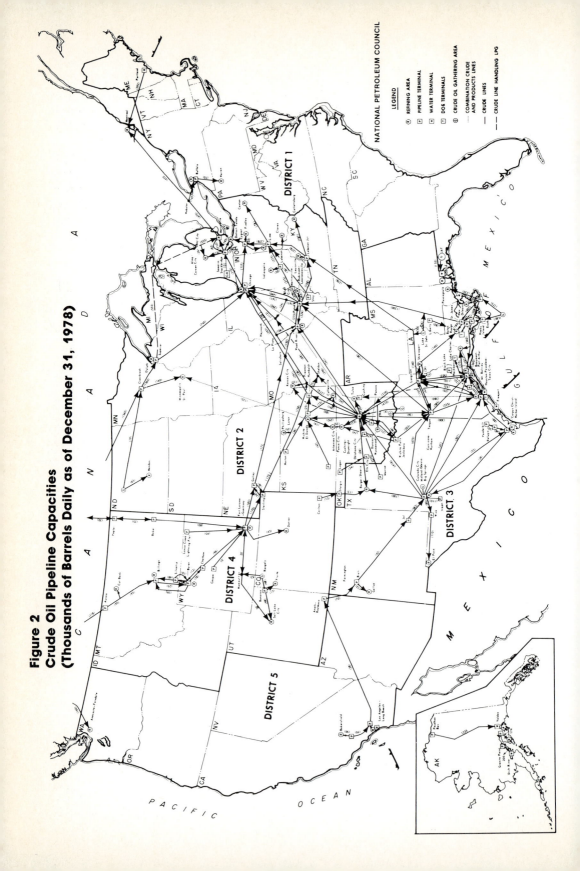

Figure 2
Crude Oil Pipeline Capacities
(Thousands of Barrels Daily as of December 31, 1978)

Method	U.S. dollars
150,000 ton ocean tanker (3000 mile trip)	$ .04
30,000 ton ocean tanker (3000 mile trip)	.06
42 inch diameter pipeline	.10
12 inch diameter pipeline	.51
Inland barge (500 mile trips)	.52
Rail (500 mile trips)	1.54
25 ton payload truck (50 mile trips)	4.42
15 ton payload truck (50 mile trips)	5.11

Again, the superiority of pipelines over everything but tankers is evident. Consequently, petroleum products in the United States are characteristically transported by pipeline (or less frequently, barge) to terminals (marked **T** in Figure 1) located near refineries or substantial metropolitan areas. The typical terminal contains at least several storage tanks, and several companies often use a particular company's terminal to store and distribute their products. In 1981, Marathon operated 50 terminals to serve the 21 states in which it marketed petroleum products. From such terminals, products are transported to market (in the case of motor gasoline, to service stations or bulk storage depots) in tank trucks. The cost of transporting gasoline 45 miles by tank truck in 1981 was estimated by witnesses as ranging from 0.7 cents to 2.5 cents per gallon, depending upon road conditions and the size of the truck.[13]

Terminals are a key pricing node in the petroleum distribution system. Companies set "terminal rack" prices varying from terminal to terminal. Surcharges applied to the terminal rack prices determine the effective prices at which the various marketing channels—in ascending order of price paid, jobbers, distributors, and dealers—obtain their supplies. Rack prices effective October 27, 1981, for regular gasoline in Marathon's southern region ranged from $0.990 per gallon at the Garyville, Louisiana, refinery terminal to $1.019 in Taft, Florida.[14] In the northern region, prices ranged from $1.003 in Chicago to $1.060 at the Chillicothe, Illinois, terminal (near Peoria). According to Marathon's manager of wholesale marketing, the factors affecting price levels at the diverse terminals included refining cost, transportation cost, and "the competition that we have in the gasoline market."[15]

Intercity Price Relationships

Gasoline moves from terminals to individual cities, where the prices consumers pay are set by retailers, most (but not all) of which are independently owned businesses—that is, without ownership ties to the refiners. However, the refiners in turn adjust their terminal prices to reflect competitive conditions in their customers' urban markets. Marathon's economist showed that prices in 1981 varied widely from city to city, often in directions inconsistent with transportation cost differences. Mobil responded by offering in evidence nine charts like Figures 3 and 4, plotting the trends of unleaded regular gasoline wholesale prices between city pairs over the two years from October 1979 through September 1981.[16]

By any criterion, the movements were highly correlated between cities. Much of the trend element common to the price series stemmed from a common cause. Throughout much of the period covered, crude oil costs were rising rapidly as a result of Iranian revolution-induced supply disruptions, OPEC's reaction to them and the phaseout of U.S. crude oil price controls. The sharp increase in prices triggered demand

Figure 3
Wholesale Price Plots, Chicago/Detroit (October 1979–September 1981)

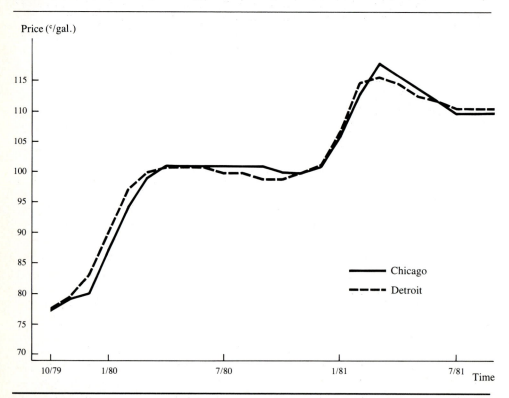

Source: Defendant's Exhibit.

Figure 4
Wholesale Price Plots, Chicago/New Orleans (October 1979–September 1981)

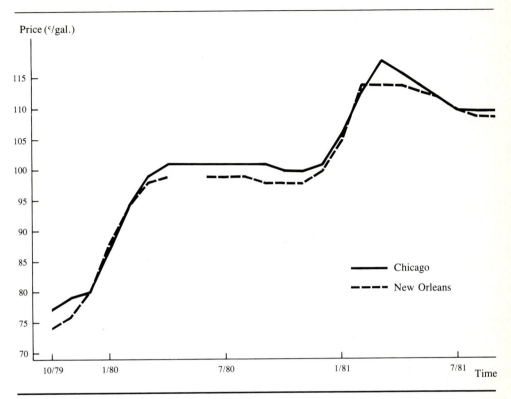

Source: Defendant's Exhibit.

cutbacks that, when decontrol ended, left refiners with substantial excess capacity and that in turn led to price competition and falling wholesale prices.

Of greater evidentiary interest were the deviations from trend between the city pairs. For several months running, Detroit prices were above Chicago prices by as much as four cents, reversing the pattern in subsequent periods. More curiously, New Orleans prices were virtually identical to Chicago prices in many months, despite the close proximity of New Orleans to crude oil deposits and hence its lower transport costs. In other periods, a differential in the expected direction materialized.

Mobil's economist viewed these deviations from price uniformity, net of transportation costs, as short-lived and unstable:[17]

[O]n a week-to-week basis, they have substantial autonomy. . . .
On the other hand, let me make [the time units] years, and I'm
going to get a much closer congruence. . . .I don't really have
any concern over whether this month has a set of alternative
markets that is narrow or wide to anywhere near the degree I
have a concern over next year or the year after. There is nothing
anyone can do—the most sovereign of our federal power can't
change the world in a week or two.

Marathon's economist argued that price patterns of the previous
several years, and indeed, over the decade following the imposition of
price controls in 1971, were so severely distorted by government intervention that they had little relevance to predicting gasoline pricing behavior once the transition to a free market was completed. For evidence
on free-market behavioral tendencies, he said, one had to go back to the
period before 1971. In support, the Marathon economist cited two
studies from that period.

Learned and Ellsworth (1959) of the Harvard Business School published an extremely detailed analysis of gasoline pricing behavior over
the period 1948–57. The research had special relevance to the
Marathon-Mobil case because it focused on Ohio, in which Marathon
had then, and subsequently retained, a particularly strong position. The
authors found important differences in pricing between such metropolitan areas as Akron and Toledo, depending upon the intensity of competition, and even within subsections of a metropolitan area. A ten-year
comparison of wholesale prices in Ohio, Chicago, and northern Oklahoma showed differentials varying by from three-tenths of a cent to two
cents that lasted for as long as two years and that "cannot be explained
on the basis of transportation costs."[18]

The other study, by Howard Marvel (1978), analyzed movements
in retail gasoline prices across 22 cities over the period 1964–71. Nationwide price leadership by Texaco in 1965 successfully raised gasoline prices following a period of intense price competition. The
questions posed by author Marvel was, how long did it take gasoline
prices to return to competitive levels in the various cities, and upon
what did the speed of adjustment depend? He computed regression
equations in which the average price in some city and time period was
the dependent variable, with dependent variables including city population, transportation costs, state and local tax levels, and a Herfindahl-
Hirschman index of seller concentration in the various cities. Marvel
found (1978, p. 258) that it took roughly five years before "competition
had become so widespread in some of the markets. . .that its effect on
prices could no longer be confined to the lower tail of the offer price distribution." Prices eroded first among the lower-price (i.e., unbranded)

sellers, and even more importantly, "competition's impact was felt first in the low concentration markets," spreading more slowly in the more highly concentrated markets. Thus, the adjustment to supracompetitive price increases required several years, not merely a few months, and it was systematically related to differences in seller structure between cities. Marathon's economist emphasized these results in concluding that competitive conditions varied sufficiently from city to city and that individual cities were reasonably viewed as separate, meaningful markets.[19]

With individual metropolitan areas taken as a reasonable approximation to economic markets, the proposed merger had more dramatic structural implications. Data were presented on the 1981 market shares of Marathon and Mobil in 36 Standard Metropolitan Statistical Areas.[20] Selected examples include the following:

Location	Marathon's Share	Mobil's Share
Chicago	9.6%	5.4%
Detroit	13.8	10.7
Cleveland	10.0	2.9
Milwaukee	15.6	9.3
Indianapolis	19.3	2.8
Springfield, IL	28.3	4.6
Ann Arbor, MI	18.5	6.8
Columbus, OH	24.7	2.8
Madison, WI	6.0	11.0
South Bend, IN	19.3	2.8

Among the 36 cities for which data were available, the Department of Justice Merger Guidelines market share thresholds were overstepped in 24 cities.[21]

The Decision

Weighing the conflicting interpretations of the evidence, the District Court concluded on November 30, 1981, that:

> The persistence of price differentials in various areas of the nation demonstrates that motor gasoline does not move from area to area in response to price changes easily or as readily as Mobil asserts. Rather, they indicate that the relevant geographic market for motor gasoline is something less than nationwide. Clearly, such an analysis must be more fully developed at a trial on the merits.[22]

The court went on to rule that, for purposes of the preliminary injunction determination, individual midwestern states were relevant markets. This compromise definition had been emphasized by neither party's economist, but it conveniently could be described by the most complete concentration and market share data. The court decided further that the combined market shares of Mobil and Marathon in six states approached or exceeded the thresholds found illegal in previous merger cases. In finding that markets were less than nationwide, the Court recognized that the price differentials persisting between cities were only one or two cents per gallon. This was a small amount in relation to the price of gasoline (well over a dollar per gallon) at the time. However, testimony had shown that Marathon's profits in a good year were four cents per gallon.[23] And from this, the court concluded, the magnitude of the intercity price differentials "is significant when compared to a petroleum company's profits."[24]

Marathon's Role as Supplier to Independent Retailers

Marathon argued that the contemplated acquisition by Mobil had competitive significance beyond the changes reflected in raw market concentration ratios. In addition, Marathon's role as a principal supplier of gasoline to independent gasoline marketers could be jeopardized.

Although it is difficult to draw a fine line, it has been customary to distinguish between major brand gasoline and gasoline offered by independent marketers. The major brands are offered by large (usually nationwide) refiners, receive considerable advertising support, and are often backed by credit card services. The independents traditionally avoided advertising and credit card services, stressing lower prices and their ability to operate at high per-station volumes. Before the sharp rise in gasoline prices precipitated by OPEC beginning in 1973, the independent marketers customarily sold gasoline of comparable quality two cents per gallon below the major brand price. In the late 1970s and early 1980s, a price differential of three to five cents per gallon was typical. The independent marketers, providing roughly 20 percent of all American gasoline at retail, injected competition not only by offering an alternative that was attractive to price-conscious consumers, but had been the industry's "mavericks," originating many if not most of the industry's localized retail price wars. Price wars were typically provoked when a widening of the major-independent price differential drew away more sales volume than the majors were willing to concede.

Of the 6.55 million gallons of motor gasoline sold by Marathon in

1980, approximately 15 percent went to dealers (mostly independently owned) who sold under the Marathon brand, mostly in the Midwest, and the remainder moved into the market as unbranded gasoline. Thirty-five percent of Marathon's sales were through wholly or partially owned Marathon subsidiaries selling under such low-price logos as Gastown, Speedway, Bonded, and Consolidated, and half were to some 1100 businesses satisfying fully the appellation "independent marketers." Marathon's independent customers had retail outlets in a total of 21 states, all in Petroleum Allocation Districts (PADs) I, II, and III, and all but two east of the Mississippi River. Marathon's gasoline sales to independent marketers were estimated to be approximately 10 percent of the total supply to such marketers in PADs II and III.

Being a reliable source of supply to the independents was an important facet of Marathon's business strategy. The price and quantity controls applied to petroleum products by the federal government during the 1970s had on occasion led to severe shortages. Marathon's policy under those conditions was to treat its independent customers exactly as it treated its own branded outlets. From 1974–76, when gasoline supplies were often only 80 to 85 percent of quantities demanded at the controlled prices, Marathon's branded and unbranded customers received equal percentage allocations. In 1979, when shortages were precipitated by the Iranian revolution, Marathon maintained a 100-percent allocation rate by buying additional gasoline in the spot market at 12 to 37 cents per gallon above the wholesale price at which it sold to its marketer-customers.[25]

Mobil, like other members of the petroleum industry Big Eight, pursued a quite different policy. A Federal Trade Commission investigation (U.S. Senate 1973, p. 8) revealed that from 1967 through 1971, independent marketers purchased only 1.1 percent of their gasoline requirements directly from Big Eight members. Several Big Eight representatives stated to the FTC that they would not sell to independents, regardless of price. Two independent marketer executives called by Marathon as witnesses testified that they had sought to buy from Mobil, but were rebuffed on asserted Mobil company policy grounds.[26] The president of the Independent Gasoline Marketers Council also testified that Mobil did not sell directly to independents, although in times of excess supply (as 1981 was), major companies' gasoline found its way into independents' tanks through jobbers and other intermediaries.[27] A 1981 internal Mobil staff study found that the price-depressing effects of a full Mobil shift from branded to unbranded marketing would more than outweigh the cost savings. As a result, the study concluded, "abandonment of our historic branded marketing mode was not warranted."[28]

Mobil's president testified that although he knew of no formal company policy preventing sales to independent marketers, Mobil in fact provided very little gasoline to the independents. He added, however:

> . . .[W]hen we first looked at Marathon and discovered they sold a lot of gasoline outside of normal branded outlets like Mobil does, we understood we would have to continue to supply. . . .What I'm trying to say is, Mobil now has a policy, if we acquire Marathon, we will supply those same types of people that Marathon is supplying, and I don't know why we should have to define it further.[29]

Mobil's economist testified that even if Mobil did not continue supplying independents, contrary to its promise, "if there is a commercially successful demand for the product. . .[someone] will cater to it and. . .provide gasoline at prices that are marketable. So it is. . .my belief that the supplies would be forthcoming as long as the demand is there."[30]

Marathon witnesses agreed that under the market conditions prevailing during 1981, independent marketers would have no difficulty obtaining gasoline supplies, whether or not Mobil chose to be their supplier. Gasoline prices had soared with U.S. price decontrol and the increase in OPEC's crude-oil prices from $15 per barrel in 1978 to $34 in 1981. Quantities demanded fell, and as a consequence, U.S. petroleum refineries utilized only 66 percent of their effective capacity in October 1981—far below the 90–95 percent rate at which they preferred to operate. The burden of excess capacity triggered price warfare, leading a Mobil witness to characterize "the competitive conditions that exist today as the most ruthless and tough and difficult that I have ever seen."[31] In sharp contrast to the situation in 1979, crude oil was also in abundant supply, and so price-competitive refined products were available in abundance to majors and independents alike.

The key question was, what would the future hold? Twice during the 1970s, gasoline supplies had been extremely tight, and partly because of perverse incentives built into the original government price controls,[32] major petroleum companies with scarce or low-priced crude oil tended to favor their own retail outlets over those of rivals. Possessing the Yates field and other domestic crude oil reserves, Marathon was a particularly reliable gasoline supplier to the independents. If crises occurred in the future, would Mobil be as reliable as Marathon, and would it sell to independents at equally favorable prices? And would crises recur? OPEC had set its prices so high that the immediate prognosis was glut, not scarcity, in world oil markets. But war could curtail supplies, as it had (briefly) in 1973 and 1979, and fighting had already erupted between two important OPEC members, Iran and Iraq. And sooner or later, demand would catch up to supply again, leaving tight crude oil markets. The refining industry was also undergoing structural change. Federal price controls and crude oil allocations had encouraged the construction of small-scale, so-called teakettle refineries whose economic viability in a period of uncontrolled competition was dubious. Marathon's economist witness estimated that small-scale refineries accounted for approximately 10 percent of U.S. refining capacity.[33] He predicted that at least half of that capacity was likely to exit the industry in the future.[34] If in addition Mobil ceased supplying independent marketers, the independents would lose a third of the capacity they currently tapped. A future supply squeeze on the independents could not be ruled out under pessimistic but not improbable assumptions.

Bandwagon Effects

A third allegation by Marathon Oil was that if its acquisition by Mobil were permitted, a bandwagon effect would be triggered. Additional oil company acquisitions would ensue, each citing the Mobil-Marathon case as a favorable precedent. Conoco, the nation's 16th largest refiner, had barely slipped through Mobil's fingers earlier in 1981. The financial pages carried reports that other oil giants had arranged lines of credit with which they too could make acquisitions: Texas had $5.5 billion, Gulf Oil $5 billion, Pennzoil $2.5 billion, and Cities Service $1 billion. In passing the Celler-Kefauver Act, Congress in 1950 had expressed clearly its intent to intervene against a "series of acquisitions" whose "cumulative effect. . .may be a significant reduction in the vigor of competition."[35] This, Marathon argued, was exactly what was occurring in the petroleum industry.

The Outcome

Addressing only the question of whether the combined gasoline market shares in six midwestern states exceeded those found to breach the limits of tolerance defined in previous merger cases, the Federal District Court in Cleveland enjoined Mobil from carrying out its plan to acquire Marathon.[36] A day later, on December 1, Mobil announced to the court that it was willing to sell off all of Marathon's refining and marketing operations in the six offending states. It asked therefore that, since the basis of the antitrust violation would be eliminated, the injunction be removed. The court refused. Under heavy time pressure because of its pending tender offer, Mobil appealed. On December 23, the Circuit Court of Appeals ruled against Mobil. It found that "the District Court did not err in analyzing concentration ratios in defining relevant markets by state rather than limiting its consideration to the nation as a whole."[37] In addition, it opined:

> Mobil Corporation did not convince the District Court that the merger would benefit the economy, increase operating efficiency, bring advantages of scale, or substitute better management. Mobil's reasons for the acquisition. . .seem to be that Marathon stock was underpriced in the market and that Marathon's valuable Yates Field in Texas would provide Mobil with additional needed domestic crude oil reserves. We do not see that it is of particular benefit to the national economy to substitute Mobil ownership of the Yates Field for Marathon ownership, and it may be disadvantageous. It may reduce Mobil's incentives to explore and find its own new domestic reserves.[38]

It went on to note that "any conceivable benefits are more than offset by the potential elimination of Marathon as a supplier of price conscious independents." Mobil's appeal to the Supreme Court for an emergency stay was similarly unsuccessful.

Meanwhile, there were important developments on two other fronts. While the Marathon-Mobil preliminary injunction hearing was underway, other Mobil attorneys were presenting information to, and negotiating with, the Federal Trade Commission, which was responsible for the federal government's antitrust enforcement with respect to the merger. Mobil's offer to divest domestic refining and marketing operations fell upon more receptive ears in Washington than in Cleveland. On December 1, Mobil announced that it had reached an agreement in principle to sell all of its American refining, transportation, and marketing assets to the Amerada Hess Corporation. Amerada had refineries in Port Reading, New Jersey; Purvis, Mississippi; and St. Croix, Virgin Islands. It had no marketing operations in the midwestern states singled out in the District Court's opinion. The announced price, for assets with an accounting book value of $1.4 billion, was $400 million. Mobil was willing to accept a low price because intense competition had rendered refining and marketing operations unprofitable and because its main objective in offering $5.1 billion for Marathon shares was to acquire Marathon's rich oil reserves. An assumption implicit in the Federal Trade Commission's acceptance of this plan was that the integration of Marathon's oil reserves with "downstream" product refining and marketing operations was unimportant. Amerada's domestic oil production in 1980 was 80,000 barrels per day, much less than Marathon's and far too little to supply its refineries, with a total capacity of 730,000 barrels per day. Thus, if another crude oil supply crisis materialized, it was implicitly assumed that Amerada Hess would somehow secure the petroleum necessary to keep its Marathon refineries competitive. On December 3, the FTC filed a preliminary injunction plea charging that the intended Mobil-Marathon merger would reduce competition in numerous Midwestern metropolitan areas and reduce supplies to independent marketers.[39] But this was a formality, for the FTC simultaneously announced its intention not to prosecute its complaint until it reached a final decision on the adequacy of Mobil's divestiture plan.

Marathon's management officials were also busy. They did not want to be acquired by Mobil, but once their company was put in play at a substantial stock price premium above previous levels, it would be difficult to avoid being taken over. They therefore sought "white knights" to come to the rescue. Gulf Oil secretly offered to pay $120 per share, but only on the condition that Marathon's antitrust challenge to Mobil *failed*—something Marathon's management deemed unlikely.[40] On November 19, as the testimony in the Cleveland antitrust hearing neared completion, the U.S. Steel Corporation emerged as the favored white knight. It offered Marathon stockholders a package of cash and debentures valued at $106 per share—$21 more per share than Mobil's original proposal. On November 25, Mobil retaliated by raising its offer to $108 per share in a package similar to, but slightly more attractive than, U.S. Steel's tender.

Mobil, however, was held back by two constraints. The first and eventually fatal limitation was its inability to break free from the Cleveland District Court's preliminary injunction. Also, the agreement reached between U.S. Steel and Marathon management gave U.S. Steel a binding option to purchase Marathon's Yates Field interest for $2.8 billion if U.S. Steel's full offer did not succeed and if a third party (e.g., Mobil) gained control of Marathon. Without its crown jewel, Marathon was much less interesting to Mobil, and so Mobil attempted to have the option declared illegal through a suit filed in the Federal District Court in Cincinnati. Mobil eventually won the battle, but by the time the appellate court ruled against the option,[41] the war was lost, since U.S. Steel was already far along in its bid to acquire all of Marathon without invoking the Yates option. And since Mobil remained blocked by the antitrust injunction, the option issue became moot. In a last-ditch effort, Mobil began purchasing shares of U.S. Steel and threatened to acquire a 25-percent interest, leaving the longer-run implications uncertain. It abandoned the effort in early 1982.

Thus, Marathon Oil became an essentially autonomous unit within the U.S. Steel Corporation. Reflecting the fundamental change in business orientation the merger effected, U.S. Steel changed its name in 1986 to USX Corporation. Whether the acquisition was a wise one from the standpoint of U.S. Steel shareholders is too difficult a question to explore here. The $35 per barrel crude-oil prices that made Yates Field and related Marathon properties such an attractive target fell dramatically as OPEC nations, saddled with enormous excess capacity, chiseled on their cartel agreements. In June 1986, with the cartel in disarray, prices FOB Saudi Arabia dropped as low as $8 per barrel. A recovery to approximately $18 followed by mid 1987. As a result of the merger, Marathon's profits were in large measure shielded from federal income taxation, since depressed conditions in the steel industry led to heavy losses that could be offset against the Marathon division's tax liabilities. The acquisition cost USX a considerable amount of ill will on Washington's Capitol Hill, where U.S. Steel's representatives had successfully pleaded for protection against steel imports with an argument that the increased revenues would be invested in modernization. The company's $6.5 billion investment in already discovered oil was seen as a betrayal. But USX ignored the criticisms and continued to diversify away from its traditional but declining industry.

The antitrust decision against Mobil's acquisition of Marathon did not put an end to major petroleum industry mergers. Mobil subsequently acquired crude-rich Superior Oil for $5.7 billion. U.S. Steel acquired Texas Oil & Gas Company. Texaco acquired Getty Oil after agreeing to divest some Getty marketing operations; Gulf Oil was acquired by Standard Oil of California; and Cities Service was acquired by Occidental Petroleum. Phillips Petroleum and Unocal narrowly escaped takeover attempts. Numerous smaller acquisitions also occurred. Merger activity slowed only when the intense bidding drove oil company stock prices to levels that, combined with the collapse of crude oil prices in 1986, made the remaining petroleum companies less attractive takeover targets.

Notes

1. *Marathon Oil Co.* v. *Mobil Corporation et al.,* Northern District of Ohio, 530 F. Supp. 315 (1981).
2. See "Yates' Last Laugh, Or Humble Origins of a 'Crown Jewel,' " *Wall Street Journal,* 7 December 1981, p. 1.
3. Testimony of Mobil President William P. Tavoulareas in *Marathon* v. *Mobil,* transcript (hereafter cited as TR), 448.
4. U.S. Department of Justice, Merger Guidelines, May 30, 1968. The guidelines were substantially amended in 1982 and again in 1984—too late to have any influence on *Marathon* v. *Mobil.*
5. Testimony of George J. Stigler, Walgreen Professor of Economics at the University of Chicago, TR at 634.

6. See especially *United States* v. *Von's Grocery Co. et al.,* 384 U.S. 270 (1966).
7. See Roush (1976) and Kalt (1981).
8. TR 305–308 and 335.
9. For various views, see Elzinga and Hogarty (1973), Boyer (1979), Landes and Posner (1981, 963–972), Horowitz (1981), Werden (1983), Harris and Jorde (1984), and Stigler and Sherwin (1985).
10. TR 225–227.
11. TR 629, 687.
12. Drawn with appropriate conversions from Hubbard (1967). The original Hubbard estimates were presented in British pounds sterling for typical European conditions.
13. The 2.5 cent estimate was provided by Marathon's economist. The 0.7 to 1.3 cent estimates were cited by a Mobil witness who was president of a retailing company. TR pp. 599–600. The 0.7 cent estimate was for 17,000 gallon (52 ton payload) trucks which, although operated by his firm at the time, had been outlawed by most states because of their accident proneness and highway damage.
14. Defendant's exhibit 1.
15. Testimony of Richard E. White, TR pp. 67–68.
16. Defendant's exhibit 16, drawing upon Platt/Lundberg survey data presented in defendant's exhibit 15. On the implied analytic methodology, see Stigler and Sherwin (1985).
17. TR 690–698.
18. TR 245, referring to Learned and Ellsworth (1959, 38).
19. TR 235–237. The Mobil economist had been a member of the dissertation committee under which the Marvel analysis was carried out. Mobil's witness explained that "the results were the opposite of what he [Marvel] wished to show, and I find that he must have left uncontrolled portions. . . .The results are so improbable that [Marvel] himself quickly scurried into another direction for an explanation." TR 710–711. Asked under cross examination whether he provided advice as a member of Marvel's committee, the Mobil economist allowed that "I now believe I did not assist him enough."
20. Plaintiff's Exhibit D.
21. TR 274.
22. 530 F. Supp. 315, 322.
23. TR 247.
24. 530 F. Supp. 315, 322. In this respect the Court anticipated the Justice Department's revised Merger Guidelines (1982), which stated (p. 8) that in defining markets, the Department would "hypothesize a price increase of five percent and ask how many sellers could sell the product to such customers within one year." Note that the Marathon-Mobil court accepted a price increase threshold of roughly one percent relative to price—considerably less than the Justice Department's five percent.
25. Testimony of Richard E. White, Marathon's manager of wholesale marketing, TR at 77.

26. Testimony of Herbert A. Mahne and Clayton L. Lhuillier, TR 137–157.
27. Testimony of Jack Blum, TR 178–182.
28. "Branded versus Unbranded Marketing," Plaintiff's exhibit EE, undated, but including April 1981 price comparisons.
29. Testimony of William Tavoulareas, TR 506–508.
30. TR at 720.
31. Testimony of William H. Boutell, TR at 604.
32. See Roush (1976, pp. 45–48 and 72–73); and Kalt (1981, pp. 10–19 and 35–48).
33. TR 308–307.
34. Lloyd (1986) found that between 1979, when decontrol commenced, and 1986, 110 refineries, or 39 percent of the United States total by number, were closed. They accounted for 11 percent of 1979 capacity. A logit analysis revealed that the closed refineries were characteristically small (below 30,000 barrels per day in capacity) and new (built after 1973). A disproportionate number of the closed refineries were located in PAD II—Marathon's home territory.
35. See generally the discussion of legislative history in *Brown Shoe Co.* v. *United States,* 370 U.S. 294, 317–318 (1962), especially footnote 32.
36. *Marathon Oil Company* v. *Mobil Corporation et al.,* 530 F. Supp. 315, 326 (1981).
37. *Marathon Oil Company* v. *Mobil Corporation et al.,* 669 F. 2d 378 (1981).
38. Ibid., at 382.
39. See "FTC Opposes Mobil Takeover of Marathon Oil," *Wall Street Journal,* 9 December 1981, p. 3.
40. "Mobil's Marathon Loss, Its Second in 6 Months, Is Tied to Blunders," *Wall Street Journal,* 8 January 1982, p. 1.
41. *Mobil Corporation* v. *Marathon Oil Co. et al.,* 669 F. 2d 366 (1981).

References

Boyer, Kenneth D. "Industry Boundaries." In *Economic Analysis and Antitrust Law,* edited by Terry Calvani and John Siegfried, 88–119. Boston: Little, Brown, 1979.

Elzinga, Kenneth G., and T. F. Hogarty. "The Problem of Geographic Market Definition." *Antitrust Bulletin* 18 (Spring 1973): 45–81.

Harris, Robert G., and Thomas M. Jorde. "Antitrust Market Definition: An Integrated Approach." *California Law Review* 72 (January 1984): 3–67.

Horowitz, Ira. "Market Definition in Antitrust Analysis: A Regression-Based Approach." *Southern Economic Journal* 48 (July 1981): 1–16.

Hubbard, Michael. "The Comparative Cost of Oil Transport to and within Europe." *Journal of the Institute of Petroleum* 54 (January 1967): 1–23.

Kalt, Joseph P. *The Economics and Politics of Oil Price Regulation.* Cambridge, Mass.: MIT Press, 1981.

Landes, William M., and Richard A. Posner. "Market Power in Antitrust Cases." *Harvard Law Review* 94 (March 1981): 937–996.

Learned, Edmund P., and Catherine C. Ellsworth. *Gasoline Pricing in Ohio.* Boston: Harvard University, Graduate School of Business Administration Division of Research, 1959.

Lloyd, Neil. "The Impact of the Small Refiner Bias on the Structure of the U.S. Petroleum Industry." Econometrics seminar paper, Swarthmore College, 1986.

Marvel, Howard P. "Competition and Price Levels in the Retail Gasoline Market." *Review of Economics and Statistics* 60 (May 1978): 252–258.

Pearl, D. J., and J. L. Enos. "Engineering Production Functions and Technological Progress." *Journal of Industrial Economics* 24 (September 1975): 55–72.

Roush, Calvin T., "Effects of Federal Price and Allocation Regulations on the Petroleum Industry." In Federal Trade Commission Staff Report. Washington, D.C., December 1976.

Stigler, George J., and Robert A. Sherwin. "The Extent of the Market." *Journal of Law & Economics* 28 (October 1985): 555–586.

U.S. Department of Justice. Merger Guidelines. May 30, 1968.

U.S. Department of Justice. Merger Guidelines. June 14, 1982.

U.S. Senate, Committee on Government Operations, Permanent Subcommittee on Investigations. *Investigation of the Petroleum Industry.* Washington, D.C., July 12, 1973.

Werden, Gregory J. "Market Delineation and the Justice Department's Merger Guidelines." *Duke University Law Journal* (June 1983): 514–579.

2 International Joint Venture: General Motors and Toyota

case

John E. Kwoka, Jr.

Introduction

As the 1980s unfolded, General Motors could see trouble on its automotive horizon. For the second time in seven years, Middle Eastern politics had driven up oil prices and driven down sales of large U.S. cars. The Japanese were satisfying the demand for small cars, and imports' share of U.S. auto sales shot up from 18 percent in 1978 to 28 percent in 1980. In October 1981, GM embarked on a "beat Toyota" project, seeking to re-establish its superiority over the leading Japanese importer. But within sixteen months, GM decided instead to "join Toyota" in a joint venture to produce small cars in this country.

The agreement signed on February 17, 1983, by the chairmen of General Motors and Toyota set in motion one of the largest and most controversial antitrust investigations of recent years. The essential question was whether it was likely that the joint venture would result in more domestic small cars, produced more efficiently, with valuable insights that could be used by GM and possibly other companies in their automotive plants, or whether it might lead to coordination of pricing and other behavior between the powerful parent companies and merely substitute for less more anticompetitive alternatives by which GM could achieve its objectives.

Examination of this question, in turn, focused attention on several issues: the relevant market and the likelihood of cooperative behavior in that market, the economic effects of joint ventures, the alternatives available to GM, the changes in conduct that might result from the joint venture, and the magnitude of the efficiencies from the joint venture. Some novel economic tools were developed in order to

John E. Kwoka, Jr., consulted and wrote a report for the Federal Trade Commission in this matter. Gratitude is expressed to Joseph Brodley, George Douglas, Philip Nelson, Lawrence White, and Walter Vandaele for comments on this case study. The usual disclaimer applies.

analyze this joint venture. They did not, however, produce agreement as to its consequences.

The Parents and the Progeny

The parents of the joint venture were two very well known companies. General Motors became the country's largest automobile manufacturer in the 1930s, and it held between 40 percent and 50 percent of U.S. sales for a half century. Except for a few years, it has always ranked as the largest domestic manufacturing company. In 1983, for example, GM grossed nearly $75 billion in sales, earned $3.7 billion in profits, and employed almost 700,000 workers.

General Motors' overall success in the auto industry has not been without some weaknesses. In particular, its traditional promotion of large-size cars left it more vulnerable than other U.S. producers to the oil-price shocks of the 1970s. Like the other U.S. auto companies, however, GM did see a future in the production of small cars despite the smaller per-unit profits on such vehicles. This was partly because of the large size of this market segment, but also the fact that small cars filled out a company's product line-up, and this meant that it could offer product variants (e.g., cars of many sizes) tailored to the preferences of different consumers. As with multiple pricing (i.e., price discrimination), this is generally more profitable than trying to satisfy all preferences with only one product variant. In addition, small cars were often young consumers' first purchases, and it was widely believed (though less and less the case) that ownership instilled loyalty and enhanced the likelihood of repeat purchases from the same manufacturer. Moreover, small, less expensive cars helped attract customers to showrooms and also kept dealers from affiliating with foreign auto companies. Finally, federal government fuel economy regulations (which were based on the average fuel economy of a company's annual sales) essentially required companies to sell small, high-mileage cars in order to raise the average enough to sell more profit-yielding large cars. For all these reasons, no U.S. auto company believed it could safely abandon the production of small cars.[1]

Toyota's history was much different from GM's. Although it began producing automobiles in the 1930s, it was turning out less than 250,000 cars annually as late as the 1960s. By the 1970s, however, Toyota had established itself as the leading automobile company in Japan, with a market share of about 30 percent. In the 1980s, it became the world's third largest motor vehicle producer, manufacturing almost entirely small cars and with a heavy emphasis on exports. During this time, the American consumers purchased over one-half million

Toyotas annually, making Toyota the fourth (and very briefly, during Chrysler's travails, the third) largest seller of automobiles in the United States.

The realization that Toyota and the other Japanese auto manufacturers were doing something right came slowly to the traditional domestic auto producers. They believed, as Henry Ford II put it, that Detroit's new small cars would "drive the Japanese back to the sea."[2] Detroit's small cars came (Ford's Escort/Lynx, Chrysler's K-cars, and GM's X- and J-cars), but the Japanese held their position. Attention then focused on the Toyota production system, and analysts were uncovering evidence of remarkable efficiency in Japanese auto plants in everything from labor utilization to quality control techniques. Better cars were being built because better *and* less expensive techniques were being employed.

During this time, pressure mounted on the leading Japanese auto companies to invest in the United States by manufacturing automobiles there. Most were reluctant to do so, since costs in Japan were considerably lower than in the United States; but protectionist sentiment was running very strong in 1980, and actual import restraints on Japanese cars were imposed in 1981. In this environment, Honda announced plans in 1979 and began U.S. production in 1982. Nissan followed shortly thereafter, but Toyota continued to stall.

Toyota eventually decided to respond to this pressure, and talks between Toyota and GM were announced in March 1982. Final matters were resolved directly between Roger Smith, GM's Chairman, and Eiji Toyoda, the Chairman of Toyota, in December 1982 and January 1983. In February of that year, an official signing ceremony committed the two companies to the joint venture.

The joint venture, ultimately named New United Motor Manufacturing, Inc. (NUMMI), was to be a separate company with ownership stock shared 50-50 between General Motors and Toyota. The initial capitalization of the joint venture was $300 million. GM's contribution consisted of $20 million plus an assembly plant in Fremont, California, that had been shut down in 1982 due to slow demand for the larger cars it was producing. The new funds, primarily from Toyota, were to be spent on conversion of the existing plant to the Toyota system of production, together with construction of an adjacent stamping plant to produce large sheet-metal body parts. About 200,000 joint-venture vehicles were to be produced annually and sold to General Motors for retail distribution through its Chevrolet division. The joint venture was not intended to be open-ended, but rather to last no more than twelve years.

By design, Toyota was the lead firm in NUMMI. The vehicle was a Toyota design. Indeed, it was nothing more than a slightly restyled version of the new Corolla model. All major components (e.g., engines and transmissions) were to be imported from Toyota in Japan. The chief executive officer, the chief operating officer, and most other senior officials of the joint venture were to be Toyota personnel. The intent behind this arrangement was to make the facility a full embodiment of the Toyota system. This would ensure that the vehicles were of high quality, that GM could observe Toyota manufacturing first-hand, and that Toyota was responsible for labor relations in the plant.

The Investigation

Most proposed mergers, acquisitions, and joint ventures above a certain size must be brought to the attention of the Department of Justice and the Federal Trade Commission under the provisions of the Hart-Scott-Rodino premerger notification act of 1976. This process provides the agencies (the FTC and Justice Department decide which one) with a certain amount of time to investigate an arrangement prior to its consummation. In this case the FTC was designated to conduct the investigation. General Motors and Toyota filed initial information in April 1983 and responded to requests for additional information during that summer. The Federal Trade Commission's investigation of the joint venture was termed "one of the most intensive, thorough antitrust reviews ever conducted."[3]

The final judgment by the five Federal Trade Commissioners was based, as usual, on separate memoranda from the Bureau of Economics and the Bureau of Competition (the legal staff). But unlike most cases, this joint venture was also independently analyzed by an outside consulting economist. The two bureaus essentially recommended approval of the joint venture, whereas the consultant's report concluded that it should be challenged. With these analyses in hand, the Commissioners of the FTC voted 3-2 in December 1983 provisionally to permit the joint venture to proceed, subject to some minor modifications. Final approval was granted (by the same 3-2 margin) in April 1984.

The absence of a court proceeding means that there was no formal account by General Motors or Toyota of their positions, no public disclosure of documentary evidence, and not even a direct joining of the issues between proponents and critics of the joint venture. What did exist was a set of documents totaling 1364 pages released by the Federal Trade Commission in January 1984.[4] These included the memos by the two FTC Bureaus analyzing the joint venture, a cover memo from the Director of the Bureau of Competition, a dissenting memo from a staff attorney, and the consultant's report. Release of such internal documents from an antitrust investigation was without precedent. All information that the companies considered "confidential" was blacked out from these memos, however, resulting in deletion of many of the factual bases for the various analysts' conclusions.

Additional information may be gleaned from statements issued by all of the Commissioners of the FTC at the times they voted, as well as from congressional testimony that some of them subsequently offered. From these diverse sources, a relatively comprehensive outline emerges of the issues debated within the FTC regarding the General Motors-Toyota joint venture. It should be remembered, however, that GM's and Toyota's views have to be inferred from these sources, rather than found directly in public documents.

The Issues

Market Definition and Cooperative Behavior

The first issue in the analysis of the General Motors-Toyota joint venture was the likelihood of cooperative behavior in the relevant market. This, in turn, involved the determination of the relevant product and geographic market and then an assessment of the probability that the firms in that market could cooperate to the detriment of consumers and market efficiency. Clearly if the relevant market were competitive, or at least one sufficiently difficult in which to sustain cooperation, then the joint venture—regardless of what it was or did—would have no adverse effects. In fact, a useful analytical question was whether a full *merger* between General Motors and Toyota would be objectionable. If not, then clearly a joint venture—a less complete consolidation of operations—would be acceptable.

The question of cooperative possibilities might seem easy to answer. After all, even allowing for imports, total U.S. auto sales were very concentrated. In 1982 the top four companies accounted for 76 percent of total sales. GM's historical leadership role in the industry could hardly be questioned, although imports represented an important competitive force. But that fact might just heighten concern over a GM-Toyota arrangement, since the joint venture might lead to moderation of the competitive behavior of the leading importer.

All facets of this simple picture underwent careful examination by the parties. First, with respect to product market definition, the logical starting point for analysis was subcompact cars. Based on the Justice Department Merger Guidelines (DOJ 1982, 1984), the essential question was: If subcompact car prices were raised by a conspiracy of sellers, would consumers switch in sufficient numbers to some other kinds of cars (or trucks, motorcycles, public transit, etc.) so that the price rise would be defeated? Those alternatives to which consumers would switch in sufficient numbers would have to be included in the relevant product market, since a price rise could not be sustained without their cooperation.

Persuasive evidence on these questions was unavailable, and different analysts came to somewhat different conclusions. Some argued for a market consisting of all new cars, while others proposed a division into large and small cars. The latter definition was ultimately adopted, although the lack of agreement on product market definition was not crucial. Almost regardless of the choice, the evidence on market shares and overall concentration told a similar story (reviewed below). Rather, the crucial issue proved to be the proper definition of the *geographic* market, since treatment of Canadian, European, and Japanese production and imports made a substantial difference to the calculations.

First, with respect to Canada, all parties agreed that its production should be added to U.S. output, given the unique U.S.-Canada Automotive Agreement that permits duty-free movement of most motor vehicles and parts between the two countries (FTC 1984, 589–591). Although there are some differences in automotive regulation between the two countries, there is nearly complete integration of manufacturing and marketing.

Imports from other countries raised more difficult problems. Existing sales of cars produced in Japan and Europe seemed relevant, and so one might simply include import shares in the United States. But some antitrust analysts have argued that merely including current sales understates the constraining effect of foreign producers, who after all can augment their sales in response to a domestic price rise (Landes and Posner 1981). In principle, the whole of their capacity anywhere might be devoted to the United States under some circumstances. That approach would have the effect of defining the market as "the world," with consequent reductions in market concentration and shares of GM and Toyota. For several reasons, a world market went too far.[5] Cars are differentiated goods, and not all capacity is dedicated to the kinds of vehicles that will sell in the United States. Moreover, port facilities, dealer networks, and U.S. regulations constitute constraints on the free flow of vehicles in response to an American price rise. Even the profitability of foreign sales plays a role in the decision as to how much output to supply to the United States. Finally, and perhaps most importantly, the existence of import restraints can make a decisive difference in the proper economic treatment of foreign production, implying that even current sales may overstate their restraining effect.

With respect to European auto companies, there was general agreement that cost differentials, dealer networks, and vehicle characteristics limited their competitive influence. The FTC legal staff placed the Europeans at the "outer fringe of a continuum of competitive influence" (FTC 1984, 184). The consulting economist proposed only "minor additions" from European production (FTC 1984, 370). Expressing somewhat greater ambivalence, the FTC economics staff calculated shares and concentration both with and without European capacity (FTC 1984, 593).

The remaining issue was the appropriate treatment of Japanese production. Beginning on April 1, 1981, all Japanese imports were subject to a quota ostensibly agreed to by the Japanese government (permitting the fiction of a "voluntary restraint agreement," or VRA). This was set at 1.68 million cars for the next two years, at which time it was extended at a slightly higher level. The key question in defining the geographic market relevant to the GM-Toyota joint venture was whether the VRA would persist. Economic analysis demonstrates the importance of this question.

Consider a geographic region like the United States, with substantial domestic production facilities, plus imports limited to exactly 1.68 million units. The pertinent question for market definition is, who can augment sales in the face of a price rise? Since imports cannot expand production, their capacity not currently dedicated to U.S. sales is unambiguously *not* part of the relevant market. The *current* sales of the constrained importers, however, do affect pricing in the domestic market, although in a special way. Figure 1 shows domestic demand curve $D_1D'D_2$, with domestic marginal production cost C (for simplicity taken to be horizontal), and foreign quota-constrained supply Q_U. The effect of the quota is that the initial segment of domestic demand D_1D' is automatically satisfied from foreign production. Domestic companies that supply the remaining demand segment $D'D_2$ therefore set price. If they act competitively, the quantity Q_C will pass through the market at price P_C, equal to marginal cost. Alternatively, if they collude, the quantity will be Q_M where C intersects the marginal revenue curve to demand $D'D_2$. In either case, importers will sell the quota quantity Q_U, but at different prices determined by the degree of competition among *domestic* companies.

It should be emphasized that in the presence of the fixed-quantity quota, the price charged by domestic firms who collude *is* affected by imports. Looking at Figure 1, it should be clear that if imports did not exist at all, the entire demand curve D_1D_2 would be available to domestic companies, rather that just the segment to the right of Q_U. In that case, domestic firms would optimally set a yet higher price. The difference stems not from the degree of domestic collusion (we have assumed perfect collusion in both cases), but from the elasticity of the demand curve available to domestic firms in each case.

Figure 1
Effects of Quota—Constrained Imports on Domestic Market Power

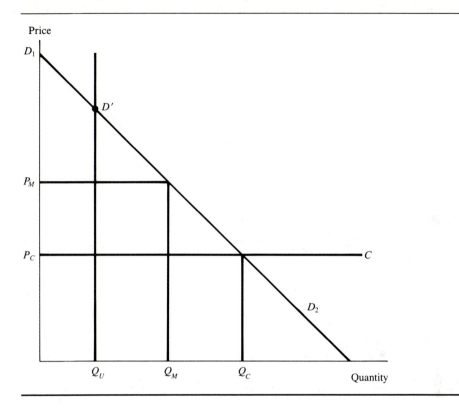

In the presence of such a quota, therefore, the relevant measure of market concentration would seem to depend in part on the concentration *among the unconstrained firms.* This concentration would capture the competitive threat to pricing among the firms that have pricing discretion, while the magnitude of imports affects the elasticity of their demand and hence the profit-maximizing price. Using the Herfindahl-Hirschman Index (HHI) of concentration, the proper calculation of pricing discretion can be derived (Kwoka 1984). This involves calculating the HHI strictly among the unconstrained (i.e., domestic) producers and then multiplying by the domestic share of the total market. This correction embodies the common-sense notion that a larger import share does reduce domestic market power, even if the domestic firms collude perfectly.[6]

The proper treatment of quota-constrained Japanese companies was the focus of considerable, but inconclusive, debate among the analysts of the General Motors-Toyota joint venture. The consultant predicted (correctly) the continuation of quotas over the next several years, and proceeded to calculate shares and concentration among the unconstrained domestic auto producers.[7] General Motors' share of subcompact plus compact ("small") cars became 44.6 percent, Ford's 28.3 percent, and Chrysler's 22.1 percent. He observed, "One cannot help but be struck by the similarity of these shares to traditional market positions by the "Big Three" U.S. producers. And if the pattern of price leadership which characterized their postwar behavior holds in the current small car market, there are ample grounds for [competitive] concern" (FTC 1984, 393).

The FTC economic and legal staffs noted that the long-run possibility that constrained Japanese producers could establish American assembly facilities (as indeed they have done), but that in the short run the import constraint was largely binding. The legal staff was therefore largely content to exclude production above current import levels. The economics staff, however, was more ambivalent, calculating market shares and concentration both with and without Japanese production, thereby bracketing the adjustment factor described above (FTC 1984, 184, 968–1042).

Table 1 gives raw data for analysis of the small-car market. The apparent four-firm concentration is 69 percent and the apparent HHI is 1589, both in the medium to upper range of concentration in manufacturing. Limiting the calculation strictly to domestic firms, one finds the domestic HHI to be 3302. Multiplying by the domestic share yields a measure of market concentration equal to 2028. This is clearly above the threshold for highly concentrated industries (1800) established in the Department of Justice Merger Guidelines (DOJ 1982, 1984).

The conclusion therefore was inescapable that the relevant market showed substantial concentration. An important ancillary question was the magnitude of increase in concentration that would be caused by the consummation of the joint venture. The FTC economics staff observed that the increase would be no greater than $2s_1s_2$, where s_1 and s_2 denote the two firms' market shares. This formula captures the magnitude of increase in the HHI due to full merger. Construing full merger as the equivalent of divesting *all* capacity to a joint venture, the staff proposed to represent the increase by $2ks_1s_2$, where k was the percentage of the two parent companies' capacity devoted to the joint venture. A sample calculation along these lines produced a modest 45-point increase in the HHI as the result of the GM-Toyota joint venture (FTC 1984, 621–622).

A somewhat different analysis was provided to the FTC by a consultant to Chrysler in this matter.[8] Beginning from the theoretical roots

Table 1
American Small Car Market Shares, 1982 Model Year

Category	Units (thousands)	Share
GM	1251	27.4
Ford	793	17.4
Chrysler	622	13.6
AMC/Renault	136	3.0
Domestic Total	2803	61.4
Toyota	480	10.5
Nissan	452	9.9
Honda	352	7.7
Mazda	151	3.4
VW	151	3.3
Subaru	139	3.0
Isuzu	15	.3
Fiat	15	.3
Import Total	1759	38.6
Total	4563	100.0

Note: These numbers, and others used later, include sports and sporty cars in the small-car market. Little difference results from their exclusion, however.

Source: FTC 1984, p. 329.

of the HHI, this analysis considered various degrees of control that the parent companies might exercise over a joint venture and the implications of each for the Herfindahl calculation. Depending on these control mechanisms, and compared to the establishment of a *new* firm with the production capacity of the joint venture (not necessarily the correct benchmark), changes in the HHI ranged from a decrease of 37 points to an increase of 672, with the most likely scenarios in the vicinity of 100- to 200-point increases.

Given the concentrated nature of the market and at least the possibility of significant increase in effective concentration from the joint venture, economic theory and empirical evidence implied that anticompetitive behavior among U.S. producers was a distinct concern. Indeed, the history of the domestic automotive industry underscored this likelihood (White 1971). Alternatively, of course, it could be that other factors so mitigated against cooperation that no real grounds for concern existed. Economic research over the preceding decade had emphasized the importance of factors other than concentration in determining the outcome of firm interactions in a market, and all parties considered their effects.

The economic consultant noted five factors that would tend to hinder cooperative behavior in the auto market. These were the number of firms, cost differences, product heterogeneity, demand instability, and technological change. As he observed, the number of relevant firms was reduced by the VRA, as was the impact of cost differences. Moreover, product heterogeneity and demand instability had not prevented cooperative behavior in the past. He concluded that, except for the VRA, the small car market was "functioning in a tolerable fashion. . .but that there are many factors suggesting the potential for anticompetitive behavior" (FTC 1984, 395–398). The FTC legal staff reached much the same conclusion: "As long as import restraints remain, the market should be carefully monitored for evidence of possible collusion in pricing and product planning" (FTC 1984, 216).

The economics staff held a much different view of the market. Even in the presence of import restraints, it contended that component importation and new-plant construction had to be considered as part of the price restraint exercised by the Japanese. Indeed, it went on to state that "the U.S. automobile market has become highly contestable in recent years, and it is likely to remain so if protectionist sentiment does not grow"[9] (FTC 1984, 612). Of course, if this were true, there would have been no need to engage in further analysis of the joint venture.

In the end, most parties within the FTC concluded that there was reason for concern with the state of competition in the market. More than any other single factor, the VRA was seen as the culprit. Given the prospect that the VRA would continue, analysis of the other issues concerning the GM-Toyota joint venture was undertaken.

The Effects of a Joint Venture

The next step in the process was an examination of the competitive effects of a joint venture—particularly the effects of this joint venture. The initial question was the general definition of *joint venture.* A leading legal scholar had defined a joint venture as "an integration of operations between two or more separate firms, in which the following conditions are present:

1. The enterprise is under the joint control of the parent firms, which are not under related control;
2. Each parent makes a substantial contribution to the joint enterprise;
3. The enterprise exists as a business entity separate from its parents; and

4. The joint venture creates significant new enterprise capability in terms of new productive capacity, new technology, a new product, or entry into a new market" (Brodley 1982).

Interestingly, the author of this proposed definition, while consulting for Ford in this case, concluded that the GM-Toyota arrangement did not even qualify as a joint venture since it was not clear that any new capacity, technology, product, or entry resulted. The FTC legal staff agreed that, based on legal precedents as well as this definition, "the question is indeed a close one" (FTC 1984, 230). Yet it rightly pointed out that whether or not the arrangement was a joint venture by some standard did not dispose of the real issue: what effect the arrangement had on competition.[10]

In many antitrust cases, the question of pro- or anticompetitive effects is the same as the question of whether total market output rises or falls.[11] This criterion appears to have been adopted in this case by all parties. The output effects of a joint venture had only begun to be analyzed in the economics literature (Reynolds and Snapp 1982), and hence, considerable original research was undertaken in this case. One such analysis follows.

Consider first an oligopoly with firms who act upon the Cournot assumption; that is, each firm expands its output as much as is profitable based on the presumption that its rivals will hold output constant. Now let each of two firms hold an equal ownership share in one of the existing, competing production facilities—i.e., the joint venture. (The case of a *new* production entity is considered later.) It should be apparent that, relative to the independent entity, each parent now has less incentive to expand its own output, since added output lowers market price and causes a revenue loss on the joint venture's output in addition to the usual revenue loss on its own output previously sold at a higher price (the marginal revenue effect). This ripple effect implies that the parent firm must subtract the profit loss incurred by its joint venture from its direct profit gain on added output.

This disincentive effect may be illustrated with a simple arithmetic example. Consider a homogeneous product market with a demand curve given by $P(Q) = 100 - Q$. Let there be five identical firms in the market, each producing with constant costs $c = 10$, under the Cournot assumption. Each firm maximizes profits with respect to its own quantity q, thus

(1) $$\Pi_i = [P(Q) - c] \, q_i.$$

One can show that each firm's optimal output is given by

(2) $$q_i = (100 - c)/(n+1) = 90/6 = 15 \text{ units.}[12]$$

Thus there is a total of 75 units of output in the market.

If firm 1 and firm 2 form a joint venture and each holds a 50-percent equity stake in firm 5, each of their profits is given by

$$(3) \qquad \Pi_i = [P(Q) - c]\,q_i + .5[P(Q) - c]q_5.$$

At a first approximation, the optimal output for each is now

$$(4) \qquad q^{**} = q^* - .5(q^*),$$

where q^* is derived from equation (2) above. This implies total production of 7.5 units, clearly less than the output chosen under independent maximization.

This is only a first approximation for the following reason: output q^* was chosen by each independent producer because all produced five times q^*, which led to a market price making q^* optimal. If now some firms (e.g., firms 1 and 2) contract their output as shown in equation (4), *ceteris paribus* the market price will rise and all other firms (those numbered 3, 4, and 5) will see fit to increase their outputs.[13] That means that the "q^*" in equation (4) *understates* the output choice of independent producers as well as that portion of the joint venture parents' output choice. The net effect of these forces is nonetheless an unambiguous decrease in total market output. In the present example, it can be shown that total output falls to 67.5.[14] Each of the three independent firms (including the joint venture) now produces 16.875 units (compared to 15.0 before), and each joint venture parent produces 8.4375 = 16.875 − .5(16.875).

Therefore, it seems apparent that the establishment of a joint venture can alter producers' incentives and result in a diminution of their output. It is important to note that these effects do not stem from increased cooperation or collusion between any firms. The changes described result entirely from the structural realignment within the market that replaces an independent competitor with the joint venture, but with identical (Cournot) behavior throughout. If the joint venture enhanced the degree of cooperation by eliminating one independent producer or a particularly disruptive firm, the output-decreasing effects would be all the more serious.

The story thus far has considered the case where a joint venture replaces an existing firm. Many, perhaps most, joint ventures involve the creation of a new production entity in the market, and the output effects in this case may be quite different. The essential reason is very simple: the creation of new production capacity (i.e., a sixth entity, to extend the previous example) clearly increases total industry capacity. If the new joint venture's parents wished to increase price (i.e., decrease output), *increasing* capacity is not a strategy well suited to doing so.

Thus, in contrast to the case of a joint venture that replaces an existing firm, purely *structural* considerations imply that a new firm joint venture is almost certainly output-increasing and hence procompetitive. A major implication of the economic analysis of joint ventures, therefore, is to focus attention on the question of whether the General Motors-Toyota joint venture represented new capacity. Although the joint venture involved opening (or reopening) a production facility, that event does not establish the capacity to be a net addition against the relevant alternative. For example, the venture might have substituted for independent expansion by either GM or its Japanese partner. If so, it would be competitively suspect. If not, competition problems may still exist, but they must lie elsewhere.

The "elsewhere" lies in the possibility of *behavioral* changes induced by the joint venture. The joint venture might somehow serve to increase the degree of cooperation between the parents and/or within the industry as a whole. If the increase in cooperation is sufficient in magnitude, it may offset the structural incentive toward larger output inherent in a joint venture that represents new capacity, resulting in a net anticompetitive effect. And of course, if such behavioral changes occur in a joint venture that replaces an existing firm, the anticompetitive effect is that much greater.

There are a number of ways in which a joint venture may increase the degree of cooperation and coordination between the parents and within the industry generally. The joint venture may serve to improve communication between the parents and thereby foster cooperation that was previously weaker or absent. The joint venture may also provide better means for enforcing discipline between the parents, since each now has a commitment that exposes it to retaliation by the other party. Or the joint venture, by expanding and partially combining the market presence of the parents, may permit them to enforce better discipline among the other firms in the market.

Thus, economic analysis did help to identify the basic questions involved in the General Motors-Toyota joint venture: 1) did it substitute for other expansion plans by either firm? and 2) did it increase the degree of cooperation within the market? With hindsight, the novelty of these insights is subject to some question. Twenty years previously in the *Penn-Olin* case, the Supreme Court required a close examination of whether either or both of two parties to a joint venture would have entered the market *de novo,* and if only one, whether the second firm would have remained "waiting in the wings" as a potential competitor. It declared both outcomes preferable to a simple joint venture, a thoroughly sound economic conclusion by the Court.[15]

Moreover, the Court clearly recognized the likely behavioral consequences of joint ventures, stating

The joint venture. . .often creates anticompetitive dangers. It is the chosen competitive instrument of two or more corporations previously acting independently and usually competitively with one another. The result is "a triumvirate of associated corporations." If the parent companies are in competition with one another, . . .it may be assumed that neither will compete with its progeny in its line of commerce (*Penn-Olin* 1964).

It was against these overlapping legal principles and economic reasoning that the General Motors-Toyota joint venture was assessed.

General Motors' Alternatives to the Joint Venture

This analysis underscored the central nature of the question as to what GM and Toyota would do in the absence of the joint venture. In particular, if it were clear that either (or both) would enter or expand, then the joint venture would almost certainly be competitively inferior in its output effects. This follows since, for example, if General Motors would otherwise have produced small cars by itself, the net effect of the Toyota joint venture would be given by the comparison between a no-joint-venture industry and one with a joint venture that replaces an existing firm. That comparison showed output to decline. In fact, good arguments could be made for the likelihood of entry by both GM and Toyota.

There were several reasons Toyota might enter U.S. production in the absence of the joint venture. First, calculations showed that such entry would be profitable for Toyota (FTC 1984, 287, 567). Moreover, it was the largest auto manufacturer in the world not to have a U.S. facility, and it was running some risk that others might exploit its lack of a U.S. presence. The FTC legal staff and the economic consultant nonetheless agreed that Toyota did not appear likely to enter by itself anytime soon. Toyota was a very conservative company that resisted foreign investment. Even the joint venture with GM seemed to be an effort to find the cheapest way to respond to protectionist sentiment in the United States. Only if that sentiment remained very strong and quotas very tight for some time did these analyses conclude that Toyota might establish its own U.S. assembly operation (FTC 1984, 291, 419–420).

An entirely different argument subscribed to by some within the FTC was that the joint venture with GM might actually *hasten* Toyota's independent entry into U.S. production (FTC 1984, 25). By learning about domestic labor relations and supplier relationships, Toyota might resolve its doubts and actually initiate full production sooner than would otherwise be the case. There was, however, no real evidence to support this possibility, and it remained in the realm of speculation.

The major debate involved GM's alternatives to the joint venture with Toyota. As previously noted, the joint venture arose from GM's search for ways to satisfy a large demand for small cars during the late 1980s. Its own offerings consisted of Chevettes plus J-cars and X-cars, the latter two of which were selling well. But the Chevette—the only true subcompact of the three, but an antiquated vehicle—was fading fast in the marketplace, and GM was widely known to have devoted much time and effort to the search for a replacement.

In various places in the FTC materials, the major alternatives considered by GM are disclosed to be the S-car, imports from Isuzu, imports from Suzuki, and domestic assembly with Isuzu. The S-car was launched in 1982 by GM's European subsidiary, Opel, and became an immediate market success there. GM had been considering producing the S-car in the United States, but in January 1982, the Chevrolet Division's chief engineer for small-car programs publicly stated that GM had abandoned further consideration. The reason given was "financial difficulties," reflecting the growing realization that U.S. production of subcompacts was no longer financially viable.[16]

Simultaneously, GM was pursuing arrangements for importing subcompacts from Japan for resale through its dealer network. One obvious source was Isuzu, a relatively small Japanese auto company in which GM had taken a 34-percent interest in 1971. Isuzu had previously supplied GM with small pickups for the U.S. market, cars for Europe, and knock-down kits (unassembled vehicles) for various countries. Now it would be asked to develop and produce 200,000 units annually of new subcompacts, known as the R-car and eventually sold as the Spectrum, to be shipped to the United States for sale in 1984. In order to ensure this plan, GM loaned $200 million to Isuzu and increased its investment state to about 40 percent.

The companion to this plan was one by which GM would import from Suzuki of Japan about 90,000 minicars for resale in the United States under the name Sprint. Know mostly for its motorcycles, Suzuki produced very small cars as well. The Sprint would be a new vehicle, to be sold in Japan in 1983 and exported to the United States the following year. In order to sponsor this undertaking, GM acquired a 5.3 percent interest in Suzuki and, further, arranged a stock swap between Suzuki and Isuzu.

Soon, however, it became clear that GM's Japanese strategy would fall victim to the Voluntary Restraint Agreement. GM had counted on no more than three years of import restraints, at which time the Isuzu and Suzuki programs would be fully operational. It was becoming apparent that this assumption was unrealistic. The quotas were being extended, at slightly greater volumes, but there was no prospect that GM's affiliates would get much of the increase (FTC 1984, 87).

This unforeseen development posed serious problems for General Motors. It faced the dismal possibility of having no new small car at all. Moreover, having induced Isuzu into production of a vehicle designed for itself, GM might have no market for the car. At a minimum it would damage GM's investment in the company and constitute an embarrassing breach of trust, and at worst it could jeopardize Isuzu's financial viability. The solution to these overlapping problems was a GM plan for U.S. assembly of R-cars.[17] That is, the very car to have been built by Isuzu would instead be shipped in component form to the United States (components were not subject to the VRA) and assembled in a facility much like the ultimate joint venture with Toyota. This would fulfill GM's commitment to Isuzu while providing GM with the necessary small cars for the U.S. market.

More to the point, domestic assembly of the R-car also was viewed as an alternative to the joint venture with Toyota. The FTC legal staff asked, "If such a plan is GM's response to a desperate shortage of small cars caused by the VRA, might it not also be GM's response to a desperate shortage of cars caused by the failure of the joint venture?" (FTC 1984, 108). Although it concluded that "no definitive answer. . .is possible," others drew firmer inferences. The economic consultant listed "pre-emption of GM's domestic R-car" as a "substantial" competitive risk from the joint venture (FTC 1984, 424–425). Two FTC Commissioners cited blacked-out passages of the released materials as supporting the conclusions that "absent the joint venture, GM would very likely satisfy its small car needs by a variety of options, including domestic assembly of the 'R' car" (Bailey 1983, 12).

The economic logic behind this position is clear: with small car requirements of apparently great magnitude, it is not likely that GM would have done *nothing* if the joint venture failed to go forward. Domestic assembly of the R-car was the obvious alternative and clearly something that GM saw as a contingency plan. The only remaining questions were whether that alternative arrangement posed any competitive problems, and whether that arrangement was equivalent to the joint venture from GM's viewpoint.

No one doubted that a domestic venture between GM and Isuzu would be competitively innocuous. After all, Isuzu was already 40 percent owned by GM, and hence not an altogether independent entity. Moreover, Isuzu was a minor factor in the U.S. auto market, without obvious potential to become a major competitor. GM plus Isuzu equaled (approximately) GM, whereas GM plus Toyota was an entirely different matter.

But would Isuzu accomplish for GM everything that the joint venture with Toyota would? There were certain added risks to GM from R-car assembly. For one, it involved a new vehicle, and regardless of how well it appeared, it was a less well-known commodity than the new Corolla. Moreover, Isuzu was not an experienced large-scale producer of passenger cars and components. General Motors might have reason for concern over Isuzu's ability to follow through on production that it needed desperately. Yet GM had relied on Isuzu before, and its continued use of its affiliate might be construed as satisfaction with Isuzu's performance.

On balance, it was probably true that from a production point of view, a GM joint venture with Isuzu was not a perfect substitute for one with Toyota. On the other hand, it was not at all clear that the difference was substantial. The other facet of this, of course, was GM's objective of learning more about Japanese production techniques. Isuzu more clearly was not the full equivalent of Toyota in this respect.

Based on these considerations, the economic consultant concluded that the GM-Toyota joint venture was anticompetitive because GM had a close alternative that was competitively preferable. The versions of the economic and legal staff memos that were released are quite unclear as to their views of the likelihood of the domestic R-car alternative, but the cover memo from the Director of the Bureau of Competition is more revealing. It argues that "GM has a business need to obtain a minimum of 200,000 additional subcompacts, even if its estimate of needs is somewhat overstated and *even if it could profitably assemble R-cars in the U.S.*" (FTC 1984, 19; emphasis added). In short, the memo's implication was that the joint venture with Toyota and R-car assembly were not alternatives, but *both* necessary ingredients of GM's small-car strategy. This became the majority view by the FTC Commissioners and, as we shall see, was an important premise for the final resolution of the investigation.

Behavioral Effects of the Joint Venture

All parties within the FTC analyzed the possible behavioral effects of the joint venture. The particular concern was that the joint venture might somehow cause a tolerably competitive industry to become significantly more cooperative. The principle areas of investigation were the transfer pricing mechanism for the joint venture vehicle and direct information exchanges between GM and Toyota. Both of these attracted attention because they represented devices by which firms generally can dispel uncertainty regarding their rivals' likely response. Fear of uncooperative response (e.g., failure to follow a price increase) is an important competitive restraint in an oligopoly environment.

A transfer price mechanism was required since the joint venture was producing cars for sale to GM (which then, of course, sold them to its dealers who in turn sold them to retail consumers). This made the joint venture, and ultimately Toyota, a supplier to GM. Like all long-term supply contracts between companies, the one between the joint venture and GM had to set a price. The way it did so was through two basic provisions: 1) the initial transfer price of the joint venture vehicle was to be set in accordance with the wholesale price of Toyota's U.S. Corolla; after adjustments for differences in features, the transfer price was to be between 8 percent and 11 percent less than the net price Toyota charged its U.S. dealers; and 2) the subsequent transfer price would be the initial price modified annually in accordance with a market-basket index of wholesale prices of U.S. small cars. The index would consist of the ten largest-selling small cars, with the Corolla weighted 30 percent and the other 70 percent divided among the remaining nine models.[18]

This pricing mechanism was defended by GM and Toyota as avoiding the necessity for direct and frequent negotiations regarding U.S. small-car prices. In reality, it would not appear to accomplish that, since the Memorandum of Understanding between the parent companies included some provisions ensuring negotiations between them. For example, computation of the market-basket index required adjustment for "the value of equipment changes and product improvements"[19] from year to year. Common understanding of such values on the ten best-selling small cars, determined by annual discussions, could result in greater commonality to GM's and Toyota's small-car feature pricing. Moreover, the parties explicitly reserved the right to reject the computed transfer price whenever it became, in their judgment, "at significant variance with then current market conditions" or if "the JV [joint venture] would incur losses which could endanger the normal operations of the JV." In such cases, they would directly negotiate an alternative price, raising all the concerns the mechanism ostensibly avoided.

But even if the transfer pricing mechanism worked as claimed, some important competitive issues remained. After all, the index had the effect of guaranteeing an increase, and of a known amount, in GM's wholesale price in response to an increase in the price of a Corolla or any other large-selling small car. For example, if the Corolla's wholesale price rose by $100, that automatically would result in a $30 increase in the joint-venture car price to GM. And if (as other evidence seemed to indicate) Toyota was the small-car price leader, other companies might follow its $100 price increase, with the ultimate effect on the joint-venture car price approaching $100.

The competitive consequences of such pricing are clear. The transfer pricing formula reduces the fear among the leading small-car companies that others might not follow their price increase. Toyota would know that if it raised the Corolla price, the price of the joint-venture car must necessarily follow. Ford, Honda, and others would know that if they raised their prices, the joint-venture car would do whatever Toyota did. Effectively, the price of the joint-venture car would no longer be independently set. Rather, it becomes a strict Toyota-price follower, so that GM (or at least that important part of GM's output) is eliminated as a separate player in the oligopoly game. The fact that this has been accomplished without explicit collusion is beside the point. The result is what Toyota's own lawyer conceded to be "lockstep" pricing (Bailey 1983, 6).

Two factors mitigate, but do not eliminate, these concerns. First, the formula does not involve exact matching of Toyota and the joint-venture car price changes. As noted, a $100 increase in the price of a Corolla by itself results in only a $30 increase in the joint-venture car price. Furthermore, the prices in question are at the wholesale (i.e., sale from manufacturer to dealer) level. The relationships between wholesale prices and list prices, and between list prices and transaction prices at the retail level are not perfectly tight. These factors imply that the pricing formula will not achieve perfect cooperation, but of course perfect cooperation is not necessary for anticompetitive effects.

In addition to the transfer pricing formula, the second major concern over enhanced cooperation involved the possibility of direct information exchange between GM and Toyota. The companies, previously arms-length competitors, now would be in close, daily contact on matters involving a major common product. Although the joint venture was limited to production, the opportunities would be enormous for possible spillovers into such competitively sensitive topics as retail pricing, future product plans, and research and development. Remarkably, there was already evidence that these concerns were well founded.

The documentary record of the negotiations leading up to the joint venture contained examples of precisely the anticompetitive information exchanges that one might fear would ensue. For one, Toyota was said to have offered suggestions on retail pricing of the joint-venture vehicle to GM. In particular, the suggestions apparently involved recommendations for the appropriate price differential at retail for that vehicle relative to the older model Corolla (Bailey 1983, 10; Pertschuk 1983, 8). This topic was quite unrelated to the operation of the joint venture and seemed transparently an effort at price cooperation between the joint-venture car and the new model Corolla, whose price

Toyota would be setting. Moreover, GM was supposed to have "acted upon" these suggestions, implying that GM's retail price differential may have been constructed or modified in accordance with Toyota's proposal (Bailey 1983, 10).

That example was not the only illustration of anticompetitive information exchange. The joint-venture negotiations were said to have involved another episode in which Toyota supplied GM with "certain detailed product information which otherwise would certainly not be exchanged between these competitors" (Bailey 1983, 9). These are further described as analyses of Toyota's forthcoming 1983 and 1984 models, including "improvements and design characteristics" (Pertschuk 1983, 8). Exchange of product information raises the possibility of coordinating product offerings so as not to be too directly competitive, or matching technological improvements, or at least altering marketing efforts in mutually beneficial ways.

The FTC economics staff was vigorous in defending these information flows as somehow necessary to the joint venture, or of little value to the other party, or without effect given the strongly competitive nature of the market. It also argued that the companies could exchange such information without the joint venture if they so chose, and thus the joint venture must be unimportant (FTC 1984, 624–657, 1092–1099). A more realistic position was adopted by the legal staff, which concluded, "the point here is that the joint venture facilitates discussions about price that GM conceded were forbidden and this is the only example we happen to know about; should the joint venture proceed, others may well occur. . ." (FTC 1984, 252). Its conclusion that information exchange was "the most troubling feature of the joint venture" (FTC 1984, 254) was ultimately echoed in the FTC's majority position.

One additional possible anticompetitive effect from the joint venture received some attention (FTC 1984, 408–410). Cartel theory emphasizes the importance of disciplinary or enforcement mechanisms among firms attempting cooperative actions. A joint venture is a device that can serve that purpose, because it simultaneously makes each party vulnerable to punitive actions by the other. That vulnerability (which has come to be called "the taking of mutual hostages") is, of course, a weapon exchanged with extreme caution, but it has the potential to promote adherence to mutual goals by otherwise independent companies (Schelling 1960; Williamson 1983).

The source of the mutual vulnerability is clear. GM and its dealers might become dependent on the joint-venture vehicle for a sizable fraction of GM's small-car offerings for as many as twelve years. Through its supply of key components and through its management of the production process, Toyota assumed a considerable measure of control over the vehicle, and hence over GM's offering. For its part, GM gained certain advantages relative to Toyota. GM became part owner of and supplier to a venture on which Toyota was counting to mollify its protectionist critics in the United States. Moreover, GM was to market the joint-venture vehicle as a Chevrolet, raising risks to Toyota (which was widely known as the co-manufacturer) if the vehicle did not live up to expectations.

The effects of such mutual vulnerability in terms of its enforcement potential were not likely ever to be witnessed. Explicit threats were less likely than subtler signs and reminders, but they would be no less real or effective. For example, if Toyota wished to raise its own prices but feared that GM might not raise its prices, Toyota might only have to mention the possibility of "component supply problems" to the joint venture in order for GM to get the intended message. Such possibilities, however, weighed little in the final analysis of this joint venture.

Efficiencies from the Joint Venture

If the joint venture posed no competitive concerns, there would be no need to evaluate efficiencies. But if, as most analysts concluded, there were risks to competition, then the question became whether they were larger or smaller than any cost savings properly attributable to the joint venture. The conceptual and empirical facets of this question were among the most fascinating and troublesome aspects of the GM-Toyota joint venture.

The importance of efficiencies for antitrust policy is usually illustrated as in Figure 2 (Williamson 1968; Fisher and Lande 1983). The market price is raised from P_1 to P_2 as the result of a merger, for example, with a corresponding decline in quantity demanded. Deadweight loss from the merger is given by the area labeled D, representing the amount of surplus lost by consumers and not recovered by anyone else. Area E is surplus lost by consumers but gained by producers as profit and hence is not lost to the market system. It may raise equity concerns but does not represent a change in market efficiency. Finally, area C denotes cost savings due to a decline in unit production costs from MC_1 to MC_2 resulting from the merger. In the case of the GM-Toyota joint venture, where the cost savings accrue only to joint-venture output, then the rectangle representing attributable economies will be correspondingly smaller. In any event, since both areas C and D are efficiency effects, an overall assessment of a merger or joint venture on efficiency grounds requires netting these out.

Figure 2
Economic Effects of a Merger that Creates Market Power

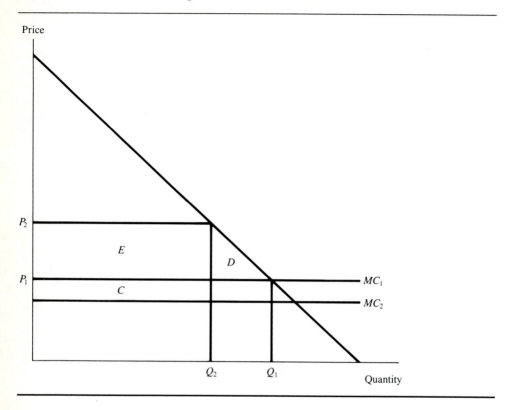

It is important to recognize at the outset that many of the conventional efficiency reasons for joint ventures simply did not apply to the GM-Toyota arrangement. No one contended that scale economies would be better realized, since both companies were well above minimum efficient scale for an auto plant (FTC 1984, 1263–1290). Nor was a new product being created by pooling resources, since the vehicle was clearly a minor variant of an existing model. Rather, the essence of the efficiency argument was that Toyota had mastered the process of manufacturing automobiles, that GM needed to learn that process in order to regain competitiveness, and that the joint venture was uniquely suited to realizing that objective.

There was no doubt about Japanese production superiority. It was widely agreed that the aggregate cost differential between U.S. and Japanese small-car manufacturing was about $2000 per car. But for various reasons, that number bore little relationship to the cost savings attributable to, and reasonably expected from, the GM-Toyota joint venture. Certain cost savings realized *by* the joint venture could not be properly attributed *to* it. In particular, the joint venture intended to import many components, perhaps totaling 50 to 60 percent, from Japan. By all accounts, these would be significantly cheaper than identical U.S. components. Yet these cost savings cannot be attributed to the joint venture, since it is not a saving generated by the joint venture, but merely an external or pecuniary economy gained by out-sourcing. As such, it would be achievable by any U.S. manufacturer through out-sourcing, as indeed all "Big 3" auto companies were doing from their Japanese affiliates.

Furthermore, the joint venture was limited to final assembly and certain major body stampings. Accordingly at a first approximation, only those aspects of the Toyota manufacturing system would be revealed to GM. Assembly and stamping operations typically constitute no more than 20 percent of total value added, implying that the relevant cost differential was not likely to exceed $400 (i.e., 20 percent of $2000). Beyond that, about 40 percent of the differential consisted of wages. The joint venture was known to have agreed to pay its workers according to existing union wage scales, and therefore only the remaining 60 percent, or $240, was even a candidate for savings through the joint venture.

This $240 figure had to be further discounted by three factors. First, certain aspects of the Toyota production system in Japan simply could not be replicated in the United States. These included an inventory system that relied on close proximity of facilities, uncharacteristic of U.S. manufacturing, and cultural differences in employment, such as "lifetime employment" in Japan. Second, some ingredients of the total cost saving were already well known to GM, and GM was pursuing them unilaterally. GM was fully cognizant of the savings associated with coordinating worker break times (so-called mass relief), with reducing the number of job classifications, with better plant layout, and so forth. In fact, simultaneous with the joint venture, GM was touting its progress on exactly these fronts in its new Lake Orion, Michigan, and Wentzville, Missouri, assembly plants.

Corrections for these factors could proceed either by 1) subtracting from the $240 cost-saving figure those portions that could not be done or were being done unilaterally by GM, or 2) comparing costs at GM's new state-of-the-art facilities with projections of joint-venture costs. These alternatives yielded remarkably similar conclusions. The economic consultant, employing the first approach, proposed that perhaps one-third of the remaining differential was achievable by GM unilaterally and concluded that the relevant cost saving was in the range of $100 to $200 per joint-venture car (FTC 1984, 444–445). The economics staff compared the joint venture with state-of-the-art GM plants and arrived at a figure of $197 per vehicle (FTC 1984, 669, 676).

The final discount factor involved the portion of this amount that GM could learn in some other, less anticompetitive manner. The key alternative again involved Isuzu, GM's longstanding Japanese affiliate which was to produce the R-car. No one argued that Isuzu was the equivalent of Toyota, but GM had used Isuzu as a source of vehicles before without apparent cost or quality problems, and the new R-car was projected to be cost-competitive with the best. The economic consultant concluded, "All of these factors clearly imply some considerable capabilities by Isuzu" (FTC 1984, 446), and the FTC economics staff at one point went so far as to state, "It is not clear that Toyota has information that GM does not already have" (FTC 1984, 539).[20]

Regardless of one's view of Isuzu's potential contribution, this efficiency calculation inevitably resulted in some rather modest benefits from the joint venture. Even $200 per car resulted in only $40 million annually—not trivial, but clearly not an overwhelming magnitude. If there were large efficiencies from the GM-Toyota joint venture, therefore, they had to result from additional factors.

FTC staff advanced several related arguments along these lines. One focused on the possible diffusion of these cost savings, claiming in particular that they would spread over time to 1) other GM assembly plants, 2) component production plants within GM, or 3) non-GM plants throughout the United States auto industry. Transfer of some new techniques to other GM assembly plants was not implausible, and indeed GM stated that it wished to rotate certain supervisory personnel through the joint-venture plant for exactly that purpose. Yet its plans for doing so were vague and in part dependent on the cooperation of the United Auto Workers—no certain matter. Much less clear were the prospects for transferring what was learned to component manufacturing plants. True, such matters as just-in-time inventory systems were relevant to both assembly and component manufacturing, but most cost savings were less obviously generic.

The largest estimates of additional cost savings were based on the contention that GM's adoption of these cost-saving techniques would force Ford, Chrysler, and AMC to respond in kind. This ripple effect from competitive forces, if attributable to the initial joint venture, resulted in apparent efficiencies of truly astronomical proportions. The problem with such calculations is obviously that they are highly speculative, depending on the mere assertion of multiple effects and neglecting a host of likely impediments.

In addition to this story concerning the *extent* of diffusion, arguments were made as to the benefits of the joint venture in speeding up the *process* of diffusion. In particular, it was claimed that the joint venture with Toyota would hasten change within GM by providing a "demonstration effect" to the United Auto Workers, whose wage scales and work rules contributed to the cost differential with Japan, and also by shaking up hidebound middle managers at GM, so that they would realize the growing urgency of responding to the Japanese cost challenge (FTC 1984, 23, 24, 686).

Factually, these contentions are subject to some reservations. For example, if demonstration projects were therapeutic for the UAW, preexisting Honda and Nissan plants should serve the purpose—perhaps even better, since they were nonunion. If the therapy is more effective coming from a major U.S.-based auto company, then the specific need for GM and Toyota to combine was unproved, since Ford and Chrysler were known to be negotiating with their Japanese affiliates over joint domestic assembly facilities.

Apart from their factual validity, these arguments starkly raise the question of what kind of cost savings should be recognized as an efficiency for policy purposes. These alleged gains are a long way from the concrete, demonstrable production cost savings that constitute conventionally acceptable efficiencies.[21] Rather, they represent the relaxation of institutional and behavioral rigidities that had arisen in cooperative oligopoly. It might be asked whether structural change in an industry, with attendant anticompetitive risks, should be permitted in order to remedy a company's own management deficiencies (hidebound managers, etc.). Apart from this conceptual issue, the indisputable *practical* problem with such claims is that they are virtually impossible either to disprove or to prove, since they consist of little more than an acknowledgment of management problems and the assertion that benefits will be realized. Acceptance of such claims would represent an open invitation to companies to make bad-faith claims and quite possibly create an enormous loophole in the efficiency defense.

Consequently, the clear and attributable cost savings from the joint venture were quite modest, perhaps no more that $40 million. Possible but certainly unquantifiable benefits included spillovers to other GM assembly facilities. Cost savings at other GM facilities remained in the realm of "hope" and spillovers to non-GM plants were surely "dreams." Acknowledging these varying probabilities, the Director of the FTC Bureau of Competition nevertheless adopted the novel position that they deserved weight. He stated, "[I]t seems clear that the potential long-term efficiency gains are quite substantial. GM's 'expected efficiency value' from the venture is therefore high—even if it has less than a certain chance of success. . ." (FTC 1984, 25).

Out of concern for creating large loopholes and unenforceable standards for the efficiency defense, the economic consultant endorsed a relatively narrow efficiency measure. Acknowledging other possibilities, he nonetheless advocated the $40 million figure. He then proceeded to explore the trade-off between this cost saving and the surplus losses from price increases (FTC 1984, 456). The usual formula for deadweight loss is $W = .5\,(PQem^2)$, where P and Q are product price and quantity, respectively, e is market demand elasticity, and m is percentage markup over competitive price.[22] Using figures of $700 for small-car P, 4.562 million for Q, and 2.0 for e, he calculated that a 3.5-percent ($245) price rise in small cars would create $40 million in deadweight loss, offsetting the cost saving. If consumer welfare were the criterion, so that the area designated E in Figure 2 also represented a relevant loss, the price rise necessary to offset fully the cost savings was a mere $9 per small car. And even if other firms failed to follow their lead, GM and Toyota still needed only to raise their own small-car prices by $23 to offset fully the cost saving. The relatively modest price effects that could offset the efficiency gains seemed quite possible.

The Outcome

The FTC Decision

The decision before the Federal Trade Commissioners was whether or not to issue a complaint alleging an antitrust violation against General Motors and Toyota and thereby send the matter to a full administrative trial. The five commissioners were split. Two opposed the joint venture on the grounds that the transfer pricing formula, the likelihood of information exchange, and GM's alternatives demonstrated clear competitive risks not outweighed by any demonstrable efficiency benefits. Reflecting on this combination of the first and third largest auto manufacturers in the world, one commissioner summed up thus: "If this joint venture. . .does not violate the antitrust laws, what does the Commission think will?" (Bailey 1983, p. 15).

The remaining three commissioners, constituting a majority, saw the GM-Toyota joint venture as basically procompetitive. They claimed that it would likely increase the number of small cars and that it would produce cars more cheaply (Miller et al. 1983, 4). The validity of these assertions, of course, depended crucially on the nature and viability of GM's alternative plans, those with Isuzu in particular. Unfortunately, there was simply no reference to this in the majority's statement, and so the basis for its conclusion remains unclear.

The majority also asserted that the joint venture would provide GM the necessary opportunity to learn Japanese production and management techniques and that GM would "attempt to implement these lower-cost techniques at its other plants" (Miller et al. 1983, 4). In support, it cited the recognized superiority of Japanese production, the advantages of "hands-on experience" through the joint venture, and the inducement ("demonstration effect") to GM managers and the UAW. It also asserted, somewhat cavalierly, that "the Commission's investigation has established that Toyota is a far superior source of this knowledge than other possible Japanese partners" (Miller et al. 1983, 5). The majority went on to claim that these techniques, "by assimilation, [would be transferred] to the manufacturing facilities of other U.S. manufacturers" and that this would in turn lead to "the development of a more efficient, competitive U.S. automobile industry" (Miller et al. 1983, 6).

No one doubted that the joint venture would have lower costs and that this should be recognized as a benefit. The transfer of known production techniques from Toyota to the joint venture was a novel efficiency argument, but seemed supportable in this instance. The remaining "benefits," however, were based on the most optimistic, and probably unrealistic, speculation. For reasons described before, acceptance of arguments for transfer to other GM plants and other companies' plants as efficiencies attributable to this joint venture represented a radical, and quite possibly dangerous, expansion of the efficiency defense.

In contrast to its own staff, the FTC majority did have concerns over certain anticompetitive possibilities. The first of these was the concern that the joint venture might eventually reduce small-car output by undermining GM's incentives to produce its own in the United States. The majority went on to make the following, rather clever argument: GM's small-car needs were far larger than the 200,000 units planned for the joint venture, and so the joint venture would be strictly inframarginal as long as it stayed at that volume. That is, unless the joint venture expanded to satisfy more of GM's requirements, it would not undermine GM's incentives to develop its own small car. This logic led, somewhat paradoxically, to a competitive concern over output *expansion* by the joint venture.[23]

The second concern expressed by the FTC majority involved information exchange. Without commenting specifically on the documented exchanges of competitively sensitive information, it asserted that the Memorandum of Understanding between GM and Toyota "lacks adequate safeguards to prevent the flow of [sensitive] information." It rejected as insufficient voluntary guidelines proposed by the two companies to regulate their communication (Miller et al. 1983, 9).

In order to remedy these perceived problems, the FTC needed a legally binding agreement with General Motors and Toyota. The process required that a complaint be filed against the joint venture as originally proposed, but simultaneously the companies would sign a consent order stipulating certain modifications to the agreement. The consent order of December 22, 1983, had two relevant parts. The first limited the joint venture to production and sale to GM of automobiles from one "module," or assembly line, effectively about 200,000 units. The second prohibited GM and Toyota from discussing or exchanging information on a list of topics judged not central to the operation of the joint venture.

The substance of the order was immediately denounced by critics of the joint venture as largely irrelevant. The information-barrier provision, in particular, appeared not to constrain the parties in ways beyond their original Memorandum, and moreover, it continued to rely on self-enforcement by the parties. This was even acknowledged by the companies themselves. General Motors Chairman Roger Smith told the *New York Times* that the consent order simply repeated what the companies had pledged to do, and he went on to remark, "If it gives them [the FTC] some comfort and seals the deal, then it's OK."[24] Toyota's U.S. counsel observed, "The precise terms of the order. . .are likely to include no more than a written agreement to abide by three elements of the venture that have already been publicly announced."[25]

Consent orders do have procedural advantages to the antitrust agencies by reducing their burden of proof in the event a violation by a company is later discovered. But here the real question was whether a violation of the information-exchange provision of the order was ever likely to be discovered. If not, and many thought not, procedural advantages were simply irrelevant.

As the FTC decision process wound to a close, Chrysler filed a private antitrust suit against the joint venture. Their complaint alleged numerous possible anticompetitive consequences. The joint venture might raise prices above normal levels, or it might cause prices to fall to predatory levels. Moreover, Chrysler claimed that the joint venture might permit coordination between GM and Toyota with respect to products, marketing, technological improvements, or other crucial areas.

Many antitrust observers were becoming deeply skeptical of competitor suits, for the simple reason that if price increases resulted from a merger or joint venture, it would be beneficial to rival companies and cause them to favor such an arrangement. By contrast, rivals' opposition could be interpreted as fear that the joining parties will achieve efficiencies and become stronger competitors. This view, while overly simplistic, led the Justice Department to file a legal brief attempting to disqualify Chrysler from filing its suit, but its position was rejected by the court. Chrysler eventually dropped its suit after obtaining minor concessions from GM and Toyota on production volumes and the longevity of the joint venture.[26]

Epilogue to the Joint Venture

A comparison of the assumptions and conclusions of the GM-Toyota investigation with the facts that have emerged is revealing. First, the assumption that import restraints would persist was borne out for the next four or five years, although they were overtaken by other events. The absolute volumes under the quotas rose, and more importantly, the appreciation of the yen drove up import prices so high that Japanese cars ceased to be scarce commodities after 1986. Moreover, under the threat of continued import restraints and a stronger yen, seven (of nine) Japanese auto companies committed themselves to some form of U.S. production. These included Isuzu, and even Toyota, which at last recognized its increasing market vulnerability without a U.S. facility of its own.

More to the point, joint-venture cars came onto the U.S. market in mid-1985 as Chevrolet Novas. As a potential answer to GM's small-car requirements, they seemed ideal—well-designed, well-built, fuel-efficient. *Consumer Reports* labeled the Nova and the Toyota Corolla as the best small cars available in the United States. Ironically, they did not sell well. True, small-car sales were not as brisk in 1985 as projected, but even by comparison with the Toyota Corolla, Nova sales were poor. Over the next two years, Nova production had to be cut three times by a total of 30 percent to prevent excessive inventories from developing.[27]

Furthermore, the belief that limiting the size of the joint venture would preserve GM's incentives to pursue its other small-car plans was not supported by subsequent events. GM never began domestic assembly of the Isuzu R-car, the clear alternative plan. Nor did it pursue any other domestic small-car program for the 1980s.[28] Although changing market demand made all the reasons difficult to disentangle, the joint venture with Toyota did not appear inframarginal, as proclaimed by the FTC majority.

The other objective of the joint venture, of course, was to build small cars less expensively and thereby to provide GM with insight into state-of-the-art Japanese auto production and management techniques. There is no doubt that the GM-Toyota joint venture embodies efficient techniques. It employs about 2500 workers, compared to 4700 when the same facility was run by GM three years earlier.[29] There are no more than four job classifications in the plant, whereas the standard U.S. assembly facility under UAW contract has nearly fifty. It is reported to assemble cars with 23 hours of labor (including stamping), compared to standard GM practice of 40 hours, or even 29 hours at its best "conventional" facility.[30]

By this criterion, clearly the GM-Toyota joint venture has been a success. GM has made efforts to rotate supervisory personnel through the plant in order to spread what it learns to other facilities. Public information about the extent and success of these efforts is limited to a few anecdotes. They suggest that Toyota production techniques have indeed made some inroads at other GM assembly facilities.[31] Nonetheless, UAW staffing requirements represent a constraint, and there is little evidence of the transfer of technique to component manufacturing facilities, much less to other auto companies. And perhaps most importantly, the counterfactual—what GM would have accomplished without the joint venture—remains unknown.

The more grandiose claims—that the joint venture would reinvigorate GM and ultimately the entire American automobile industry—seem fanciful indeed. Four years after enjoying the benefits of watching Toyota firsthand, General Motors has been declared the "sick man" of the domestic auto industry,[32] with unit costs far higher than Ford and Chrysler. But if the demonstrable benefits of the joint-venture have been slight, so too have been the competitive risks. Intensified competition in small cars and mediocre market acceptance of the joint-venture vehicle make some of the original fears of anticompetitive pricing seem exaggerated. Both sets of facts—the modest benefits and the modest risks—represent an ironic conclusion to the major antitrust inquiry into the General Motors-Toyota joint venture.

Notes

1. These reasons are elaborated upon in Federal Trade Commission, Materials Released in Conjunction with the General Motors-Toyota Joint Venture, January 1984 (hereafter cited as FTC), pp. 379–387.
2. Paraphrased in "Detroit Falls Far Short in its Effort to Match Japan's Smaller Autos," *Wall Street Journal,* 1 November 1983, p. 1.
3. Memorandum of the Director of the Bureau of Competition of the Federal Trade Commission, FTC p. 1.
4. These Federal Trade Commission materials, cited *supra* note 1, constitute the principal source for this case study.
5. These reasons are elaborated upon, with further references, in Kwoka (1984).
6. This correction may not perfectly represent remaining market power. For example, if the likelihood of successful collusion increases sharply at some value of HHI, then "discounting" that value by the import share may lower the calculated value below that threshold even though domestic firms' ability to collude is still high. Furthermore, to the extent that policy is concerned with domestic welfare, even the lower price-cost margin associated with the discounted HHI leaves a significant profit transfer to foreign sellers. This is ignored by the

adjustment described. Gratitude is expressed to Larry White for bringing these points to my attention.

7. Taken literally, this fact would make GM and Toyota nonrivals, thereby eliminating any anticompetitive possibilities from the joint venture. This, however, is too abstract a view of the auto market, in which firms compete (and may avoid competing) by physically differentiating their products and by marketing them differently. Moreover, the fixed quantity quota gave importers considerable discretion as to the "mix" of vehicle types and prices they chose to sell in the United States.

8. The consultant's analysis was subsequently published as Bresnahan and Salop (1986). Also see FTC, pp. 621–622 and Kwoka (1985).

9. A contestable market is one with no entry or exit barriers, and where existing firms' price responses are slower than actions by new entrants. It has been shown that under such conditions, prices will not exceed marginal costs, even with only a single incumbent firm. The model bears no obvious relationship to the facts of the automobile market.

10. Brodley also emphasized the more permissive legal standards for joint ventures as a reason for concern whether the GM-Toyota arrangement was so classified.

11. This need not be true, for example, if price discrimination or predation are concerns, if products are differentiated, or if criteria other than static economic efficiency are important.

12. Proof: Differentiating equation (1) by q_i and solving, one obtains profit-maximizing $q_i = p - c$. But $P = 100 - Q$, and Q is merely $n*q_i$, where n is the number of identical firms, five in this example. Substitution yields equation (2). See Kwoka (1985) for an elaboration and correction of partial proofs in FTC, pp. 399–402, 961–967.

13. This presumes the joint venture ("firm 5") is instructed to operate independently—i.e., to behave as any other separate profit-maximizing firm. Alternative assumptions are, of course, possible.

14. Proof: Each parent's optimal output is given by $q_i = P - c - .5(P - c + q_5)$. The independent firms and the joint venture each produce $q_j = P - c$. Again, summing and relying on the market-demand equation, one obtains total $Q = 4(100 - c)/5$, or 67.5 units. From this, individual outputs are readily determined. See Kwoka (1985).

15. *United States* v. *Penn-Olin Chemical Co. et al,* 378 U.S. 158 (1964). The Court also stated that the joint venture was competitively no less desirable than independent entry, a conclusion not necessarily supportable.

16. *Automotive News,* 18 January 1982, p. 1.

17. *Automotive News,* 8 August 1983, p. 4.

18. These figures were inadvertently disclosed in FTC, p. 536, and in Pertschuk (1983), 5. They were subsequently disclosed voluntarily by GM in court filings in a suit brought by Chrysler.

19. This language, and that later in this paragraph, is from the Memorandum of Understanding signed by General Motors and Toyota on February 15, 1982.

20. Indeed, even if Toyota did possess unique knowledge, one might doubt that it would willingly disclose it to one of its principal competitors.

21. Both the FTC Statement Concerning Horizontal Mergers and the then-operative 1982 Department of Justice Merger Guidelines declared their receptivity to claims of efficiencies in exceptional cases, with compelling evidence and limited to production-type savings. These standards were clearly not met in this case.

22. For derivation and discussion of this formula, see (e.g.) Scherer (1980), 459–464.

23. This argument first appears in the Memorandum of the Director of the Bureau of Competition, FTC pp. 31–32.

24. *New York Times,* 21 December 1983, p. D1.

25. *Washington Post,* 21 December 1983, p. D1.

26. *Automotive News,* 15 April 1985, p. 4. The day following, Chrysler announced its own joint venture, with Mitsubishi.

27. See "An Unexpected Flop," *National Journal,* 12 April 1986, p. 888; "GM, Toyota Venture to Cut Production of Chevrolet Novas," *Wall Street Journal,* 23 October 1987, p. 16; and "GM, Toyota Plant Expects 1988 Loss Up to $100 Million," *Wall Street Journal,* 8 February 1988, p. 10. In the interim, Toyota had begun production of a different model of its Corolla at the joint-venture facility, for sale through its own dealer network. This was explicitly permitted to Toyota under the initial terms of the agreement with GM.

28. GM's much-ballyhooed Saturn project was correctly recognized by the FTC as a long-term undertaking with no prospect of building American small cars until the 1990s, FTC p. 15. See also "Will Saturn Ever Leave the Launch Pad?" *Business Week,* 16 March 1987, p. 107.

29. The GM facility had built larger cars, typically requiring more labor. Hence, the comparison somewhat exaggerates the difference.

30. See "U.S. Auto Makers Get Chance to Regain Sales From Foreign Rivals," *Wall Street Journal,* 16 April 1987, p. 1.

31. See, for examples, "GM's Big Burden in Toyota Venture," *New York Times,* 7 May 1987, p. 34; and "Detroit Is Trying, but Its Image Lags," *Business Week,* 8 June 1987, pp. 138–139.

32. "General Motors: What Went Wrong," *Business Week,* 16 March 1987, pp. 102–110.

References

Bailey, Patricia. "Dissenting Statement of Commissioner Patricia P. Bailey: GM/Toyota Joint Venture." Federal Trade Commission, Washington, D.C., December 22, 1983.

Bresnahan, Timothy, and Steven Salop. "Quantifying the Competitive Effects of Production Joint Ventures." *International Journal of Industrial Organization* 4 (1986): 155–175.

Brodley, Joseph. "Joint Ventures and Antitrust Policy." *Harvard Law Review* 95 (May 1982): 1521–1590.

Federal Trade Commission, Materials Released in Conjunction with the Proposed General Motors-Toyota Joint Venture, File No. 821–0159, Washington, D.C., January 15, 1984.

Fisher, Alan, and Robert Lande. "Efficiency Considerations in Merger Enforcement." *California Law Review* 71 (December 1983): 1580–1696.

Kwoka, John. "Antitrust Policy and Foreign Competition." Department of Economics Discussion Paper D87–11, George Washington University, 1984.

Kwoka, John. "Market Power from Horizontal Mergers and Joint Ventures." Department of Economics Discussion Paper D84–13, George Washington University, January, 1985.

Landes, William, and Richard Posner. "Market Power in Antitrust Cases." *Harvard Law Review* 94 (May 1981): 937–996.

Miller, James, et al. "Statement of Chairman James C. Miller III, Commissioner George W. Douglas, and Commissioner Terry Calvani Concerning Proposed General Motors/Toyota Joint Venture." Federal Trade Commission, Washington, D.C., undated, but released December 22, 1983.

Pertschuk, Michael. "Dissenting Statement of Commissioner Pertschuk: GM/Toyota Joint Venture, File No. 821–0159," Federal Trade Commission, Washington, D.C., December 22, 1983.

Reynolds, Robert, and Bruce Snapp. "The Economic Effects of Partial Equity Interests and Joint Ventures." Department of Justice Economic Policy Office Discussion Paper 82–3, August 1982, published in *International Journal of Industrial Organization* 4 (1986): 141–153.

Schelling, Thomas. *The Strategy of Conflict.* Cambridge, Mass.: Harvard University Press, 1960.

Scherer, F. M. *Industrial Market Structure and Economic Performance.* Boston: Houghton Mifflin, 1980.

White, Lawrence J. *The U.S. Automobile Industry Since 1945.* Cambridge, Mass.: Harvard University Press, 1971.

Williamson, Oliver. "Economics as an Antitrust Defense." *American Economic Review* 58 (March 1968): 18–36.

Williamson, Oliver. "Credible Commitments: Using Hostages to Support Exchange." *American Economic Review* 73 (September 1983): 519–540.

Application of the Merger Guidelines: The Proposed Merger of Coca-Cola and Dr Pepper

Lawrence J. White

Introduction

On February 20, 1986, the Coca-Cola Company announced its intentions to purchase the Dr Pepper Company and merge the operations of the two companies. Three and a half weeks earlier, PepsiCo had announced its intentions to purchase the Seven-Up Company, which was a subsidiary of the Philip Morris Corporation. These two mergers would have meant the consolidation, respectively, of the first and fourth and the second and third largest sellers of concentrate for carbonated soft drinks in the United States.

Exercising its antitrust enforcement responsibilities, the Federal Trade Commission in June 1986 decided that these mergers were likely to be anticompetitive and declared its preliminary decision to oppose them. In the face of this opposition PepsiCo and Seven-Up called off their merger, but Coca-Cola and Dr Pepper persisted to the point of a small-scale trial in Federal District Court.

This case is important in at least two respects. First, it represented a federal government antitrust challenge to a major merger at a time when critics of the Reagan administration's antitrust enforcement agencies were claiming that these agencies had largely abandoned enforcement. Second, it is a case in which sophisticated economic reasoning shaped and influenced the structure of many of the arguments advanced by both sides, as well as much of the trial opinion written by the judge in this case.

This case study will provide the background, analyze the economic arguments advanced by both the plaintiff (the FTC) and the defendant

Lawrence J. White was an expert witness for the Federal Trade Commission in the mergers described in the text. The views and opinions expressed in this chapter, however, do not necessarily represent those of the Federal Trade Commission nor of the FTC staff lawyers and economists who worked on the cases. Thanks are due to Marilyn Frankel, John Kwoka, William Lynk, Gordon Spivak, and Gregory Werden for their helpful comments on an earlier draft.

(Coca-Cola) in this antitrust case, and evaluate the outcome. Though reference will also be made to the merger of PepsiCo and Seven-Up, our primary focus will be the merger of Coca-Cola and Dr Pepper.

Industry Background

Coca-Cola, Dr Pepper, PepsiCo, and Seven-Up are usually identified as producers of carbonated soft drinks (CSD). Whether CSD was the appropriate market for judging the competitive consequences of these mergers—or whether, for example, the market should have been construed to be much wider and encompass all potable liquids—was an important issue in the FTC's investigation and the eventual trial. But, because of the companies' primary identification as CSD producers (and because the FTC and the trial judge did conclude that CSD was the relevant market), some background information on the CSD industry should prove useful for the discussion that follows.

The national CSD producers are, for the most part, manufacturers of flavoring concentrate.[1] They sell the concentrate to independent local bottlers, who add carbonated water and sweetener and package the finished CSD into bottles and cans. Bottlers provide the subsequent distribution function, delivering the packaged CSD to food stores, vending outlets, and other retail outlets. Many bottlers also deliver syrup (concentrate plus sweetener) to restaurants and other "fountain" accounts. Bottlers frequently handle the brands of more than one concentrate manufacturer, but most manufacturers place "flavor restrictions" on the ability of bottlers handling their brands to handle competing companies' brands with similar flavors. Thus, in some areas the local Coca-Cola bottler may handle Seven-Up, but he would never also distribute Pepsi or Royal Crown. The concentrate manufacturers generally restrict their bottlers to distribution in local geographic areas. Finally, in the 1980s a few concentrate manufacturers—especially Coke and Pepsi—began absorbing some of their bottlers into the parent companies, so that the latter were becoming more vertically integrated.

The CSD industry involves large dollar sales volumes. The wholesale value (at the bottler level) of CSD sales in 1984 was approximately $23.5 billion.[2] The comparable value of concentrate sales in the same area was approximately $3.5 billion, and the retail value of that CSD was probably around $35 billion. Table 1 provides an estimate of the 1985 retail sales shares of the leading CSD producers.

Table 1
U.S. Retail Sales Shares of Leading Producers*
of Carbonated Soft Drinks, 1985

Producer	Share
Coca-Cola Co.	37.4%
PepsiCo	28.9
Philip Morris (Seven-Up)	5.7
Dr Pepper Co.	4.6
R. J. Reynolds	
(Sunkist, Canada Dry)	3.0
Royal Crown Cola	2.9
Procter & Gamble	
(Orange Crush, Hines Root Beer)	1.8
Others	
(including supermarket brands)	15.7

*Sales shares for each company include all brands produced by that company.
Source: *F.T.C.* v. *Coca-Cola Co.*, 641 F. Supp. 1128, 1134.

The Legal and Procedural Background

Section 7 of the Clayton Act instructs the Department of Justice and the Federal Trade Commission to prevent those mergers and acquisitions "where in any line of commerce in any section of the country, the effect of such acquisition may be substantially to lessen competition or to tend to create a monopoly." The 1976 Hart-Scott-Rodino Amendments to the Clayton Act require that the two agencies be given advance notice of any merger or acquisition that is above a specified size. With only a few exceptions,[3] the division of cases for investigation of potential violations is largely arbitrary. Historical expertise in handling cases in the relevant industry is the major criterion.

After notification of the proposed merger, the agencies usually have thirty calendar days to conduct an initial investigation.[4] At the end of that period (or sooner), the agency can indicate that it will not oppose the merger. Or the agency can make a request for more information (e.g., about detailed sales data, entry experience) from the merging parties. After the new information is received, the agency has another twenty days for analysis.[5] At the end of this second period,[6] the merger can automatically proceed unless the agency obtains a preliminary injunction (PI) from a Federal District Court. Frequently, the simple announcement by the DOJ or the FTC that they intend to seek a PI will cause the merger partners to cancel their deal. But some merger candidates persist and contest the PI. The legal dispute over the PI usually involves a relatively rapid "mini-trial" on the merits of the antitrust issues; in order to grant a PI the court need not resolve all issues, but it must find "that a challenged acquisition is reasonably likely to lessen competition substantially,"[7] so that a full-length investigation and trial would be warranted. If the merger candidates win the mini-trial, they can proceed with their merger, but the agencies can still try to prosecute to unscramble the merger through a full-length legal proceeding (which can often extend, including pre-trial depositions and document requests, for two or three years or even longer).[8] If the agencies win the mini-trial for the PI, the merger is temporarily stopped, but the merger candidates can nevertheless persist with their legal efforts, hoping to reverse their fortunes through a full-length legal proceeding. Most merger candidates, though, cancel their plans if they lose the mini-trial and thus fail to prevent the agencies from obtaining the PI.

For the two proposed carbonated soft drink industry mergers under discussion, the FTC was the logical agency to conduct the investigation. The FTC in the 1970s had conducted an extensive investigation of the carbonated soft drink bottling industry and the practice of the syrup manufacturers of granting exclusive sales territories to their bottlers. In 1978 the FTC declared that this practice was anticompetitive. (The Congress in 1980, however, legislatively overruled the FTC and carved out a special exemption in the antitrust laws — the Soft Drink Interbrand Competition Act — for the territorial exclusivity practices of the syrup manufacturers.)

The FTC's investigation of the two mergers lasted approximately four months.[9] At the end of June 1986 the Commission decided unanimously[10] that the mergers were likely to be anticompetitive and instructed the FTC's lawyers to seek a preliminary injunction to halt the proposed mergers.[11] Faced with this challenge, PepsiCo and Seven-Up cancelled their merger plans. Coca-Cola and Dr Pepper persisted and indicated their willingness to contest the granting of the PI. Under such circumstances the parties are usually granted an expedited hearing before a Federal District Court judge. In mid-July Judge Gerhard Gesell conducted a mini-trial in Washington, D.C., on the merits of the FTC's claim that the merger between Coca-Cola and Dr Pepper was likely to be anticompetitive. The FTC presented four witnesses: an executive from Procter and Gamble (which owns a soft-drink company, Crush International, that has a comparatively small market share); a Dr Pepper bottler; an owner and operator of snack- and lunchwagons, who buys soft drinks from bottlers and resells them to consumers; and an economist, as "expert" witness. Coca-Cola presented three defense witnesses: the president of Coca-Cola's American operations and two economists, as expert witnesses. The trial lasted four days.

On July 31, 1986, Judge Gesell delivered his opinion. He found in favor of the FTC and granted the PI, effectively halting the merger. Coca-Cola initially wanted to appeal Judge Gesell's ruling, but Dr Pepper decided to withdraw from the acquisition. Apparently, the latter company did not want to take its chances in a potentially lengthy proceeding that would first have to be heard by an FTC administrative law judge and then by the Commission itself. The proposed merger was effectively dead.

The Parties' Arguments

The economic arguments advanced by both sides at trial[12] were largely structured by the Department of Justice's Merger Guidelines[13] (discussed in the introduction to this section): the market-definition paradigm (including a price-increase standard), a quantitative focus on market shares, an analysis of entry conditions, and a discussion of other market conditions that might help or hinder coordinated behavior among the CSD producers.

The FTC's Arguments

The FTC's economic case against the mergers rested on four propositions: 1) the relevant product markets were CSD concentrate and CSD itself, and the relevant geographic markets were a national market and also local markets that could be approximated by metropolitan areas; 2) these markets were highly concentrated, and the proposed merger would increase the levels of concentration substantially; 3) entry by new producers or expansion by small existing producers—that might otherwise thwart efforts at exercising market power—was difficult, risky, and time consuming; and 4) consequently, the merger was likely to result in a substantial lessening of competition.

Market definition. The FTC's product-market-definition claim was based on deposition (interview) and discovery (document) evidence. CSD company executives, when asked, indicated that their primary competitors were other CSD producers. Their pricing and marketing strategies were developed with an eye toward other CSD producers—not (as claimed by the defendant) toward the sellers of fruit juices, milk, coffee, tea, or other beverages. The information on rivals' prices and sales volumes that they regularly collected pertained almost exclusively to other CSD producers — and not the producers of the other beverages. The marketing documents uncovered by the FTC's discovery requests (see footnote 9) told the same story.

Further, many industry executives, when asked if they thought the CSD producers could collectively raise the retail prices of CSD by 10 percent (a more conservative standard than that of the Merger Guidelines) and not be thwarted by consumers' switching to other beverages, replied affirmatively. Also, the cost of the CSD concentrate was only a small fraction—approximately one-tenth—of the retail price of CSD, and there was little room for substitution of other inputs for concentrate. Thus, there appeared to be considerable room for an industry-wide increase in the price of *concentrate*—well beyond the 5 percent DOJ benchmark—that would not decrease industry sales appreciably and would be jointly profitable for the concentrate manufacturers. Hence, both CSD concentrate and CSD itself appeared to be relevant antitrust markets for the purposes of analyzing the competitive effects of a merger.

The economics staff at the FTC had also developed econometric studies of CSD retail prices in local metropolitan areas that were based on marketing data collected by the A. C. Nielsen Co. on a weekly and bi-weekly basis. The estimation results appeared to indicate that CSD sellers could, collectively, exercise market power.[14] But, in the very limited time available to prepare for the mid-July trial, some of the potential weaknesses in the estimations could not be adequately corrected, and these results were not part of the evidence introduced by the FTC to support its market-definition claim. If the case had subsequently gone to a lengthy trial, modified forms of these estimations would likely have been used to support the FTC's position.

Since the merging entities were sellers of CSD concentrate, the FTC claimed that CSD concentrate was a market. Also, because the CSD sellers could influence the wholesale and retail prices of CSD itself through sales promotions and direct discounts, CSD itself was a market.[15] Further, because the CSD-concentrate manufacturers appeared to be able to influence prices separately (e.g., through specific rebates and promotions) in bottlers' sales to food stores, sales through vending machines, and sales to fountain accounts, these three distribution lines were also designated as separate markets.

With respect to geography, the FTC claimed that the United States was a market that met the Merger Guidelines criteria; imports were negligible. Further, the FTC argued, individual local areas—for which metropolitan areas, as measured by the Nielsen marketing surveys, could be a suitable proxy—were also relevant markets. Through their adjustments of marketing promotions, rebates, and discounts, the CSD producers could charge effectively different prices in different areas. The producers' practice of requiring their bottlers to sell only within the latters' designated marketing areas ensured that arbitrage shipments of concentrate or CSD by bottlers would not foil efforts at price discrimination. The Nielsen marketing data mentioned above, along with similar data shown to the Commission by the merging parties (but intended to demonstrate other things), supported this view.

The claim that local areas were markets was not a contradiction to the claim that the entire United States was also a market. The CSD producers appeared to be capable (if they could coordinate their behavior) of raising prices significantly in individual local areas as well as nationally, and thus both levels constituted markets.

Levels of seller concentration.   Table 1 indicates that the leading four sellers accounted for over 75 percent of national market sales. With the merger, the HHI for this national market would have risen by 341 points to a level of 2646.[16] This was well above the Merger Guidelines' 1800 decision point. In addition, of the 91 local areas for which the FTC had food store sales data,[17] all 91 had market seller concentration levels such that the postmerger HHIs would have been above 1200, and for 81 areas the postmerger HHIs would have been above 1800. Of these 81 market areas, 66 would have experienced HHI increases of over 100 points as a consequence of the merger, again exceeding the Merger Guidelines' criteria.

Entry.   The FTC argued that meaningful entry in CSD concentrate sales and/or significant expansion by smaller firms was difficult, risky, and time-consuming. These problems stemmed from a number of sources.

First, though no specialized resources or talents were required for CSD formulation and production, substantial sums were required for the advertising and promotion of a new soft drink. In the early 1980s Seven-Up had spent $57 million in the first two years of promotion for its Like Cola brand. Coca-Cola documents indicated that the company intended to spend $44 million and $42 million, respectively, on first-year promotional efforts on its new Cherry Coke and Minute Maid soft-drink brands in the mid 1980s. (By comparison, the first-year promotional expenditures for new products in other food lines are typically in the range of $5 to $10 million.[18])

The significance of these advertising and promotion numbers is that they represent "investments" that are highly risky; they are sunk. Unlike an investment in plant and equipment, which usually has substantial salvage value even if the planned product fails, investments in advertising and promotion have little salvage value if the product fails — as, indeed, Seven-Up's Like Cola did. An alternative to undertaking large-scale (risky) promotional expenditures would have been a slower, less costly (and hence less risky) "roll out" of a soft drink in a few regional markets, with the process extending over four or five years or more. This was the strategy chosen by some smaller CSD sellers. But this slower expansion would be less likely to be an effective check on the exercise of market power that might follow a merger of Coke and Dr Pepper. Also, even before the marketing effort began, product formulation and testing could take approximately two years, thus delaying entry and impeding the ability of entrants to check rapidly the exercise of market power.

Second, for sales to food stores and through vending outlets, access to distributors—the bottlers—appeared to pose difficulties to entrants. To be an effective distributor, a bottler appears to need a sales volume (from all its brands) of at least 10 to 20 percent of a local market.[19] Thus, an entrant, with a small market share, would initially have to "piggyback" on the brands of others and use existing bottlers. But the flavor restrictions imposed on bottlers by most producers would have made this difficult or impossible in many markets. While an entrant trying to sell a new banana cream soda might not face this problem, someone trying to sell a "new, improved cola" would. Though alternative forms of distribution—through beer distributors, dairies, independent food brokers, or direct distribution to supermarket warehouses—were possible and had been or were being used by some smaller CSD producers, these alternatives appeared to be less effective. All of the larger companies (and most of the smaller ones) used only bottlers. The direct promotional effort provided by a bottler seemed to be the best way of winning the battle for supermarket shelf space and marketing cooperation.[20]

Third, for vending and fountain sales, the limited number of buttons on a machine and spigots at a fountain posed entry barriers for smaller entrants. A company with, say, 2 percent of sales of CSD in a local market might be able to convince food retailers elsewhere to give it approximately 2 percent of the shelf space in their soft-drink section. But with only six or eight buttons on most vending machines (which are usually owned and operated by bottlers), and about the same number of spigots on most fountain dispensers, the small entrant with 2 percent sales would be unlikely to gain access to these limited slots.[21] (The alternative strategy, of course, would be to try for the big marketing push that would generate a large enough market share to justify vending machine and fountain spigot allocations; but, as explained above, this large effort would be considerably more risky.)

Overall, then, entry was not easy. It was true that a few brands had entered the market, and some regional or niche brands had enjoyed brief periods of success; but neither individually nor collectively could they be expected to serve as a competitive check on the exercise of market power by the larger CSD procedures. Even a marketing giant like

Procter and Gamble, through its ownership of Crush International, had not been able to make much of a dent in the market; P&G's brands accounted for less than 2 percent of retail sales. Also, though private-label supermarket brands of CSD accounted for 10 to 15 percent of food-store CSD sales in some areas, they too were unlikely to be a check on the exercise of market power, even in food-store sales,[22] and certainly not in vending and fountain sales.

Competitive consequences. The FTC argued that the merger of the first- and fourth-largest sellers of CSD in a highly concentrated market was likely to reduce the level of competition and make coordinated behavior among CSD producers easier. Direct competition between Coca-Cola's Cherry Coke and Mr. Pibb brands and Dr Pepper's brands would be eliminated. And, with one fewer major player in the soft-drink markets, coordinated behavior—higher list prices for CSD concentrate and/or reduced rebates and promotional expenditures—would be more likely, as the major firms would find it easier to police themselves and hence would be less fearful that one among them might "cheat," cut prices, and expand promotion.

As an indicator that such behavior was already occurring to some extent, the previous decade's profit data—return on stockholders' equity—showed comparatively high rates of return for the major CSD producers. A number of critics has claimed that these accounting data may not be accurate indicators of competitive or noncompetitive profits.[23] The FTC did not use these data as evidence, largely because the Guidelines approach argues that Section 7 of the Clayton Act should be forward-looking: Will this merger make things worse? Past profit rates are not strictly relevant in addressing this question. Still, these data suggested (at least to this author) that noncompetitive, coordinated behavior was possibly already occurring in this concentrated industry and could become worse after the merger.

Also, to the extent that the Coca-Cola Company decided to consolidate its distribution through one local bottler in areas where Coke and Dr Pepper had previously used separate bottlers, the smaller CSD manufacturers who had piggy-backed with Dr Pepper might find that their volume alone was insufficient to achieve adequate economies of scale in distribution and thus would suffer higher costs; the same would be true for potential entrants. And if the Dr Pepper brand continued to be distributed through a separate bottler that was also used by Pepsi, that bottler might serve as a device for the exchange of information between Pepsi and Coke and thus facilitate the coordination of behavior between the two.

The fact that CSD is not an absolutely uniform product—each company's brands and flavor formulations are different, and most brands come with at least two alternative sweeteners, in a variety of sizes, and with a variety of promotional possibilities—did not appear to be a bar to the possibility of coordinated behavior among the major CSD producers, with anticompetitive consequences. The CSD producers might simply raise wholesale prices of CSD concentrate, without changing promotional activity. Or they might cut back on the latter, reducing the frequency of special promotions or reducing advertising efforts. Again, the previous decade's profits data were suggestive that such behavior was possible.

The FTC did not directly address the efficiencies arguments raised by the defense (see discussion following), considering them largely irrelevant to its case. If the case had gone to a full trial, the FTC surely would have tried to develop evidence to refute Coke's claims.

Coca-Cola's Arguments

The Coca-Cola Company, as defendant, argued that the merger would not have anticompetitive consequences. Its defense centered on three propositions, any one of which, if valid, would imply that the merger could not adversely affect competition: 1) the relevant market was all potable beverages, not just CSD; 2) even if the market was just CSD, entry was easy into CSD; 3) even if entry was difficult, the only competition that mattered was the head-to-head rivalry of Coke and Pepsi. Further, the merger would achieve efficiencies for the combined entity and hence would promote competition.

Market definition. The defense argued that Coke (and other CSD brands) competed against all other beverages, not just against each other.[24] They noted that CSD consumption had expanded substantially in the past few decades, apparently at the expense of more traditional beverages, such as coffee. All these beverages were actual and potential substitutes for CSD and hence competed with CSD. Also, because beverage manufacturers typically operated and sold their products nationwide, as did Coke and Dr Pepper, the geographic market should be the entire United States. In this larger market, CSD was only 25 percent of all beverage consumption, and the post-merger HHI was only 739,[25] well below the Merger Guidelines' minimum decision point of 1000. Hence, the merger did not increase the likelihood of the exercise of market power.

Like the FTC, Coca-Cola did not offer any quantitative evidence to support its market definition claim. PepsiCo, in defending its merger, however, had presented the FTC with an econometric study that used time series price and quantity data to estimate a demand curve for

CSD. The study indicated that the demand for CSD was sensitive to the prices of other beverages. This, PepsiCo claimed, showed that the market should be defined to include other beverages. (What they did not demonstrate, however, was whether the cross-elasticity was high enough to thwart a concerted effort by CSD producers to raise prices.)

Entry. Coca-Cola argued that even if the market were defined as only CSD, entry into CSD production and sale was nevertheless easy, as was expansion by smaller producers. There were no specialized resources involved in the production and sale of CSD, and economies of scale were not significant. It was easy to develop a flavor and produce the concentrate, or specialized "flavor houses" could be hired to do it. Bottlers and bottling capacity were available for distribution; and warehouse distribution, independent food brokers, and beer distributors were suitable alternatives.

The defense pointed to large, diversified food-products manufacturers—such as Kraft, Beatrice, and Borden—as potential entrants, as were beer producers. Further, R. J. Reynolds was in the process of selling its Canada Dry and Sunkist brands to Schweppes; and though its attempt to sell Seven-Up to PepsiCo had been stopped by the FTC, Philip Morris would surely try to sell Seven-Up to someone else. Both of these companies were possible re-entrants if the existing CSD producers tried to raise their prices and thereby earn extraordinary profits.

Coca-Cola also pointed to recent entrants and smaller CSD producers—such as Shasta, Fanta, Hansens, Soho Natural, Canfield, Seagrams, and others—who either had or were capable of expanding their sales significantly. In addition, supermarket private-label brands were important in some areas.

In sum, entry was easy, so the high apparent HHI levels in the CSD market (if it were a market) were competitively irrelevant. Easy entry would keep in check any effort by the CSD producers, even after the merger of Coke and Dr Pepper, to coordinate their behavior and raise prices.

Structural characteristics of the market. Coca-Cola further argued that, even if entry were difficult, the characteristics of the CSD industry made difficult any coordinated behavior to raise prices. There were too many product types and sizes and too many promotional opportunities. It would be difficult for any one firm to police or monitor the others in any informal understanding to raise prices or reduce promotion, and thus each firm would have a great incentive to cheat on any such arrangement. Coordinated efforts to raise prices and profits were therefore doomed, even if Coke merged with Dr Pepper. Only the merger of Coke and Pepsi might stifle competition and cause prices to rise.

The defense pointed to the decline in the real (inflation-adjusted) price of CSD over the previous two decades and argued that this showed the great competitive vigor of the CSD producers, which had persisted despite an increase in Coke's market share (through internal growth) that was greater than the increase in Coke's market share that would occur through the purchase of Dr Pepper.[26] Coke offered an econometric study that combined time series and cross-section data on weekly and biweekly prices and market shares of CSD sellers in local metropolitan areas. The study indicated that prices and concentration were inversely correlated—the opposite of what a coordinated-behavior hypothesis would imply.[27] Finally, Coke offered evidence on the stock market's reaction at the time of the announcements of the Pepsi-Seven-Up and Coke-Dr Pepper mergers; Coke argued that the stock prices of its rivals in the CSD industry fell, indicating that the stock market believed that the mergers would be pro-competitive rather than anticompetitive.[28]

In sum, as long as Coke and Pepsi did not merge, they would slug it out with each other, and the market would remain competitive. The Coke-Dr Pepper merger could only aid this process by making the combined entity more efficient.

Efficiencies. Coca-Cola argued that the merger would allow the combined entity to consolidate the operations of Coke and Dr Pepper and thus achieve cost savings and efficiencies. Also, Coke felt that it could use its marketing skills and resources to improve the profitability of Dr Pepper's operations.

Judge Gesell's Opinion

On July 31, 1986, Judge Gerhard Gesell delivered his decision.[29] He found in favor of the FTC, accepting many of the agency's crucial propositions and supporting arguments.

First, the relevant product market was CSD.[30] The relevant geographic markets were the entire United States and thirty-two "significant population areas" in the seven contiguous states of Texas, Louisiana, Mississippi, Alabama, Georgia, Tennessee and Arkansas. "The major participants in the market. . .make pricing and marketing decisions based primarily on comparisons with rival carbonated soft drink products, with little if any concern about possible competition from other beverages such as milk, coffee, beer or fruit juice."[31]

Second, these markets were highly concentrated, and Coke and Dr Pepper were active competitors in them. "There is general agreement that the market for carbonated soft drinks is already highly concentrated. It consists of a few major concentrate companies and a number of minor concerns, not all of which do business nationally."[32] "The stark, unvarnished truth is that Dr Pepper brand has been a staunch effective competitor in the market, that Coca-Cola Company has tried to stifle it by developing its own pepper drink and by seeking to replace it with its new Cherry Coke brand in fountain accounts at considerable expense and that it has failed. It is now seeking to buy out its competitor."[33]

Third, entry into the market was not easy. Access to effective bottlers was one problem. "Other companies seeking to seriously challenge the dominance of Coca-Cola Company and PepsiCo by entering in the major flavor segments would probably have serious difficulty finding effective distribution. . . .Relatively few independent bottlers have the strength to compete on a major scale. Moreover, the strong independent bottlers are unlikely to be available for major entry due to their own flavor restrictions. . . .Alternative channels of distribution are unproven and of dubious effectiveness. . . .As a further concern, effective access to bottlers is likely to become even more difficult in the future as dominant companies increasingly focus their energies on controlling their distribution network even more tightly."[34] Further, "To establish a major new brand requires large expenditures for advertising to fix the brand name and image in the mind of the consumer—expenditures that cannot be recovered if the introduction fails. . . .Effective entrants must also match the considerable promotional budgets of the dominant companies in targeting their brands for effective distribution through retailers. . . .Finally, it has been the experience of the industry that effective entry against the dominant companies is likely to require years of sustained effort for any continuing success. . . ."[35]

Fourth, the merger would have anticompetitive consequences. Judge Gesell focused primarily on the loss of competition between Coke and Dr Pepper. "Once the Dr Pepper brand joins the Coca-Cola Company line much of this direct rivalry will probably cease."[36] He was clearly uncomfortable, however, with the FTC's proposition that greater concentration would lead to reduced competition generally in the market.[37] "No tendency in that direction has yet been evidenced and there is no proof that the mere addition of Dr Pepper to Coca-Cola Company's line, standing alone, will trigger a foreseeable development of this kind. The present intensity of competition between Coca-Cola Company and PepsiCo does not seem likely to diminish in the immediate future."[38] "But," he also added, "the fact remains that if the proposed acquisition is consummated there will be one less independent factor in the market to challenge the dominance of Coca-Cola Company."[39]

Instead, he was more comfortable with the legal argument that had been advanced by the FTC at the trial. Citing an earlier Supreme Court antitrust decision,[40] he wrote that "[g]iven [Congress'] dominant legislative desire to curb the economic concentration of power, it is unnecessary to speculate about the economic effect of the proposed acquisition. Without more, substantial mergers of this kind in heavily concentrated industries are presumed illegal. . . .A court must be guided by the view that 'a merger which produces a firm controlling an undue percentage share of the relevant market, and results in a significant increase in the concentration of firms in that market, is so inherently likely to lessen competition substantially that it must be enjoined in the absence of evidence clearly showing that the merger is not likely to have such anticompetitive effects.' "[41]

Finally, he paid little attention to Coca-Cola's efficiency arguments. "Any federal judge considering regulatory aims such as those laid down by Congress in Section 7 of the Clayton Act should hesitate before grafting onto the Act an untried economic theory such as the wealth-maximization and efficiency-through-acquisition doctrine expounded by Coca-Cola Company. . . .To be sure, efficiencies that benefit consumers were recognized as desirable but they were to be developed by dominant concerns using their brains, not their money by buying out troubling competitors."[42]

In sum, "The acquisition totally lacks any apparent redeeming feature."[43] "A preliminary injunction in the form attached shall issue forthwith."[44]

Aftermath

The FTC's successful challenge to the Pepsi-Seven-Up and Coke-Dr Pepper mergers did not spell the end of the restructuring of the carbonated soft drink industry. Philip Morris was determined to sell Seven-Up. In mid-July 1986 it sold the international operations of Seven-Up to PepsiCo,[45] and later in the year it sold Seven-Up's domestic operations to a private investor group headed by the venture capital firm of Hicks & Haas. Dr Pepper, thwarted in its attempt to merge with Coca-Cola, was soon bought by a different group of private investors that was also headed by Hicks & Haas. Earlier, Hicks & Haas had also bought A&W Brands, and in November 1986 Hicks & Haas bought Squirt. Thus, the market shares of the companies over which Hicks & Haas had acquired some influence, when combined, would constitute the third largest CSD producer. How much influence Hicks & Haas will exercise over these four companies, and what the competitive consequences in the CSD market will be, is as yet unclear. Finally, in July 1986, while the Coca-Cola case was under challenge, Schweppes bought the Canada Dry and Sunkist brands from R. J. Reynolds.[46]

Thus, despite the FTC actions, the CSD market has undergone changes and some consolidation. But these changes do not appear to offer the same level of competitive threat as was posed by the two challenged mergers.

Also, since the middle of 1986 the Department of Justice has begun grand-jury investigations and succeeded in obtaining criminal indictments and convictions of bottlers for price fixing in a number of local markets. As of this writing these investigations are continuing. There has been no indication, however, of any direct involvement by any CSD concentrate company.

Conclusion

The FTC's challenge to the Coca-Cola–Dr Pepper merger represented a fruitful application of microeconomics. The Department of Justice's Merger Guidelines structured many of the arguments advanced by both sides. Sophisticated reasoning and econometric studies buttressed much of the analysis. The economics experts hired by each side differed in their interpretations of the relevant facts and of the weights that should be put on various arguments, but there was little disagreement on the fundamental economic propositions that should be applied. And, from an economic perspective, Judge Gesell's decision was largely a sensible one, except for his reluctance to accept the FTC's argument concerning the likely competitive consequences of an increase in market concentration.

From this same economics perspective, however, one discordant note in his decision should be mentioned. In his discussion of the likely effects of the merger, Judge Gesell wrote the following:

> At the preliminary injunction hearing economists, drawing on experience in this multi-faceted discipline, flatly disagreed as to the significance of the proposed acquisition upon competition in the market. These sincere professionals are theoreticians in an imprecise field. They have never sold a can of carbonated soft drink and indeed the principal economist for Coca-Cola Company frankly admitted he had little knowledge of the underlying facts.

> The Court should not, in any event, rely on the economic testimony in reaching a conclusion about the probable effects of the proposed acquisition given the concentrated nature of the

market just outlined. Section 7 of the Clayton Act was not designed to support a particular economic theory; it was directed at what Congress in the exercise of its own common sense perceived.[47]

Yet, as we have argued in this chapter, economic theory importantly structured many of the arguments that were presented to Judge Gesell by both sides and was an important influence on his eventual decision. It can only be hoped that future antitrust litigants and judges will listen more to the "music" of the general nature of the arguments and the opinion and less to the specific words quoted above.

Notes

1. The discussion that follows is in terms of generalities. There may be a few minor exceptions to the general descriptive elements provided.
2. *F.T.C.* v. *Coca-Cola Co.*, 641 F. Supp. 1128, 1133 (1986).
3. For example, mergers in regulated industries are largely the province of the Department of Justice.
4. If the proposed merger involves a cash tender offer, the relevant time is 15 days.
5. If a cash tender offer is involved, the period is 10 days.
6. The actual time from announcement to agency decision can extend for more than 50 days if the merging parties require time to respond to the agency's request for more information, or if they agree to a delay in consummating the merger in the hopes of thereby eventually obtaining a favorable decision. This is a frequent occurrence.
7. *F.T.C.* v. *Coca-Cola.*, 641 F. Supp. 1128, 1134 (1986).
8. For a DOJ challenge, the full trial would be in a Federal District Court. For a FTC challenge, the full trial would be before an administrative law judge, with eventual review before the full Commission. For both routes, appeals could then be made to a Federal Circuit Court of Appeals and then possibly to the U.S. Supreme Court.
9. Most of the extension beyond 50 days was due to the companies' delays in responding to the FTC's information requests. In the end the four companies delivered over 600 file boxes of documents to the agency.
10. The vote was 4–0; the fifth commissioner did not participate in the case because of a possible conflict of interest.
11. A few weeks before the FTC decision the Royal Crown Cola Company filed suit in Federal District Court in Georgia to stop the two mergers, but that suit was held in abeyance pending the FTC's actions.
12. In most cases, the witnesses (if any) for each side testify at trial through a process of direct examination by their own side's attorney (to draw out the witness's story) and then cross-examination by the other side's attorney (to try to undermine or cast doubt on that story). In the Coca-Cola case, which was tried only before a judge and not before a jury, Judge Gesell asked the economic experts for both sides to submit

affidavits to him (and to the other side) before the trial, which he read and entered into the court record. Thus, the experts did not have to go through direct examination but only through cross-examination by the other side. This procedure saved valuable court time, allowed each side to present its economic arguments in a relatively polished fashion, yet also allowed the opposing side to receive and review those arguments with adequate time for rebuttal. It is a procedure that should be copied in other judge-only trials.

13. In June 1982, at the same time that the DOJ issued its Merger Guidelines, the FTC issued a "Statement on Horizontal Mergers." It was the DOJ Guidelines, however, that largely shaped the FTC's investigation of the CSD mergers and its prosecution of the case.

14. The econometric studies were similar to those done by Baker and Bresnahan (1985) for beer brewers.

15. The FTC also considered the possibility that only branded CSD—i.e., excluding private label CSD sold by supermarkets—might be a market. But this proposition was never formally advanced by the Commission.

16. By using a slightly different base for total sales, the FTC developed other HHI estimates that were somewhat different but not appreciably so. The FTC also developed a post-merger HHI estimate for the fountain market that was even higher.

17. These were areas that were monitored by Coke or Dr Pepper.

18. Also, among all of the categories of food producers listed by the Internal Revenue Service's *Statistics of Income, Corporate Returns,* the advertising-to-sales ratio of the carbonated soft drink producers is second only to that of the producers of distilled spirits—and well above all of the remaining categories.

19. The interview data indicated that this minimum efficient scale was a relative concept—a market share concept—in these local markets. It appeared that a bottler needed to attain this 10 to 20 percent of the local market in order to gain supermarkets' attention and cooperation in promotional activity.

20. Dr Pepper itself had tried warehouse delivery methods in a few markets in the 1950s and had abandoned it as ineffective. Also, in the 1980s Coke and Pepsi began buying some of their bottlers' franchises and thus vertically integrating into distribution. These actions meant even greater difficulties for potential entrants.

21. Coca-Cola presented data on its profit margins in the fountain and retail areas that were consistent with this proposition. The profit margins were appreciably higher in the former area.

22. Either the supermarkets might go along with the major producers in raising prices or, even with lower prices, they might not attract enough customers to foil the major producers' price rise. In this latter event, the relevant market would therefore be restricted to branded CSD.

23. See Benston (1982), Fisher and McGowan (1983), and Fisher (1984). For a rebuttal, see Horowitz (1984), Long and Ravenscraft (1984), Martin (1984), and van Breda (1984).

24. When first informed of this position by Coca-Cola's counsel at trial, Judge Gesell responded by saying, "So we've got everything in [the market], milk and tea, Pepto Bismol, anything potable." Coca-Cola's

counsel replied, "I'll concede that Pepto Bismol is not in the market, your honor." (Trial transcript, p.18.)

25. These data pertain to a beverage market that excludes wine and distilled spirits.

26. In response, the FTC pointed out that declining real prices were not automatically or necessarily a sign of competitive vigor. Elementary microeconomic theory indicates that even a monopolist would lower its price if (other things remaining unchanged) the costs of inputs decreased or productivity improvements caused production costs to decrease. It was quite likely that these cost decreases and productivity improvements were the driving forces behind the real price declines in CSD, and thus no implications about competition could be drawn from these claims.

27. In response, the FTC argued that the very short-term nature of the data—weekly and biweekly observations—cast doubt on the implications that Coca-Cola tried to draw from the study. Instead, the inverse relationship between prices and market shares might be largely (or entirely) the result of periodic "specials" on various brands, with many consumers buying large inventories of those brands at that time (and thus increasing the very short run market shares of those brands at those times). The coordinated behavior hypothesis, by contrast, is a proposition about long-run relationships and should be tested with longer run (e.g., annual) data. Coca-Cola offered another econometrics study, using the same data, that showed that market share stability was not positively related to market concentration (which, again, would be inconsistent with an implication of the coordination behavior hypothesis). The FTC offered a similar critique.

28. In response, the FTC argued that a slightly different interpretation of the data yielded the opposite conclusion. The methodology of looking at rival companies' share price reactions was first suggested by Baxter (1980). For some applications, see Eckbo (1983) and Eckbo and Wier (1985).

29. The full opinion is found in *F.T.C.* v. *Coca-Cola Co.,* 641 F. Supp. 1128 (1986).

30. Judge Gesell did not make any distinction between sales of CSD concentrate and sales of CSD itself.

31. 641 F. Supp. 1128, 1133 (1986).

32. 641 F. Supp. 1128, 1133 (1986).

33. 641 F. Supp. 1128, 1139 (1986).

34. 641 F. Supp. 1128, 1135–6 (1986).

35. 641 F. Supp. 1128, 1137 (1986).

36. 641 F. Supp. 1128, 1139 (1986).

37. Based on his questioning of the witnesses at the trial, he seemed to expect that the anticompetitive behavior resulting from the merger would be in the form of predatory price-cutting or predatory promotions by Coke. But this was not the FTC's theory.

38. 641 F. Supp. 1128, 1138 (1986).

39. 641 F. Supp. 1128, 1138 (1986).

40. *U.S.* v. *Philadelphia National Bank,* 374 U.S. 321 (1963).

41. 641 F. Supp. 1128, 1138 (1986).
42. 641 F. Supp. 1128, 1141 (1986).
43. 641 F. Supp. 1128, 1139 (1986).
44. 641 F. Supp. 1128, 1141 (1986).
45. Because there were unlikely to be any domestic competitive consequences from this sale, the FTC did not challenge it.
46. There had been some thought within the FTC of challenging the Schweppes purchase on the grounds that mixers might constitute a separate market, but this notion was not pursued very far. Among the arguments that could be marshalled against challenging the purchase was that Coke, Pepsi, and the other large non-mixer CSD producers were potential entrants into that mixer "market," and hence the merger was not likely to permit the exercise of market power.
47. 641 F. Supp. 1128, 1138 (1986).

References

Baker, Jonathan B., and Timothy F. Bresnahan. "The Gains from Merger or Collusion in Product-Differentiated Industries." *Journal of Industrial Economics* 33 (June 1985): 427–444.

Baxter, William F. "The Political Economy of Antitrust." In *The Political Economy of Antitrust: Principal Paper by William Baxter*, edited by Robert D. Tollison, 3–49. Lexington, Mass.: Lexington Books, 1980.

Benston, George J. "Accounting Numbers and Economic Values." *Antitrust Bulletin* 27 (Spring 1982): 161–215.

Eckbo, B. Espen. "Horizontal Mergers, Collusion, and Stockholder Wealth." *Journal of Financial Economics* 11 (April 1983): 241–273.

Eckbo, B. Espen, and Peggy Wier. "Antimerger Policy under the Hart-Scott-Rodino Act: A Reexamination of the Market Power Hypothesis." *Journal of Law and Economics* 28 (April 1985): 119–149.

Fisher, Franklin M. "The Misuse of Accounting Rates of Return: Reply." *American Economic Review* 74 (June 1984): 509–517.

Fisher, Franklin M., and John J. McGowan. "On the Misuse of Accounting Rates of Return to Infer Monopoly Profits." *American Economic Review* 73 (March 1983): 82–97.

Horowitz, Ira. "The Misuse of Accounting Rates of Return: Comment." *American Economic Review* 74 (June 1984): 492–493.

Long, William F., and David J. Ravenscraft. "The Misuse of Accounting Rates of Return: Comment." *American Economic Review* 74 (June 1984): 494–500.

Martin, Stephen. "The Misuse of Accounting Rates of Return: Comment." *American Economic Review* 74 (June 1984): 501–506.

Van Breda, Michael F. "The Misuse of Accounting Rates of Return: Comment." *American Economic Review* 74 (June 1984): 507–508.

The Importance of Entry Conditions: Texas Air's Acquisition of Eastern Airlines

George W. Douglas

Introduction

With the passage of the Airline Deregulation Act (The Federal Aviation Act of 1978), Congress brought the legal review of air carrier mergers into conformity with the same antitrust standards that are applied to the unregulated sector. Section 408 of the Act requires approval of any acquisition that: 1) will not result in a monopoly, further an attempted monopoly, or likely lessen competition substantially in any region of the United States; and 2) is not inconsistent with the public interest.

Authority to enforce the Act's antitrust provisions was originally vested with the Civil Aeronautics Board (CAB) but was transferred to the Department of Transportation (DOT) with the end of the CAB's existence on December 31, 1984. The statute requires the DOT to make a final determination within six months of an application. If the Department determines that significant factual contentions are at issue, it can set a formal oral evidentiary hearing before an administrative law judge (ALJ). In such instances, the DOT's investigatory staff takes a position as an active party in the proceedings. Otherwise, the DOT may make a determination based on the written filings of the staff and interested parties.

Texas Air Corporation (TAC) is a holding company whose operating entities at the time were New York Air and Continental Air Lines. Prior to the acquisition it was the eighth largest air carrier, with 5.1 percent of the industry's RPMs (revenue passenger miles); and Eastern was the third largest carrier, with 9.5 percent of the industry's RPMs (see Table 1). Although Eastern was in financial distress, a point stressed by Texas Air in seeking expeditious approval, the case was not structured as a failing-firm exception.[1] While not expressly at issue in assess-

---

George W. Douglas consulted for and filed written testimony on behalf of Texas Air in its application before the Department of Transportation.

Table 1
Air Carrier Market Shares: Revenue Passenger Miles

Carrier	% 1985 System RPMs
American	12.6%
United	11.9
Eastern	9.5
Trans World	9.2
Delta	8.6
Pan American	7.8
Northwest	6.6
Texas Air	5.1
People Express	4.5
Republic	3.1
Western	3.0
USAir	2.9
Piedmont	2.4
Southwest	1.8
World	1.5
PSA	1.0
Ozark	0.9
Braniff	0.8
Pre-acquisition HHI (Herfindahl-Hirschman Index)	743.2
Post TAC/EA acquisition HHI	839.9
Post TAC/EA, TWA/Ozark, and Northwest/Republic acquisitions HHI	896.6

Source: DOT Forms 41, Table T2.

ing the competitive impact of the acquisition, it was widely perceived that Texas Air's motivation for acquiring Eastern was to transform the airline from a high-cost, low-productivity carrier that had proved unsuccessful in adapting to the heightened competition in the era of deregulation to an efficient, low-cost competitor. If it were to succeed in such a turnaround, the financial gains compared to the low acquisition cost could be enormous; and further, the resultant size of the low-cost TAC carriers could have a profound effect on the competitive level of fares nationally.[2]

Even though the Airline Deregulation Act vests the Department of Transportation with antitrust jurisdiction over the airline industry, the Antitrust Division of the Department of Justice (DOJ) also takes an active advisory interest (and has intervened) in most airline merger cases. Indeed, the DOJ position may be—and in this case was—pivotal in affecting the outcome. In addition, any other carriers, airline unions, civic parties (e.g., cities, airport authorities, state attorneys general), and others may also intervene in the proceeding.

These interventions are generally motivated by private or political—as opposed to antitrust—interests and frequently provide an interesting byplay.

Since deregulation, a series of merger proceedings at the CAB and the DOT has resulted in standardized requirements for submissions of competitive information by the applicants. This reduces the time and scope required for discovery by a substantial amount. As is typical in current airline mergers, the 400-page application for approval filed by Texas Air on February 28, 1986, contained essentially the complete competitive analysis relied on by the applicant in the proceeding.

Thus, the joining of competitive issues in an airline merger takes place at an early stage—in the interested parties' initial comments on the application—and frequently through various procedural motions filed with DOT and through discussions and negotiations with the Antitrust Division. Although the TAC-Eastern acquisition was the largest airline merger or acquisition to come before the DOT, the case never came to "trial" but was in fact disposed of through written filings.

A Preliminary Analysis: Competitors and the Securities Markets

As noted, airline competitors frequently intervene in merger proceedings in opposition to the proposed merger. The degree of their opposition can in itself reveal much about how the industry views the merger's effect on competition. Where the result is perceived as anticompetitive, facilitating collusion, and resulting in elevated prices and reduced output, rivals would be expected to benefit instead of fearing injury. Alternatively, if the merger is perceived as efficient, with the likely consequences of increasing competition and exerting downward pressure on prices, rivals would be expected to avoid competitive injury and seek to quash it.

The only theory by which a rival might find its interest served by opposing an anticompetitive merger is the realistic fear of subsequent predation—but the economic circumstances for successful predation in this industry are largely absent. In this instance the competitors who intervened in opposition to the acquisition included those who would most likely suffer injury if the merger were successful in transforming Eastern into a low-cost, low-fare competitor along the same lines as TAC's Continental—namely, Delta, People Express, Presidential, and to a lesser extent USAir and Piedmont. The other opposing carriers included several larger airlines that may have wanted to purchase all or part of Eastern themselves or that may have simply preferred to see the carrier fail, providing them thereby the opportunity to scavenge the wreckage for the pieces best fitting into their plans. These airlines included American, United, and TWA.

Similarly, the financial market may enable us to distinguish between a merger motivated by increased efficiency versus one motivated by an attempt to obtain market power. Recent contributions to antitrust analysis have sought a more direct means of analyzing the competitive effect of mergers by examining the effect of the merger's announcement on financial markets (see, for example, Stillman 1983; and Eckbo 1983).

One problem that has hampered economists in attempting to conduct statistical analyses of the relationship between profits and firm size or market structure has been the inability to discriminate between two alternate explanations for the relationship: efficiency (i.e., lower costs) and market power. One can, however, often obtain significant information about the likely competitive effects of a proposed merger by turning the focus of attention from the merging firms to their competitors.

An extensive literature in economics and finance allows us to conclude that financial markets efficiently incorporate the perceived or expected results of economic events into the current prices of securities. Most simply, an unanticipated event that is likely to increase investors' expectations of future earnings will cause the price of the common stock to rise, and an event that causes investors to expect decreased earnings would cause the stock price to decline (other factors being held constant).

This suggests a means for distinguishing between efficient (procompetitive) mergers and market power (anticompetitive) mergers: if the announcement of the merger depresses the prices of the stock of competing firms, the market perceives the merger as procompetitive, depressing product prices and increasing output. Alternatively, a merger announcement that causes a statistically discernible increase in the competitors' stock suggests that the merger may be anticompetitive, increasing prices and profits for all firms in the industry. An increase in the price of some competitors' stocks is not an unambiguous signal of a market power merger, however. For example, the announcement of the transaction may cause the stocks of inefficient competitors to increase based on the perception that *they* too may be acquired by an efficient firm.

Financial markets are adept at developing and processing information, which is continuously incorporated into stock prices (i.e., a merger may be rumored before it is announced, having an effect on prices before the announcement). For this reason it may be difficult to measure accurately a merger proposal's effect on stock prices. Thus, analyses of the financial market's assessment of a merger's competitive implications are likely to prove most fruitful when the proposed merger is not anticipated prior to its announcement.

The mechanics of an examination of the financial market's analysis in the TAC-Eastern case were fairly straightforward. The first step was to examine the effect of the merger's announcement on the prices of the proposed merger partners' stocks. Significant increases in the prices

Table 2
Announcement Effects: Texas Air's Acquisition of Eastern (announced February 24, 1986)

Carrier	Stock Price		% Change	Beta[1]	Expected % Change[2]	Actual − Expected Change
	2/21	2/28				
Texas Air	17	28-1/2	+67.64	1.35	+1.39	+66.25
Eastern	6-3/8	8-3/8	+31.37	1.10	+1.13	+30.24
Other Carriers						
Delta	45-5/8	41-1/8	− 9.86	1.15	+1.18	−11.04
People Express	10-1/4	9-7/8	− 3.66	1.30	+1.34	− 4.99
Presidential	17-1/4	16-7/8	− 2.17	1.00[3]	+1.03	− 3.20
Northwest	50-3/4	49-7/8	− 1.72	1.15	+1.18	− 2.91
United	59-3/4	58-7/8	− 1.46	1.35	+1.39	− 2.85
USAir	37-1/8	36-5/8	− 1.35	1.35	+1.39	− 2.73
Piedmont	40-3/8	39-7/8	− 1.24	1.25	+1.28	− 2.52
Republic	15-5/8	15-1/2	− 0.80	1.10	+1.13	− 1.93
Ozark	17-1/2	17-1/2	0.00	1.35	+1.39	− 1.39
PSA	27-1/4	27-5/8	+ 1.38	1.20	+1.23	+ 0.14
Pan Am	8-3/8	8-1/2	+ 1.49	0.95	+0.98	+ 0.52
American	52-1/8	53	+ 1.68	1.35	+1.39	+ 0.29
America West	12-1/8	12-7/8	+ 6.19	1.00[3]	+1.03	+ 5.16
Alaska	18-3/8	19-7/8	+ 8.16	1.00	+1.03	+ 7.14
Southwest	20-3/4	22-5/8	+ 9.04	1.35	+1.39	+ 7.65
Midway	8-1/4	9	+ 9.09	1.00[3]	+1.03	+ 8.06
Trans World	14-1/4	16-5/8	+16.67	1.00[3]	+1.03	+15.64
Aloha	20-1/4	24	+18.52	1.00[3]	+1.03	+17.49
Western	8-3/8	10	+19.40	1.40	+1.44	+17.96
NYSE Composite	129.41	130.74	+1.028			
Value weighted average, other carriers[4]			+0.487		+1.270	−0.783
Value weighted average, Aloha & Western deleted			−0.085		+1.266	−1.351

[1]Value Line Investment Survey, 4/4/86

[2]Beta times percent change NYSE Composite Index

[3]Not available, assumed to equal 1.00

[4]Sum of % change times value weights

of both stocks provided a preliminary indication that the merger was unanticipated (and that the analysis would prove useful) and that the merger would be profitable—whether via significant efficiency gains or market power.

Of course, many other economic factors also affect the stock market, and the stocks of the partners may rise or fall for reasons wholly unrelated to the merger. Much of these effects may be screened out, however, by estimating the expected change of the stocks' prices due to overall changes in the market. A useful tool for this is the stock's "Beta"—the time series regression coefficient of the return of that stock relative to the return of all stocks (or a broad composite index). By multiplying a stock's Beta by the percent change of the composite index we can calculate the statistically expected change in the stock's price.

The TAC-Eastern merger announcement was made on Monday, February 24, 1986. An examination of the stock prices of Texas Air and Eastern before (Friday, February 21) and after (Friday, February 28) the announcement indicated a substantial increase in their prices. Texas Air's stock appreciated by 67 percent; Eastern's, by 31 percent. These increases exceeded by far any increases that could have been attributed to changes in the stock market averages (up 2.8 percent between the two respective Fridays), tending to confirm that the merger was unanticipated.

Analysis of the prices of the merger partners' competitors' stocks strongly suggested that the financial markets perceived the effects of the proposed merger to be procompetitive. Prices of the stocks of Eastern's closest competitors were substantially affected. These effects are arrayed by magnitude on Table 2. The pattern is dramatic.

The list is topped by Delta, People Express, and Presidential—three carriers whose profits would be most susceptible to competitive incursion by an efficient, low-cost, low-fare Eastern. The carriers relatively unaffected—Ozark, PSA, Pan Am, and American—faced either little direct competition from TAC or Eastern or were already in competition with TAC's low-cost Continental (thus having little added effect on future prices and profits). The carriers whose stocks appreciated following the announcement—American West, Alaska, Southwest, Midway, Aloha, and Western—comprised a group whose value might be enhanced because of the enhanced prospect of *their* acquisition, not because they stood to benefit from the exercise of putative market power.[3] TWA's stock also increased significantly that week—probably due to the rumor (circulating that week) of TWA's impending acquisition of Ozark, rather than any perceived benefit to TWA from the TAC acquisition of Eastern.

In conclusion, the reaction of the financial markets suggests that the proposed merger was widely perceived as procompetitive. This inference is corroborated by the correlation of the identity of the carrier protestants and their implied financial stakes in blocking a procompetitive merger.

The Structural/Functional Analysis

The provision of scheduled air transportation has several distinctive economic characteristics that make it inherently competitive, even though in most circumstances only one or at most a few firms may be actively producing any given service—i.e., transportation from point A to point B, referred to in the industry as a "city pair." Since the "plant"—the aircraft—is not inherently dedicated (or configured) to produce any specific service and is by design quite mobile, firms may convert production from serving one set of points to another easily and, in most instances, at little cost. This is especially so if a carrier already has stations at both end-point cities, which is commonly the case for at least one carrier not currently providing service over the city pair.

If the product market is viewed solely from the consumers' perspective, service between point A and point B would rarely be seen as a substitute for service between points A and C. Under such circumstances the routes would be considered as two separate product markets—forcing the conclusion of high concentration in both markets, whatever the measured used. Based on a sample of 5053 city-pair markets in 1981, Bailey, Graham, and Kaplan found that the average Herfindahl-Hirschman Concentration Index (HHI) was 7780—over four times the DOJ "highly concentrated" threshold (see Bailey, Graham, and Kaplan 1985, 161; and U.S. Dept. of Justice 1984, 23). If markets so defined were the relevant benchmark for structural analysis, one would have to conclude that the industry should be earning substantial rents. As the pervasive fare discounting and low industry profits attest, this does not appear to have been the case—although some commentators believe that significant rents yet persist in the form of excessive compensation for labor and management (see Levine 1987).

It was in grappling with this paradox that William Baumol, R. D. Willig, and Elizabeth Bailey (1982) and others derived the notion of "contestable markets." The theory of contestability holds that, in circumstances where entry and exit are instantaneous and devoid of sunk costs, the equilibrium price would approach (or equal, in the polar case) the competitive price, regardless of the number of actual competitors.

Some observers—including Baumol, Willig, and Bailey—have identified the airline industry as an example of "perfect contestability." In the author's view, this is not a useful characterization. Clearly the force of potential competition is exceedingly powerful and works to prevent sustained supracompetitive pricing in individual markets regardless of the number of actual competitors. Nonetheless, it seems inescapable that the actual price level at any point in time is equally (if not more) reflective of such other factors as the dynamics of recent entry (which often results in substantial increases in capacity and fare-cutting before an equilibrium emerges) and the presence of aggressive low-fare carriers.

Although the CAB and the DOT have never endorsed the concept of contestability, they have recognized the inappropriateness of mechanically evaluating city-pair markets on the basis of concentration statistics. Instead, both have adopted what has been termed a "functional analysis," by which the possible effects on the degree of competition are evaluated at various geographic levels. At the national level, every merger so far proposed has fallen well short of the region of concern defined by the DOJ Merger Guidelines. Thus, the issue of the appropriate level of aggregation or output definition has never been reached. Similar to previous airline mergers, the proposed TAC-Eastern merger fell well within the DOJ "safe harbor" in terms of the national market, with a post-merger HHI of 839.9 and with an indicated change in the HHI of 96.7. No opponent challenged the merger based on excessive concentration at the national level.

Following the review of the national market, the "functional analysis"—as it has evolved in previous airline mergers—proceeds to examine other, narrower competitive foci. The CAB and the DOT have both found the provision of scheduled airline service between city pairs to be "relevant markets" for antitrust purposes, each city pair constituting a separate market. At this point the analysis turns to an examination of "overlap city pairs," where both carriers provide service (either nonstop or without a change of planes) and the merger would eliminate a direct competitor. Recognizing the futility of drawing inferences from the HHIs calculated at the city-pair level, the analysis also examines the air services supplied by the merger applicants' competitors. This service is conventionally characterized by three levels: "nonstop," "single plane" (implying one or more stops but no plane changes), and "connecting" (implying one or more plane changes and, possibly, additional stops as well).

Absent any unusual conditions inhibiting entry on city-pair routes directly served by only one or two carriers, the existing service should be subject to competitive discipline as long as there is a sufficient number of potential entrants—particularly those already serving both end points of the city pair.[4] Factors such as the limited availability of terminal space (ticket counters, hold rooms, and gates) and restraints on service to the airport (e.g., due to statutes or regulations) are examples of potential entry barriers.

Concentration at Hubs

The Department of Justice has articulated a theory of competitive injury relating to the concentration of services at hub airports. To understand the theory one must first understand the economic function of hub-and-spoke networks. There is a distinct "lumpiness" problem in the *production* of airline services, caused by scale economies relating to aircraft size. Thus, the minimum size of an efficient jet aircraft is approximately 115 to 125 seats (Bailey, Graham, and Kaplan 1985, 50–52). Most point-to-point traffic flows are small fractions of that number—frequently one to twenty-five passengers per day. Service can be efficiently provided between the majority of such thin demand segments by aggregating large numbers of diverse destinations from any single point to a hub city, where connections are made with incoming passengers from many other points to those diverse destinations.

To aggregate adequate flows may require serving a number of points, typically twenty or thirty in a schedule pattern that meets at the hub—a schedule "bank." This suggests the existence of a threshold problem in hub operations and that potential entry might provide discipline in any *single* city linked to the hub only by entry into a sizable number of cities from the hub simultaneously.[5] Thus, the creation by merger of a dominant carrier at a hub might raise concerns that entry by other carriers would be incapable of disciplining the dominant carrier's putative market power, particularly if other constraints, such as limited gate space, came into play.[6] Although the DOJ advanced this theory in the contemporaneous merger applications of TWA-Ozark and Northwest-Republic, the facts in the TAC acquisition of Eastern raised no such concerns. The TAC carriers had hubs at Denver, Houston, and Newark, while Eastern had hubs at Atlanta, Miami, and Kansas City. Thus, however one construed the effect of hub dominance on competition, the proposed merger had no effect whatsoever under the DOJ's theory.

International City Pairs

In contrast with domestic service, international routes are not readily open to entry. While the American preference for competition has significantly expanded competition in fares and over alternate gateways, one cannot rely on potential entry to discipline competition. The antitrust analysis of the impact on international routes is important because a substantial reduction in *direct* competition may necessitate the designation of an alternate U.S. carrier on the affected routes. Since only rarely do two or more U.S. carriers serve the same foreign city from the same U.S. gateway, any direct competition would arise from hinterland-originating traffic that could route foreign travel over alternate (or competitive) gateways served by the two carriers.

For example, Eastern and Continental both provided service to London: Continental from Houston, and Eastern from Miami. To ascertain the extent of direct competition for U.S.-London service by the two carriers required an analysis of actual traffic flows. (The actual routings of passengers originating at United States points to London is available from the DOT's Origin-Destination Surveys.) All U.S. cities with five or more passengers per day were analyzed by routing to ascertain what cities had significant traffic flows to London over *both* Houston and Miami. Only one city, New Orleans, had a significant flow (over 5 percent of its total flow) over both Houston (13 percent) and Miami (7 percent). Since approximately 80 percent of New Orleans-London traffic was routed over *other* gateways, one could conclude that adequate (if not superior) competitive alternatives were available to New Orleans-London travellers. Analyses of the common Mexico destinations, Cancun and Mexico City, had similar results. Thus, the author concluded that the merger could not cause any injury to competition in international routes, and no party challenged that result.

Service from Capacity-Controlled Airports

Clearly the direct competition between Eastern and the TAC carriers that was the focus of antitrust concern involved their hourly shuttle services in the Northeast corridor. New York Air and Eastern both provided hourly services between New York (LaGuardia) and Washington (National Airport) and between New York (LaGuardia) and Boston (Logan Airport). Both carriers were the principal carriers between Boston and Washington National.

Both LaGuardia and Washington National are subject to the Federal Aviation Administration's (FAA's) High Density Rule, which limits the operations at several capacity-constrained airports. To operate an arrival or departure requires a certificate (or "slot") denoting the right to operate within a given hour at National, or within a given half-hour at LaGuardia. Other airports not subject to slot constraints also serve the New York and Washington areas: Newark, White Plains, and Islip in the New York area and Baltimore-Washington International (BWI) and Dulles in the Washington area. Other carriers were actively competing for the traffic flows between the city pairs from these alternate airports, and *de novo* entry was possible in the same fashion as at any other city pair.

A theory of competitive injury from the merger then required a determination that:

1. a relevant market could be defined as *airport pairs,* rather than city pairs,
2. the other incumbents at the airport pair in question would be unable or unlikely to provide competitive discipline, and
3. entry barriers were sufficiently high to foreclose or substantially mitigate a disciplining effect of potential competition by *de novo* entrants at the airport pair.

The merger applicants contended that an airport pair did not constitute a relevant market and that competitive services from other airports in the cities could not be excluded from the relevant market. In support of their contention, they presented the following arguments:

1. Within a metropolitan area airports are much closer substitutes for many travellers than is generally believed. Although the conventional wisdom is that National is *the* preferred airport for Washington, D.C., because of location, this ignores the fact that many trip origins/destinations are not in downtown Washington. Mappings of "indifference zones" in which the difference in ground access time between airports is ten minutes or less were executed. The indifference zones included many regions in Northern Virginia with very high travel origins/destinations that proved equivalently accessible between National and Dulles; regions in Montgomery County, Maryland, that were equivalently accessible between Dulles, BWI, and National; and areas on the east side of the Capitol Beltway that were equivalently accessible to BWI and National. The only clear access advantage for National turned out to be the origins/destinations within the District itself and portions of Northern Virginia adjacent to the airport.

In the New York area, the analysis of ground access time also revealed that for most areas there were one or more unconstrained airports with roughly equivalent or superior access times. Even within Manhattan, Newark was "closer" than LaGuardia on the west side and was "closer" in terms of travel time by bus and train from lower Manhattan.[7]

2. The traffic flows between other airports over New York-Washington has increased both absolutely and relatively compared to LaGuardia-National flows. Over the period 1982 to 1985, LaGuardia-National traffic fell from 59 percent of the New York-Washington total to 35 percent of the total. This occurred while the total New York-Washington traffic was increasing by 62 percent—meaning that the increase was picked up by other airport pairs, because LaGuardia-National traffic actually declined. For example, traffic flows increased substantially over Dulles, Newark, and BWI. Fueled by rapid suburban growth—particularly along the beltway around Washington, the traffic increases at the outlying airports necessitated higher frequencies, which worked synergistically to make those airports closer substitutes for the downtown terminals—as higher frequencies of operations are also relevant in a traveller's choice of airport.

3. A close—or even perfect—substitute in consumption does not require "equality." Even were all travellers in the city destined to downtown Washington or to New York's East side, it does not follow that the "preferred" airport is a distinct market. In such a circumstance the products could be in the same market, with the price of the "preferred" service commanding a fixed premium over the other. The scarcity premium at the preferred airport would be expected to equal the difference in access costs, and if the supply elasticity of the disadvantaged service were high, the demand elasticity for the preferred service at that price would also be high.

As to the second requisite finding (point 2 on page 109), the merger applicants simply pointed to the history of hit-and-run entry over the years following deregulation and argued that the existence of other strong incumbents at the end-point airports in question could adequately discipline any attempted exercise of market power by initiating service between those airports.

The third requisite finding addressed the more compelling question of whether the necessity of holding "slots" at an airport created a barrier to entry for service to that airport. Prior to 1986 this was a fair characterization because the slots were allocated by a nonmarket process—a committee of the carriers themselves. In 1985 the DOT, recognizing the competitive problems inherent to the slot allocation process, established a "buy-sell" rule that allowed carriers to transfer slots. Thus, beginning on April 1, 1986, carriers could freely buy, sell, or trade slots at capacity-constrained airports.

The existence of a free market for slots transformed the slot requirement from an entry barrier to an ordinary asset requisite for production. Thus, while the acquisition of a slot might be expensive (perhaps on the order of one-half million to one million dollars each), such costs would be identical for incumbents and new entrants alike and thus not a true entry barrier. Whether or not an incumbent's slot holdings were obtained without cost prior to the rule is irrelevant. Since the slots are transferable, the opportunity cost of retaining one is the same as the price of obtaining one. Thus, one would expect that services from slot-constrained airports would bear prices (here, the average yield over the various service offerings) reflective of the scarcity rents and that the exercise of market power to elevate yields further would attract entry—even *de novo* entry requiring the purchase of slots.

The Voluntary Divestiture of Slots to Pan Am

As noted, all interested parties had an initial opportunity to submit written comments concerning the legality of the merger following the filing of the application and its accompanying data and analysis. Significantly, all adverse comments concerned the effect on competition in the Northeast corridor to the exclusion of all other concerns.

Discussions with the staff of the Justice Department's Antitrust Division and Charles F. Rule, the Deputy Assistant Attorney General for Antitrust, indicated that this was their concern as well. Although the Department had not informed the applicants that it would oppose the acquisition, Texas Air offered to sell slots at LaGuardia and National to another carrier for the establishment of a competitive shuttle service—if that would entirely alleviate the Department's concerns. The divestiture was thus arranged on the very eve of the submission of direct testimony.

In a letter to Texas Air dated May 13, 1986, Mr. Rule summarized the Department's position and intent in arranging the spin off of slots to Pan Am. He reconfirmed that the Department's chief concerns focused on the possible diminution of competition in the Northeast corridor. He noted two potential problems: "First, the evidence as to the substitutability of Newark and LaGuardia airports and of National and Dulles airports is at best inconclusive. . . .Second, entry into these markets may be uniquely difficult" (U.S. Dept. of Transportation, *Letter* 1986, 2). What seemed to bother the Department most was the possibility that competitive discipline could not be effected in the corridor absent a credible threat of entry. To the Department, this meant entry on a massive scale, with the immediate provision of high-frequency service:

> Even assuming an efficiently functioning "buy-sell" market in landing and take-off rights (so-called slots) at the slot-constrained LaGuardia and National airports, the provision of high-frequency service on these airport-pairs appears to require entry on such a significant scale that it is unclear whether a third carrier (or carriers) would enter in response to a small but significant, nontransitory price increase by TAC after the merger (*Letter* 1986, 2).

Mr. Rule conceded that it was "conceivable that after examining the record developed at a hearing before DOT the Department might conclude that the prepared acquisition creat[ed] no significant competitive problem in the Northeast corridor." Given this uncertainty, the Department agreed to balance Texas Air's concerns in expediting a decision with safeguarding competition within the Northeast corridor by *creating* a new entrant through the spin off of TAC's slots. Thus, under the agreement endorsed by DOT, TAC would sell to Pan Am 46 slots and two gates at LaGuardia, 18 slots at National, and one gate at Logan Airport in Boston. TAC also agreed that, for at least 18 months, it would fly no more than 20 round trip frequencies between each of the two airport pairs, LaGuardia-Logan, and LaGuardia-National. Pan Am in turn agreed to fly at least 12 daily round trip flights over each airport pair for two years.

Thus assured of the existence of a new entrant into the market, Mr. Rule summarized the Department's conclusions:

> The Department has concluded that this divestiture to Pan Am will alleviate any conceivable competitive problem arising out of TAC's acquisition of Eastern. The divestiture agreement is roughly equivalent to a spin off of the shuttle service of either Eastern or New York Air. If market conditions necessitate that Pan Am expand the number of its scheduled flights from 12 to 15 (the number currently offered by Eastern and New York Air), Pan Am should be able to shift service involving slots it already has or to obtain the necessary additional slots without difficulty. Moreover, Pan Am's willingness to commit itself to operating a shuttle for at least two years indicates that it intends to become a serious competitor in those markets.

> We believe the divestiture creates a credible new competitor in the markets for high-frequency air service between LaGuardia and National and between LaGuardia and Logan. As a result, it eliminates any possible anticompetitive effects from this transaction. We therefore will not oppose TAC's acquisition of Eastern and will support TAC's proposal to expedite the proceedings currently pending before DOT (*Letter* 1986, 2, 5).

Tactically, the divestiture and its timing appeared brilliant. The opponents of the acquisition, having failed to raise any issue *except* the effect on the Northeast corridor, had the rug pulled from under them. Texas Air immediately filed a motion with DOT to employ an expedited "show-cause" procedure since the only contested matter of fact had been resolved. The DOT suspended the proceedings from the Oral

Evidentiary Hearing and subsequently issued on July 9 an Order to Show Cause. This order requested that parties submit replies as to why the divestiture did not resolve all competitive issues and why the DOT should not approve the merger.

The Unresolved Issues of Market Definition and Entry Barriers

Since the applicants' voluntary divestiture was a "cure" for a theory of injury that, at that time, neither the DOT staff nor DOJ had formally adopted or addressed through testimony, the contested issues of market definition and entry barriers were never joined. Rather, the DOT's Order to Show Cause did set out *tentative* findings on these issues consistent with the DOJ's theory of injury—which the applicants naturally did not oppose.

In reaching its conclusion, the DOT found as follows:

> [The merger applicants' arguments to the contrary, a] specific airport will nonetheless constitute a separate market if there is a large number of travellers who will rarely consider using alternative airports and, importantly, if the carriers serving that airport can disregard the level of fares and service offered at other airports in determining their fares and service levels (U.S. Dept. of Transportation, *Order,* 1986, 13).

The DOT noted that while many corridor travellers exhibited no preferences among airports, the record showed "a large number of business travellers" preferring National and LaGuardia and who did not consider the suburban terminals as practical alternatives: "[A]s a result," the DOT found, "the services offered at the other airports do not discipline the level of fares and service offered by carriers on the [National-LaGuardia] and [LaGuardia-Logan] routes" (*Order* 1986, 13).

The DOT then invoked a fundamental principle of market definition: "The key question in deciding whether services are in the same market is whether (and to what extent) the prices for one service respond to changes in prices for the other service" (*Order* 1986, 13). The DOT concluded that the record indicated that fares for National-LaGuardia and LaGuardia-Logan service were not affected by fares offered at Dulles or Newark—suggesting that the shuttle routes were separate markets.[8]

As corroborative evidence, the DOT also found that New York Air's and Eastern's competitive behavior—particularly their advertising—also supported placing the "suburban" airports outside of the shuttle market definition.

Given the loss of actual competition on the shuttle routes, the DOT was less than sanguine about the likelihood of new entry, but it could not tie its fears to actual evidence: "Entry would require a large block of slots at both [National] and [LaGuardia], for competition for business travellers on these routes *apparently* requires the operation of frequent flights throughout the day" (*Order* 1986, 15, emphasis supplied). Attempting to spell out its reasoning, the DOT wrote:

> Without Texas Air's agreement to transfer a large block of slots to Pan Am, entry on such a scale would be unlikely. A carrier not already holding a substantial block of slots at both DCA and LGA could not practicably begin competitive service within a reasonable period of time, because it could probably not obtain the large block of slots required for frequent service. Most slots are being used by carriers to provide feed traffic to their hubs or international flights or in markets not served by another carrier. Because such operations substantially improve a carrier's ability to obtain profits, relatively few slots are likely to be available at any one time at a price which a new entrant would be willing to pay.

> Although a few carriers already holding a substantial number of slots (for example, USAir) arguably have the resources needed for establishing a shuttle-type service, doing so would require the cancellation of a large proportion of their existing service. As shown, the traffic and earnings benefits provided by their existing service would probably dissuade them from cancelling that service in order to use the slots to create a new service in competition with the Eastern shuttle, which is well-entrenched in the routes (*Order* 1986, 13, citations omitted).

The DOT thus concluded that, but for the spin off of slots to Pan Am (and, implicitly, the ensuing agreements by TAC to limit frequencies and by Pan Am to maintain certain frequency levels), the acquisition would have substantially reduced competition in the two shuttle routes.

Remaining Issues

People Express and the Commonwealth of Massachusetts complained that the divestiture was an inadequate remedy because, *inter alia*

1. Pan Am would not likely be a successful competitor, and People Express should be the replacement carrier, and
2. the divestiture would not remedy competitive injury in the Boston-Washington National market.

With respect to People Express, the DOT found their argument "unpersuasive" as it was based on "the contention that we should select it as the replacement carrier since it would allegedly provide the most vigorous competition for the Eastern shuttle" (U.S. Dept. of Transportation, *Order,* 16). As the DOT pointed out, Congress instructed it to approve all acquisitions that did not lessen competition and were not adverse to the public interest—a charge that clearly did not embrace disapproval of acquisitions where an alternate transaction *might* create better competition.

Massachusetts submitted expert economic testimony in support of the second point—that the merger would injure competition in the Boston-National airport pair. The expert witness retained by the state raised (for the first time in the proceeding) the results of a series of empirical analyses that had been previously performed by several economists for the purpose of testing the contestability hypothesis. Drawing on these studies, the expert witness argued that one could infer competitive injury from the reduction in *actual* competition in the airport-pair market (see Call and Keeler 1985; Strassman 1986; Bailey, Graham, and Kaplan 1985; and Morrison and Winston 1986). As pointed out by the author, however, in every case the empirical results were either contradictory or raised doubts about their validity in airline markets. The author's response was two-fold:

1. The empirical analyses were all based on *city-pair,* not airport-pair markets; thus *arguendo,* one could not necessarily extend their results to airport-pair markets. To do so would imply that Dulles service has no greater discipline on National Airport service than does service from other cities, such as Philadelphia.
2. Each of the cross-section regressions was incapable of distinguishing statistical *association* from *causation.* The finding of a significant relationship between price and market concentration could be, for example, an artifact of the omitted relationship of market size and costs. That is, while larger markets are served at lower unit costs than smaller ones, they are also likely to be less concentrated because of the minimum threshold of service by any single carrier.

More fundamentally, cross-section regression analysis of this sort contains an implicit statement of competitive equilibrium that is fundamentally incorrect. Each such analysis is founded on the implicit assumption that the unit cost of service in each city-pair market can be independently defined and that actual and potential competition (in the polar case of perfect contestability) drive price to that unit cost. This grossly mischaracterizes the production process for airline services, which is, as described above, with perhaps the single exception of shuttle service, always characterized by joint production of many services simultaneously.

In the case of joint production, neither the costs of individual services nor their prices in competitive equilibrium can be defined. Potential competition—or contestability—in the airline industry drives total revenues down to total costs and thus prevents the exercise of market power. In short, the effect of potential competition is to prevent prices from being elevated above costs for the entire collection of joint products over a significant period of time. By this process, individual prices for some or all of the joint products may be driven *below* apparent "unit" cost by new entry or the presence of an aggressive low-cost competitor because incumbent firms do not in practice withdraw capacity as quickly as the theoretic model would suggest. Thus, while the *structure* of fares that evolves may well be related to the structure of actual competition, this is not dispositive evidence of market power.

The DOT, in the Final Order, did not comment or make a finding on this issue. Rather, it dismissed Massachusetts' complaint with the following observations:

1. Neither Eastern nor New York Air provided hourly service; therefore, the threshold of competitive service was low.
2. The airport pair was currently served by Northwest and Delta, either of which could have marginally expanded service in response to any contraction of service or elevation of prices by the merged carrier.
3. USAir had announced entry into the airport pair with four daily flights.

Final Resolution

While the sale of slots and gates to Pan Am was adequate for the frequency specified in the agreement—twelve flights daily—Pan Am required additional slots to provide hourly service typical of shuttle operations. In other words, there remained some gaps in the hourly service pattern that would require acquisition of additional slots at National Airport. Texas Air refused to sell Pan Am the needed slots, but it was generally assumed that a small number could be obtained from other sources. In any event, as the time period for comment expired, Pan Am had not obtained the slots and approached the FAA for an emergency allotment of slots (to be obtained from the quota for general aviation—private planes that do not serve as common carriers). In its first Final Order, dated August 26, 1986, the DOT found that:

> The responses filed by the applicants and Pan Am to the show-cause order have failed to persuade us that Pan Am will be able

to provide effective competition in the shuttle markets, since the record shows that effective competition requires the ability to operate hourly flights, particularly at peak hours, and that Pan Am's shuttle schedule will have gaps at peak hours as well as other times. We stated in our order that we cannot approve the acquisition until we are satisfied that Pan Am has the resources necessary for effective competition. Accordingly, we must disapprove the acquisition (U.S. Dept. of Transportation, *Final Order* 1986, 1).

Whether Pan Am's failure to purchase additional slots at National represented a breakdown in the slot market or rather was strategic behavior is a fascinating question.[9] In any event, the DOT action placed the onus squarely on Texas Air, which responded by selling Pan Am additional slots on terms favorable to Pan Am. A postscript filing was made on September 12, and an expeditious Final Order approving the acquisition was issued by DOT on October 1, 1986.

Conclusion

The resolution of competitive concerns through the show-cause process and by voluntary divestiture proved satisfactory to most parties. However, the lack of a fully developed record joining the critical issues in the case leaves many critical issues to be resolved in another forum.

For example, the DOT's resolution of the question concerning the separateness of service among airports within a single city was based on casual empiricism and a subjective analytic framework that would have benefitted substantially by a case with full DOJ participation.

Also, the Final Order did not adequately discuss or resolve the issue of slots as a barrier to entry. The Order concluded that establishment of a new shuttle service would be unlikely, primarily on the grounds that it would require the use of slots that were more profitably employed by carriers in providing service to other cities (particularly their hub cities), which is perfectly consistent with an efficient allocation of slots and a competitive equilibrium in shuttle and other markets.

A more sophisticated theory that might have been advanced by DOJ (had the issue gone to hearing) is that the assembly of the requisite package of slots would cause the price of the total to exceed the efficient level and thus block efficient entry. This is analogous to the difficulties encountered in assembling a package of small tracts of land requisite for a large construction project. If the tracts are widely held, and each seller is aware of the significance of *his* holding to the buyer, each seller might "hold out" for a price above "market." (The analogy could prove strained, however, because the number of slots in each time period is numerous, and thus any particular one is not uniquely required by the buyer.)

Finally, the econometric evidence concerning "contestability" continues to grow, and its relevance for the assessment of airline mergers will soon become much clearer. All analyses of contestability at this time are of cross-section market data, which may hold as much value for merger analysis as cross-section consumption studies hold for estimating macroeconomic national income models. That is, for merger analysis, as in the national income model, it is critical to distinguish *causation* from association. With the publication of postmerger price data on markets affected by significant mergers in the past several years, a clearer resolution of these issues will be gained by direct test.

Notes

1. Under this doctrine, an otherwise unlawful, anticompetitive merger or acquisition is permitted if it can be shown that, *but for* the proposed transaction, the acquired firm would go bankrupt and thereby withdraw from the market.

2. Texas Air indicated that it would operate Eastern as a separate division and not merge it with its other operating units.

3. Western and Aloha were subjects of acquisition rumors reported contemporaneously in the press; their trading volume further suggested this explanation for the appreciation of their stock prices.

4. The presumed adequacy of potential competition to discipline prices has been challenged by a series of cross-section analyses that often find an association between prices and the level of actual competition (i.e., concentration) in city-pair markets (see, for example, Call and Keeler 1985; Strassman 1986; Bailey, Graham, and Kaplan 1985; and Morrison and Winston, 1986).

   Such results appear inconsistent with the "perfect contestability" hypothesis and raise doubts as to the actual degree of market discipline exerted by potential competition. While these results were raised by one intervenor in the case, they were not relied on by the DOJ and were never reached by the DOT in its Orders.

5. Such conditions provide an excellent example of "economies of scope," wherein the cost of producing a single product is related to the number of other product types being produced.

6. In most instances the cities are served via connections over many hubs. Therefore the likelihood of competitive injury arising from domination at one hub is slight. However, DOJ has maintained that competition may be injured for travel to and from the hub city itself.

7. By contrast, however, in terms of economic distance taxi fares to Newark from Manhattan include a surcharge arising from the distinct regulatory jurisdictions for taxi service.

8. The distinct fare differences between LaGuardia and Newark services, however, involved People Express fares for their services from Newark, which arguably represents a distinctly different product itself.
9. The term "slot-mail" has been used by some to describe the situation.

References

Bailey, Elizabeth E., David R. Graham, and Daniel P. Kaplan. *Deregulating the Airlines.* Cambridge, Mass.: The MIT Press, 1985.

Baumol, William J., John C. Panzar, and Robert D. Willig. *Contestable Markets and the Theory of Industry Structure.* New York: Harcourt Brace Jovanovich, Inc., 1982.

Call, Gregory D., and Theodore E. Keeler. "Airline Deregulation, Fares, and Market Behavior: Some Empirical Evidence." In *Analytical Studies in Transport Economics,* edited by Andrew R. Daugherty. Cambridge: Cambridge University Press, 1985.

Eckbo, B. Espen. "Horizontal Mergers, Collusion, and Stockholder Wealth." *Journal of Financial Economics* 11 (1983): 241–273.

Levine, Michael. "Airline Competition in Deregulated Markets: Theory, Firm Strategy and Public Policy." *Yale Journal on Regulation* 4 (1987): 393–494.

Morrison, Steven, and Clifford Winston. *The Economic Effects of Airline Deregulation.* Washington, D.C.: The Brookings Institution, 1986.

Stillman, Robert. "Examining Antitrust Policy towards Horizontal Mergers." *Journal of Financial Economics* 11 (1983): 225–240.

Strassman, D. L. "Contestable Markets and Dynamic Limit Pricing in the Deregulated Airline Industry: An Empirical Test." Rice University Working Paper, 1986.

U.S. Department of Justice. Merger Guidelines. June 14, 1984.

U.S. Department of Transportation. Letter to Clark Onstad, Vice President, Texas Air Corp. from Charles F. Rule, Deputy Assistant Attorney General, Antitrust Division, May 13, 1986.

U.S. Department of Transportation. Order to Show Cause, Docket 43825 (Texas Air-Eastern Acquisition), July 9, 1986.

U.S. Department of Transportation. Final Order, Docket 43825 (Texas Air-Eastern Acquisition), August 26, 1986.

2
Part

Horizontal Practices

The Economic and Legal Context
of Horizontal Practices

A firm in a competitive market has no real choice of behavior: survival requires constant attention to the constraints and opportunities of its market environment. An oligopolist or dominant firm, however, has a wider range of possible behavioral relationships that it may establish with its horizontal rivals. It may cooperate or collude with them so that the industry behaves as a monopoly. Alternatively, the firm may compete vigorously with its rivals, resulting in a competitive market outcome. The firm may even undertake deliberately hostile actions, seeking to "monopolize" or enhance its market power. The antitrust laws address this spectrum of possibilities in oligopoly. Section 1 of the Sherman Act forbids any "contract, combination, . . .or conspiracy in restraint of trade. . ," while Section 2 prohibits actions that would "monopolize, or attempt to monopolize. . ." a market. Section 5 of the Federal Trade Commission Act encompasses all of this in its ban on "unfair methods of competition."

Issues of horizontal practice differ from the problems addressed in Part 1 of this book since horizontal practices are not the result of, or enhanced by, any structural *change* in the industry. Rather, they represent behavior patterns that arise within a given industrial structure, as firms either seek to increase profitability through closer cooperation or attempt to alter that structure (e.g., through aggression against rivals) in favorable ways. The cases in this section span this spectrum. Two of the cases involve allegations of cooperative behavior among sellers with respect to price and advertising. A third case describes an alleged, multifaceted attempt by one company to monopolize an industry. Yet another case raises the issue of predatory pricing and product actions against rivals, while the remaining case combines allegations of conspiracy and predation. Here we shall begin by offering additional comment on the various behavioral possibilities themselves.

Collusion and Cooperation

Economic Theory

A simple demonstration in microeconomic theory is that a cartel of firms can achieve the monopoly level of price and quantity in the market by means of collusion. Where this takes place, the economic consequences are just as adverse as under pure monopoly. Indeed, the economic judgment is likely to be even stronger than in the case of monopoly for the simple reason that many of the cost savings possibly realized by a larger firm (e.g., a monopolist with scale economies) are logically unobtainable by a cartel of separate firms with distinct production facilities.

As noted in the introduction to Part 1, Horizontal Structure, success in efforts to collude is by no means certain.[1] Indeed, one may envision a continuum reflecting the probability of success as a function of such underlying conditions as the number of firms, entry conditions, and so forth. Where conditions are especially favorable, firms may succeed in "tacit coordination"—that is, spontaneous cooperation resulting from strongly perceived interdependence. But in most circumstances, one or more factors may represent serious impediments to purely tacit cooperation, confronting firms with the choice of realizing merely competitive profit levels or undertaking some stronger cooperative action.

In the most unfavorable circumstances, firms may be driven to outright collusion. For example, if firm numbers are large, perceived interdependence is likely to be quite weak, and nothing short of explicit agreement will suffice (and indeed, even that may fail). Thus, economics predicts that cases of explicit conspiracy are likely to arise where conditions are unfavorable to looser forms of cooperation (Hay and Kelley 1974). Between these extremes lie conditions that neither require explicit conspiracy nor permit spontaneous cooperation to succeed. The term *facilitating devices* is used to denote common institutions or behavioral patterns that firms in such markets may adopt to promote some degree of cooperation. "Most favored customer" clauses may play this role by reducing each seller's incentive to cut prices. Long-term customer contracts and exit fees from contracts may insulate existing sellers from new competitors and handicap existing firms in bidding away each other's customers. Advance announcements of price or product changes may facilitate the process of oligopolists' converging on new, higher prices. The dilemma for policy in this area is that each of these practices or devices, at least within some limits, also has a benign or procompetitive explanation.[2]

It is worth emphasizing that perfect collusion among firms is not necessary for "success." Sellers in an industry may be considerably better off simply by moderating their rivalry, even if full monopoly cooperation is not achieved. Moreover, in the case of dominant firm and perhaps some other markets, cooperation among all firms may not be necessary for above-competitive pricing. A single leading firm or core of cooperating firms may succeed in raising price by contracting their own output. If the supply elasticity of the fringe of nonparticipating firms is low enough, they may even behave like perfect competitors (producing where price equals their marginal costs) without defeating the price increase. Although the dominant firm or core would surely prefer fringe firms' cooperation in order to spread the burden of output-contraction, that firm or core may nonetheless find it advantageous to act unilaterally.

As economic literature has shown, unilateral pursuit of higher prices is likely to result in the erosion of market price, market share of the leader, and its monopoly profits, as over time new entry and expansion lead to the decline of its previous dominant position.[3] That outcome, of course, does not indicate "failure" when the alternative may be no profits at all, and it does not predict that the erosion will be sufficiently fast to make policy action moot. It does show, however, that there are temporal limits to market power.

Antitrust

The longest-standing precedent in all of antitrust policy has been the per se prohibition on explicit price fixing. Beginning with the *Trans-Missouri Freight Association*[4] case and strongly affirmed in *Trenton Potteries*,[5] the Supreme Court has ruled that price fixing is an automatic violation of the Sherman Act's ban on "contracts, combinations and conspiracies in restraint of trade." This per se approach stems from a literal reading of Section 1 of the Act, but it is also an efficient rule for violations that, though there may be variation in outcomes, never or almost never yield net social benefits. The "almost never" phrase concedes that the rule may yield occasional mistakes; but to the extent that mistakes are proportionally very few and/or very costly to distinguish from those that should be prohibited, a per se approach serves society well. There have been occasional deviations in Court opinions concerning price fixing, notably in the Depression-era *Appalachian Coals* decision.[6] Yet the broad thrust of policy in this area has little ambiguity and few critics.

Considerably more controversy has surrounded judicial treatment of information exchanges among firms—in particular, exchanges of price information among direct competitors. In the *Container Corporation* case,[7] for example, the Supreme Court articulated the rule that such exchanges were illegal when industry characteristics suggested they would have an adverse effect, but accepted very ambiguous evidence in the case itself.

This rule-of-reason approach is appropriate when a practice may have either adverse or beneficial effects, both in significant proportion, and when these alternative outcomes can be distinguished in practice. The experience of the courts in attempting to draw such distinctions, however, has not been altogether successful. Trade association cases involving information exchanges highlight the difficulties with this approach. Generally speaking, trade associations are permitted to collect and disseminate price information, but not to take actions that are intended to force compliance by its members with published prices. Many critics feel that this standard permits too much price information to pass among competitors.[8] The courts have similarly struggled with arguments that certain kinds of market transactions actually require coordination among competitors for the transaction to take place at all. In the *ASCAP/BMI*[9] and *NCAA*[10] cases, it has accepted versions of precisely that argument, causing debate about the erosion of the per se ban on price agreements.

The courts have also been recently asked to judge the competitive effects of so-called facilitating practices: those institutional arrangements and behavioral patterns among companies said to promote coordination without explicit agreements. These cases have involved such practices as adherence to common pricing books that reduce the complexity of pricing heterogeneous products (as in the *GE-Westinghouse* case[11]) and use of most-favored-customer clauses as incentive-altering devices (as in the FTC's action against four gasoline additive companies[12]). The courts have been willing to consider some of these as undue intrusions on the market process, but a common theme has been their insistence on guidance regarding circumstances in which these represent anticompetitive behavior as opposed to normal business practice. They have often found such guidance lacking.[13]

In contrast to this scrutiny of multifirm efforts to raise price, a single dominant firm that raises its price unilaterally has been subject to a relatively permissive standard. Throughout the course of antitrust policy, the courts have been reluctant to attack large companies without evidence of victimized rivals from *low* prices or some other nasty practice toward horizontal competitors. Thus, dominant firm behavior by U.S. Steel that resulted in higher prices and adverse affects on customers (but favorable reviews by its rivals) was nonetheless sanctioned.[14] In that case, like the *Standard Oil*[15] case before, the Court was looking for evidence of "brutalities and tyrannies"[16]—predation in some form against smaller rivals. Even the *Alcoa* case[17] (into which it has been said one can read anything one wishes) appears to have been decided as much on the grounds of aggressive behavior toward rivals as on the more prominent structural criteria. The prevailing *Grinnell*[18] rule on monopoly, which demands proof of "willful acquisition and maintenance" of market power, reinforces this emphasis on aggressive dominant firm conduct toward rivals.

Monopolization and Predation

Economic Theory

Oligopolists and dominant firms do not at all times seek cooperation with their rivals. Profits may be increased by any one of several aggressive actions. A firm may attempt to drive one or more of its rivals from the market through various pricing, product, or marketing strategies. Alternatively, it may seek to discipline its rivals, so that they may remain in the market but their subsequent behavior will be less competitive. Or the firm may bend its efforts to the task of deterring new competitors from entering. Most of these strategies involve conduct that is costly in the short term but is expected to result eventually in a monopolistic industry structure or, at least, a more cooperative behavior pattern by rivals.

The first of these alternatives—predation—was long thought to be a plausible strategy by which a firm could enhance its market power and ultimate profitability. A leading or dominant firm would increase its output, thereby lowering market price and imposing losses on rivals. Those rivals would then exit and leave the predator firm with unfettered market power, resulting in yet higher market price and additional consumer harm. The prototypical case of such predation (together with other alleged practices) involved the rise of Standard Oil to dominance of petroleum markets in the late nineteenth century. There has been little dispute that Standard was a harsh competitor, that many rivals exited the market, and that Standard came to possess substantial market power. But much controversy has arisen as to whether Standard did engage, or even could have engaged, in predatory pricing.

Challengers to the classic view have argued that the circumstances under which predation can succeed are so limited that it is not a significant policy problem. Because of its larger size, the dominant firm predator incurs losses proportionally greater than its target, the proportion being its share relative to that of its rivals. Thus, the would-be predator is likely to injure itself more than it damages its rival. Moreover, in order ever to benefit from this action—even if successful in driving rivals out—the dominant firm must enjoy entry barriers in the post-predation period. Without such barriers, the firm can never earn above-competitive profits sufficient to justify the initial losses incurred. All of these considerations, it has been argued, make predation rarely rational (McGee 1958).

This argument, together with some reexamination of past predation cases,[19] led a number of economists and antitrust analysts to conclude that instances of true predation are sufficiently rare that they can be safely ignored. While that view may be extreme, most economists would probably agree that predation is far less common than alleged. Most instances of alleged predation consist of rivals confronted by hard competition, often by more efficient larger firms, with adverse consequences for their own market share and profitability. But these adverse consequences for a competitor do not imply adverse consequences for competition. Thus, in a great many instances, the revisionist school's skepticism with respect to predation is justified.

More recent economic analysis, however, has identified a number of circumstances under which predation may indeed be rational.[20] A dominant firm may predate in order to deter future competitors—i.e., in order to develop a reputation as an aggressive firm. Alternatively, a dominant firm may have a deeper pocket due to differential access to capital markets by the predator and its target firm. Most recently, some economic models have shown that a dominant firm may use pricing in an effort to convince ("signal") actual and potential rivals that it has lower costs (which need not actually be the case) and hence that they would be better off in some other market.

Other new approaches reexamine the premises of the predation story. Whereas the classic story almost always has a large firm lowering price, thereby penalizing itself greatly, the crucial elements turn out to be the ability of the would-be predator to expand output readily and the inability of the target firm to decrease output easily. In these circumstances, even a smaller firm may be able to exercise profitably predation against a larger firm.[21] Apart from that possibility, the classic story presumes the dominant firm predator will simply raise quantity indiscriminately in the market. More selective or targeted competition against particular rivals is almost certainly advantageous to the dominant firm. That is, it may seek to win sales away from one particular rival, either because that rival is especially aggressive, or merely as a demonstration to other rivals.[22]

Moreover, price is only one of a large number of strategic variables available to an aggressive firm. Indeed, it may be the least attractive since it is relatively indiscriminate and may be avoidable by the target firm. This recognition has led to analyses of alternative strategies against existing rivals or against those contemplating entry. These include strategic use of capacity investment (Spence 1977; Dixit 1980), product innovation (Ordover and Willig 1981), product proliferation (Schmalensee 1979), product replacement (Menge 1962), advertising (Hilke and Nelson 1983), and cost manipulation (Salop and Scheffman 1983). Which of these might be employed depends on the circumstances—in particular, the aggressor's perception of the most readily exploited weakness of its rivals.

Finally, the classic focus on actually forcing rivals from the market may not be the most likely scenario. The dominant firms may benefit substantially merely by convincing their rivals to act in a less competitive manner—i.e., "disciplining" them. Successful discipline consists of using any of the above strategies in order to modify the response function of rivals—neither forcing them from the market nor requiring complete cooperation. Rather, the objective is to secure enough output restraint so that the dominant firm's output contraction is no longer offset by its rivals' expansionary responses.

Antitrust

The problem that has always faced antitrust policy in the area of predatory and disciplining behavior is how to distinguish such behavior from hard, but honest and procompetitive, conduct by large firms. A policy that treats dominant firm actions too harshly is likely to stifle the very market conduct that antitrust was designed to foster. A policy that is too lenient, on the other hand, risks harm to competitors and consumers alike. The enforcement agencies and courts have pursued a variety of different policies during the history of antitrust.

As previously noted, early monopoly cases like *Standard Oil* emphasized conduct aspects ("monopolization") of leading firms. In that case, where the dominant firm was seen as having engaged in nasty practices toward rivals (whether this was true or not), the Supreme Court found that it "monopolized" its market. But where a dominant position was achieved without victimized rivals, as in *U.S. Steel,* the opposite verdict was reached. And, as noted above, even the *Alcoa* case, often viewed as the high water mark of a structural standard for monopoly, was probably decided as much on the basis of that company's conduct as its large market share.

Judicial hostility toward the conduct of large firms may have reached its peak during the 1960s. Merger cases, price discrimination cases, and monopolization cases routinely included allegations of predatory actions or potential by the leading firm in the market, or sometimes the largest multimarket firm. In the *Utah Pie* case,[23] for example, large, diversified food manufacturing firms were convicted of predatory price discrimination against a local firm that remained the leading firm and remained profitable throughout the period of alleged predation. Such decisions gave rise to concern that price competition itself was being sacrificed to protect specific—often smaller—firms.

In an effort to advance the debate concerning predatory conduct, two leading antitrust scholars published an analysis seeking to establish enforceable rules for predation. In their analysis, Areeda and Turner (1975) did not claim that predation would never occur. Rather, they sought to limit judicial prohibitions on low prices to those cases that they believed were demonstrably anticompetitive by contemporary economic standards. Their survey of various possible price and cost patterns led them to conclude that anticompetitive effects were likely only if the leading firm priced below its own marginal cost, and they proposed using average variable cost as a surrogate for marginal cost.

This Areeda-Turner rule now has many critics, but the criticism in no way detracts from the importance of its contribution. For one thing, in the confusion that pervaded judicial opinions with respect to predation, the concreteness of the Areeda-Turner rule had an immediate attraction, and many (but by no means all) courts seized upon it for their own use.[24] Moreover, that original rule caused an explosive growth in research attempting to make operational the economics of predation.[25] The difficulties with the analysis described above, not surprisingly, are mirrored in the problems of finding acceptable rules for judicial proceedings.

Despite these ongoing difficulties, one broad theme emerges from recent judicial opinion. Most generally, actions by dominant firms that may harm rivals are now accorded a much more sympathetic hearing than previously. The *Kodak* case,[25] quickly followed by the FTC ruling in the *DuPont Titanium Dioxide* case,[27] consolidated the policy position that dominant firms have much the same degree of discretion in their behavior as competitive firms. In particular, they are under no obligation to avoid hard competition with smaller or newer competitors, regardless of the fate that might befall the latter. These cases validated a line of reasoning that arose in increments in various cases against IBM by peripheral equipment manufacturers.[28]

The Cases

The cases in Part 2 serve to illustrate most of the issues just outlined. In the first case, Steven Cox recounts the *Bates-O'Steen* case, in which anticompetitive practices were alleged against a state bar association for restricting informational advertising of legal services. The case is noteworthy for many reasons: it established the position that antitrust scrutiny could be applied to the professions. Also, unlike most antitrust cases, the impact of the decision could be evaluated after the fact.

The second selection is authored by Gerald Brock and describes the just-mentioned series of cases by peripheral equipment manufacturers against IBM during the 1970s. Known collectively as the West Coast cases, these arose in opposition to IBM's allegedly predatory actions when confronted with new competition from makers of attachments to IBM's computers. Brock explains why, despite the injury sustained by those firms, the presiding courts found IBM's actions consistent with the competitive process.

In a case involving cooperative action, George Hay discusses a number of facilitating practices among gasoline lead additive companies and the FTC case that ensued. Unable to sustain cooperation through purely tacit means, the companies were alleged to have employed various practices in the industry that allowed them to support prices above competitive levels. Hay's analysis illuminates the economic theory underlying the case and the legal difficulties that this theory encountered.

The fourth case, by John Hilke and Philip Nelson, describes the alleged attempted monopolization of the market for ground coffee by General Foods, the maker of Maxwell House. At issue were actions taken by General Foods against a principal rival at the time the latter was seeking to market its product in new cities. Crucial to the understanding of this case are several elements of the market setting in which the two rivals found themselves, including mobility barriers, first-mover advantages, and the relationship between manufacturers and retailers.

Finally, a very recent case combines allegations of both predation and conspiracy. Kenneth Elzinga describes the relationship between these charges in the *Matsushita-Zenith* case, noting the various difficulties associated with the supposed scheme among Japanese electronic manufacturers. He offers some novel calculations demonstrating the implausibility of the predation argument.

Notes

1. See, e.g., Posner (1976) for a review of the factors influencing success. A further problem worthy of note is that a cartel is likely to be less efficient at producing any given output, since it cannot unilaterally close down high-cost facilities. Rather, some profit accommodation must be made to each separate participant.

2. Discussions of these various practices may be found in Salop (1986) and Cooper (1986).

3. The first to sketch the theory of the declining dominant firm appears to have been Worcester (1957). The modern version of that story springs from work by Gaskins (1971) from which has followed a large literature. For a review, see Encaoua, Geroski, and Jacquemin (1986).

4. *United States v. Trans-Missouri Freight Association,* 166 U.S. 290 (1897).

5. *United States v. Trenton Potteries Co., et al.,* 273 U.S. 392 (1927).

6. *Appalachian Coals, Inc., v. U.S.,* 288 U.S. 344 (1940).

7. *United States v. Container Corp. of America et al.,* 393 U.S. 333 (1969).

8. See Scherer (1980) for some of these concerns.

9. *American Society of Composers, Authors, and Publishers, et al., Inc., v. Columbia Broadcasting System, et al,* 441 U.S. 1 (1979).

10. *National Collegiate Athletic Association v. Board of Regents of the University of Oklahoma and University of Georgia Athletic Association,* 104 S. Ct. 2948 (1984).

11. *United States v. General Electric Co. et al.,* Civil No. 28,228 (E.D. Pennsylvania, December 1976).

12. *In re Ethyl Corp., et al.,* FTC Docket No. 9128, 1978.

13. *E.I. duPont de Nemours v. F.T.C.; Ethyl Corp. v. F.T.C.,* 729 F.2d 128 (1984).

14. *United States v. United States Steel Corporation,* 251 U.S. 417 (1920).

15. *Standard Oil Company of New Jersey v. United States,* 221 U.S. 1 (1911).

16. Phraseology is from *U.S. Steel.*

17. *United States. v. Aluminum Co. of America,* 148 F.2d 416 (1945).

18. *United States v. Grinnell,* 384 U.S. 563 (1966).

19. See Koller (1971), but also Zerbe and Cooper (1982) for contrary evidence.

20. For a good review of these scenarios, together with relevant references, see Ordover and Saloner (1988).

21. For a possible example of this scenario, see Pittman (1984). This possibility is so universally overlooked that some economists and the courts have sought to establish *minimum* shares for predation cases. See *Monfort of Colorado, Inc., v. Cargill, Inc.,* 107 S. Ct. 484 (1986).

22. This can be done, for example, by instructing sales agents to underbid one particular rival supplier, or by giving special incentives to sales agents for such activities.

23. *Utah Pie Co. v. Continental Baking Co.,* 386 U.S. 685 (1967).

24. For example, it was adopted without equivocation in *Northeastern Telephone Company v. AT&T,* 651 F.2d 76 (1981).

25. For reviews, see Hay (1981) and Ordover and Saloner (1987).

26. *Berkey Photo, Inc., v. Eastman Kodak Company* 603 F.2d 263 (1979).

27. *In re E.I. duPont de Nemours and Co.,* FTC Docket 9108 (1980).

28. See, for example, *California Computer Products, Inc., et al. v. International Business Machines Corp.,* 613 F.2d 727 (1979).

References

Areeda, Philip, and Donald Turner. "Predatory Pricing and Related Practices Under Section 2 of the Sherman Act." *Harvard Law Review* 88 February 1975: 697–733.

Cooper, T.E. "Most Favored Customer Clauses and Tacit Collusion." *Rand Journal of Economics* 17 (Autumn 1986): 377–388.

Dixit, Avinash. "The Role of Investment in Entry Deterrence." *Economic Journal* 90 (March 1980): 95–106.

Encaoua, David, Paul Geroski, and Alexis Jacquemin. "Strategic Competition and the Persistence of Dominant Firms: A Survey." In *New Developments in the Analysis of Market Structure,* edited by J. Stiglitz and G.F. Mathewson, 55–86. Cambridge: MIT Press, 1986.

Gaskins, Darius. "Dynamic Limit Pricing: Optimal Pricing Under Threat of Entry." *Journal of Economic Theory* 3 (September 1971): 306–322.

Hay, George, and Daniel Kelly. "An Empirical Survey of Price-Fixing Conspiracies." *Journal Of Law and Economics* 17 (April 1974): 13–38.

Hilke, John, and Philip Nelson. "Noisy Advertising and the Predation Rule in Antitrust." *American Economic Review* 74 (May 1984): 367–371.

Koller, Roland. "The Myth of Predatory Pricing." *Antitrust Law and Economics Review* 4 (Summer 1971): 105–122.

McGee, John. "Predatory Price Cutting: The Standard Oil (N.J.) Case." *Journal of Law and Economics* 1 (October 1958): 137–169.

Menge, John. "Style Change Costs as a Market Weapon." *Quarterly Journal of Economics* 76 (November 1962): 632–647.

Ordover, Janusc, and Robert Willig. "An Economic Theory of Predation." *Yale Law Journal* 91 (November 1981): 8–53.

Ordover, Janusc, and Garth Saloner. "Predation, Monopolization, and Antitrust." In *Handbook of Industrial Organization,* edited by R. Schmalensee and R. Willig. North-Holland, 1988.

Pittman, Russell. "Predatory Investment: *U.S. v. IBM*." *International Journal of Industrial Organization* 2 (December 1984): 341–365.

Posner, Richard. *Antitrust Law: An Economic Perspective.* Chicago: University of Chicago Press, 1976.

Salop, Steven. "Practices That (Credibly) Facilitate Oligopoly Coordination." In *New Developments in the Analysis of Market Structure,* edited by J. Stiglitz and F.G. Mathewson. Cambridge: MIT Press, 1986.

Salop, Steven, and David Scheffman. "Raising Rivals' Costs." *American Economic Review* 73 (May 1983): 267–271.

Scherer, F.M. *Industrial Market Structure and Economic Performance.* Boston: Houghton Mifflin, 1980.

Schmalensee, Richard. "Entry Deterrence in the Ready-to-Eat Breakfast Cereal Industry." *Bell Journal of Economics* 9 (Autumn 1978): 305–327.

Spence, Michael. "Entry, Capacity Investment, and Oligopolistic Pricing." *Bell Journal of Economics* 8 (Autumn 1977): 534–544.

Worcester, Dean. "Why 'Dominant Firms' Decline." *Journal of Political Economy* (August 1957): 338–347.

Zerbe, Richard, and Donald Cooper. "An Empirical and Theoretical Comparison of Alternative Predation Rules," *Texas Law Review* 61 (1982): 655–715.

Advertising Restrictions among Professionals: *Bates* v. *State Bar of Arizona*

Steven R. Cox

Introduction

Advertising by attorneys was strictly prohibited in every U.S. jurisdiction either by legislation, court rule, or court decision until June 1977 when the U.S. Supreme Court handed down its decision in *Bates* v. *State Bar of Arizona*.[1] That decision extended constitutional protection to attorneys' right to advertise their availability and fees to perform certain routine legal services.[2]

By declaring state prohibitions of attorney advertising unconstitutional, the *Bates* decision made it possible for such advertising to occur throughout the United States for the first time in almost seventy years.[3] In addition, it created a climate of doubt about the legality of advertising prohibitions in other professions. Since *Bates,* many such prohibitions have been relaxed, permitting other professionals besides lawyers to advertise.[4] One need only compare the Yellow Pages of any telephone directory today to a pre-*Bates* volume to observe the effect that the *Bates* decision has had on lawyer advertising in particular and professional services advertising in general.

Because of the long history of state prohibitions against all attorney advertising, no one knew at the time of the *Bates* case what effects such advertising would have on legal service markets. In fact, no one even knew whether and to what extent attorneys would advertise if permitted to do so.[5] The findings of a few studies on the price effects of product price advertising restrictions were available, but for the most part attorneys for both sides had to rely on economic theory for supporting arguments. Following the *Bates* decision, a team of researchers at Arizona State University conducted a major national study of the market effects of attorney advertising. Their findings along with other post-*Bates* empirical evidence will be discussed later in this case study. In the inter-

---

Steven R. Cox testified on behalf of the law firm of Bates and O'Steen in a disciplinary proceeding of the State Bar of Arizona.

vening sections, some background information on the *Bates* case is provided; the potential market effects of attorney advertising are discussed; and the actual arguments and evidence presented in the *Bates* case are examined.

The *Bates* Case: Some Background Information

The sequence of events that led to the *Bates* case began in 1972 with the graduation of John R. Bates and Van O'Steen from Arizona State University's College of Law. Following their admission to the bar in September 1972, Bates and O'Steen went to work as attorneys for the Maricopa County Legal Aid Society. In March 1974, they left Legal Aid and formed the Legal Clinic of Bates and O'Steen. The stated purpose of their clinic was to provide quality legal services to moderate and low-income people who did not qualify for legal aid and who consequently had trouble finding a lawyer at affordable fees.

Bates and O'Steen's theory was that an efficiently operated legal clinic would be able to assist people with limited means and relatively routine legal problems at fees well below that which attorneys in a typical law firm were charging at the time. What Bates and O'Steen soon discovered, however, was that 1) a large volume of legal business was needed to break even (i.e., to reduce costs per client served to a level equal to the fees that they felt were consistent with their firm's objective), and 2) the traditional means by which a law firm obtained business (namely, word-of-mouth reputation) was not sufficient to yield such a volume.

After almost two years of operation, Bates and O'Steen concluded that their legal clinic needed to advertise. Yet, both knew that advertising by attorneys was strictly prohibited, not only in Arizona but also in every state in the country. The dilemma that Bates and O'Steen faced, therefore, was the following: if they advertised their law practice, they could possibly be disbarred for violating a disciplinary rule of the Supreme Court of Arizona; but, if they did not advertise, their law practice would almost certainly go bankrupt.

In February 1976, Bates and O'Steen decided to challenge the legality of the court rule against attorney advertising. They placed an advertisement in the February 22, 1976 issue of *The Arizona Republic* (a Phoenix metropolitan daily newspaper). Their ad contained some basic information about their availability and fees to perform certain routine legal services (see Figure 1). On March 2, 1976, the State Bar of Arizona, in accordance with court rules pertaining to the discipline of attorneys, filed a complaint against Bates and O'Steen and initiated a disciplinary proceeding. The case eventually was appealed all the way up to, and decided by, the U.S. Supreme Court.

Figure 1
Bates & O'Steen Advertisement

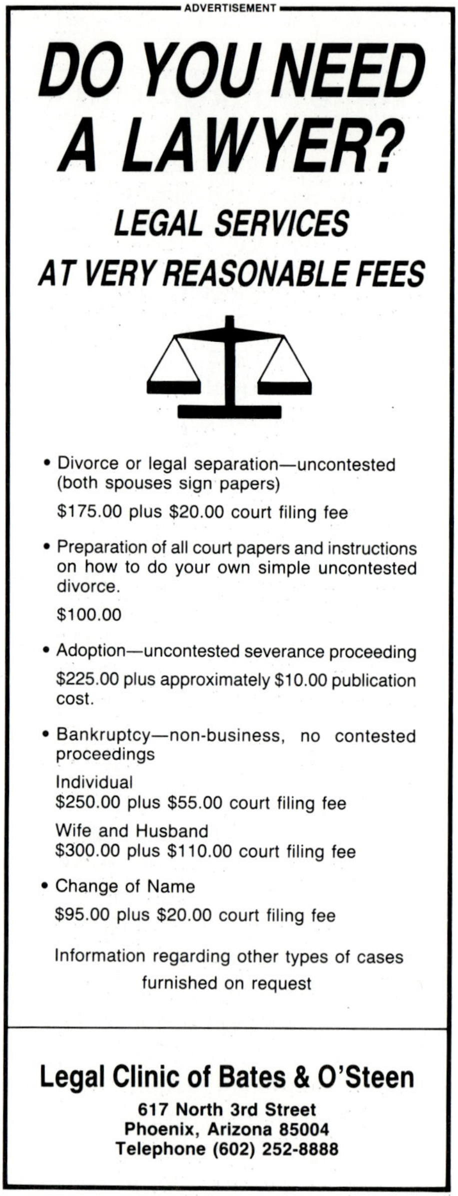

Source: *The Arizona Republic*, February 22, 1976.

The Market Effects of Seller Advertising: Economic Theory and Pre-*Bates* Evidence

As noted earlier, the long history of state prohibitions on attorney advertising made it impossible to say with any certainty what effects such advertising would have on either individual law practices or on legal service markets generally. Bates and O'Steen hypothesized that it would help save their law practice by increasing demand for their services, and the attorney for Bates and O'Steen argued at trial and in his case briefs that the elimination of advertising prohibitions would increase competition among attorneys in legal service markets. The attorney for the State Bar of Arizona, on the other hand, argued that advertising had great potential for public deception, especially in markets for nonstandardized professional services. In the following discussion, four possible market effects of attorney advertising are examined: buyer search, seller competition, entry barriers, and service quality.

Advertising and Buyer Search

The *Bates* decision extended constitutional protection to a particular type of attorney advertising: fee advertising. It did not compel all attorney advertisements to include fee quotes, but it did acknowledge that consumers would be better off with more rather than less such information. A principal benefit to consumers of seller advertising in general, and price advertising in particular, is a reduction in search costs; and, the lower the search costs are, ceteris paribus, the more prepurchase comparison shopping consumers may be expected to do.

In a seminal article on the economics of information, George Stigler examined the role of advertising in what may be referred to as the low-price search process.[6] Stigler's model assumes that consumers operate in a market for a homogeneous commodity and face a distribution of seller-quoted prices for that commodity. The consumer, under these circumstances, wants to find the lowest possible price, but to do so involves some costs as well as benefits. The rational consumer will continue his or her search process as long as the marginal benefits exceed marginal cost. By reducing search costs, therefore, advertising should stimulate more price comparison shopping and lead more consumers to obtain the commodity at lower prices.[7]

The relevant question for the *Bates* case is: How applicable is Stigler's theory to legal service markets? The *Bates* advertisement involved relatively routine legal services, the quality of which (by definition) varies little, if at all, from one attorney to another. Hence, such services may be sufficiently standardized for the Stigler theory to apply. On the other hand, no legal service is ever fully routine and fully standardized, and so it is also possible that attorney advertisements (and, especially those containing prices) may be more misleading than they are informative. If advertising increases rather than decreases perceived service differentiation across attorneys, it could lead to less, not more, comparison shopping.[8]

Advertising and Seller Competition

The relationship between advertising and competition among existing sellers in a market has been the subject of considerable debate in the industrial organization literature. In a recent review of published research on that subject, Comanor and Wilson point out that the key to the advertising-competition relationship lies in the connection between advertising and sellers' individual demand elasticities.[9]

One view of advertising's effect on price elasticities is the "information/search theoretic" view. It hypothesizes that advertising will increase the price elasticity of individual seller demand curves. In markets for relatively homogeneous products, advertising will stimulate consumer price search activity, which in turn will cause the demand curve facing each seller to become more price elastic. The logic here is that more price comparison shopping by consumers will lead to greater reductions in sales experienced by any seller who raises price. In markets for relatively nonhomogeneous products, advertising will aid consumers' quality comparison information gathering. It will do so by increasing consumers' familiarity with a wider variety of market options, again causing the demand curves facing individual sellers to become more elastic. In the case of search goods, this will be accomplished by directly informing consumers of the availability and qualities of alternative sellers' products, and in the case of experience goods advertising will indirectly increase consumer information by encouraging experimentation with more market brands.[10]

An opposite view of advertising's effect on price elasticities is called the "product differentiation" view. The premise here is that if advertising is to occur, sellers must reap some benefits from it. One such benefit would be greater market power. By differentiating a firm's product in the eyes of consumers, advertising will insulate, to some extent, a firm from competition with its rivals. In this view, firms that advertise will enjoy lower demand elasticities than non-advertising firms.

There is one major problem with each of the above views. The "information/search theoretic" view applies least well to goods or services, such as legal services, the quality of which cannot be thoroughly assessed by typical consumers. Such commodities are sometimes described to as credence goods.[11] In such markets, the typical consumer is particularly vulnerable to fraud and deception because of the high costs of quality comparison information. Seller advertising of credence goods, therefore, may do more to mislead than inform consumers.

The "product differentiation" view suggests that firms may obtain greater market power and higher profit margins through advertising. If that is so, then one would expect all firms to advertise in the long run. Absent any significant barriers to entry associated with advertising, the inevitable result would be a profitless monopolistic competition equilibrium. Hence, if a firm is to derive any long-run benefits from advertising, it must have some entry barrier effects.

Advertising and Entry Barriers

Does advertising provide new competitors with the means by which to enter a market, or does it generate barriers to their entry? Bates and O'Steen claimed that without the right to advertise, their legal clinic would not be able to attract the number of clients needed to reduce average total costs to a low-price breakeven level. Their experience had taught them that some means other than referrals from previously satisfied customers, other lawyers, and/or local bar associations was needed to generate a breakeven volume of business.

Informing potential customers of their availability is one of the first tasks that new entrants to any market face, and advertising is one means of accomplishing that task. However, if there are real economies of scale associated with advertising, then over time advertising may serve more as a barrier to new competition than as a means of entry.[12] Either of two phenomena may lead to real advertising economies of scale. Advertising may generate consumer brand loyalty, discouraging consumer search and experience. Or, there may be some threshold or accumulative effect to advertising (i.e., increasing returns to advertising). In either case, existing sellers' promotion costs per client served will be less than those of new entrants to the market.

Advertising and Service Quality

The effect of advertising on the entry of new competition and on the price elasticity of existing sellers' demand curves will influence the long-run market equilibrium level of output price and quantity. The more competition that attorney advertising stimulates, the lower will be the mean of the distribution of seller prices and the higher will be the number of cases handled. The impact of advertising on service quality, however, may depend more on factors like buyer information costs than seller competition in a market.

Phillip Nelson, in his work on advertising as a source of information, developed a theory that suggests that sellers who advertise will offer higher product quality on average.[13] By familiarizing consumers with a wider variety of available market options, advertising increases consumer search and/or experience. In other words, it encourages consumers to buy and try a brand at least once. Consumer repeat purchases of a product brand, however, will depend on its relative quality/price ratio. Since advertising expenditures are a sunk cost, advertisers will depend to a greater extent on future, repeat purchases than will non-advertisers. Consequently, the former will tend to offer brands of higher quality than the latter.

The problem with Nelson's theory as applied to legal service markets is its assumption that consumers can determine product quality, at least ex post, if not ex ante. Practically speaking, this is a troublesome assumption. Any legal service may be divided into two parts, the tangible and the intangible. Let the tangible element be defined as the outcome of the service (e.g., the legal documents produced) and the intangible element consist of factors such as an attorney's personal attention and/or relevant counseling. Even if we assume that the typical consumer of legal services can judge the quality of the latter service dimension, he or she certainly lacks the expertise necessary to judge the quality of the former dimension.[14] Also, others on whose past experience one might rely for some quality information may be unreliable and invalid sources because of their own lack of expertise.

In legal service markets, therefore, two conditions exist. One is asymmetrical information concerning service quality, and the other is high buyer information costs. The former refers to the fact that sellers of legal services possess more knowledge of relative output quality than buyers do, and the latter refers to the fact that the cost to buyers of becoming better informed about relative service quality is very high, even ex post. When we further acknowledge that a high quality version of a legal service costs more to produce than a low quality version, two possible conclusions emerge. One is that of George Akerlof's lemons model: bad products (or services) may drive out good ones under conditions of quality uncertainty.[15] Consumers would be willing to pay for quality if they could determine it ex ante, but they cannot, and so they purchase low-price market options. The other possible conclusion is that the opportunity for seller fraud is greater. Market competition, moreover, as Darby and Karni showed in their research on the optimal amount of seller fraud in credence goods markets, does not mitigate the incidence of such an outcome.[16]

Pre-Bates Evidence

At the time of the initial *Bates* case proceedings, the supply of available empirical evidence on any of the possible market effects of advertising (or advertising bans) was limited to just three studies. Each examined the price effects of different product price advertising bans. One study, conducted by Lee Benhan, investigated various state bans on eyeglass prescription price advertising.[17] Another, conducted by John Cady, examined the product price and pharmaceutical service effects of state prohibitions of prescription drug price advertising.[18] Both studies compared the prices of standardized products across states and found that price levels were significantly higher on average where price advertising was prohibited than where no such prohibition existed. For eyeglasses, the average difference was $5 to $6 on a pair selling for $30 to $40. At the extreme, eyeglasses in the state with the strictest advertising regulations sold for $19 per pair more than in the state with the least strict regulations.[19] For prescription drugs, prices were about 3 percent higher in states with advertising bans than in those without such bans.[20] Cady estimated the aggregate potential savings to consumers of eliminating prescription drug price advertising bans to be about $135 to 150 million.[21] The third study, conducted by Alex Maurizi, tried to assess the impact of city ordinances prohibiting on-premise advertising of retail gasoline prices. In the two cities surveyed where such a prohibition existed (namely, New York City and Boston), Maurizi found that the dispersion in gasoline prices was higher, but the average price quoted was significantly lower, than in the seven other cities sampled.[22]

The price findings of the Maurizi study are mixed, but those of the Benham and Cady studies are consistent with the hypothesis that advertising increases competition among sellers in a market (or, alternatively, advertising prohibitions decrease market competition). The only study to deal at all with possible quality effects of advertising was the Cady study. It investigated the relationship between pharmacy services (such as delivery, credit, and emergency service), firm size as measured by sales volume, and advertising regulation. The study's findings were threefold. First, significant differences in service levels were found across firm sales size classifications. Small pharmacies tended to offer services more frequently than larger pharmacies, although very small pharmacies offered services less frequently than intermediate-size pharmacies. Second, service level differences, except those for prescription records, were not significant across regulated and unregulated states. Third, no significant relationship was found between the sales size distribution of pharmacies and advertising regulations. These findings, then, together with the study's price findings, suggest that advertising regulations affect prices directly, rather than indirectly through service quality.[23]

The *Bates* Case: Arguments and Evidence

The initial *Bates* case proceedings were conducted by a Special Local Administrative Committee of the State Bar of Arizona rather than a court of law. This Committee, from the outset, took the position that it could not consider an attack on the validity of the rule that Bates and O'Steen admittedly and purposely violated. Thus, the sole purpose of the Committee's proceedings was to permit both parties to develop a record on which such a challenge could be based.

The Committee's proceedings began and ended on the same day, April 7, 1976. The reasons for their brevity were threefold. First, the case involved no disputed factual issues. The accused admittedly placed an advertisement of their law practice in *The Arizona Republic,* and their action clearly violated the Arizona Supreme Court's rule against such behavior. Second, only a court of law could and would deal with the case's central legal questions, and so no time had to be devoted to the presentation of legal arguments. They would be made in the legal briefs that each party would prepare when the case was appealed to the Supreme Court of Arizona. Third, no direct evidence on the economic effects of attorney advertising was available to either side of the case, and the amount of relevant indirect evidence available at the time was very limited.

Only one economist was called to testify at the *Bates* case proceedings, and he was a witness for Bates and O'Steen. During direct examination, he was asked to discuss the findings of the Benham and Cady studies and to render an opinion on the possible price and competition effects of prohibitions against attorney advertising. His opinion was that they reduced seller competition in legal service markets and thereby increased legal service fees on average.[24]

Upon cross examination, the attorney for the State Bar of Arizona pursued two subjects. One was advertising's potential for public deception, especially in nonstandardized professional service markets, and the other was the competitive nature of legal service markets. His objectives were to undermine the relevance of the Benham and Cady studies to the case at hand and to argue that legal service markets, even with an advertising ban, were highly competitive because of the large number of licensed, practicing attorneys in Arizona.[25]

On the day after the case proceedings, the Administrative Committee issued its findings of fact and conclusions of law, both of which were essentially predetermined by the position that the Committee took regarding the limits of its responsibility. The penalty that the Committee recommended was that Bates and O'Steen be suspended from the practice of law for not less than six months. About three weeks later, the Board of Governors of the State Bar of Arizona reviewed the Committee's decision and reduced the recommended penalty to a one week suspension. The weeks were to run consecutively and not simultaneously so that Bates and O'Steen could continue their law practice.

Following the Board's decision, Bates and O'Steen sought review of their case in the Supreme Court of Arizona. Specifically, they sought review of the legality of 1) the court rule that their advertisement violated and 2) the procedures that the court had established for enforcing that rule. The legal grounds on which judicial review was sought were antitrust and constitutional in nature. With regard to the court rule itself, therefore, the *Bates* case raised two major questions. One was whether the rule violated either state or federal antitrust laws, and the other was whether it infringed on lawyers' constitutional right to free speech. On July 26, 1976, the Supreme Court of Arizona issued its opinion.[26] The majority concluded: 1) that the court rule prohibiting all attorney advertising amounted to state action (i.e., was a requirement of a state entity, acting on behalf of the state's citizenry) and, therefore, the Sherman Act did not apply; and 2) that restrictions on professional advertising had survived constitutional challenges before and this one, too, passed constitutional muster.

As support for its first conclusion, the Arizona Supreme Court cited the U.S. Supreme Court's decision in *Parker* v. *Brown.*[27] In that decision, the Court held that the antitrust laws do not apply to activity that otherwise might be regarded as a violation of antitrust law but that is required by the state. The *Parker* case involved a California state program designed to restrain competition among raisin growers and thereby maintain raisin prices.

In declaring that constitutional protection did not extend to professional service advertising, the Arizona Supreme Court distinguished the *Bates* case from two contemporary cases in which the U.S. Supreme Court had extended first amendment protection to commercial advertising. In *Bigelow* v. *Virginia,* the U.S. Supreme Court overruled a lower court conviction of a newspaper editor for running an advertisement of a commercial abortion referral service.[28] The Court held in *Bigelow* that a Virginia statute that prohibited the publication of information on abortion violated the first amendment right to free speech of the newspaper publisher. The Arizona Supreme Court noted, however, that the *Bates* case did not involve the right of *The Arizona Republic* to publish the *Bates* ad but rather the right of attorneys themselves to advertise.

One year later, the U.S. Supreme Court held again (this time in *Virginia Pharmacy Board* v. *Virginia Consumer Council*) that commercial speech was entitled to certain first amendment protections.[29] In this case, the Court specifically struck down as unconstitutional a state prohibition of prescription drug price advertising, but in a footnote the Court made a point of the fact that it was extending constitutional protection to advertising by pharmacists who dispense a standardized product and not to other professionals such as physicians and attorneys who render "services of almost infinite variety and nature."[30] The Arizona Supreme Court relied on this distinction in ruling that its disciplinary rule against all attorney advertising passed constitutional muster.

As a last resort, Bates and O'Steen appealed their case to the U.S. Supreme Court, which granted jurisdiction (*certiorari*) in October 1976. Oral arguments were heard on January 18, 1977, and the Court's opinion was issued on June 27, 1977 (about sixteen months after the publication of the *Bates* advertisement). Mr. Justice Blackmun, writing for the majority, upheld the Supreme Court of Arizona's decision on the inapplicability of the Sherman Act, but reversed its decision on the constitutionality of blanket prohibitions of attorney advertising.

In reaching its decision, the Court considered 1) whether attorney advertising would be misleading or informative in nature and effect; 2) whether it would tend to increase or decrease legal service fees because of its anti- or pro-competitive effect on legal service markets; and 3) whether it would adversely or favorably affect service quality. In rejecting the argument that attorney advertising would be inherently misleading, the Court made two points. First, it claimed that "the only services that lend themselves to advertising are the routine ones"[31] and that such services are sufficiently standardized to permit attorneys to quote meaningful and comparable fixed fees.[32] Second, even though an attorney's fee for any legal service is but one aspect of that service, consumers are better off with some information rather than none. The prohibition of all advertising by attorneys, furthermore, serves only to restrict the free flow of information to the public that, presumably, is sophisticated enough to realize the limitations of seller advertising when it comes to making a purchase decision.[33] In short, the Court felt that attorney advertising would facilitate rather than hinder consumer search in routine legal service markets.

With regard to the price and competition effects of attorney advertising, the Court accepted the arguments put forward by the attorney for Bates and O'Steen and rejected those offered by the attorney for the State Bar of Arizona. That is, the Court indicated that it believed attorney advertising would tend to increase competition among sellers in routine legal service markets, thereby decreasing routine service fees on average, rather than raising cost barriers to entry that might lead to higher fee levels[34] While noting that no studies had been conducted on the price effects of professional service advertising, the Court did cite the results of the Benham and Cady studies of eyeglasses and prescription drugs, respectively.[35]

Finally, concerning the service quality effects of attorney advertising, the Court expressed two opinions. One was that the use of standardized procedures in the handling of routine legal problems may increase rather than decrease service quality by reducing the probability of error. The other was that prohibitions of attorney advertising are an ineffective means of "deterring shoddy work" by lawyers because those who are inclined to cut quality will do so regardless of whether advertising is or is not permitted.[36] It is important to note here that the latter opinion differs from both of the theoretical arguments presented earlier. The Court's opinion implies that advertising will have no effect on the incidence of market "lemons," whereas economic theory suggests that advertising will tend either to increase or to decrease that incidence depending on the costs to consumers of determining the quality of legal services.[37] The apparent lack of influence of both theoretical possibilities on the Court's opinion may be due, in part, to the fact that neither side of the *Bates* case referred, at trial or in its legal briefs, to any of the research that economists had done on the relationship between consumer information and product quality.

The Market Effects of Seller Advertising: Post-*Bates* Evidence

The *Bates* decision did not take away the states' right to regulate attorney advertising. It only required that some advertising be permitted everywhere. Predictably, then, various states responded quite differently to *Bates*. A few adopted highly restrictive regulations that virtually limited the *Bates* ruling to its own facts, or nearly so. Others adopted highly permissive regulations that prohibited only false or misleading attorney advertising. Most, however, adopted regulations of varying degrees of moderate restrictiveness. Their differences concerned 1) the types of services that attorneys were allowed to advertise, 2) the information that advertisements could or must contain, and 3) the media that attorneys were permitted to use in the promotion of their services and fees.

In early 1978, less than one year after *Bates*, the National Science Foundation (NSF) funded a pilot study of attorney advertising and pricing behavior in Phoenix. The study's objectives were twofold. One objective was to produce useful information on existing price patterns for certain routine legal services, and the other was to provide a foundation for a subsequent study of the impact of lawyer advertising on the fees consumers pay for such services. Four routine legal services were included in the study. They were reciprocal simple wills with and without a trust provision, an uncontested divorce, and an uncontested personal bankruptcy. The study's results showed that each service market was characterized by substantial fee variation and that each service tended to be priced on a flat fee basis. The former finding suggested that consumers of routine legal services in the immediate post-*Bates* era were largely ignorant of available market alternatives and, thus, the potential impact of advertising was great. The latter finding suggested that it would be possible to measure actual attorney charges for routine legal services via fee surveys.[38]

Meanwhile, state regulatory developments made it possible to examine the market effects of attorney advertising in much the same manner as earlier studies had done for eyeglasses and prescription drugs. In 1980, the NSF funded a follow-up to the Phoenix pilot study to compare attorneys' fees and advertising practices across six cities with widely differing attorney advertising regulations. Those surveys were conducted in 1981. One year later, Louis Harris and Associates on behalf of the Federal Trade Commission replicated the NSF study research design in eleven additional cities. By prior agreement, the NSF-funded team of researchers at Arizona State University and officials at the Federal Trade Commission exchanged their data so that each would have the largest possible database to analyze. Three of the four possible market effects of attorney advertising discussed earlier have been studied using the data collected.

Advertising and Buyer Search

One of the benefits that the U.S. Supreme Court assumed that consumers would realize from fee advertising is an increased ability to shop for, and obtain, lower prices. In other words, the Court assumed that Stigler's model would pertain to attorney advertising of routine legal services.

The critical assumption of Stigler's model is product homogeneity. As long as there are no significant quality differences across sellers, consumers have some incentive to engage in costly search for low price quotes. Routine legal services may be defined as ones for which quality is not a significant variable from either the attorney's or client's perspective; but, do consumers know when their legal problem is routine, and do they know that the quality of services required to solve such problems varies little, if at all, from one attorney to another? If so, or if advertising helps consumers become better informed about the nature of their legal problems and the services required to solve them, then advertising may be expected to increase consumer price comparison shopping, as the U.S. Supreme Court assumed it would.

One possible strategy that consumers may follow in searching for low price quotes is called the reservation price search strategy.[39] According to this strategy, a consumer will continue sampling quoted prices until one is found that is equal to or less than a critical level, known as the consumer's reservation price. This reservation price will depend on, among other things, the search costs that are incurred in randomly sampling individual sellers' quoted prices. Advertising, by decreasing search costs, reduces consumers' reservation prices and thereby increases the amount of prepurchase price comparison shopping conducted. Empirically, then, one would expect to find lower reservation prices, relative to quoted prices, and more search activity in areas where advertising is relatively extensive.

An empirical study of advertising and buyer search in routine legal service markets was conducted to test these hypotheses.[40] Two types of services were included in the study—namely, uncontested personal bankruptcies and uncontested divorces. The study's results show no evidence of a positive relationship between attorneys' use of advertising and buyers' price search activity. In fact, the study's findings show a tendency toward very high consumer reservation prices, even relative to attorney quoted prices, and thus very low estimates of both of the study's indexes of consumer price search. Estimates of the mean reservation price in some cases even exceeded the highest sample price quote, indicating that the "average" consumer in those areas would be content to pay the first price sampled.[41]

If routine legal service advertising, in its initial stages at least, did not have the expected effect on buyer price search behavior, what effect did it have? Unfortunately, we cannot answer that question on the basis of available data. However, one theoretical possibility is worth mentioning because of its implications for the long run. It begins with the supposition that all consumers of legal services—routine and nonroutine—face some quality uncertainty when selecting an attorney to help them with their legal problem. That is, because of high information costs, consumers are unaware of the exact nature of their legal problem (i.e., its relative complexity or routineness) and the type of service required to solve it. They are also ignorant of the lack of degree to which routine services are performed.[42]

Under such market conditions, as Benjamin Klein and Keith Leffler have shown, firms may reduce quality uncertainty for consumers through reputation signals or brand name differentiation.[43] In other words, by investing in brand name capital, a firm may create for consumers some quality guarantee. The guarantee arises from the "sunk" nature of the investment in firm-specific capital that would be sacrificed if the firm were to cheat on its quality guarantee.[44] Advertising is one possible mechanism through which a firm may create such brand name capital and thereby offer consumers some quality guarantee.

According to the theory of brand name capital, advertising should have a number of pro-efficiency effects in the long run. First, it will facilitate buyers' quality search by reducing quality uncertainty. Second, it will increase seller competition by rendering firm demand curves more price elastic. Third, and ultimately, it will lead to a more efficient market distribution of price-quality alternatives. As some firms establish a market reputation for quality through advertising, more certain buyer choices among differentiated sellers will emerge. Consumers will be able to choose between high price sellers who offer some quality guarantee and low price sellers who offer no such guarantee.

Advertising and Seller Competition

The relationship between advertising and seller competition, in one manifestation or another, has been explored in dozens of empirical studies.[45] A subset of those studies has concentrated on advertising's effect on price levels in various product and professional service markets. Three studies were conducted prior to *Bates.* Their results were discussed earlier. Eight additional studies have been completed since *Bates.*[46] Two of these studies extended earlier work on the relationship between advertising and prices for eyeglasses and retail gasoline, while the other six explored advertising's effect on the prices of two professional services (namely, optometric and legal services). The results of all eight studies, like those of the earlier Benham and Cady studies, are consistent with the hypothesis that advertising increases market competition.

The general subject matter of the post-*Bates* Maurizi-Kelley study of retail gasoline prices was the same as that of the pre-*Bates* Maurizi study. That is, both examined the effect of posting price information on retail gasoline prices. In every other respect, however, the two studies differed. The Maurizi-Kelley study used a better (i.e., more reliable) data set; its city sample size was larger; and its results showed that prices on average were negatively related to posting intensity (i.e., the higher the proportion of retail gasoline stations in an area that posted price information, the lower were retail gasoline prices on average in that area). By measuring the price effect of posting intensity, the Maurizi-Kelley study was able to calculate an estimate of the potential dollar savings to consumers of universal posting. The estimates calculated ranged from a low of about $500 million to a high of more than $800 million annually.[47]

The post-*Bates* eyeglass study by Alex Maurizi and Ruth Moore extended Lee Benham's earlier work by examining the relationship between advertising and prices, using various behavioral measures of advertising itself rather than the mere permissibility to advertise. Its results showed that eyeglasses, contact lenses, and component lenses are generally less expensive if the dispensing optician or optometrist provides price information by telephone and advertises outside the telephone book.[48]

Four studies in all examined the price effects of restrictions on advertising by optometrist and opticians. The results of the first Feldman and Begun study showed that state restrictions on optometric service price advertising raise the price of an eye examination by optometrists for a presbyopic patient (presbyopia is a deterioration in focusing ability).[49] A second Feldman-Begun study encompassed restrictions on opticians as well as optometrists. The authors found that states with bans on advertising by both groups had prices for their services that were about 11 percent higher than states that either had no bans or had restrictions on only one group but not the other.[50]

Like the two Feldman-Begun studies, the FTC and Kwoka studies constitute another pair of studies on the price effects of optometric service advertising. The major difference between the two pairs of studies lies in the manner in which their data were collected. Their major similarity lies in the nature of the relationship found between advertising and prices. The FTC and Kwoka studies were based on experimental rather than survey data. Trained subjects with routine visual problems were sent to a sample of 12 different cities across the United States to purchase eye examinations and eyeglasses.[51] When prices in the most and least restrictive cities were compared, both studies found that prices on average for an eye examination plus eyeglasses are significantly higher in the former compared to latter areas. The same holds true when prices charged by non-advertising optometrists only are compared across permissive and restrictive areas.[52]

Finally, two studies dealing directly with advertising's effect on routine legal service prices have now been completed.[53] Both studies analyze the price and advertising data that were collected as part of the Arizona State University initiated study on the market effects of attorney advertising, and their findings support the pro-competitive view of seller advertising. The FTC study examined four different routine legal services (reciprocal simple wills with and without a trust provision, an uncontested personal bankruptcy, and an uncontested divorce) and one nonroutine service (a plaintiff personal injury case). It employed linear multiple regression analysis to estimate, for each service, the relationship across markets between prices and advertising restrictions and between prices and advertising use, holding other possible influencing factors constant. The former relationship was significantly positive for all five services examined, while the latter relationship was significantly negative for three of the five services studied. For the two simple will cases, the latter relationship was not significantly different from zero.[54]

The Schroeter-Smith-Cox empirical investigation of the relationship between advertising and competition in routine legal service markets differed from the FTC study in two important respects. First, it employed a different modeling and estimation technique; and, second, it examined only three routine legal services (namely, reciprocal simple wills without a trust provision, an uncontested personal bankruptcy, and an uncontested divorce). The specific model estimated assumed that profit-maximizing attorneys set their service fees optimally in view of individual demand elasticities and that those elasticities are influenced by 1) an attorney's own advertising effort, 2) the general level of advertising intensity in the market, and 3) other characteristics of the seller or market such as firm size (a proxy for firm reputation) and the number of attorneys per capita in the market (a variable reflecting market concentration).[55]

The "information/search theoretic" view predicts that advertising will render seller demand curves more elastic, thereby reducing seller prices on average, ceteris paribus, whereas the "product differentiation" view predicts that advertising will render seller demand curves more inelastic, thereby raising seller prices on average. Conventional wisdom regarding market structure and firm performance suggests that seller prices will be positively related to firm size because of the market power effects of firm reputation and negatively related to the number of sellers per capita in the market because of the effects of market concentration on seller demand elasticities.

The study's findings provide considerable support for the "information/search theoretic" view of advertising's effect on market competition. The dependent variable in each estimated regression equation was the price that the ith attorney in the jth area quoted for performing each service, adjusted for area cost-of-living differences. The sign and statistical significance of the two independent variables of primary interest (namely, market advertising intensity and an attorney's own advertising effort) are given in Table 1. As indicated, the estimated coefficient on market advertising intensity was negative and significant for all three services. The coefficient on attorneys' own advertising effort, on the other hand, was positive and significantly different from zero, as predicted by the "product differentiation" view, for the uncontested divorce case only. For the other two cases, the coefficient was insignificantly different from zero.[56]

Table 1   The Relationship Between Advertising and Legal Service Prices

Legal Service	Independent Variable	
	Market Advertising Intensity	*Attorneys' Own Advertising*
Reciprocal simple wills without a trust provision	Negative and significant	Positive and insignificant
Uncontested personal bankruptcy	Negative and significant	Negative and insignificant
Uncontested divorce	Negative and significant	Positive and insignificant

Advertising and Service Quality

The third issue raised in *Bates* on which some empirical evidence now exists concerns the relationship between advertising and service quality. Economic theory suggests that there are two distinct aspects of the relationship between advertising and product or service quality. One concerns the correlation, across sellers within a market, between individual advertising practices and product quality. The other pertains to the correlation, across markets, between average advertising intensities and average quality levels. The theory sketched by Phillip Nelson suggests that both correlations will be positive.[57] A more recent model by Richard Schmalensee, however, shows that both correlations may be negative.[58] According to Schmalensee's model, as long as a high quality version of a product costs more to produce than a low quality version and the cost to consumers of judging quality, even after purchase, is relatively high, then producers of low quality products will be able to advertise and sell their market offerings for a lower price than non-advertising producers of high quality products. As a result, advertising and product quality at any moment in time will tend to be inversely related, and over time bad products may drive out good ones.

Four studies have examined either or both of the above aspects of the advertising-quality relationship. Their results are mixed. The first study compared two alternative measures of the quality of legal service rendered by a legal clinic and a sample of more traditional law firms in the Los Angeles area.[59] One measure was subjective in nature and the other objective in nature. The subjective measure consisted of consumers' reactions to the manner in which their divorce cases were handled. The objective measure was the estimated difference in amount of child support awarded in divorce cases handled by the legal clinic versus more traditional law firms, holding other possible determinants constant. To the extent that any differences in service quality were found, they tended to favor the one legal clinic studied. Thus, since it was the only firm in the sample that advertised and since it was the low price service provider, the study's authors claimed that their findings contradicted the proposition that advertising would lead to both lower prices and lower service quality.[60]

The next two studies examined the relationship between advertising and quality for optometric services. In the FTC study, service quality was measured by 1) thoroughness of eye examination, 2) accuracy of eyeglass prescription, 3) accuracy and workmanship of eyeglasses, and 4) extent of unnecessary prescribing. The study's findings with respect to all four measures do not support the view that advertising reduces service quality in the marketplace.[61] John Kwoka's findings, too, are "inconsistent with the view that high-quality service is endangered by advertising."[62] He found that the mean time spent on eye examinations in advertising markets was greater than that spent in restrictive markets.[63]

The most recent study of the advertising-quality issue involves the same three routine legal services as those included in the Schroeter-Smith-Cox competition study.[64] Because of the lack of any direct measures of service quality, attorney time input data had to be used as a proxy for output quality. Total attorney time estimates were available for all three services studied, and for one service (uncontested divorce) estimates of attorney time spent counseling clients were also available.[65] Regression analysis was used, and a number of control variables were included in each estimated regression equation. Two advertising variables were included in each estimated equation to test the relationship between advertising and routine service quality across markets and across attorneys within a market.

None of the study's estimated coefficients on attorneys' own advertising efforts was significantly different from zero, implying that advertising and service quality are unrelated across attorneys within routine legal service markets. Across markets, however, the study's overall findings suggest that advertising and average output quality are *inversely* related.[66] These results are contrary to those found by Kwoka.

As the study's authors discuss in the conclusion to their paper, two interpretations of the apparent inverse relationship between advertising and average output quality for the uncontested divorce and personal bankruptcy cases are possible.[67] One is that the estimated inverse relationship is simply a spurious correlation arising from systematic misreporting of the time spent performing a service.[68] The other begins with the assumption that the data were reliably reported. Therefore, the study's empirical findings are accurate in showing an inverse relationship between advertising and quality. The critical question, then, for policy purposes is: Does advertising move the average level of quality closer to, or father away from, economic efficiency?

In a monopolistically competitive, excess capacity environment, attorneys may have an incentive to offer inefficiently high levels of service quality as justification for their relatively high, noncompetitive price. The fact that consumers may not be able to judge adequately the quality of some service, even ex post, will prevent clients from detecting offers of superfluous "quality"; and excessive quality will help justify the monopoly prices charged. Once in a more competitive environment, however—perhaps brought about by advertising—attorneys may be forced to reduce their fees for routine legal services; and, as their offered prices fall, so too will their incentive to offer inefficiently high quality. In other words, by increasing market competition, advertising may bring about not only lower prices but also more efficient levels of service quality.[69]

Conclusions

More than a decade has passed now since the U.S. Supreme Court handed down its *Bates* decision. Nevertheless, its full impact has probably yet to be felt. All states had to revise their prohibitions of attorney advertising in light of *Bates,* but the new regulations that many states adopted following *Bates* did not create the most favorable environment for attorney advertising. Two other U.S. Supreme Court opinions concerning the legality of newly adopted attorney advertising regulations have been issued since *Bates,* and both decisions have further eased state restrictions on attorneys' right to advertise.[70] Eventually, perhaps, legal service advertising in all U.S. jurisdictions will be subject only to the false and deceptive standard applicable now in states like California and Wisconsin.

Restrictions on advertising by professionals other than attorneys have also been relaxed since *Bates.* Some optometric, dental, and medical-service advertising, for example, is clearly permissible now in every state as a result of court decisions and of new professional association rules with respect to advertising by optometrists, dentists, and physicians.

Questions concerning the use and market effects of professional service advertising present rich opportunities for future research. Available evidence from past studies suggests that the U.S. Supreme Court, in extending constitutional protection to fee advertising of routine legal services, significantly advanced the cause of antitrust in professional services markets. Advertising may not increase substantially the amount of low-price search that consumers conduct in such markets, as the U.S. Supreme Court predicted would occur in routine legal service markets; but it may reduce quality uncertainty for consumers and thereby facilitate their quality search. As buyer choices among differentiated sellers become more certain as a result of advertising, seller competition should increase (i.e., firm demand curves should become more price elastic). The results of empirical studies of the price effects of professional service advertising consistently support the pro-competitive hypothesis. Finally, even though advertising's effect on average output quality in markets with high buyer information costs is a relatively unsettled issue theoretically and empirically, it is likely that the long-run equilibrium distribution of price-quality choices in such markets will be more efficient with advertising than without it.

Notes

1. *Bates* v. *State Bar of Arizona,* 433 U.S. 350 (1977).
2. A routine legal service may be defined as one for which a) the marginal productivity of legal skill is negligible, b) the time required to complete it may be estimated with known and little variance, and c) the quality does not vary significantly across attorneys. See Cox, DeSerpa, and Canby (1982, 306).
3. The first Canons of Ethics adopted by the American Bar Association in 1908 contained a prohibition against advertising by attorneys, and within a few years that provision was adopted in every state.
4. For a discussion of changes in restrictions on advertising by various health care professionals, see Cox (1985, 63).
5. Everyone assumed that some attorneys would advertise if such a practice were permitted, and the U.S. Supreme Court believed that attorney advertisements would be limited largely, if not solely, to the promotion of routine legal services. *Bates* v. *State Bar of Arizona,* 433 U.S. 350, 375 (1977).
6. See Stigler (1961).
7. Also, the more price comparison shopping consumers do, the smaller will be the price variance that the market will be able to support over time and, thus, the more price competitive sellers will have to become. More will be said about the competitive effects of seller advertising later in this section.
8. The ultimate concern here is that differences in seller prices will not reflect actual service quality differences. For a discussion of the necessary and sufficient conditions for heterogeneous search goods markets to behave competitively, see Schwartz and Wilde (1982).
9. See Comanor and Wilson (1979).
10. Search goods are ones whose quality may be ascertained prior to purchase. Experience goods are ones whose quality can only be determined by buying and trying them. See Nelson (1970).
11. Credence goods are ones whose quality is costly to ascertain even ex post. See Darby and Karni (1973).

12. Also, because advertising is nonsalvageable, it is a riskier investment than normal plant and equipment. Thus, entry barriers in markets with advertising, ceteris paribus, will be greater than in markets without advertising.

13. See Nelson (1974).

14. Even in the event of "victory" in a contested matter, the typical consumer cannot determine the relative quality of service he or she received (i.e., whether other legal counsel would have produced a "similar victory" for a lower price or a "better victory" for the same price).

15. See Akerlof (1970).

16. See Darby and Karni (1973).

17. See Benham (1972).

18. See Cady (1976).

19. See Benham (1972, 342–344).

20. See Cady (1976, 501).

21. Ibid., 508.

22. Maurizi's findings, especially his price means, are somewhat clouded by the poor wholesale price data available to him. See Maurizi (1972).

23. See Cady (1976, 499–502).

24. See Appendix to Jurisdictional Statement filed in the Supreme Court of the United States, No. 76–316, pp. 187–188.

25. Ibid., 196–213.

26. *In re Bates,* 113 Ariz 394, 555 P.2d 640 (1976).

27. *Parker* v. *Brown,* 317 U.S. 341 (1943).

28. *Bigelow* v. *Virginia,* 421 U.S. 809 (1975).

29. *Virginia Pharmacy Board* v. *Virginia Consumer Council,* 425 U.S. 748 (1976).

30. Ibid., at 773.

31. *Bates* v. *State Bar of Arizona,* 433 U.S. 350, 372 (1977).

32. Ibid., at 372–373.

33. Ibid., at 374–375.

34. Ibid., at 377–378.

35. Ibid., at 377.

36. Ibid., at 378–379.

37. Recall that if legal service qualities can be ascertained by search or experience, then economic theory suggests that advertising will have a favorable effect on service quality. If, however, sellers enjoy an information advantage vis-à-vis buyers and if buyer information costs are high, then economic theory suggests that advertising's effect on service quality will tend to be unfavorable.

38. See Cox, DeSerpa, and Canby (1982).

39. Reservation price search strategies are optimal in market settings characterized by the following conditions: 1) consumers have a perception of the quoted price distribution, which they take to be correct throughout the search process; 2) they begin the search process without any information about the prices charged by particular sellers; 3) they proceed to gather seller price information by sequentially and

randomly sampling individual sellers' quoted prices, incurring a constant incremental cost for each such sampling; 4) buyers regard all sellers' versions of the good or service to be purchased as identical in all respects except price; and 5) consumers' sole objective of search is to locate a seller who quotes a suitable low price.

40. See Schroeter and Cox (1986).

41. See Schroeter and Cox (1986, 16–17 and Tables 2 and 3).

42. Information about the exact nature of individuals' legal problems and the services required to solve them cannot be disseminated efficiently through advertising. Attorneys, therefore, have no incentive to do so. They also have no incentive to advertise the quality comparability of routine services across attorneys (at least in terms of service outcome) because consumers have no way of verifying the truthfulness of such information, and hence may not use it when selecting an attorney.

43. See Klein and Leffler (1981).

44. This line of reasoning assumes that firms face some probability that fraud will be detected either by consumers themselves or by some interested third party such as the Bar.

45. For a survey of the literature, see Comanor and Wilson (1979).

46. See FTC (1980), FTC (1984), Feldman and Begun (1980), Feldman and Begun (1978), Kwoka (1984), Maurizi and Kelley (1978), Maurizi and Moore (1978), and Schroeter, Smith, and Cox (1987).

47. See Maurizi and Kelley (1978, 47).

48. See Maurizi and Moore (1978).

49. See Feldman and Begun (1978).

50. See Feldman and Begun (1980, 491).

51. For a discussion of the experimental method used in the FTC study, see FTC (1980, 39–47).

52. See FTC (1980, 4–5) and Kwoka (1984, 213–214).

53. See FTC (1984) and Schroeter, Smith, and Cox (1987).

54. See FTC (1984, 109–120).

55. Due to data deficiencies, few empirical studies have explored directly the relationship between advertising and demand elasticities. The careful and comprehensive work of J. J. Lambin (1976) is one exception. Also, not many econometric investigations of advertising's effects consider firm and industry advertising variables separately. One exception is a paper by Vernon and Nourse (1973).

56. All signs of the coefficients on firm size and number of attorneys per capita conformed to conventional wisdom, but only one of the negative point estimates of the latter variable approached statistical significance at conventional levels while all three positive point estimates of the former variable were statistically significant. See Schroeter, Smith, and Cox (1987, Table 1, 56).

57. See Nelson (1974).

58. See Schmalensee (1978).

59. See Muris and McChesney (1979).

60. Ibid., 196–206.

61. See FTC (1980, 6–26.).

62. See Kwoka (1984, 215).

63. Ibid., 215.

64. See Cox, Schroeter, and Smith (1986).

65. The use of attorney time input data to measure the output quality of legal services would, under most circumstances, present a number of problems for an advertising-quality study like the one conducted. However, because of the very special nature of the services examined, attorney time was a rather reasonable and useful measure of output quality. A routine legal service, by definition, is one for which the marginal productivity of legal skill is negligible. Thus, the quality of the tangible element of such a service (i.e., its outcome) will not vary significantly from one attorney to another. The quality of the intangible element (the personal attention and counseling offered to the client) may vary across sellers; but, generally speaking, higher quality will be associated with greater time devoted to client counseling and greater total time spent performing the service.

66. See Cox, Schroeter, and Smith (1986, 345–346, and Table 1).

67. Ibid., 347–348.

68. The Schroeter, Smith, and Cox (1987) study findings show that advertising and the average price offered are inversely related across markets with differing advertising intensities. An attorney who charges a relatively high, noncompetitive price for a service while in a non-advertising environment may attempt to justify that price, both to himself and his clients, by inflating his reported time spent in performance of the service. Once in an advertising environment, however, that same attorney, who is now forced by competition to reduce his price for the service, may deflate reported time spent. In this way, he would rationalize a lower price offered without conceding a reduction in his price per hour or the opportunity cost of his time.

69. Some empirical evidence consistent with this scenario is presented in Kwoka (1984) and Feldman and Begun (1985). Specifically, both studies find that the marginal price of optometric service quality (i.e., the difference in price between a high and low quality eye examination) is less in regulated than unregulated markets. One possible reason for such a finding is that sellers in regulated markets have to rely on quality competition to attract new customers. Deregulation, therefore, by increasing market competition, may not only bring about lower price levels but also price differences more reflective of consumer valuation of quality.

70. *In re R.M.J.*, 455 U.S. 191 (1982); and, *Zauderer* v. *Office of the Disciplinary Counsel of the Supreme Court of Ohio*, 105 S. Ct. 2265 (1985).

References

Akerlof, George A. "The Market for 'Lemons': Quality Uncertainty and the Market Mechanism." *Quarterly Journal of Economics* 84 (August 1970): 448–500.

Appendix to Jurisdictional Statement filed in the Supreme Court of the United States, No. 76–316.

Benham, Lee. "The Effect of Advertising on the Price of Eyeglasses." *Journal of Law and Economics* 15 (October 1972): 337–351.

Cady, John F. "An Estimate of the Price Effects of Restrictions on Drug Price Advertising." *Economic Inquiry* 14 (December 1976): 493–510.

Comanor, William S., and Thomas A. Wilson. "The Effect of Advertising on Competition: A Survey." *Journal of Economic Literature* 17 (June 1979): 453–476.

Cox, Steven R. "Some Reflections on the Possible Use and Nature of Advertising by Health Care Professionals." In *Advertising by Health Care Professionals in the 80's: Proceedings of a National Symposium Sponsored by the Federal Trade Commission.* Washington, D.C.: Federal Trade Commission, 1985.

Cox, Steven R., Allan C. DeSerpa, and William C. Canby, Jr. "Consumer Information and the Pricing of Legal Services." *The Journal of Industrial Economics* 30 (March 1982): 305–318.

Cox, Steven R., John R. Schroeter, and Scott L. Smith. "Attorney Advertising and the Quality of Routine Legal Services." In *Review of Industrial Organization,* no. 4 (1986): 340–354.

Darby, Michael R., and Edi Karni. "Free Competition and the Optimal Amount of Fraud." *Journal of Law and Economics* 16 (April 1973): 67–88.

Federal Trade Commission. *Effects of Restrictions on Advertising and Commercial Practice in the Professions: The Case of Optometry.* Washington, D.C.: Federal Trade Commission, 1980.

Federal Trade Commission. *Improving Consumer Access to Legal Services: The Case for Removing Restrictions on Truthful Advertising.* Cleveland: Federal Trade Commission, 1984.

Feldman, Roger D., and James W. Begun. "The Effects of Advertising Restrictions—Lessons from Optometry." *Journal of Human Resources* 13 (Supplement 1978): 247–262.

————. "Does Advertising of Prices Reduce the Mean and Variance of Prices?" *Economic Inquiry* 18 (July 1980): 487–492.

Feldman, Roger D., and James W. Begun. "The Welfare Cost of Quality Changes Due to Professional Regulation." *The Journal of Industrial Economics* 34 (September 1985): 17–32.

Klein, Benjamin, and Keith B. Leffler. "The Role of Market Forces in Assuring Contractual Performance." *Journal of Political Economy* 89 (August 1981): 615–641.

Kwoka, John E., Jr. "Advertising and the Price and Quality of Optometric Services." *American Economic Review* 74 (March 1984): 211–216.

Lambin, J. J. *Advertising, Competition and Market Conduct in Oligopoly Over Time.* Amsterdam: North-Holland Publishing Company, 1976.

Maurizi, Alex R. "The Effect of Laws Against Price Advertising: The Case of Retail Gasoline." *Western Economic Journal* 10 (September 1972): 321–329.

Maurizi, Alex R., and Kelley, Thom. *Prices and Consumer Information.* Washington, D.C.: American Enterprise Institute for Public Policy Research, 1978.

Maurizi, Alex R., and Ruth L. Moore. "Price Advertising of Eyewear: An Analysis of Legal Restraints in California." A paper presented at the Western Economic Association annual meeting, June 1978.

Muris, Timothy J. and Fred S. McChesney. "Advertising and the Price and Quality of Legal Services: The Case for Legal Clinics." *American Bar Foundation Research Journal* (Winter 1979): 179–207.

Nelson, Phillip. "Information and Consumer Behavior." *Journal of Political Economy* 78 (March 1970): 311–329.

———. "Advertising as Information." *Journal of Political Economy* 82 (August 1974): 729–754.

Schmalensee, Richard. "A Model of Advertising and Product Quality." *Journal of Political Economy* 86 (June 1978): 485–503.

Schroeter, John R., and Steven R. Cox. "Estimating the Distributions of Search Costs and Reservation Prices: An Application to Routine Legal Service Markets." A paper given at Arizona State University, 1986.

Schroeter, John R., Scott L. Smith, and Steven R. Cox. "Advertising and Competition in Routine Legal Service Markets: An Empirical Investigation." *The Journal of Industrial Economics* 36 (September 1987): 49–60.

Schwartz, Alan, and Louis L. Wilde. "Competitive Equilibria in Markets for Heterogeneous Goods under Imperfect Information: A Theoretical Analysis with Policy Implications." *Bell Journal of Economics* 13 (Spring 1982): 181–193.

Stigler, George. "The Economics of Information." *Journal of Political Economy* 69 (June 1961): 213–225.

Vernon, John M., and Robert E. M. Nourse. "Profit Rates and Market Structure of Advertising Intensive Firms." *The Journal of Industrial Economics* 22 (September 1973): 1–20.

6

case

Dominant Firm Response to Competitive Challenge: Peripheral Equipment Manufacturers' Suits Against IBM

Gerald W. Brock

Introduction

In the mid-1970s, a number of IBM's competitors filed private antitrust suits against IBM seeking triple damages for IBM actions of the early 1970s in defending its peripheral products against competitive attack. The first case to trial was the suit by Telex Computer Products. It resulted in a stunning initial defeat for IBM with a damage award far greater than Telex's total stock market value. Telex's success inspired other plaintiffs to file similar suits. Although the reversal of the Telex victory in the appeals court dampened enthusiasm for suing IBM, several of the cases were pursued through the trial and appeals stage. In the end, IBM's actions were vindicated in all the cases.

The central question at issue in the related cases was the extent to which a dominant firm can take explicit actions to protect itself from the attacks of competitors without incurring the offense of "monopolization" or "attempted monopolization." Existing case law left considerable uncertainty over the distinction between the allowable actions of a dominant firm and those of any other firm, but could be interpreted to place strict limits on the ability of a dominant firm to defend itself. The plaintiffs alleged that practices designed to maintain monopoly power, even if these were ordinary practices when used by competitive firms, were illegal if used by a firm with monopoly power. IBM responded that its actions were evidence of competition rather than monopoly and that it should be allowed to react to its competitors.

IBM's victories in the peripherals cases were important for overall antitrust policy because they increased the freedom granted to dominant firms to protect their markets while narrowing the range of prac-

Gerald W. Brock served as an economic consultant to Transamerica, California Computer Products, and Memorex in their litigation against IBM. The views expressed here are those of the author alone and do not necessarily represent the views of the FCC (where he is currently Chief of the Common Carrier Bureau) or of any of the author's former employers or clients.

tices considered predatory. The cases indicated that a dominant firm is allowed actively to protect its market. It is not required to freeze its actions and allow competitors to profit from particular prices or practices that the firm adopted prior to the advent of competition.

IBM's Incentives

Computers of the 1960s were generally sold or leased as complete systems, combinations of central processing units (CPUs), tape drives, disk drives, programs, and other components necessary to supply the customer's needs. IBM was the dominant systems manufacturer, with about 70 percent of the market. The remaining 30 percent was divided among seven major systems competitors (Sperry Rand, Control Data, Burroughs, Honeywell, General Electric, NCR, and RCA, known collectively as "the seven dwarfs") and a number of smaller specialized or partial line suppliers. Although separate prices were charged for individual system components, the major competition was on a systems basis because of the impossibility of mixing components from different systems manufacturers. A Control Data disk drive did not provide direct competition to an IBM disk drive because the Control Data unit would not work with the IBM central processing unit and software, but there was competition between Control Data systems (including disk drives) and IBM systems. Because customers made substantial investments in software and personnel for a particular manufacturer's standards, switching among systems suppliers was a major event undertaken only with the expectation of long-term advantage. Each systems supplier had substantial brand loyalty and a reasonable expectation of supplying the additional needs of its established customers.

With systems competition, individual components need not be priced to meet competition directly from other components, but can instead be priced to maximize overall profit from the system. Even with no explicit effort to do so, the components are tied together. Each component has a well-defined demand curve, given a set of prices for the other components, but the firm only achieves profit maximization by considering the interaction effects as well as the individual demand curves.[1]

In the late 1960's several companies developed tape and disk drives very similar to those produced by IBM and designed them to work on the same interface and software as the IBM units. This allowed the companies to sell a tape drive or disk drive in direct competition with the corresponding IBM tape or disk drive rather than only as part of a complete competitive system. The new competitors were known as plug-compatible manufacturers (PCMs) because they claimed that their products allowed a customer simply to unplug the IBM drive, plug in the competitive drive, and continue all operations as if the IBM drive were still in place. The arrival of plug-compatible competition significantly increased the competitive constraints on IBM because it now had to respond to competition on each piece of equipment as well as competition for entire systems. The barriers to entry were substantially lower for plug-compatible manufacturers than for systems suppliers because the PCMs had only to produce a single component rather than all parts of a system. They could also sell the component with more direct emphasis on price advantages because switching from IBM to a PCM did not require the long-term confidence in the competitor that switching systems did.

The reduction in barriers to entry caused by the development of plug-compatible peripherals reduced IBM's market power in the peripherals market. Because the peripherals companies at that time could not produce a compatible CPU, IBM continued to possess market power in the systems market. However, it could no longer follow a profit-maximizing strategy based on the interaction of demand for peripherals and CPUs because at any peripherals price above the limit price (the price at which competitors are indifferent between entering and not entering), competitors would enter the peripherals market. With a limit price below the monopoly profit-maximizing price and above the marginal cost, IBM's new profit-maximizing strategy was to drop its peripherals price to the limit price. That price cut would expand output in the peripherals market and reduce profits in that market while excluding competitors.

The relationship between the limit price and IBM's marginal cost is of both economic and legal significance. If the limit price were below IBM's marginal cost, then IBM's straightforward profit-maximizing strategy would be to exit the peripherals market, allow the competitors to supply the entire peripherals market demand, and take all of its profits in the CPU market. In that case, an IBM strategy of pricing at or below the limit price would be clearly predatory (because it is below marginal cost) and would only be undertaken in the expectation of future profits from higher prices after the competitors were driven out. If the limit price is above marginal cost, then it is in IBM's interest to drop the price to the limit price even if it must be left there permanently to guard against future entry. The reduction in price in the peripherals market increases the quantity demanded in that market and therefore shifts the demand curve to the right in the complementary CPU market. The result would be greater profits in the CPU market, reduced profits in the peripherals market, and reduced profits in total. The quantity of peripherals would be higher and the price lower. The price of CPUs would be higher and the quantity could be either higher or lower.

An alternative strategy, if feasible, is to tie the products together either through explicit contractural arrangements or alternative arrangements that have the same effect. If, for example, IBM were able to condition the lease of its CPUs on the customers using only IBM storage equipment, then IBM would be able to continue a joint profit-maximizing strategy. Such explicit contractural limitations, known as "tying," have generally been suspect under the antitrust laws. However, more subtle arrangements can have a similar economic effect. If IBM was able to change the interface between the CPU and the storage devices to render the competitive machines useless, or was able to change the physical arrangements of the various pieces to increase the difficulty of attaching competitive devices, it could achieve at least a partial tie and limit the competitive impact of storage entrants. If such a strategy has some plausible technological purpose other than pure defense against competition, it is likely to survive antitrust scrutiny.

IBM's Defensive Actions

As PCM competition began to develop, IBM instituted a series of studies on alternative responses. Because those studies and the records of management meetings that evaluated them have been made public in the antitrust litigation, we have a fairly complete record of IBM's reasons for undertaking the actions that it did. IBM developed three types of responses to the new competition. All three responses were challenged by competitors as anticompetitive and violations of the antitrust laws.

The Price Cut Strategy

The most straightforward (but also expensive) response to increased competition is to cut prices. Standard economic analysis would predict that a reduction in barriers to entry would lead to a price cut so long as the price remains above marginal cost. The amount of the price cut is determined by the limit price in static analysis, but may be more complex if there are limitations on the speed at which competitors can enter. If entry takes time (as it generally does either because of the time required to market the competitive product effectively or because of capacity constraints that limit the amount of competitive products available), then the profit-maximizing strategy would be to hold price somewhat above the limit price and allow some entry (Gaskins, 1971).

IBM's first study of the new competition in June 1968 (soon after the initial competitive PCM deliveries) concluded that already planned new products would be adequate to meet competition and no specific response was required. That first analysis was soon shown to be overly optimistic about the strength of IBM's market position. IBM's inaction and the attractive target presented by IBM's prices spurred a number of competitors to offer replacement tape and disk drives. By the beginning of 1970, the competitors had captured six percent of IBM's installed base of tape drives and four percent of its base of disk drives for smaller computers. They were just beginning deliveries of replacements for IBM's high capacity 2314 disk drive for larger computers. The credibility of the PCM companies was improved at that time when the General Services Administration began encouraging government agencies to replace IBM products with competitive products.

In February of 1970, IBM designated the peripheral competition as a "key corporate strategic issue"—an IBM method of focusing attention on major problems that required intensive study and management attention. This review of the peripherals competition led IBM to the conclusion that no action was necessary to protect the large base of System/360-installed peripherals and that attention should be focused on protecting the peripherals for the announced but undelivered System/370 computers. However, the unexpectedly high growth rate of competitors for IBM's highly profitable base of high-capacity 2314 disk drives during 1970 induced a second study designed to calculate the lowest price at which competitors could produce a 2314 disk drive.

Because the 2314 system also required a specialized controller that rented for about three times the price of a single drive, the 2314 system was only used by customers who needed the capacity of multiple 2314 drives. IBM's late 1970 task force concluded that the break-even monthly rental for a 2314 competitor was $381 per month per drive. At that time, IBM rented a 2314 disk drive for $485 per month. In December 1970, IBM announced the new 2319B disk drive. The 2319B consisted of three 2314 disk drives placed in a single box and offered at a price of $1000 per month. The $1000 price for three drives effectively cut IBM's price per drive from $485 per month to $333 per month, below the computed competitive break-even point for competitors of $381 per month.

The 26-percent price cut on 2314 drives was not available to installed equipment. In order to get it, the customer had to order a 2319 system and have it physically exchanged for the installed 2314 system. This arrangement restricted IBM's revenue loss from the announcement. Customers who were not particularly aware of the marketplace and who were satisfied with their current equipment were likely to miss the announcement or fail to give it serious consideration. Customers who were planning a relatively quick upgrade to a new generation of equipment were not likely to accept the disruption of ordering and installing new equipment with the same performance as the old for a short-term reduction in rental. But customers who were actively considering switching to a PCM would find the announcement attractive because the $333 price per drive was below the lowest competitive price at that time. Repackaging the 2314 as the 2319 allowed IBM to offer a price cut to the most competitively vulnerable customers while maintaining higher prices for many of its customers because of transactions time and IBM's control of the 2319 delivery rates.

Although the 2319 price cut was below the competitive average cost computed by the IBM study group, there is no reason to believe that it was below IBM's opportunity cost. A new high-performance disk drive for large computers in the System/370 series had been announced in June 1970, six months before the 2319B announcement. IBM could reasonably expect to get the 2314 disk drives for repackaging into 2319s from its existing base that was being replaced by the competition or IBM's own new drives. Because the drives returned to IBM had little alternative value, the opportunity cost of the 2319 disk drive to IBM was low.

The Fixed Term Plan

Despite the IBM estimate that the 2319 price cuts would be adequate to eliminate the profitability of the competitors, competition continued to accelerate. The competitors apparently had a lower break-even point than the one computed by IBM's analysts, and they cut their prices in response to IBM. The differential between the IBM price and the competitors' prices for 2314 type disk drives was narrowed from about 25 percent to about 15 percent, but the competitors were still able to attract customers. The number of installed competitive 2314 type disk drives rose from 2600 in December 1970 (at the time of the 2319 announcement) to 4600 in April 1971 at which time new competitive drives were being ordered at the rate of 1000 per month.

IBM convened a new study group to find a solution to the competitive losses. The new study found competition a much greater threat than had the earlier studies and recommended drastic price cuts— about 50 percent on 2314 type disk drives and up to 80-percent cuts on particularly vulnerable tape drives. In early May 1971, IBM's top management rejected the recommendation and ordered the task force to develop a term lease plan as an alternative.

At that time, all IBM lease products were cancellable on thirty days' notice, while many competitive products were on one-year or longer lease plans. An IBM long-term lease plan would have been both a convenient excuse for cutting prices and a method of protecting the installed inventory. With appropriate penalty provisions in the lease, a customer would not consider a PCM replacement except at the time his lease was up. This would sharply reduce the demand available to the PCM companies during any given period of time, and in particular it would restrict their attacks on the new devices being delivered with the System 370. Because of the need for compatibility, the PCM companies could not deliver a replacement for a new product until after IBM had delivered the product, and if the products were under a two-year lease, the PCMs would be prevented from marketing a replacement until two years after deliveries began. An IBM analysis showed that a term lease plan that protected the market for twenty months would turn PCM profits on the initial placement into losses. The IBM analyst concluded that a term lease plan would be so effective that it would lead to inadequate funds for rivals' investments and would result in a "dying company."

At the recommendation of the task force, IBM's top management approved the Fixed Term Plan on May 25, 1971, and announced it two days later. The Fixed Term Plan (FTP) allowed one- or two-year leases on most tape, disk, and printer products. The customer received an 8-percent discount for a one-year lease and a 16-percent discount for a two-year lease. Penalties for early termination of a fixed lease were 2½ times the monthly rental charge for a one-year lease and 5 times monthly rental charge for a two-year lease. IBM expected the FTP to reduce its profits in 1971 and 1972 but to increase profits in later years by avoiding losses to competition.

The FTP was highly popular with IBM's customers. Within a month of the announcement, 40 percent of IBM's eligible customers had signed up for the plan, and 90 percent of the new System/370 tape and disk drives (not yet subject to competition) were being installed under the FTP.

The FTP and its associated price reduction was available only to peripheral equipment, not to central processing units. Two months after the FTP announcement, IBM announced increases in its prices for central processing units and related equipment. An IBM analyst concluded that no change in the expected number of IBM systems should be expected because the net effect of the reductions on peripheral equipment and increases on central processing units would produce little change in the price of an entire IBM system. As predicted by the economic analysis, the reduction in barriers to entry on one of two complementary goods led to a decrease in the price of that good and an increase in the price of the good for which barriers to entry remained the same.

The FTP marked the end of the PCM companies as highly successful growth companies. The combination of reduced prices and restricted market flexibility limited the ability of the competitors to lure customers away from IBM. The threat to the PCMs was widely recognized at the time of the announcement. The stock of the major PCM companies plummeted about 15 percent at the time of the announcement and continued to sink. In the two years following the FTP, Telex's aggregate stock market value dropped from $198 million to $48 million. The plan was interpreted in the trade press as a sign that IBM would take whatever action necessary to protect itself and that further action would be taken if the FTP was not enough. The financial and trade press evaluation of the significance of the plan reduced the ability of the companies to raise capital for growth. In the year following the FTP, the PCM order rate was 44 percent lower than for the year preceding the announcement.

Bundling of Previously Separate Units

IBM announced the high performance 3330 disk drive as a component of the new System/370 computers in June 1970 just as competitive deliveries of the older technology 2314 drives began. Each 3330 disk drive had over three times the storage capacity of a 2314. The initial 3330 announcement was an expected new product announcement for a new generation of computers. While the PCM companies were vigorously replacing the older 2314 disk drives, they were also developing a replacement for the 3330.

By mid-1972, competitors succeeded in developing replacement 3330 disk drives and in duplicating the interface specifications necessary to allow the competitive drives to work on an IBM system. In August of that year, IBM announced a series of new products and product modifications that were collectively referred to in internal IBM documents as the SMASH program. The disk drive portion of the SMASH program rearranged the packaging of the 3330 system. The original system consisted of a separate box of control electronics and boxes of two-drive 3330 disks. The August 1972 announcement introduced a modified controller with greater capacity, but that also required a modified 3330 disk drive with additional electronics for each set of eight drives. The upgraded controller was a typical minor technological enhancement. The modified distribution of control functions between the controller box and the first disk drive had no significant competitive effect because competitors generally replaced the controller and drives as a unit. It was the interface between the controller and the channel connecting it to the CPU that was crucial for competitors.

However, the August 1972 announcement also included an option to include the new 3330 controller as an integrated part of the central processing unit rather than as a separate box. The new controller that rented for $2025 per month as a separate box was priced at $700 per month if integrated into a small scale 370/135 and at $1150 per month if integrated into a larger 370/145. The massive price cuts for the integrated version provided a strong incentive for customers to order the integrated controller with their CPUs. The integrated controller not only substantially cut the price of a 3330 system but also changed the interface between CPU functions and peripheral functions. It consequently limited the ability of competitors to replace the 3330 disk drives.

The Cases and Basic Contentions

The three events discussed—cutting prices, instituting term leases, and modifying product interfaces—effectively protected IBM from the continued inroads of the competitors. The PCM companies' expectations and stock market prices plummeted. As the companies found themselves relegated to a niche in the computer industry and incurred difficulty in raising capital because of investor fears of further IBM actions, they began considering private treble damage antitrust suits against IBM.

Private antitrust suits alleging monopolization or attempted monopolization are difficult and complex to prosecute because they involve a comprehensive examination of the state of competition in the relevant markets. They require a huge commitment of management attention and financial resources, but they can be very lucrative because the successful plaintiff is awarded three times the adjudicated damages plus costs of the suit. If both the plaintiff and the defendant are rational, then only cases in which there is real uncertainty about the outcome or a difference in expectations will go to trial. Cases in which the outcome can reasonably be predicted will be settled prior to trial in order to save on litigation expenses. Companies contemplating the filing of a suit will carefully evaluate the probability of either a successful outcome in court or a favorable settlement agreement and compare the expected value of that outcome against the expected cost of litigation expenses and countersuits that may be inspired by the original suit.

A complicating factor in the evaluation of the benefits of filing suit in the peripherals case was the existence of a government monopolization suit against IBM. The government suit was filed in 1969, prior to the actions described above, and thus did not complain of IBM's peripherals actions. However, if the peripherals companies could reasonably expect the government to win its suit, then they would have a far easier time with private suits because the government would have done most of the work for them. Although the PCM companies could thus reduce their risk by waiting for the outcome of the government suit, the slow pace of preparation in that case meant that waiting for its outcome could foreclose the opportunity to pursue their grievances against IBM.[2]

The viability of the private antitrust suits depended upon the interpretation that could be put on IBM's actions. Two fundamentally different interpretations were possible. The first interpretation (favored by IBM) was that IBM's actions were a proper competitive response to an increasingly competitive industry. Under this interpretation, the entry of the PCMs was a sign of reduced barriers to entry, and IBM's actions were necessary competitive actions that benefited consumers. The alternative interpretation (favored by the PCMs) was that IBM's actions were predatory in intent and evidence of IBM's monopoly power and of its abuse of that monopoly power. Under this interpretation, IBM's actions were expensive efforts to eliminate its competitors and discourage future entry with the expectation of making future profits from renewed monopoly control of the peripherals products. The empirical difference between the two versions consisted of the long-term effects: prices should be expected to remain low in the IBM version, while in the competitors' version prices should be expected to rise again once competition was eliminated.

Legal Standards

The cases charged IBM with the offenses of "monopolization" and "attempted monopolization" in violation of Section 2 of the Sherman Act. It was well established at the time that the offense of monopolization required some action to acquire or maintain monopoly power, but actions that were legal for a firm without monopoly power could constitute monopolization for a firm with monopoly power. Judge Hand's decision in *Alcoa* found that Alcoa had "monopolized" when its only exclusionary practice was "to embrace each new opportunity as it opened, and to face every newcomer with new capacity already geared into a great organization, having the advantage of experience, trade connections and the elite of personnel. . . ."[3] Judge Wyzanski's decision in *United Shoe Machinery* found the company guilty of monopolization, even though he found no evidence of predatory practices, because United was able "to exercise effective control of the market by business policies that are not the inevitable consequences of its capacities or its natural advantages."[4] In the *Grinnell* case, the Supreme Court specified a two-part test for the offense of monopoly: "(1) the possession of monopoly power in the relevant market and

(2) the willful acquisition or maintenance of that power as distinguished from growth or development as a consequence of a superior product, business acumen, or historic accident."[5]

The offense of "attempted monopolization" as interpreted at that time did not require a showing of monopoly power but placed a greater burden of proof that the challenged acts were designed to eliminate competition. Attempted monopolization requires "a specific intent to destroy competition or build monopoly" along with specific predatory acts and a "dangerous probability of success."[6] For either monopolization or attempted monopolization, a private plaintiff must also prove that it was damaged by the specific acts found to be illegal.

The economic meaning of the two tests is that there is a trade-off between the allowable degree of monopoly power and the severity of acts undertaken to establish or maintain that monopoly power. A firm with a great deal of monopoly power is severely constrained in its ability to respond to competition without "monopolizing." A firm with a substantial market presence, but one that does not meet the legal requirements for possession of monopoly power, has a greater range of freedom in responding to competition; but if too aggressive it may incur the offense of an "attempt to monopolize." A firm in a highly competitive market is free of the constraints of Section 2 because it neither has monopoly power nor a significant probability of success in achieving market power regardless of its acts.

The Telex Suit

Telex Computer Products enjoyed spectacular initial success in the plug-compatible business. As a leader in the competition with IBM, its revenues rose from under $1 million in fiscal 1967 to over $56 million in fiscal 1971. It remained a small company compared to IBM and other industrial giants, but its rapid growth and profitability made it a favorite in financial circles. When Telex's prospects and stock market price plummeted in 1971 after IBM's defensive actions, Telex filed an antitrust suit charging IBM with monopolizing and attempting to monopolize the market for peripheral equipment plug compatible with IBM peripheral equipment.

Telex focused narrowly on plug-compatible products and largely ignored the question of IBM's monopoly power in the larger markets for all peripheral products or for all data processing equipment. Telex's case depended on two critical factors: 1) the ability to define the market very narrowly and to infer market power from a high market share in that market, and 2) an interpretation of the existing case law that strictly limited the freedom of a firm with monopoly power to respond to competition.

By defining the market narrowly, Telex found that IBM had approximately 90 percent of the relevant market and argued that such a market share was in itself evidence of monopoly power. Telex made no attempt to show that IBM's competitive products were priced below any measure of cost, but argued that IBM's actions were predatory because they were taken after an explicit evaluation of the competitive capabilities and were designed to reduce or eliminate the competition.

IBM's response included the following: 1) Telex's plug-compatible peripherals market was not a "relevant market" because it ignored the competitive effects of other peripheral equipment; 2) market power cannot be inferred from market share alone but must include an analysis of barriers to entry; 3) the relevant market should be broadly defined as all "electronic data processing," a market that showed rapid growth and extensive entry with an increasing number of competitors and an IBM market share steadily declining from 64 percent in 1952 to 35 percent in 1970; and 4) IBM responses to the PCM competition were not predatory in nature but were ordinary business actions brought about by the increased competitiveness of the industry.

IBM's economic analysis of the case was contained in an affidavit by their economics expert. He contended that because of demand and supply substitutability the market ought to be defined broadly and that "no responsible person with any training in economics would attempt to define such arbitrarily separate markets as Telex has."[7] After reviewing various measures of IBM's market share, he concluded:

> The number of competitors in the industry and their strength is growing. The industry itself is growing dramatically in absolute size. Customers are sophisticated and becoming more so. Finally IBM's share of the market, however that market is reasonably defined, is decreasing rapidly. All this suggests a competitive industry which grows more competitive with each passing day."[8]

In addition to its defense against Telex's antitrust charges, IBM responded to the Telex suit with a countersuit charging that Telex had stolen IBM trade secrets, violated IBM patents, and infringed IBM's copyrighted manuals. Telex and other PCM companies based their product development in part upon the efforts of former senior IBM peripherals engineers who were attracted to the peripherals companies with promises of stock and bonuses if they could develop copies of IBM products on which they had worked under tight time schedules. IBM alleged that such personnel improperly transferred IBM trade secrets to Telex.

After a brief trial (by antitrust standards—29 days) Judge

Sherman Christensen in September 1973 found both parties guilty of the respective charges. Judge Christensen accepted Telex's narrow definition of the market and inferred market power from IBM's 90-percent share. He then found the acts to be predatory even though prices remained above IBM's cost because they were designed to reduce the viability of IBM's competitors. With regard to the Fixed Term Plan, the court found:

> Defendant's officers at the trial expressed the view that FTP was simply to render the company "more competitive" and to obtain more business by meeting the competitive efforts on a basis similar to that of plug-compatible suppliers. It is the court's view that such justification, which could be convincing under different circumstances, is overpowered by IBM's monopoly position in the particular markets involved and the rather clear indication that its action was directed not at competition in an appropriate competitive sense but at competitors and their viability as such.[9]

Christensen awarded Telex actual damages of $118 million which by law were then tripled to determine a damage award of $353 million plus costs and attorney's fees. The decision was a stunning blow to IBM. Not only was it the largest antitrust damage award ever granted as of that date, but it induced numerous other private suits and renewed activity in the government suit. The damages awarded to Telex were the equivalent of $25 per share of Telex stock to a company whose stock was then selling for around $3 per share. IBM's only consolation was that Christensen also found Telex guilty of violating IBM's trade secrets and ordered a judgment against Telex of $22 million. After further legal proceedings, the numbers were adjusted somewhat to develop a net payment obligation from IBM to Telex of $260 million.

Following Telex's victory, other peripherals companies filed similar suits, and the government amended its suit to include the Telex claims that were for actions taken after the original government suit was filed. However, in January 1975 on appeal, the Court of Appeals for the Tenth Circuit reversed the Telex decision. With regard to market definition, the court ruled that the plug-compatible peripherals market was too narrow because of evidence of both supply and demand substitutability with other products. The court emphasized trial testimony that interfaces for other types of computer systems could be developed at reasonable cost and that Telex had even offered to supply peripherals to non-IBM manufacturers and absorb the cost of producing the required interfaces. The court also noted that indirect demand substitutability existed between peripherals compatible with IBM systems and those not compatible because of the competition of alternative systems including peripherals. Because Telex had provided no backup evidence regarding IBM's share of the "all peripherals" market, the court was left with only the IBM evidence on the very broad "electronic data processing market." That evidence indicated a declining IBM market share reaching 35 percent in 1970 and led the court to conclude that IBM did not have market power.

The court's conclusion that IBM did not have market power in the "relevant market" was sufficient in itself to overturn the district court verdict because the district court had only found IBM's actions predatory in the context of possession of market power. However, the Court of Appeals also analyzed the acts under the assumption that IBM did have market power and concluded that the acts should be exonerated. The trial court had concluded that monopolization occurs when a company with monopoly power "willfully acquired or maintained" that power. Actions that maintained monopoly power were illegal unless they fell under one of three exceptions: a superior product, business acumen, or historic accident. The Court of Appeals ruled that the emphasis on involuntary actions unnecessarily constrained the actions of a monopolist and limited real competition. It stated:

> The "predatory" conclusion was expressed after the trial court had given extended consideration to the creation of "task forces" by IBM, and the direction of their attention and study to Telex especially and other corporations in the business. . . .The record demonstrates that these acts of IBM are again part of the competitive scene in this volatile business inhabited by aggressive, skillful businessmen seeking to market a product cheaper and better than that of their competitors. To do this, the record shows it was customary for them to study their competitors, all their capabilities, and what may be expected of them when a new product appears on the market. It is IBM's participation in this marketing that the trial court termed "predatory," but the record shows this was no more than engaging in the type of competition prevalent throughout the industry.[10]

Although the Tenth Circuit reversed Judge Christensen's award of antitrust damages from IBM to Telex, it let stand his award of trade secret damages from Telex to IBM. What had been a minor reduction in a huge Telex damage award now threatened to bankrupt the company. Telex appealed to the Supreme Court, but before a decision on a hearing was announced both companies agreed to drop all litigation against each other.

Areeda and Turner on Predatory Pricing

During the same year as the Telex reversal, Professors Areeda and Turner published an analysis of predatory pricing that was widely cited in later cases. Areeda and Turner noted the economic literature suggesting that predatory pricing is unlikely in theory and rare in practice (McGee 1958, Telser 1966, Koller 1971). They felt that the existing legal standards encouraged frivolous suits because of the restrictive interpretation of the actions allowed a dominant firm and believed that restrictive standards impeded beneficial competition. They stated:

> That predatory pricing seems highly unlikely does not necessarily mean that there should be no antitrust rules against it. But it does suggest that extreme care be taken in formulating such rules, lest the threat of litigation, particularly by private parties, materially deter legitimate, competitive pricing (Areeda and Turner 1975, 699).

Areeda and Turner noted that predation consists of sacrificing current revenues in the expectation of greater future gains after the rivals are driven out of business. They asserted that predation only makes sense if the predator has both greater financial power than his rivals and also a "very substantial prospect that the losses he incurs in the predatory campaign will be exceeded by the profits to be earned after his rivals have been destroyed" (Areeda and Turner 1975, 698). Consequently, predation is only profitable when barriers to entry are so strong that new firms cannot enter once the successful predator attempts to recoup its losses through higher prices. Areeda and Turner proposed that predatory pricing be determined only by the relationship between short-run average variable cost and price: if price is below short-run average variable cost it should be presumed predatory and if above should be presumed not to be predatory. They suggested that all other limitations on the pricing freedom of dominant firms that had been proposed by courts or the economic literature (such as limit pricing to block entry, differential returns on products subject to different degrees of competition, or excessive investment in capacity) should be considered irrelevant to the analysis of predatory pricing for antitrust purposes.

The Areeda-Turner standard clearly exonerated IBM. Although it was only a law review article, the prestige of the authors meant that their analysis might well influence future court decisions. The Appeals Court's reversal of the Telex victory, combined with a proposed stringent burden of proof for future predatory pricing cases, severely reduced the prospects for the remaining PCM plaintiffs. Despite the dashed hopes of easy victories based on Telex's initial success, three other peripherals companies—Memorex, California Computer Products, and Transamerica Computer, known collectively as the West Coast plaintiffs—decided to press forward with their allegations that they had been illegally damaged by IBM's efforts to protect its market position.

The West Coast Cases

The West Coast cases presented similar but not identical issues. They all challenged IBM's actions in defending its peripheral market against PCM competitors, but each company had a somewhat different legal strategy and economic theory of case. The cases were combined for initial pretrial work and then separated for trial. All three cases were tried before juries, a common but controversial practice in complex antitrust litigation. Companies that believe they have been damaged by far larger competitors frequently believe that they will receive a more sympathetic hearing before a jury than a judge. Although no legal requirements are changed by the presence of a jury, the use of jury trials in antitrust is a severe constraint on the level of sophistication and technical detail that can be used in the trial.

California Computer Products (CalComp) was the first of the West Coast cases to reach trial, beginning at the end of 1976. The *CalComp* trial repeated basic elements of the *Telex* trial with added theatrics designed to impress the jury and with close attention by both sides to the insights gained from the Telex experience. Once the jury was chosen, IBM hired a complete "shadow jury" of people who IBM's consultants felt matched the real jury as closely as possible. The shadow jury went in and out of the courtroom with the real jury and reported to IBM lawyers on its perception of each part of the case at the end of each trial day.

CalComp used the basic Telex theory (IBM's dominant position in the plug compatible market; acts designed to maintain that position constitute illegal monopolization), but developed the market and acts in a broader framework in order to distinguish the *CalComp* case from the market definition problem noted by the *Telex* Appeals Court. CalComp devoted a great deal of effort to establishing a computer systems market and proving IBM's market share in that market, with submarkets of disk drives and of disk drives compatible with IBM CPUs. By emphasizing IBM's market power in the broader market, CalComp was able to avoid reliance on the plug compatible market rejected by the Tenth Circuit and still place IBM in the context of a firm with monopoly power taking actions to defend its monopoly position.

The Telex Appeals Court's conclusion that IBM had only a 35-percent market share was based on a census of the broadly defined Electronic Data Processing Industry conducted by IBM under court authority. The census included detailed questionnaires sent to 2700 companies that IBM claimed were part of the industry. The 2700 companies ranged from IBM's major systems competitors to companies in related industries (such as AT&T and aerospace companies) to small software companies. The census produced a massive amount of information on the industry, including year-by-year revenue figures on each individual product. IBM's 35-percent market share was derived essentially by dividing IBM's total revenue according to the census by the total "electronic data processing" revenue of all companies included in the census. Telex had considered the census irrelevant to its case and had made no effort to analyze it or introduce its own version of the census evidence of IBM's market share.

As part of its effort to establish IBM's market share in the computer systems market, CalComp hired an economic consultant to supervise a detailed analysis of the census data and to determine IBM's market share from that data. Market definition consists of an analysis of supply substitutability and of demand substitutability. As part of the analysis of supply substitutability, the census data were used to determine the pattern of diversification in the industry. If companies in one segment of the industry frequently entered another segment, that was taken as evidence supporting supply substitutability. Combining the evidence of supply substitutability with other analyses of demand substitutability, a variety of reasonable market definitions were created. The detailed data from the census allowed the easy computation of market shares for any set of products that were considered a potential relevant market.

At trial, CalComp introduced two different markets based on the census. The narrower (and preferred) market definition consisted of all general-purpose CPUs and general-purpose peripherals. That set of products produced an IBM market share that averaged 78.4 percent in the 1961 to 1965 period and declined to 70.7 percent in the 1966 to 1970 period. The broader market was introduced to provide evidence of IBM's market share if the court found the preferred definition too narrow. The broader market included all products in the narrow market plus a large number of more specialized products that were frequently used in computer systems but had limited substitutability with the products in the narrow market. IBM's share of the wider market was slightly lower and falling faster; it fell from an average of 75 percent during the years 1961 to 1965 to an average of 65.6 percent from 1966 to 1970. CalComp also introduced market share evidence from industry experts that yielded similar but not identical market shares and used somewhat different market definitions.

Aside from challenges to the sufficiency of CalComp's proof of relevant market, damages, and other aspects of its case, IBM's defense rested primarily on the proposition that the actions complained of by CalComp were indications of competition rather than of monopoly. On the day that CalComp rested its direct case, IBM made a motion to dismiss the case, backed up by a one-hundred page printed brief including a vast number of citations to the record and including evidence even from that day's testimony. The IBM brief presented a detailed argument that the evidence presented by CalComp, even if accepted as true, did not add up to a violation of the law. IBM portrayed its own actions as necessary and legitimate responses to competition and dismissed CalComp's arguments as efforts to suppress competition: "The fundamental defect in CalComp's theory and proof. . .is its failure to distinguish between competition on the merits and predatory conduct" (IBM Memorandum in support of its motion for a directed verdict, p. 12).

After brief consideration of the opposing arguments, Judge McNichol granted IBM's motion for a directed verdict. The directed verdict was a striking loss for CalComp because it meant that even accepting CalComp's view of the facts, the judge did not find an antitrust violation and therefore there was no reason for IBM to present its defense or to submit the case to the jury. CalComp appealed the directed verdict.

In June 1979, the Ninth Circuit Court of Appeals upheld the IBM victory and established an important precedent granting new freedom to dominant firms. The Ninth Circuit noted that proof of monopolization required both the possession of monopoly power and the willful acquisition or maintenance of that power. It ruled that although there were problems with CalComp's proof of IBM's possession of monopoly power, the evidence was not so poor as to justify a directed verdict. Consequently, the court analyzed the legality of IBM's acts on the assumption that they were the acts of a monopolist. Even using this standard, the court exonerated IBM's actions. The court cited the Areeda-Turner analysis approvingly and noted that

> Price reductions up to the point of marginal cost are consistent with competition on the merits, since in this case only less efficient firms will be disadvantaged, while a firm pricing below marginal cost by definition incurs losses, so that competition on the basis of efficiency in this situation is frustrated.[11]

The court noted that departures from the marginal cost standard might be necessary and suggested that limit pricing could in some contexts be an impermissible practice. However, it concluded that because CalComp had made no showing that IBM's prices were below marginal or average variable cost, IBM's actions should not be condemned.

The court accepted IBM's position that its actions were a sign of competition.

> IBM's price cuts were a part of the very competitive process the Sherman Act was designed to promote. To accept CalComp's position would be to hold that IBM could not compete if competition would result in injury to its competitors, an ill-advised reversal of the Supreme Court's pronouncement that the Sherman Act is meant to protect the competitive process, not competitors.[12]

With regard to CalComp's claim that IBM's product changes were designed to prevent competition, the Court concluded that because the product changes had a technological rationale, they were acceptable even if they disadvantaged CalComp.

> IBM, assuming it was a monopolist, had the right to redesign its products to make them more attractive to buyers—whether by reason of lower manufacturing cost and price or improved performance. It was under no duty to help CalComp or other peripheral equipment manufacturers survive or expand. IBM need not have provided its rivals with disk products to examine and copy. . .nor have constricted its product development so as to facilitate sales of rival products."[13]

The court's ruling on technological changes gave a dominant firm extensive freedom to modify its products in ways that disadvantage competitors so long as there is some plausible technological rationale for the changes. The product changes at issue were improvements over the existing products. Although the evidence indicated that protecting the market from competitors was a factor in the design of the products, the court ruled the changes were legal because they provided some potential benefit to consumers. In a later case (*Transamerica*) the court later clarified the technological rationale when it found one minor product change unjustified because it actually degraded the product in order to protect it from competition. IBM redesigned the channel that attached peripherals to the smallest System/370 computers in order to slow the data transfer speed to below that used by competitive peripherals. The court held that because the change degraded the product with no purpose except to exclude competitors, it was illegal. However, no damages were awarded because Transamerica failed to quantify its injury from the design change in question.[14] The cases placed the burden of proof on the plaintiff to show that the only purpose of the change was to harm competitors and allowed any showing of technical benefit as a defense for the dominant firm.

Between the time of the *CalComp* trial and the *CalComp* appeals decision, the *Memorex* and the *Transamerica* cases went through separate trials. IBM's request for a directed verdict in the *Memorex* case was denied, and the case was submitted to the jury at the end of the trial. After the jury deadlocked on a 10 to 2 vote in favor of Memorex, the judge directed the entry of a verdict in favor of IBM. Similarly, in the *Transamerica* case the jury deadlocked, and the judge then entered a verdict in favor of IBM.

Transamerica's appeal to the Ninth Circuit, decided in February 1983, provided further clarification of the standards for predatory conduct while upholding IBM's victory. Transamerica had developed its theory of IBM's predatation in part around the "dead body" theory: the fact of PCM companies being forced out of business by IBM's actions is in itself evidence of predatory conduct. The Ninth Circuit accepted Transamerica's version of the facts and noted, ". . .there is no doubt that IBM's strategy worked. Transamerica, along with fifteen out of seventeen companies involved with plug-compatible peripherals, left the market after suffering huge losses."[15] The court declined to treat "dead bodies" as evidence of predatory conduct and instead focused on the relationship between price and various forms of cost. The trial court had been presented with IBM's evidence that the prices in question were above average total cost and with Transamerica's evidence (after accounting adjustments to the IBM data) that the prices were below average total cost but not necessarily below average variable cost. The trial court had accepted IBM's version of the cost numbers and had ruled as a matter of law that prices above average total cost were per se legal. After an extensive discussion of the Areeda-Turner and related tests for predatory pricing, the Ninth Circuit in *Transamerica* backed off from the almost per se rules in *CalComp* and focused on the burden of proof rather than absolute rules. The court ruled:

> [C]ost categories should be used to allocate the burden of proof on the issue of predation. By this approach, we give due weight to the economic considerations which suggest that prices are presumptively lawful if they exceed marginal or average variable cost and presumptively predatory if they do not. And, of course, this approach does not preclude a litigant from introducing evidence sufficient to overcome these presumptions. . . .
>
> The test for determining the antitrust legality of prices that exceed average total cost. . .should be consistent with the economic analysis of Areeda and Turner. Their analysis indicates that prices above average total cost will rarely be predatory. . . . We therefore hold that if the challenged prices exceed average

total cost, the plaintiff must prove by clear and convincing evidence—i.e., that it is highly probably true—that the defendant's pricing policy was predatory.[16]

After reviewing the evidence in the light of its legal conclusions on the requirements for predatory pricing, the Appeals Court concluded that Transamerica had presented insufficient proof of predatory pricing to overcome the presumption that IBM's prices were legal because they were above average total cost. The court took particular note of the absence of evidence that IBM raised its prices once competitors were driven from the market. The court retained the suggestion it first made in the *CalComp* appeal that "limit pricing" might be illegal, but it defined limit pricing more stringently than is common in economics. The court asserted that limit pricing only occurs when entry barriers are very high and when the dominant firm cuts prices below that of competitors in order to prevent entry. Because the court found that entry barriers into the peripherals business were low and that IBM did not undercut the PCM prices, it dismissed Transamerica's effort to prove that IBM had engaged in limit pricing.[17]

Conclusion

IBM's victories in the peripherals litigation were an important part of a trend toward far greater freedom for dominant firm actions and far stricter standards of proof for predatory pricing. In an analysis of 73 predatory pricing cases decided before 1971, Koller (1971) found that the plaintiffs won 45, or 62 percent. Ten years later, Hurwitz, Kovacic, and Lande (1982) analyzed 38 predatory pricing cases decided after the 1975 Areeda-Turner article and found only 4 plaintiffs' victories, a decline in the success rate from 62 percent to 11 percent. IBM's 1970 to 1972 peripheral protective actions were of doubtful legality by the standards of that time, but by the end of the litigation eleven years later the legal standard had shifted clearly to condone IBM's responses.

The key to the shift was the widespread court acceptance of the economic attitude of Areeda and Turner, even if rejecting their specific tests for predation. Areeda and Turner's assertions that "predatory pricing seems highly unlikely" and strict predatory pricing rules may "materially deter legitimate, competitive pricing" were far from the old standards that monopoly power must be maintained virtually involuntarily in order to be legitimate. Although the Areeda-Turner approach was a substantial departure from then existing predatory pricing law, it was backed up by extensive economic literature and pressed in court by prestigious economists testifying that a variety of defendants' actions

(IBM and others) were the essence of competition rather than inappropriate behavior. Consequently, many judges were convinced that the old standards should be modified to allow dominant firms an opportunity to respond to their competitors. The new standards indicated an increased emphasis on the competitive process and an abandonment of the idea of protecting small firms from the competitive advantages of larger ones, which appeared to be implicit in some of the older case law.[16]

Under the new predatory pricing standards developed in the IBM cases, there is a presumption that practically any behavior has a legitimate competitive purpose. The plaintiff alleging predatory pricing must overcome that presumption by providing credible evidence that the dominant firm has the ability and desire to reap greater profits in the future after driving the competitor out of business. Such proof is difficult, but is justified by the assumed rarity of true predatory pricing and the assumed frequency with which competitors complain of hard competition.

Notes

1. This is a standard result of microeconomic theory. For a derivation see Allen (1960, 359–362).
2. The government case was filed at the end of the Johnson administration, was in preparation throughout the Nixon administration, began trial in the Ford administration, continued trial throughout the Carter administration, and was abandoned in the Reagan administration, thirteen years after it began. Six months after the end of the trial, but before the initial court decision was issued, the government dismissed the case. Consequently, the peripheral companies would not have gained support for their cases by waiting for the completion of the government case, but they would have saved considerable legal expenses if they had judged the validity of their cases by the final outcome of the government case.
3. *United States* v. *Aluminum Co. of America,* 148 F.2d 416 at 431 (1945).
4. *United States* v. *United Shoe Machinery Corp.,* 110 F. Supp. 295 at 345 (1953), *aff'd per curiam,* 347 U.S. 521 (1954).
5. *United States* v. *Grinnell Corp.,* 384 U.S. 563 at 570–571 (1966).
6. *Times-Picayune Publishing Co.* v. *United States,* 345 U.S. 594, 626.
7. Fisher (1972, paragraph 132).
8. Fisher (1972, paragraph 137).
9. *Telex* v. *IBM,* 367 F. Supp. 258 at 296 (1973).
10. *Telex* v. *IBM,* 510 F.2d 894 at 928 (1975).
11. *California Computer Products* v. *International Business Machines Corporation,* 613 F.2d 727 at 743 (1979).
12. Ibid., at 742.
13. Ibid., at 744.

14. *Transamerica Computer Co., Inc.* v. *IBM Corp.* 698 F.2d 1377 at 1383 (1983).
15. Ibid., 1381.
16. Ibid., at 1388.
17. Ibid., at 1389.
18. The Areeda-Turner analysis and the court cases discussing it inspired an extensive academic literature on the meaning of predatory pricing in both law and economics. A number of important contributions to that literature were first presented at a Federal Trade Commission conference in the summer of 1980. Although many of the papers were later published in revised form, the 700-page conference volume (Salop, 1981) provides a good introduction to the literature.

References

Allen, R. G. D. *Mathematical Economics.* London: Macmillan, 1960.

Areeda, Phillip, and Donald Turner. "Predatory Pricing and Related Practices under Section 2 of the Sherman Act." *Harvard Law Review* 88 (February 1975): 697–733.

Fisher, Franklin. Affidavit of Franklin M. Fisher in *The Telex Corporation* v. *International Business Machines Corporation.* (1972).

Gaskins, Darius. "Dynamic Limit Pricing: Optimal Pricing under Threat of Entry." *Journal of Economic Theory* 3 (September 1971).

Hurwitz, James, William Kovacic, and Robert Lande. "Judicial Analysis of Predation: The Emerging Trends." *Vanderbilt Law Review* 34 (January 1982).

Koller, Roland. "The Myth of Predatory Pricing—An Empirical Study." *Antitrust Law & Economic Review* 4 (Summer 1971).

McGee, John. "Predatory Price Cutting: The Standard Oil (N.J.) Case." *Journal of Law and Economics* 1 (October 1958): 137–169.

Salop, Steven, ed. *Strategy, Predation, and Antitrust Analysis.* Federal Trade Commission, Bureau of Economics and Bureau of Competition, 1981.

Telser, Lester. "Cutthroat Competition and the Long Purse." *Journal of Law and Economics* 9 (October 1966): 259–277.

Practices That Facilitate Cooperation: The *Ethyl* Case

George A. Hay

Introduction

Section 1 of the Sherman Act makes "every contract, combination. . .or conspiracy in restraint of trade" illegal. The most obvious application of Section 1 is to price-fixing agreements, and through its prohibition of price-fixing agreements Section 1 seeks to protect consumers against supra-cometitive prices. However, the economic theory of oligopoly teaches us that there are circumstances in which a group of firms can achieve supra-competitive prices without the need for any formal agreement. In such cases, what is the antitrust response?

This case study is about this "oligopoly problem" and the efforts of the antitrust authorities to deal with it. It involves an antitrust case brought by the Federal Trade Commission (FTC) against the four manufacturers of lead-based antiknock gasoline additives, who were alleged to have succeeded in substantially eliminating price competition among themselves without entering into any formal price fixing agreement.

Lead-based antiknock compounds have been used in the refining of gasoline since the 1920s. The compounds are added to gasoline to prevent engine "knock", the premature detonation of gasoline in the engine's cylinders. Resistance to knock is measured by octane ratings, and for a gasoline refiner the use of lead-based compounds is the most economical way to raise the octane rating of gasoline for cars that take leaded gas. From the 1920s until 1948, the Ethyl Corporation was the sole domestic producer of lead-based antiknock compounds. Demand for the compounds increased with the increase in gasoline use, however, and in 1948 Du Pont entered the industry and captured a substantial market share. In 1961, PPG Industries began to manufacture and sell the compounds, followed by the Nalco Chemical Company in 1964. From 1974 to 1979 (the relevant period for the case), these were the

---

George A. Hay consulted with and testified on behalf of the FTC in the *Ethyl* Case.

only four domestic producers of lead antiknock compounds. Du Pont had 38.4 percent of the market, Ethyl 33.5 percent, PPG 16.2 percent, and Nalco 11.8 percent. There were no significant imports into the United States.

Beginning in 1973, the federal government initiated steps that would lead to a dramatic decrease in the demand for lead-based antiknock compounds. At that time, the Environmental Protection Agency (EPA) required that all automobiles manufactured in the United States beginning in 1975 be equipped with catalytic converters. Since the lead in antiknock compounds fouls such converters, almost all new cars sold in the United States since 1975 have required unleaded gasoline. At the same time, in order to reduce the amount of lead in the atmosphere, the EPA imposed severe limitations on the amount of lead that could be used in "leaded" gasoline. As a result of these two measures, the use of lead antiknock compounds declined from more than one billion pounds in 1974 to approximately 400 million pounds in 1980.

The drop in demand in an industry with substantial sunk costs resulted in substantial excess capacity, a situation that economists would normally expect to lead to intensified price competition as companies vied against one another for the available business. Nevertheless, the FTC claimed that during the 1974 to 1979 period the companies substantially eliminated price competition among themselves and charged uniform supracompetitive prices. The FTC did not claim that this was the result of an agreement among the firms. Rather the absence of effective price competition could be traced to several practices that some or all of the firms employed, within the framework of a highly oligopolistic market structure.

The specific practices identified by the FTC were: quoting prices on a uniform delivered price basis, announcing price changes to customers and to the press well in advance of the effective date, and including in contracts with individual customers a clause requiring the seller to extend to that customer any discount offered to any other customer. The FTC asserted that these practices "facilitated" the elimination of horizontal competition and ought to be prohibited.

Antitrust and Oligopoly: The Policy Dilemma

A traditional horizontal price-fixing agreement is an effort by a group of firms explicitly to coordinate their activities so as to eliminate competition among themselves and thereby achieve noncompetitive prices and supranormal profits.[1] These kinds of price-fixing agreements have long been regarded as unlawful, and there is widespread agreement that this is the appropriate policy.[2]

The classic economic theories of oligopoly, on the other hand, do not focus on explicit efforts to coordinate conduct but instead on the profit-maximizing behavior of individual firms in an interdependent environment. The typical oligopoly model posits a number of firms, each deciding what level of a homogeneous output to produce. Since the market price depends on the sum of all firms' output, each firm must make certain assumptions about the combined output of its competitors and how that output will change in response to its own decision. Based on these assumptions, the firm chooses its own profit-maximizing course of action. The collective result of all such individual decisions can be a price above the competitive level.[3]

The emphasis of oligopoly theory on individual profit maximization, as opposed to explicit coordination, is highly significant for antitrust policy. Since the applicability of the Sherman Act seems to turn on the existence of an agreement, and since by assumption there is no explicit agreement in a classic oligopoly situation, it would appear possible that firms can enjoy the supracompetitive prices and profits that are associated with price fixing without violating the Sherman Act. If so, there is a potentially troublesome gap in the coverage of the antitrust laws.

One could argue that oligopolistic behavior leading to supracompetitive prices could be brought within the scope of the Sherman Act by characterizing the end result of oligopolistic interdependence as "tacit" or "implicit" agreement and applying the antitrust laws not merely to explicit agreements but to tacit or implicit agreements as well. It is not unusual for the law to recognize tacit or implicit agreements outside the antitrust context, and there is ample precedent in the economics literature for referring to situations of oligopolistic interdependence in this way (Blair and Kaserman 1985, 200). Unfortunately, the semantic simplicity of such a solution masks a very serious underlying difficulty.

The problem can be illustrated with a simple example. Consider two essentially identical gas stations selling private brand gasoline directly across the road from one another on a long isolated highway with no rivals for miles around. Prior to today, both stations have been charging $1 a gallon, which we assume to be the competitive price. Since the two stations are regarded by consumers as offering virtually identical products, we assume that at the $1 price each enjoyed 50 percent of the total gasoline sales.

One station (station A) is contemplating raising the price to $1.25, which its resident economist has computed to be the profit-maximizing monopoly price: the price that would maximize total profits if both stations were to charge the identical price. The scheme will be profitable for A only if station B matches the $1.25 price, since if A raises the price and B does not follow, all of A's customers will switch to B.

At first glance, it appears risky for A to go ahead with the price increase without prior assurance (i.e., agreement) that B will follow, since a possible strategy for B is not to match A's price increase and to capture all the business. However, if A raises the price to $1.25, it will learn very quickly whether B has followed since the same signs that communicate B's price to potential customers can be seen by A.[4] If B has not followed the increase, A can promptly restore its $1 price.[5]

Station A's ability to detect and respond quickly to B's failure to match A's price affects B's optimal strategy. By keeping the price at $1, B enjoys a brief period where it captures nearly 100 percent of the business. However, once A has retracted its increase, the firms go back to sharing the market at $1. If instead B were to match A's increase (which it can do easily by observing A's prices directly), it forgoes the brief period of extra business, in return for a possible long-term equilibrium in which it shares the market with A at $1.25.[6] Hence, B has an incentive to go along with an increase by A, and A, knowing that B's best strategy is to follow, can initiate the price increase with minimal risk.[7]

If the scene unfolds as described, the firms jointly achieve monopoly profits without the need for any formal agreement of the kind usually involved in a Section 1 price-fixing case. What we want to consider is whether it is feasible to bring the situation within the reach of the Sherman Act by labeling it a tacit or implicit agreement and arguing that the antitrust laws ought to extend to such agreements.

In dealing with the question, recall that the essence of pure oligopoly behavior is individual profit maximization based on certain assumptions about how rivals will react to changes in the individual firm's price or output level. In terms of the example, A's price increase is based on its calculations as to the most profitable course of conduct *given* the way in which it expects B to react. Since A expected that B would follow a price increase to $1.25, initiating such an increase was A's profit-maximizing strategy.

To see the difficulty of applying the Sherman Act to such conduct, consider how one would explain to a judge or jury precisely what A did that is objectionable or how one would fashion an effective remedy. It seems foolish to argue that A should have ignored the fact that B would likely follow an increase by A. This is essentially requiring A to pretend that it is in perfect competition rather than in a situation of duopoly. What the argument comes down to, then, is that A should have kept its price at $1 even though it knew that $1.25 would be more profitable.

But if that is the argument, what is the criterion for determining when A has acted illegally? Is it simply the fact that B followed A's price increase? Surely not, since that would essentially make any price increase that is not subsequently rescinded (because rivals failed to follow) illegal. Can A never initiate a price increase without risking a violation of the antitrust laws in the event its rivals follow? (Of course if rivals do not follow, the price increase is useless to A.) Would we interpret the law to mean that A can increase prices only when costs go up? (And if so, must the price increase be the absolute amount of the increase in costs or can it be the same percentage, and who must bear the burden of showing that the price increase did or did not reflect the cost increase?)

Similarly, it is difficult to argue that B committed an antitrust violation when it matched A's increase, knowing that if it failed to match, A would simply retract the increase. Can B ever follow an increase by A without itself violating the antitrust laws? Can it follow A's increase only if it is cost-justified? (Is the cost justification based on A's costs or B's? Or B's estimate of A's cost?) Finally, if the relationship between price and costs is to be determinative, are the federal courts equipped to carry out this regulatory function?

These questions suggest the great difficulty of attempting to apply the antitrust laws to classic oligopolistic behavior.[8] If there are many real-world markets that resemble our example, or that in other ways fit the classic oligopoly model, there would appear to be a serious policy problem that cannot be solved without more drastic measures.[9]

The Difficulty of Oligopolistic Coordination in Complex Markets

Although the policy dilemma posed by the classic oligopoly model as described in the preceding section is analytically troublesome, the dilemma may be more theoretical than real. In this section we focus on the difficulties faced by an industry seeking to achieve supracompetitive prices and profits and assess how likely the industry is to achieve those prices and profits without some kind of explicit effort at coordination. We then seek to describe an antitrust approach that "picks up" most such efforts, even those that cannot be described as "agreement."

Complicating Factors

To focus the discussion, it will be helpful to revisit the gas-station example. The key to eventual success for the gas stations was that one station—station A—was willing to initiate a price increase without any formal agreement from the other station—station B—to follow in such a way that the initial distribution of business remains unchanged.

Nevertheless, A was quite confident that B would follow and that there would be little risk associated with initiating the price increase.[10]

A's confidence that B would follow the price increase so that the initial distribution of customers would be unchanged was based on two factors: first, since B could readily observe A's price, there was no difficulty in following A's increase exactly, *if* B wanted to; second, since, if B failed to follow, A would promptly withdraw the price increase (so that B would enjoy only the most temporary gain in sales), it was in B's interest to follow A's increase, *if* B could do so. The two factors—ability and incentive—are equally important. If B is unable to follow A (because it does not know what A has done), it does not matter that B would like to follow. And, if it is not in B's interest to follow, it doesn't matter that B is able to.

However, B's ability to follow A's increase depends critically on the facts that B can easily observe A's prices and that A's prices are unambiguous in their meaning. The same mechanism that informs consumers about A's price increase (probably large signs facing the highway) promptly informs B as well. Moreover, there is little chance of any confusion on B's part as to what the signs mean. In our simple model A sells only a single variety of gasoline (e.g., regular unleaded), and there is no ambiguity about what the customer gets for the posted price (one gallon of the gasoline). Moreover, the products sold by A and B are regarded by consumers as virtually perfect substitutes, so that if B does increase its price by the same dollar amount there should be no shift in the distribution of business. And of course the fact that there are only two stations means that there is only one firm's price for B to match.

Likewise, B's incentive to follow A depends critically on the fact that B's failure to follow would be detected by A, who could retract the price increase promptly. Even if A could not observe B's prices directly, the fact that there are only two firms means that any increase in B's business would result in a corresponding drop in A's business. Hence A would immediately feel the impact of B's increase in business and is very likely to conclude that the reason for the shift in business is B's lower price. Moreover the impact on A would be substantial enough that A's only realistic strategy, once it has suspected that B has not followed the price increase, is to withdraw it; and B knows that.

Real markets, however, are frequently more complicated, so that a firm that seeks to initiate a price increase to noncompetitive levels cannot always be confident that the move will result in increased profits, either because its rivals will be unable to raise their own prices so as to preserve the preexisting distribution of business or because they will not want to do so (or both). The following is an illustrative (not exhaustive) list of the factors that are likely to complicate oligopolistic coordination.[11]

Nonpublic prices. An obvious and important characteristic of the gas station example was that station B had no trouble following A's price because it always knew precisely what A's price was. The same mechanism used to inform A's customers (signs) promptly and accurately informed B. Similarly, A had no trouble determining promptly whether B had in fact followed. While this might be characteristic of most goods sold off the shelf in retail outlets, there are many marketing contexts (e.g., sales to industrial buyers) in which the process of informing actual or potential customers of prices (and price changes) does not necessarily inform rivals. This is not to say that rivals can never find out about a price increase, but the time delay and potential for inaccurate information increases the risk to the initiator of a price increase that a rival will not follow. The same phenomenon also affects rivals' incentives to follow a price increase as well as their ability to do so. If A will not learn promptly whether B has matched the increase, the profits that B can make in the interim are higher, thereby increasing B's incentive not to follow and increasing A's risk in initiating the increase.

Lumpy sales. In the gas station example, A did not lose much business in the brief period during which its prices were higher than B's. This is because of the evenness of gasoline sales throughout the year. In some contexts, however, sales occur in large, discrete batches. An example is the process whereby the major auto manufacturers bid once or twice a year on a contract to supply the major rental car companies with new cars. Suppose Ford became aware that GM intended to raise prices during the next round of bids. If Ford were to refuse to follow GM, GM would almost certainly find out, but probably not until Ford had won a major contract for the coming year. This big chunk of sales may give Ford an incentive not to follow GM even though the result may be for GM to rescind its increase during the next round of bidding. More generally, the lumpiness of sales increases the incentive not to follow a leader's increase and thereby increases the risks in initiating one.[12]

Complex and nonfungible products. Where the product in question is simple and fungible across sellers, it is easier for rivals to follow a price increase in such a way as to maintain the preexisting distribution of sales. Where there is not a single product but a product line (such as regular, unleaded, and premium unleaded gasoline) there are more prices to coordinate. The broader the array of products, the more complicated the problem. When the products are not fungible across sellers, coordination is difficult because if A raises prices by $.25, it is not obvious that a price increase of $.25 by B will leave market shares unchanged.

To get a flavor of the difficulties that may arise, change the example so that A and B are supermarkets rather than gas stations, each selling thousands of products for which the prices frequently change weekly. Assume further that the stores differ dramatically in the amenities they offer (one has free babysitting while the parents are shopping and employees who carry the groceries to the car; the other requires customers to bag their own groceries but offers to redeem manufacturers' coupons at double face value). Now consider how confident one supermarket can be that if it increases prices by a certain amount, its rivals will follow promptly in such a way that there is no significant shift in business. Not only are there thousands of prices to be coordinated, but also it is not obvious that if the second supermarket raises prices on each product by the same dollar amount as the first store that the distribution of business will be unchanged.

One important dimension of fungibility is associated with location. For a steel customer located in Detroit, the steel from a manufacturer in Gary, Indiana, and the steel from a manufacturer in Birmingham, Alabama, are not perfect substitutes if the buyer has to pay the freight from the manufacturer's plant. Hence the fact that FOB prices are the same from both manufacturers (or are increased by the same dollar amount) does not mean that buyers will be indifferent as to their source and that market shares will not shift after a price change. Alternatively, if freight rates change frequently, market shares may shift even if FOB prices remain unchanged, and compensating changes in FOB prices will have to be coordinated to restore the preexisting distribution of sales.

Market Concentration.   A basic tenet of oligopoly theory is that the less concentrated the market, the more likely that individual firms will find it in their own self interest to undercut a noncompetitive price, and the less attractive it will be for one firm to initiate a noncompetitive price increase.[13] The reasons have to do with the potential for a small rival to increase profits significantly above its share of the "cooperative equilibrium" if it lowers price while rivals' prices remain unchanged. In an industry of many firms, rivals may not notice when one firm increases sales by taking a little from each of them, and even if they notice, retaliation may not be worthwhile. The smaller the number of firms, the more likely it is that even a "secret" price cut by one will be detected by the others (by inference from the large otherwise unexplainable loss in business to the price cutter); and the more likely are the remaining firms to feel compelled to respond by matching the price cut (because the loss in business to each is too significant to ignore).

An additional aspect of concentration is that an industry with a large number of firms, especially if they are of different sizes (with associated differences in average and marginal costs), may have many different views as to the appropriate industry price. The result may be that the firm preferring the lowest price gets its way or that disagreement results in considerable instability of industry prices with prices tending to stay close to the competitive level most of the time.

Facilitating Practices

Once we move beyond the simple oligopoly models of Cournot (1963) and Chamberlin (1933), or uncomplicated but unrealistic examples such as the gas station case, complicating factors such as those just described are likely to be present in many markets to a degree that firms in those markets are unlikely to be able to approximate the monopoly level of prices and profits solely as the result of perceived interdependence; something more will be needed. In many cases, what is required is explicit agreement—the usual stuff of a Sherman Act Section 1 price-fixing or market-allocation case—and nothing less will suffice.[14]

However, this is not the only possibility. In this paper we want to consider a situation where some explicit behavior that cannot fairly be labeled as agreement (at least in the usual Section 1 sense) will serve to *facilitate* a noncompetitive equilibrium. This is behavior that, either by design or happenstance, helps the firms in the market overcome the complicating factors that make pure oligopolistic interdependence infeasible or insufficient to yield monopoly profits.

To illustrate the concept, assume in our supermarket example, where one of the problems is the frequent change of prices (e.g., weekly), that there are thousands of prices needing to be coordinated and policed. The supermarket that intends to be the price leader routinely provides to its competitors, on the day before price changes are to be implemented, a computerized list of the prices for the following week for every item in the store. While in principle, the other stores could obtain the information by sending price checkers into the leader's store on the first day of the new prices, the list minimizes the likelihood of error and makes it possible for all stores to implement the new, higher prices on the same day, thereby negating the likelihood of a shift in business.[15]

A focus on the specific practices used to facilitate the noncompetitive result circumvents the major policy problem of dealing with oligopolistic interdependence—the absence of culpable conduct. The treatment of facilitating practices need not differ fundamentally from the treatment of agreement under Section 1, where firms are guilty not merely because they have achieved noncompetitive prices, but because they have done so by entering an agreement. Under a "facilitating practices" approach it would be unlawful to achieve noncompetitive prices via the use of one or more facilitating practices.[16]

While such an approach to dealing with oligopolistic behavior seems attractive, we need to determine if it can be implemented under the antitrust laws. Several possibilities exist. First, it will sometimes be the case that, although there is no agreement to fix prices, there is an agreement on the part of several firms to implement the facilitating practices. In our supermarket hypothetical, for example, all supermarkets may have agreed to exchange the computerized lists of the next week's prices. If so, there is no special legal issue. Section 1 applies to any agreement in restraint of trade, and it need be proved only that the exchange of prices does in fact result in a diminution of competition.[17] The agreement to exchange prices need not be contained in a formal written or oral agreement. The fact that all firms exchange the information will normally be enough for the courts to be able to find a tacit or implicit agreement to do so.[18]

Second, in the case where a noncompetitive outcome is achieved through the use by one or more firms of certain facilitating practices, without any explicit agreement on price or any explicit agreement to use the facilitating practice, one could simply define the noncompetitive outcome (the "meeting of the minds") that is achieved through the use of facilitating practices to be an illegal tacit or implicit agreement. It could be argued that using such an approach is somewhat arbitrary, when earlier we rejected the notion that a noncompetitive outcome arising out of pure oligopolistic interdependence should be labeled as a tacit or implicit agreement. As a matter of semantics, it may be hard to distinguish a "meeting of the minds" that arises from oligopolistic interdependence from one that depends on facilitating practices and therefore it may be hard to justify labeling one, but not the other, as a tacit agreement. But the major policy objection to using the tacit-agreement approach to pure oligopolistic interdependence—the absence of identifiable culpable conduct and the lack of effective remedy—is not present in the facilitating practices approach.[19]

Finally, it may be possible to avoid the Sherman Act altogether. Section 5 of the Federal Trade Commission Act prohibits "unfair methods of competition." Traditionally the FTC has interpreted Section 5 to cover more or less the same conduct as that which is covered by the Sherman Act. Specifically, in oligopolistic situations, the FTC has traditionally alleged at least a tacit, if not an explicit, agreement. But neither the statutory language nor the legislative history would appear to limit the FTC to situations involving agreement, and facilitating practices could arguably be condemned as "unfair methods of competition."[20]

Our case study involves the latter approach. It involves an action brought by the FTC under Section 5, in which the FTC specifically declined to characterize the conduct as constituting an agreement. The action was a deliberate effort to test the limits of Section 5 in relation to oligopolistic behavior.

The Lead-based Antiknock Industry and the FTC Complaint

The lead antiknock compound market had several of the characteristics generally viewed by economists as being conducive to noncompetitive outcomes. There were only four domestic sellers, with two firms dominating the industry.[21] The two larger firms apparently had similar costs of production. The product was relatively simple. There were two basic lead antiknock products—tetraethyl lead (TEL) and tetramethyl lead (TML)—that were usually combined in various proportions. Individual antiknock compounds of a given type produced or sold by one of the firms were substantially similar to those of the same type sold by the others—i.e., the product was essentially fungible. The product had no reasonably close substitutes and constituted such a small percentage of the cost of refining a gallon of gasoline that the overall industry demand faced by the sellers was highly inelastic: increases in the industry price would result in relatively small reductions in consumption.

Moreover, it seemed unlikely that high prices would be deterred or undercut by new entry. From 1964 (when Nalco, the last of the four current producers, entered the industry) throughout the 1970s there were no new entrants into the industry. Given the overcapacity that characterized the industry in 1974 and the forecasts for further substantial drops in demand due to the government regulations, there was little likelihood of new entry even if existing firms were earning "monopoly" profits.[22]

However, other industry characteristics reduced the likelihood that supracompetitive prices could result merely from oligopolistic interdependence. These are the "complicating factors" referred to earlier; they can be enumerated as follows:

1. Sales of antiknock compound were not made to the general public but to the major oil refiners in essentially private transactions. Hence, it was not inevitable that one firm's price changes would immediately be observed by its rivals. This complicated the task of coordinating price changes so that there would be no shift in the distribution of sales and provided an incentive for secret discounts (since such discounts would not necessarily be detected quickly).

2. The oil companies were sophisticated customers making large dollar amounts of annual purchases. There was ample incentive on the part of oil companies to bargain hard for discounts and to offer to shift significant business in return for discounts. Moreover, the huge excess capacity provided a strong incentive for one seller to offer a discount if it would result in significant additional sales.[23]

3. The four producers had a total of six plants: one in California, one in New Jersey, one at Baton Rouge, Louisiana, and three in Texas. The customers' plants were dispersed throughout the country. While, on average, transportation costs were not large as a percentage of the price of the product (about 2 percent), the transportation costs to any given customer from each of the four producers could differ significantly. Hence, even if FOB prices were equal for all four producers, the effective delivered price from one producer to a given customer could be substantially different from the effective delivered price from another producer to that customer. Since the product was otherwise fungible, the lowest effective delivered price would in all likelihood get the business, with no guarantee that, after all the business was allocated on this basis, the market shares would be distributed in a way that would be "satisfactory" to all producers. Moreover, nonproportional changes in freight costs to different locations could cause market shares to shift unpredictably.

In light of these complicating factors, the FTC did not believe that pure oligopolistic interdependence could be entirely responsible for the lack of effective price competition. Rather, the FTC identified four practices that contributed materially to the noncompetitive outcome.

Advance Notice of Price Changes

All four firms gave notice to their customers of price increases at least thirty days in advance of the effective date of the price increase. For example, if Ethyl were attempting to initiate a price increase to be effective on July 1 of a given year, it would notify customers of the increase no later than June 1 and typically a few days earlier. The FTC argued that such advance notice gave rivals an opportunity to respond so that uncertainty about whether rivals would follow would be eliminated *before* the price increase actually went into effect, thereby permitting modification or rollback of the price increase prior to its effective date if rivals did not follow precisely. For example, Ethyl might actually announce the increase on May 28. The other firms would then have three days to make matching announcements, which would assure that, when the price increases actually went into effect, all firms would have identical prices. Even if one or more of the rivals did not make an announcement until say, June 3, Ethyl would at least be sure that rivals would be matching the increase and that at worst they would be a few days out of phase.

Insuring that the initiator will not be alone in the market with a higher effective price prevents a possible shift of short-term business to lower-priced competitors and, as a result, reduces risk associated with the price move. It also permits time for "adjustment" if one or more of the competitors should favor a price increase of a different amount. The actual record of price increases showed that during the period 1974 to 1979 there were twenty-four price increases. In twenty instances all the firms had an identical list price that was effective on the same date. In the other four instances there was an identical price list and an effective date difference of only a day or two.

Press Notices

Until about mid-1977 (when the practice was stopped on advice of counsel), all the firms issued press notices concerning price increases. While the producers had other sources of information (customers voluntarily notified the other firms of one firm's announced price increase, so as to learn promptly if the others would follow), the FTC claimed that these other sources of information were not always timely and were sometimes inaccurate. The fact that information may be unreliable creates uncertainty about rivals' actions. It may make it difficult for a price leader to "communicate" its move or to learn whether rivals have followed. Either consequence increases the risk of initiating a price increase, and the press releases helped ease this uncertainty by providing early and accurate information of price moves.

Uniform Delivered Pricing

All the firms quoted antiknock prices only on the basis of a delivered price inclusive of transportation and quoted the same delivered price regardless of the customer's location. The effective list price for any one firm is therefore identical throughout the United States. A delivered pricing formula removes transportation cost variables from the pricing structure, thus simplifying each producer's price format. A producer seeking to match a competitor's price under this system need not deal with complications engendered by freight tariffs or speculate on its competitors' transportation cost variables. Rather, a producer seeking to have the identical effective price as its rival to *each* of its 150 actual or potential customers need only be concerned with matching the single uniform delivered price. The alternative would be to adjust its FOB price to each customer so as to compensate for the higher or lower freight costs to that customer's location from its production point as compared to the transportation costs from its rival to that same customer.[24]

The courts had recognized for years that *an agreement* to use a delivered pricing formula such as uniform delivered prices has sufficient potential for eliminating price competition. Such agreements have routinely been held illegal. The FTC argued here that the same anticompetitive consequences follow even where the common use of the pricing formula is not the result of agreement.

"Most Favored Customer" Clauses

A "most favored customer" clause in a sales contract is a promise by a seller to offer its customer the benefit of any lower price the seller gives another customer. While the precise terms of a most favored customer clause can vary from contract to contract, the essence of the clause in the present context was that any discount off the uniform delivered list price granted to a single customer would have to be extended to all customers of that seller. Ethyl and DuPont were the primary users of most favored customer clauses during the 1974 to 1979 period, although the other two firms did employ them in various ways.

As discussed earlier, one of the problems confronting any oligopoly seeking to maintain a supracompetitive price is the incentive that exists for any one firm to shade the price slightly in an effort to pick up additional sales by "stealing" them from its rivals. The incentive is particularly strong where the discount need be extended only to the incremental customer—i.e., where the firm can continue to charge the prevailing industry price to its existing customers and discount only to those customers who would otherwise buy elsewhere. In many contexts, especially in sales to consumers in traditional retail establishments (such as gas stations or supermarkets), such discrimination is often impractical.

In the case of antiknock compounds, however, where sales are made privately to each of many industrial customers (the oil refiners), discrimination in the form of secret discounts is feasible and, given the difficulty of detection and effective retaliation (because sales are secret and at least potentially lumpy), probably attractive. Most favored customer clauses effectively prohibit discrimination. This has the effect of discouraging discounting from list prices since cutting prices "across the board" to all customers would be less likely to be profitable than would selective cuts to targeted customers (to keep them loyal or woo them away from rivals). In addition, where the discount is offered widely, it is much more likely to be detected by rivals.

Most favored customer clauses not only create disincentives to discount, they also reduce uncertainty about rivals' prices and pricing actions in significant ways. Since such contractural provisions discourage discounting, a firm's knowledge that its rivals employ them provides assurance that the latters' discounting will be restrained. As a result of this reduction in uncertainty about rivals' transaction prices, most favored customer clauses facilitate noncompetitive price increases by improving confidence that information regarding a competitor's prices, gathered from only one or two sources, is applicable to all customers. Therefore if a firm that has initiated a price increase learns from a few customers that a rival has matched the increase for sales to those customers, it can be reasonably confident that the rival's matching increase applies to all customers.[25]

Issues for the Court

As structured by the FTC the case presented two main economic questions for the court: 1) was the industry performing noncompetitively; and 2) if so, was the poor performance attributable to the challenged practices? The case also presented the legal and policy issue of whether Section 5 of the FTC Act is applicable to noncollusive horizontal conduct, and if so, what are the general guidelines for when noncollusive horizontal conduct violates Section 5?[26]

Economic Issues

Industry performance.   The FTC made the following arguments about the antiknock compound industry's performance:

1. The overall level of prices was high, as evidenced by profit levels and industry statements about the profitability of the industry and the possibility of much lower prices if competition "broke out." With respect to the former, the FTC compared the profit level in this business for the 1974 to 1979 period to the average return on net assets for all manufacturing and for the chemicals industry generally and found, for example, that Ethyl's and DuPont's return exceeded 150 percent of any benchmark comparison in every year during the period. With respect to the latter, the FTC made much of a document in which an Ethyl executive characterized the business as a "golden goose," and there were similar (albeit less colorful) characterizations from some of the other firms as well.

The various courts that ruled on the case generally accepted the

FTC's claim with respect to profits. The FTC was lucky in this respect, however. Profit levels are a notoriously slippery vehicle for showing that an industry is performing noncompetitively, and it is rarely possible to show noncompetitive performance from profit levels alone.[27]

2. The structure of prices geographically was not compatible with assertions that the industry was performing perfectly competitively. Since delivered prices were uniform even though transportation costs differed depending on the seller's and the buyer's location, then even if prices to some buyers were at the competitive level (i.e., buyers for whom transport costs were relatively high), it must be the case that prices to other buyers (those for whom transport costs were relatively low) were above the relevant marginal costs. Put simply, in a competitively functioning industry, buyers who are close to the plants of two or more sellers should pay less for delivered compound than buyers located at greater distances.

3. More generally, the FTC argued that it was simply unrealistic to attribute the identical prices to an abundance of competition. While it is true that in a "perfect" market prices for identical products tend toward equality, there is generally enough friction in the system that the process does not work instantly or produce perfect equality. Especially given the presence of big, sophisticated buyers and the considerable excess capacity, one should have observed more variation in the system.

The defendants challenged the FTC's assertions about performance in two important respects. First, they established that prices were not in fact perfectly uniform. While Ethyl and DuPont consistently sold at list price, a substantial portion of Nalco's and PPG's sales were made at a discount. Overall, approximately 15 to 20 percent of industry sales during the period were at a discount from list prices. The FTC argued that these discounts could be explained by special factors (for example, Nalco continued to give discounts to the refiners who first gave Nalco some business when it entered the industry) and were not enough to rebut the overall characterization of the industry performance as noncompetitive.

Second, there was substantial evidence of nonprice competition in the form of various free services. Most were directly related to provision of the antiknock compounds (such as safety services and product equipment and inspection services) that arguably would be provided even in a competitive environment, but others were clearly disguised discounts. Examples included installing lead weigh tanks for refiners, paying architectural fees incurred by a refiner in building an employee cafeteria, and building a railroad spur to facilitate antiknock compound delivery. The parties disputed the significance of this nonprice competition. The FTC argued that customers would have preferred a straight price cut and that the nonprice concessions were actually a symptom of the elimination of direct price competition. Defendants, anticipating their main defense (discussed *infra*), argued that the nonprice competition was in many cases the practical equivalent of a price cut and, in any event, the best that could be expected in an oligopolistic industry, where direct price cuts would be quickly observed and matched, thereby rendering them unprofitable.

It is worth noting that in a conventional price fixing case, the issue of whether prices are set at supracompetitive levels does not arise. Price fixing is regarded as illegal per se; the fact that firms have agreed on the price is sufficient for the firms to be guilty of a violation of the Sherman Act. Since, however, there is no agreement in a case such as *Ethyl,* and no policy interest in a complete prohibition of the kinds of individual business practices involved in *Ethyl,* it is essential that the court in a facilitating practices case determine at the outset whether the industry is in fact performing noncompetitively.

In theory this is straightforward; the theoretical "benchmarks" for perfect competition (price equal to marginal and average cost) and monopoly (price above marginal cost and normally but not necessarily above average cost) are well established. But unless the courts wish to invoke Section 5 *any time* an industry deviates from the competitive norm, no matter how slightly, some judgment is required about how much of a deviation is "too much." There really was no dispute that the antiknock compound industry was not performing as a perfectly competitive industry would have, and in that respect, at least, the various courts did not really disagree with the FTC. In the absence of any recognized benchmark for how much of a deviation was too much to be tolerable, what the FTC's argument boiled down to was that, but for the facilitating practices, the industry performance would have been significantly improved. Hence, the issue of industry performance merged into that of causation.

Causation.   Based on the documentary evidence and the opinion of its economic expert, the FTC argued that the noncompetitive performance was attributable, at least in part, to the identified facilitating practices and that, but for the practices, industry performance would have been measurably improved. The FTC acknowledged that structure was important and that in a less concentrated industry the facilitating practices may not have mattered, but claimed that, because of the complicating factors, structure alone could not account for the poor performance. Defendants took the position that, to the extent the industry performed unsatisfactorily, it was the natural result of the oligopolistic structure of the industry.

Defendants also took specific exception to some of the FTC's claims about the importance of the practices.

1. As to the press announcements, defendants argued that information about price changes initiated by one firm would spread quickly to the firm's rivals as customers sought to inquire whether the other firms intended to go along with the increase.

2. The practice of uniform delivered prices was not significant in light of the relatively low transportation costs as a percent of the total price. Since the product was fungible, competitive forces would lead to freight absorption by more distant sellers in an effort to compete against more favorably situated sellers for a customer's business. Since freight rates between any two points could easily be determined, firms would have no trouble matching one another's effective delivered price even if prices were quoted on a delivered price basis.

3. The most favored customer clauses simply put into contractural language what the firms regarded as the sensible policy from a customer relations standpoint of not discriminating among customers by giving discounts that other customers would learn about anyway. Testimony indicated that customers *on an individual basis* desired contractural protection against discrimination.[28] Defendants also referred to their legal obligations under the Robinson-Patman Act not to discriminate in price where the effect may be to harm competition among the industry's customers.

These arguments on causation presented an interesting dilemma for the court. Given the FTC's admission that some oligopolistic interdependence was at work and that, even without the facilitating practices, it was unlikely that the industry would behave perfectly competitively, how does the court assess *how much* worse the performance was as a result of the facilitating practices? There is no obvious way to measure this factor, and the courts were left to some extent with the conflicting judgments of the parties' expert economic witnesses.[29] The FTC's expert claimed that in his opinion the industry would have performed significantly better in the absence of the facilitating practices, although he acknowledged that there was no scientific way to determine precisely how much. The experts for the defendants took the position that the practices really didn't matter much at all, but neither did they offer any "scientific" proof.

Both the administrative law judge and the Commission (with a vigorous dissent by Chairman Miller) felt that the practices contributed significantly to the poor performance. However, the Court of Appeals determined that the Commission had not carried the burden of showing that there had been a significant lessening of competition due to the challenged practices. The court felt that the degree of price uniformity was much more limited than the FTC had characterized it and that the extensive nonprice competition, combined with the frequent discounts, presented a picture of a competitive market in which large, sophisticated, and aggressive buyers were making demands on the sellers and were satisfied with the results. Even if the industry performance was less than fully satisfactory, the court was prepared to attribute that result to the underlying structure rather than the practices.

Legal and Policy Issues

While the economic issues just discussed were important to the outcome of the case, in many ways the most important questions that had to be addressed were whether Section 5 could be used at all in a horizontal context in the absence of agreement (if not an explicit agreement, then at least a tacit agreement) and, if so, under what circumstances was it appropriate for the FTC to challenge behavior that firms individually engaged in, without any prior agreement to do so. Defendants observed that each of the challenged practices was initiated by Ethyl during the period prior to 1948 when it was the sole producer in the industry. For example, Ethyl began quoting prices on a delivered price basis in 1937 in response to customer demand. Each of the three subsequent manufacturers, upon entry into the market, followed that practice. Customers demanded a delivered price because it would require the manufacturers to retain title to and responsibility for the dangerously volatile compounds during transit to the refiner's plant.

Similarly, Ethyl adopted the most favored customer clause when it was the sole producer, as its guarantee not to price discriminate among its own customers who competed against each other in the sale of gasoline. The clause assured the smaller refiners that they would not be placed at a competitive disadvantage on account of price discounts to giants such as Standard Oil, Texaco, and Gulf. For the same reason, DuPont adopted the same contractual clause when it later entered the industry. Finally, the issuance of advance notice of price increases both to buyers and the press, a common practice in the chemicals industry, was initiated by Ethyl well before the entry of DuPont or the other two producers, as a means of aiding buyers in planning their purchase decisions.

The Court of Appeals agreed with defendants' argument that, since the practices were adopted when there was no competition, it could not be that their *purpose* was to reduce competition. Furthermore, in the opinion of the court, the conduct was not inherently collusive, coercive, predatory, restrictive, or deceitful. Thus, the essence of the FTC challenge was that at some point the practices resulted in a substantial lessening of competition. The Court of Appeals expressed great concern that a test based solely on the fact of an impact on competition would be so vague "as to permit arbitrary or undue government interference with the reasonable freedom of action that has marked our country's competitive system." The court asserted that before business conduct in an oligopolistic industry may be labeled "unfair" within the meaning of Section 5 (in the absence of a tacit agreement) there must be a showing of either evidence of anticompetitive intent or the absence of independent legitimate business reason for the conduct. In a case such as *Ethyl,* where the conduct was implemented when the original firm did not confront any competition, the absence of an independent business meaning cannot be presumed.

Conclusions

The "facilitating practices" theory was enthusiastically endorsed both by the administrative law judge who conducted the hearing and by the Commission itself in its role as a review panel. In principle, the Court of Appeals did not reject the basic approach, but its reversal of the Commission's application of the theory to the antiknock industry at least raises a question about how frequently the evidence would be strong enough to satisfy the court's criteria, *except* in those situations where there is enough interaction among the firms that the plaintiff can follow the traditional approach of asserting the existence of an agreement. The only basis for optimism is that the circumstances of this industry—i.e., Ethyl's having adopted the practices as a monopolist—are somewhat unusual. Only as additional attempts are made to utilize the facilitating practices theory will it be possible to determine how much of a burden the court will place on the FTC in circumstances where there is not that basis for an inference that the practices have some significant independent business value.

Notes

1. Comparable agreements are those in which firms agree to restrict output or not to compete at all with one another for sales to certain customers or within certain geographic regions.
2. Many observers are skeptical about whether price-fixing agreements very often succeed, but even among those who believe that few agreements if any succeed for any appreciable period of time, there are few observers who do not support the current legal treatment. One rationale is that there appear to be no social benefits associated with

such private agreements and hence nothing to be lost by condemning even those that are incapable of doing serious damage to consumers.

3. The basic Cournot (1963) model is typical of the methodology and the results of the early models. Under the simple (and probably unrealistic) assumption that rivals' output will not be influenced by changes in the output level of the individual firm, Cournot established that the collective result of each firm's individual profit-maximizing output decision would be an industry output level that deviated sharply from the competitive level as the number of firms became smaller. Thus, for example, a two-firm industry—i.e., a duopoly—would yield a price that was much closer to the single-firm monopoly price than to the competitive price without the firms' having had any explicit communication or agreement. Other early models employed different reaction functions but generated similar results. Chamberlin (1933), for example, showed that if each firm expected its rivals to follow perfectly its own behavior, then the collective result of each firm's individual profit-maximizing behavior would be the monopoly price, *even with a large number of firms.*

The more recent oligopoly literature has criticized these simple reaction functions. Stigler (1964), for example, emphasized the links between industry concentration and the likelihood that rivals will follow a price increase. Others (see Waterson [1984, chapter 3] for a brief survey) have emphasized the dynamic aspects of oligopolistic interdependence and have argued, among other things, that where firms confront one another frequently over time, firms will learn something about the way their rivals will react. The model presented in this case study, if interpreted within the context of the traditional oligopoly literature, emphasizes how firms can behave so as to influence their rivals' reaction functions in an effort to produce Chamberlin-type conduct.

4. Even if A could not observe B's price directly, the immediate and large shift in business from A to B would be an almost certain indication that B was keeping its price low.

5. In the interim, A will have lost some sales but as long as it is able to detect B's price cutting and responds immediately, the losses will not be too great.

6. We assume for the sake of illustration that entry by additional stations is unlikely.

7. This model is vastly oversimplified. Modern game theory is concerned with articulating in some detail the conditions under which the joint monopoly price is in fact a stable equilibrium. See Waterson (1984) for a brief survey of this recent work.

8. For a more extended discussion of this argument, see Turner (1962). For an argument that the Sherman Act can be applied to oligopolistic pricing, see Posner (1969; 1976).

9. The two obvious choices are: first, a comprehensive scheme of price and/or profit controls for oligopolistic industries; and second, where feasible, structural relief to reduce the degree of concentration in markets. While the latter would likely not be feasible in the gas station example, there may be oligopolistic markets in which it would be feasible through divestiture to reduce concentration without

introducing significant operating inefficiencies. A third, longer run alternative is a strict horizontal merger policy designed to prevent highly oligopolistic markets from developing. Each of these alternatives has its liabilities, and one would want to be certain that the problem was in fact serious before invoking any one of them.

10. Station A also knew that, even if B did not follow, A could retract the price increase without having suffered any serious financial consequences.

11. For a more extensive treatment, see Hay (1982).

12. While lumpiness often occurs "naturally" (e.g., for business reasons on the part of the buyer or seller that have nothing to do with oligopolistic behavior), buyers sometimes have the ability to lump their purchases into big batches precisely to provide an inducement for sellers to cut prices. This can be done either by actually purchasing and storing large quantities at one time, or by entering into a long-term contract calling for delivery over the life of the contract. It is also worth noting that frequently both lumpiness and secrecy are present, and the effect is, of course, cumulative.

13. The classic derivation of this theorem is from Stigler (1964).

14. Market structure will sometimes be sufficiently unfavorable that even explicit agreement will be inadequate to produce supracompetitive prices and profits for any significant period of time.

15. Other complicating factors may mean that this particular practice by itself is insufficient to produce a noncompetitive equilibrium.

16. An exception might be permitted where it could be established that there are efficiencies associated with the practices that outweigh the anticompetitive consequences.

17. There have been several major antitrust cases along these lines, including *United States* v. *Container Corp.,* 393 U.S. 333 (1969).

18. This is because it is not necessarily in one firm's interest (especially if it is not the price leader) to provide information about its own prices without some understanding that it would receive the price lists from the other firms. To avoid the inference of agreement, defendants would want to show that there were reasons (unrelated to the goal of achieving supracompetitive prices) for making their own prices available to their rivals even if they did not receive their rivals' prices in return.

19. For an example of this approach see the Justice Department's memorandum on the degree modification governing General Electric and Westinghouse in their marketing of turbine generators, *United States* v. *GE Co.,* [1977] 1 *Trade Cas. (CCH)* 712. Sometimes the courts indicate the need for certain "plus factors" in addition to simply a noncompetitive outcome. For a discussion of this general approach and citations to some of the cases that have followed it, see Hovenkamp and Sullivan (1984 221–231).

20. These aspects of the FTC Act are discussed in some detail in the various opinions in the Ethyl case. Two major consequences of relying on the FTC Act are that there is no right of private action under the FTC Act and there are no sanctions imposed on firms that have been found to have engaged in unfair methods of competition; they are merely given an order to "cease and desist" from using the practices.

21. During the period under consideration, Ethyl's market share averaged

34 percent and Dupont's averaged 36 percent. PPG's average share was 17.5 percent and Nalco's 12.5 percent. Based on these average shares the HHI exceeds 2900.

22. The fixed costs of a plant of minimal optimal scale were large enough that new entry would substantially depress prices. Since many of the fixed costs would also be sunk costs, this would result in losses for the entrant. Although there was widespread agreement on the low likelihood of independent entry, the possibility of backward vertical integration by one or more of the major oil companies was perceived by the Court of Appeals to be a significant factor.

23. The excess capacity meant that the marginal costs of additional output were relatively low and that the incremental profits on additional sales would be substantial.

24. Scherer (1980, 329) has commented on the role that delivered pricing plays in facilitating and maintaining uniform prices:

> If each producer independently and unsystematically quoted prices to the thousands of destinations it might serve, it would almost surely undercut rivals on some orders, touching off retaliatory price cuts. But common adherence to basing point formulas in effect eliminates discretion and uncertainty, and if each firm plays the game and sticks to the formulas, price competition is avoided. Identical prices are quoted to a given customer by every producer, leaving the division of orders to chance or nonprice variables (such as delivery times, special service, the dryness of martinis provided by salesmen at business luncheons, etc.—bases on which oligopolists often prefer to compete).

25. Theoretical work and experimental evidence supporting these points can be found in Salop (1986), Cooper (1980), and Grether and Plott (1984).

26. The judicial process in an FTC matter works as follows: first, based on a staff recommendation, the Commission (5 members, each appointed by the president for a term of five years) votes whether to issue a complaint; if a complaint is issued, the matter is heard by an FTC administrative law judge, who issues what is called an "initial decision". The matter then returns to the Commission itself which, based on the record compiled at the hearing, along with subsequent argument by the Commission staff and the defendants, either issues an opinion and an order (normally a prohibition on certain conduct in the future) or dismisses the complaint. If the Commission's decision is adverse to the defendants, they may appeal to the U.S. Court of Appeals. Either party may seek to appeal a decision of the Court of Appeals to the U.S. Supreme Court. However, the Supreme Court accepts only a small percentage of the petitions it receives. In this case, both the initial decision and the Commission's opinion were adverse to defendants. The Court of Appeals, however, reversed the Commission and ordered the complaint dismissed. *E.I. du Pont de Nemours & Co.* v. *FTC*, 729 F. 2d 128 (1984). The matter was not appealed to the Supreme Court. In the text that follows, I refer to the three layers

collectively (i.e., the administrative law judge, the Commission, and the court of appeals) as "the court."

27. See Fisher et al. (1983), Chapter 7, and the discussion of the FTC's unsuccessful efforts to attack the breakfast cereals industry in Scherer (1979).

28. It can be entirely rational for each individual customer to demand such protection even if it would be in the collective interest of customers to have the practice prohibited.

29. The court also had available, from documents and from the testimony of live witnesses, perceptions from those in the industry as to whether the practices played any role in the decision-making process. This evidence was still of limited utility, however, in assessing precisely how much of a difference they made.

References

Blair, Roger D., and David L. Kaserman. *Antitrust Economics*. Homewood, Ill.: Richard D. Irwin, 1985.

Chamberlin, Edward H. *The Theory of Monopolistic Competition*. Cambridge, Mass.: Harvard University Press, 1933.

Cooper, T. E. "Most Favored Customer Clauses and Tacit Collusion." *Rand Journal of Economics* 17 (Autumn 1986): 377–388.

Cournot, Augustin. *Researches Into the Mathematical Principles of the Theory of Wealth*. Translated by N.T. Bacon. Homewood, Ill.: Richard D. Irwin, 1963.

Fisher, Franklin M., John J. McGowan, and Joen E. Greenwood. *Folded, Spindled, and Mutilated: Economic Analysis and U.S. v. IBM*. Cambridge, Mass.: MIT Press, 1983.

Grether, D. M., and C. Plott. "The Effect of Market Practices in Oligopoly Markets: An Experimental Examination of the Ethyl Case." *Economic Inquiry* 22 (October 1984): 479–507.

Hay, George A. "Oligopoly, Shared Monopoly, and Antitrust Law." *Cornell Law Review* 67 (March 1982): 439-481.

Hovenkamp, Herbert, and E. Thomas Sullivan. *Antitrust Law: Policy and Procedure*. Charlottesville, Va.: Michie, 1984.

Posner, Richard A. "Oligopoly and the Antitrust Laws: A Suggested Approach." *Stanford Law Review* 21 (June 1969): 1562–1606.

_____. *Antitrust Law: An Economic Perspective*. Chicago, Ill.: University of Chicago Press, 1976.

Salop, Steven. "Practices That (Credibly) Facilitate Oligopoly Coordination." In *New Developments in the Analysis of Market Structure,* edited by J. Stiglitz and F. G. Mathewson. Cambridge: MIT Press, 1986.

Scherer, F. M. "The Welfare Economics of Product Variety: An Application to the Ready-to-Eat Cereals Industry." *Journal of Industrial Economics.* 28 (December 1979): 113–134.

_____. *Industrial Market Structure and Economic Performance*. 2d. ed. Skokie, Ill.: Rand McNally, 1980.

Stigler, George J. "A Theory of Oligopoly." *Journal of Political Economy.* 72 (February 1964): 44–61.

Turner, Donald F. "The Definition of Agreement under the Sherman Act: Conscious Parallelism and Refusals to Deal." *Harvard L. Rev.* 75 (February 1962): 655–706.

Waterson, Michael. *Economic Theory of the Industry.* Cambridge, England: Cambridge University Press, 1984.

8

case

Strategic Behavior and Attempted Monopolization: The *Coffee* (*General Foods*) Case

John C. Hilke and Philip B. Nelson

Introduction

Since its earliest days, antitrust law and enforcement policy has evolved with changes in business practices and in economic and legal understanding of these practices. While the law changes over time, it often lags the market behavior it regulates. This lag arises because firms are free to adopt new modes of behavior that are not specifically prohibited under existing statute and precedent. Similarly, since economic understanding of business behavior frequently lags the implementation of that behavior, the law is often forced by events to deal with economic issues that are not yet well understood or are hotly debated by economists. Thus, the law must periodically revise, or even reverse, its course after discovering that "new learning" has invalidated the premises that underlie the reasoning in earlier cases.[1]

Recent changes in predatory pricing law are illustrative of these evolutionary processes and the problems they pose for courts. During the last decade, courts have been adjusting the test they use to determine whether predatory pricing has occurred. One notable movement in this direction was the Federal Trade Commission's decision in *General Foods Corp.*, followed quickly with a parallel ruling in *I.T.T. Continental Baking Co.*[2] In these cases, the Commission adjusted traditional attempted monopolization standards in an effort to reflect its reading of recent economic learning about predation.

In previous attempted monopolization cases the Commission had followed the three-element test advocated in *DuPont*[3] to determine if there was 1) specific intent to control prices or destroy competition, 2) exclusionary or anticompetitive conduct, and 3) a dangerous probability of success.

In *General Foods,* the Commission adjusted the three-part at-

John C. Hilke and Philip B. Nelson worked with complaint counsel on the *General Foods* case. The opinions expressed are their own; they are not intended to represent the view of either the Federal Trade Commission or any individual commissioner.

tempted monopolization test. Rather than dealing thoroughly with all three issues and assessing how the conduct and intent evidence might contribute toward a better understanding of the probability of success element, the Commission chose to concentrate on the dangerous probability element of the test without considering the implications of the questioned conduct. Finding that the alleged predator did not have a dangerous probability of success, based on its analysis of market characteristics, the Commission majority felt it was unnecessary to address in detail the conduct and intent evidence.

The Commission's approach in *General Foods* and *ITT Continental* represents a break from the approach used in previous cases where all three points were considered, or where intent and conduct evidence was considered as part of the assessment of the dangerous probability of success element. Moreover, while previous cases view sales below cost (particularly average variable cost) to be largely unrebuttable evidence of a dangerous probability of success element, the Commission decided:

> [p]rices above average variable cost raise a strong, often conclusive, presumption of legality. Conversely, prices below average variable cost can raise a presumption of predation, but that presumption is rebuttable. . . .[Thus] low prices alone, including prices below some measures of variable cost, do not by themselves mean the seller has violated the antitrust laws.[4]

The Commission's majority decision appears to have been based on its reading of economic analyses of predation that preceded the case. Evidently, the majority of the commissioners believed that 1) predation is extremely unlikely, 2) predation is difficult to distinguish from socially beneficial competition, and 3) sizeable social losses will result from stifling aggressive competition.[5]

While the Commission clearly felt it was advancing attempted monopolization law by restructuring it to align with the relevant economics literature, the Commission's decision did not fully reflect the existing economics literature. During the more than five years of investigation and litigation challenging the response of Maxwell House (owned by General Foods) to the entry of Folger (owned by Procter and Gamble) into eastern retail coffee markets, there were several contributions to the strategic planning literature that suggest that the theoretical and empirical basis of the Commissioners' decision may have been outdated by the time the Commission rendered its decision.

The Commission's failure to use this case to comment directly on and test the relevance of this portion of the economics literature to antitrust law is somewhat surprising, since complaint counsel drew heavily on the growing literature on business strategies in structuring their case. Among the topics discussed in the strategic planning literature that complaint counsel felt were key to understanding General Foods' behavior, but that the Commission chose to ignore, are: mobility barriers, first mover advantages, the effects of retailer behavior on competition at the manufacturing level, the tactical raising of rivals' costs, and the importance of firm reputations.

Perhaps the most important of these concepts is that of "mobility barriers."[6] The term mobility barrier is used to indicate a structural characteristic of the market that insulates some, but not all, firms in the industry from both new entry and incursions by other firms or groups. As Porter (1980) points out, where mobility barriers are present, the height of "entry barriers depends on the particular strategic group that the entrant seeks to join."[7]

The development of the concept of "first mover advantage" also proved to be important to the arguments in the case.[8] A "first mover advantage" is present when early entrants into a market have cost advantages relative to subsequent entrants. Often these advantages are associated with a lower cost of building a reputation for satisfactory quality and obtaining a loyal group of consumers.

With respect to retailers, while economists have long recognized that consumer products pass through middlemen, many models assume that retail behavior is a simple derivative of the consumer demand that retailers are trying to satisfy. There is no recognition of any strategic behavior by retailers that can affect the demand manufacturers face. However, economists have increasingly come to recognize that retailer behavior can affect the demand that manufacturers face in important ways.[9]

The development of the strategic concept of "raising rivals' costs" was important to complaint counsel's argument, since it provided a motive for at least some of General Foods' behavior. This type of strategy rests on the fact that competitors often have a different production function or face somewhat different demand curves. Because of these differences, specific input cost increases may affect competitors differently.[10] If one competitor can increase the cost of an input that is relatively unimportant to him but crucial to his rival, he can gain a relative cost advantage and cause market prices to rise and his own profits to increase. These asymmetries on the cost or demand side, leading to strategic opportunities to disadvantage one's rivals, were crucial to the FTC staff's concern over some of General Foods' tactics.

The FTC complaint counsel's argument also employed the concept of "reputation building." Recent empirical evidence suggests that predation is much more likely to be a profitable strategy if the predator can build a credible reputation as a predator.[11]

In the following sections, we will use these five strategic concepts to evaluate General Foods' response to Folger's entry. This strategic perspective will be contrasted with the economic analysis used by the Commission in this case. By comparing the results of these two different analytical techniques, we hope to obtain some insights about the Commission's decision to adjust the traditional three-part attempted monopolization test in the way it did.

Background and Chronology of Events

The events that were the subject of this case took place during the early to mid-1970s. In 1970, General Foods sold approximately 43 percent (of which 90 percent was its Maxwell House brand) of the non-instant (ground) coffee purchased by grocers in the eastern U.S.[12] A variety of other firms also did business in these areas, but their share positions were concentrated in particular groups of metropolitan areas, and even in these smaller areas they typically had less than half of the Maxwell House brand's share. General Foods was the only company that had brands in nationwide distribution. Although some companies that sold coffee in the West also did business in a number of eastern areas, the Folger's brand, which was the largest brand in the West, was not distributed in most of the eastern areas.

During all of the period, the merchandising of regular coffee was carried out by the joint efforts of manufacturers and retailers. Manufacturers sponsored media advertising and redeemed coupon offers, either offered directly to consumers (consumer coupons) or offered to the consumer through retailer ads (retailer coupons). Manufacturers also provided an assortment of other discounts directly to retailers. Retailers often promoted coffee on their own as part of efforts to draw consumers to their stores. Their support for a brand included promotional activities (principally advertisements and preferred in-store positioning) or reduced retail margins.

In 1971, Procter and Gamble (P&G) initiated efforts to sell its Folger's brand in the areas of the East where it had not sold before. Folger began its roll-out in Cleveland and surrounding areas. There were subsequent roll-outs to Pittsburgh and Philadelphia in 1973 and to Syracuse in 1974. Entry into remaining areas was not begun until 1978. Folger's national expansion was completed in 1979.

Although work on the *General Foods* case began in the early 1970s, the formal complaint was not voted out until July 14, 1976. Hearings on the case started on August 20, 1979, and ended on June 19, 1981. The administrative law judge's opinion acquitting General Foods, although finding that they did price below average variable cost, was filed on January 25, 1982. The unanimous opinion of the Commission in favor of General Foods was filed on April 6, 1984. The majority opinion, which was signed by Commissioners James Miller, George Douglas, and Terry Calvani, was joined by two concurring opinions from Commissioners Michael Pertschuk and Patricia Bailey. Commissioner Pertschuk generally agreed with complaint counsel about market power and geographic market issues, but believed that a large firm, such as P&G, could not be anticompetitively harmed by predatory behavior of a smaller firm. Commissioner Bailey concurred in dismissing the case because she found no evidence that competitors had exited as a result of the alleged predation. She specifically took exception to the majority opinion's treatment of product differentiation barriers to entry.

Issues

The two primary economic questions debated in this case were: 1) Did General Foods, principally through its Maxwell House brand, have or could it acquire economic power in this market? 2) On the assumption that market power could exist in this market context, did General Foods' actions in response to Folger's entry efforts seriously threaten to reduce competition in the long run by allowing General Foods to retain or enhance its market power?

As noted earlier, these two economic questions are traditionally examined in a three-part legal test for attempted monopolization, which requires examination of the respondent's intent, conduct, and dangerous probability of success. Of these, the Commission opinion addresses itself exclusively to the last, which focuses on the economic issue of whether General Foods had and/or could obtain market power. Because General Foods' market power is so central to the analysis of this case, we will turn to this issue first, including in this discussion the crucial market definition question. We will then turn to the evidence regarding conduct and intent.

Structural Evidence of Market Power

Analysis of General Foods' market power and efficiencies is central to the determination of whether it had a dangerous probability of successfully monopolizing the market. The analyses of market power introduced in this case not only examined key structural characteristics of the market (market shares and barriers to entry), but also included a fairly detailed evaluation of available conduct and performance evidence. While economic studies historically have had trouble distinguishing cases of efficient market performance from examples of monopolization, the analysis of the coffee industry presented in this case was able to go further in this direction than most economic studies, since a much richer data set was available.

Market definition. Calculation of the market share statistics used in the structural analysis of markets requires the definition of relevant product and geographic markets. In this case, the product market was stipulated by complaint counsel and General Foods to be "all regular coffee products packaged for sale at retail, including caffeinated, decaffeinated, and extended ground coffee products."[13] However, there was substantial debate over the relevant geographic market(s).[14] The dispute over the size of the relevant geographic market(s) reflected an ongoing debate in the economics literature over the appropriate way to define markets.[15] In previous cases, the courts had often relied on transportation costs and shipment patterns to identify the appropriate geographic markets, believing that low transportation costs or long-distance shipping necessarily indicate large markets.[16] However, at the time of the *General Foods* case, economists, especially at the FTC and Justice Department, were becoming concerned that this type of evidence was not as conclusive as had been thought, since other factors that affect geographic market definition may not be reflected in this evidence. In their search for better tests of the scope of geographic markets, economists turned to direct statistical tests of pricing behavior. Indeed, the adoption of the Department of Justice Guidelines in 1982 and 1984 institutionalized this approach.[17]

The debate in the economics literature over the reliability of shipments analysis relative to price analysis is reflected in this case. Complaint counsel, relying on a price analysis that employed techniques later adopted in the Merger Guidelines, disputed the shipments-based arguments advanced by General Foods.[18]

All parties involved in the case appear to have agreed that a geographic market is an area that is insulated from other areas in the sense that a hypothetical monopolist could profitably raise prices above competitive levels for a sustained period of time. The view expressed in the Commission's majority decision was that no ability to raise coffee prices in local areas could exist. In support of this view, the majority decision noted that the ratio of transportation costs to value for coffee is relatively low. The basic notion underlying this test is that low transportation costs, especially when the product is homogeneous, are usually associated with large geographic markets because any attempt to raise price in one area can be readily undercut by shipments from other areas. Moreover, in the case of coffee, several coffee manufacturers do ship to the entire nation from a few manufacturing facilities. As a result, as the low transportation costs suggest, the hypothesis that markets are local also fails shipment pattern tests, such as the one proposed by Elzinga and Hogarty.[19]

The Commission decision also argues that efforts to price differently in different areas would be undermined by arbitrage activities, such as transshipment, trade flow, and entry.[20] Indeed, testimony about the existence of such arbitrage activities is cited as evidence of General Foods' inability to price discriminate geographically. Several incidents of successful regional entry efforts by small brands were cited for the proposition that geographical expansion by existing brands was easy.

While the majority of Commissioners concluded that coffee markets were not as small as sales districts,[21] there is substantial contradictory evidence. General Foods' planning documents indicate that it set different prices in different areas of the country for its coffee products.[22] In particular, these documents indicated that General Foods focused exclusively on firms actively distributing products in the particular area when setting prices.

The descriptions of General Foods' pricing behavior that were found in its planning documents aligned with available pricing data. Specifically, available data suggest that the discriminatory pricing guidelines described year after year in the planning documents were successfully implemented. Prices clearly varied across areas. For example, very different price promotions were offered simultaneously in neighboring sales districts. Moreover, prices were observed to fall in entry areas and then rise later without parallel price changes in neighboring (unentered) areas. As a result, we conclude that the price data for Maxwell House are more consistent with localized, rather than national, competition.

Closer scrutiny of ongoing arbitrage activities in the ground coffee market indicate that they were quite limited, despite the sizable differences in regional prices. As a result, one could conclude that, while transshipment does occur (indicating that price differences are present), it is sufficiently constrained that it does not equalize prices. And, as will be explained in detail later, entry by fringe brands is consistent with complaint counsel's mobility barriers argument, since these firms did not obtain sizable market shares.

In sum, there appears to be contradictory evidence on the issue of geographic market definition, although the evidence, we believe, is more consistent with localized geographic markets. Here we retain the possibility that there are regional markets so that the strategic theory advanced by complaint counsel can be portrayed more fully.

Market shares.   If one concludes, as the Commission majority did, that local markets are not present, then national (or close to national) share statistics become relevant. Nationally, the market share position of General Foods and its largest brand was between 29.8 percent and 35.1 percent in the 1971 to 1977 period. Since General Foods' share in a national geographic market was not overwhelmingly large, the Commission concluded that its activities could be presumed to be competitive because it could not hope to predate and then recoup its losses in this market context. However, using localized markets, the market shares of General Foods and its Maxwell House brand fit well within the usual range for attempted monopolization cases and at the lower bound for monopolization cases, especially when its relative share position is also taken into account.[23] Specifically, General Foods' shares were typically in the 35-percent to 60-percent range in eastern sales districts. In the entry areas Cleveland/Pittsburgh and Syracuse, GF's shares, just before entry, were 46.4 and 48.6 respectively. Moreover, its Maxwell House brand's share (which was typically well over 30 percent of the sales in these areas) was two to five times as large as the next largest rival brand's shares.

Barriers to entry. FTC complaint counsel argued that there were significant product differentiation barriers to entry that insulated a dominant coffee brand from other brands in the market and from potential entrants. The principal product differentiation barrier identified by Commission staff was a featuring advantage: the established dominant coffee brand appeared to have a strategic advantage because of preferential treatment by the retail trade. This product differentiation advantage was not believed to be based on a superior quality product,[24] but rather was attributed to the fact that the dominant coffee brand in a local market was viewed by the retailer as a particularly good item to feature because of consumers' *historical* purchasing patterns.[25] Retailers engage in featuring activity in order to increase store traffic and accompanying increased sales of items with normal markups. Featuring activity is an integral part of competition between retail grocery stores. As a result of its featuring advantage, the dominant incumbent could charge the same wholesale prices as an entrant and have a lower retail price.

Several aspects of the special treatment that dominant coffee brands receive appear to be critical to understanding the operation of this industry and, as a result, have major implications for subsequent parts of the analysis as well.

1. Although product preferences on the part of consumers (either from advertising or from consumption) may reinforce or contravene the "featuring" effect, the primary connection between recent purchase experience of consumers and their recognition or aware-

ness of a price reduction is independent of these other factors since it depends on the fact that the past purchasing behavior of consumers sensitizes them to recognize price changes for that brand.

2. The product differentiation is localized. Stores care about the price recognition of consumers in their own area. The fact that brand X has 50 percent of the market elsewhere is of almost no concern to the decisions of the retailers, since a retailer's preferences will be different depending on past share portions among its own potential customers. Offering a reduced price on a new brand or on a brand used primarily in other areas will not produce the same store draw, although there might be nothing inherently different about that brand.

3. The importance of historical market share levels to retailers provides a strong advantage to a dominant firm seeking to preserve its position. It can expect to retain its advantage (special treatment) in the future as long as it retains its share today. Any firm seeking to undermine the dominant firm's position or to supplant the dominant firm must have an extraordinary commitment to gain share in the current period so that subsequently it will gain retailer support.

While the majority opinion does discuss product differentiation, this discussion never comes to grips with complaint counsel's main argument. The Commission's analysis focuses on consumer behavior and whether consumers truly preferred Maxwell House, to the exclusion of any analysis of retailer behavior. As a result, the Commission's opinion does not incorporate the fact that the wholesale price premium charged by Maxwell House need not be reflected in a parallel retail shelf-price difference. In particular, it ignores the possibility, which a number of witnesses and documents supported, that Maxwell House's retail price was often close to other brands' retail prices even when its wholesale price exceeded other brands' wholesale prices.[26]

The Commission evidently believed that product differentiation barriers to entry were unlikely to be present in this industry or was skeptical of product differentiation barriers to entry in general. This view appears to have been premised on the flawed conclusion that product differentiation will not permit the monopolistic reduction of output and maintenance of prices above competitive levels by manufacturers unless the ultimate consumers cannot turn to other brands. The flaw in the Commission's product differentiation argument can be shown by considering two questions. First, can product differentiation exist at the wholesale level and not exist simultaneously at the retail level? Second, if it can, could a manufacturer charge prices above its costs as a result?

If we turn to the first question, it appears that the Commission agreed with the FTC trial staff that Maxwell House was valued at the wholesale level as a feature item. However, they deny that this reflects any significant product differentiation advantage. To support their view, the Commission argues that the leading brand draws traffic better because of its high quality.[27] However, the facts in this case do not appear to support this explanation. The most direct evidence that the Maxwell House advantage is not due to product quality or to promotional finesse is that consumers are unwilling to pay a significant premium for the leading brand (a fact that the Commission appears to acknowledge). As a result, it does not appear to be some innate characteristic of the preparation or delivery of the leading brand that caused it to be valued by retailers as a feature item, since no parallel valuation is evident at the consumer level. A supporting fact is that in other areas of the country, where other brands have historically had leading positions, these other brands receive featuring advantages, while Maxwell House does not.

The explanation for Maxwell House's "featuring" advantage in the eastern United States, which complaint counsel accepted, was that prices of dominant coffee brands are more effective in conveying impressions of relative retail store prices to consumers than are other coffee brands and that this encourages grocery retailers to use larger coffee brands as feature items.[28]

Why would the prices of leading brands provide more consumer information and result in a greater store draw? As noted earlier, consumers have better recall of the prices of the brands that they have purchased frequently and most recently. Since leading brands have both of these memory characteristics and since virtually all stores carry the leading brand, prices of leading brands garner more attention and convey more information about the general store price/quality levels than prices on other items. Since "familiarity" and the associated value as a feature item can arise without consumers viewing Maxwell House as a particularly unique type of coffee, the elasticity of demand at the wholesale level can be substantially lower than the elasticity of demand at the retail (consumer) level.

This set of circumstances is illustrated in Figure 1, where a perfectly elastic consumer demand curve and a somewhat inelastic retailer (wholesale) demand curve are plotted. Using this figure, it is possible to illustrate the possibility, raised by the second question, that a manufacturer earns a profit as a result of wholesale-level product differentiation, despite the absence of consumer-level product differentiation. In Figure 1, it is assumed that Maxwell House's consumer demand schedule is horizontal at the competitive price level where price equals the marginal production costs of coffee manufacturers. In contrast, the current wholesale demand schedule for Maxwell House (expressed by retailers) is

Figure 1
Retailer and Consumer Demand for a Featured Brand (*MH*)

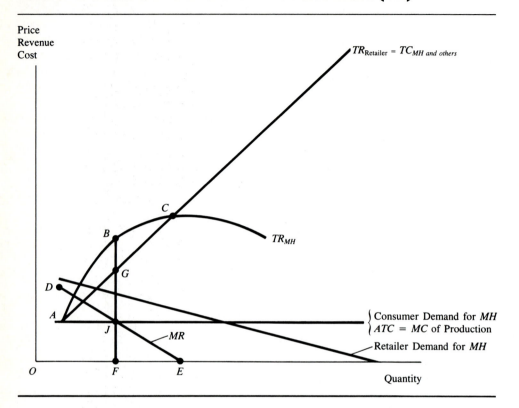

sloped downward because the attractiveness of Maxwell House as a feature item declines as its wholesale price rises. This decline in Maxwell House's attractiveness as a featuring item is attributable to the fact that higher wholesale prices imply larger retailer losses on Maxwell House (given a constant retail price) and the absence of any compensating increase in the drawing power of the brand over this range.

From this wholesale demand schedule, a total revenue curve *ABC* is drawn as well as a marginal revenue curve, *DE*. As usual, the profit-maximizing position for Maxwell House is where the marginal revenue and marginal cost curves intersect, at *J*. If Maxwell House supplies the quantity *OF*, the total revenue for Maxwell House will be *BF*. The total revenue obtained by the retailers in selling this quantity will be *FG*, with the difference being the extent of the loss leader subsidy provided by the retailers. And, as the diagram indicates, the manufacturer of Maxwell House earns a profit of *BG*. Thus, the finding of a price premium at the consumer level is not necessary to a finding of product-differentiation-based market power.[29]

To the extent that the position of dominant incumbent coffee brands is correctly reflected in Figure 1, de novo entrants and established firms that are not viewed as particularly good brands to feature are at a disadvantage. In other words, a mobility barrier insulates the dominant brand.

This mobility barrier not only arises from the difference between the incumbent's strategic position today and a potential entrant's position today, but from the difference between the position of today's potential entrant and the incumbent's position when it entered. While it is difficult to chart Maxwell House's movement to its current dominant position in the East, it appears likely that it did not face the types of rivals that Folger faced at the time it tried to enter the East. Moreover, to the extent that Maxwell House can alter the market environment so that the costs of its entering rivals are raised relative to its own costs, it can insulate itself further.[30] As a result, Maxwell House may have a "first mover" advantage. Unfortunately, historical data to test this theory more fully were not obtained, due to a ruling by the ALJ.

Perhaps because the majority never directly dealt with complaint counsel's theoretical arguments about barriers to entry in these markets, their interpretation and presentation of the facts also differs. For example, the majority opinion recited several examples of entry in the coffee industry, indicating that this undermined complaint counsel's view that barriers to entry are present. In contrast, complaint counsel viewed these entry experiences as evidence that there were mobility barriers that inhibited large-scale entry, since these entry efforts suggested that anything except entry at the "fringe" was very difficult.

Close scrutiny of the entry efforts cited by the majority reveals that in none of them did the entrant displace the dominance of the leading brand, when that brand had a sizable share advantage.[31] For example, General Foods struggled in the West to gain market share from Folger and failed. Hills, a leading brand in some areas, tried to gain on General Foods in the East after an entry effort in the 1960s and failed. Chock Full O'Nuts never achieved more than an eighteen-percent share in any retail market, despite a strong reputation in New York City.[32] And, Folger's entry was deflected, so that Folger's share came at the expense of secondary brands, not General Foods.[33] Given that those recent coffee entries resulted in only small shares for the entrants, even after several years, the evidence at the time of the trial was strongly supportive of complaint counsel's mobility barrier theory.

The majority's treatment of the entry evidence highlights another difference between the Commission's perspective and the trial staff's strategic view of barriers to entry. For the majority, entry barriers are discussed as a black and white issue. Either all entry is impossible or no barriers exist. The staff view was that potential entrants may have different skills and resources, so that what are large hurdles for most potential entrants may be manageable for a select few. In other words, the staff took the view that potential entrants could be ranked. Moreover, they believed that Procter & Gamble was at the top of the small queue of firms that had the management talent and coffee organization to mount a potentially effective challenge to General Foods in the East.[34] As a result, the deflection of Folger's entry effort seriously reduced the number of significant challengers in the lists, as well as enhanced General Foods' reputation as an effective guardian of its dominant position.

Conduct and Performance Evidence of Market Power

Economists have used profit and price data to test many of the theories proposed in the industrial organization literature. While the use of data on profit performance and pricing conduct has been a traditional part of empirical analyses, the FTC staff recognized that these data are not without flaws.[35] As a result, a variety of sensitivity analyses and confirmatory tests were performed. Moreover, the simultaneous availability of profit and price data along with market share data for the same geographic areas and time periods gave the trial staff a relatively rare data set that allowed the staff to perform some tests that are normally not feasible.

The trial staff started by asking the simple question: Were General Foods' profits higher in the eastern markets where it was thought to have market power? The basic answer appeared to be yes. Not only did General Foods think it was doing extremely well in its own analysis of the data,[36] but the actual profit numbers (both nationally and regionally) showed that General Foods was making unusually high profits in its regular coffee business.[37] Indeed, an analysis of General Foods eastern coffee profits showed it was earning over 1.5 times the "All Manufacturing" average, which would put it in the top 5 percent of profitable firms reported by Compustat.[38]

Since accounting profits, rather than economic profits, had to be used for this analysis, additional tests were performed to see if these profitability numbers made sense. Perhaps the most informative study was one that correlated profits to share, prices to share, and profits to prices.[39] This study, performed for different years, found that prices were correlated positively and significantly with market share (the simple correlation coefficient ranged from .438 to .725), as were profits (.547 to .873). Moreover, profits appeared to be positively correlated with prices (.811 to .973). These results suggested that the profits were high in the eastern United States because prices were high, not because costs were low. Furthermore, these empirical results confirmed General Foods' "pricing principles," that it could charge higher prices where it had higher market shares.[40]

The majority dismisses this analysis without directly explaining why the correlation study was not an important finding. Perhaps the Commission's disregard for these findings was due to the fact that the study employed a cross-sectional analysis of geographic markets that was thought by the Commission majority to be incorrect and the fact that the findings contradicted their view that product differentiation barriers to entry are unlikely to exist in this industry.

With respect to the first of these possibilities, the Commission's assumption that markets are local is directly refuted by these statistical results, since the statistical significance of the results suggests that the use of local markets helps to predict prices. After all, if markets were not local, it would be highly unlikely that local shares would be related to local profits and prices in the way they were in these statistical studies. And, with respect to the second possibility, it appears to be based on a flawed theoretical treatment of product differentiation barriers to entry, as was pointed out above.

In sum, the structure, conduct, and performance of the ground coffee market suggests that dominant brands may have some market power. However, this evidence should not be taken to imply that the presence of a dominant brand indicates that there necessarily is an antitrust problem. Indeed, absent evidence of predatory or other unfair activities, a brand's dominance is likely to reflect socially beneficial activities. For this case, it is hard to determine whether GF's advantageous position was the product of socially beneficial effort or historical strategic activities. However, even if one assumes that GF's market position was thrust upon it, as a result of diligent procompetitive actions, the use of anticompetitive strategies to protect its current position would not be excused. As a result, evidence of anticompetitive activities that injure competition is key to the determination of whether an antitrust problem exists. The following section addresses this issue.

Intent and Conduct

Once the Commission determined that there was not a dangerous probability of success at monopolization, their analysis stopped and no intent or conduct evidence was reviewed. In contrast, complaint counsel structured their briefs so that this evidence was encountered first, suggesting that they felt it was particularly strong. Moreover, they argued that this evidence could be used to test whether General Foods had a dangerous probability of success. Along these lines, trial staff believed that General Foods' aggressive response was consistent with their argument that General Foods' product differentiation advantage (and associated profits) was rooted in historical purchasing patterns that could be disrupted by a particularly aggressive entrant, rather than in an intrinsically superior product.

As noted earlier, the Commission's inclination to disregard the conduct and intent evidence may have stemmed from suspicion that it would be difficult to assess the reliability of this evidence.[41] Indeed, in analyzing the intent and conduct of an alleged predator, there is some dispute among economists over what types of evidence are relevant. Some economists argue that all or most company documents are useless in analyzing these types of market events.[42] While it is true that braggadocio on the part of employees can lead to overdrawn conclusions, it would appear incorrect to conclude that all internal corporate documents are misleading.[43] In particular, documents laying forth alternative strategies and expected results as part of a firm's decision-making routine may be very helpful in assessing conditions in the industry and the rationale underlying actions that are ultimately taken. After all, business executives who set prices and must survive in the market have substantial knowledge of the structure of the industry and what types of tactics will work given that structure. As a result, we do not believe that such market-tested information should be completely disregarded. Therefore, the following section includes references to several of General Foods' documents that seem particularly helpful in analyzing the events and that do not appear to be examples of braggadocio that should be dismissed.

Three aspects of General Foods' conduct warrant examination: its pricing in the entry markets, its pricing in selected other markets, and its introduction of Horizon. With respect to pricing in the entry markets, Maxwell House was clearly sold below variable cost in localized areas,[44] for long periods of time.[45] Specifically, using a fairly conservative version of this Areeda-Turner test,[46] the trial staff found sales below average variable costs in Cleveland, Pittsburgh, and Syracuse for periods of at least a year, and in some cases longer. Since some volume-based allocations were used, the staff performed some sensitivity tests. The results suggested that the finding of sales below cost was largely insensitive to numerous variations in the treatment of cost elements, including the treatment of advertising completely as a long-term investment. Documents of the firm even state that Maxwell House was sold below the firm's own price floor, which was itself below most accepted definitions of variable cost.[47] Moreover, at times the price of Maxwell House was less than the price of the green coffee beans that were roasted by General Foods and then ground and packaged to make the coffee.[48]

Complaint counsel did not limit their proof of the likelihood that GF's pricing conduct would succeed to inferences from its studies of market share and pricing relationships. They also introduced direct evidence of recoupment in the Youngstown district. Youngstown was the first area entered by Folger. After two entry programs within this district (Cleveland (1971) and Pittsburgh (1973)), including below variable cost pricing and massive promotional campaigns, Maxwell House was able to restore higher prices, characteristic of the pre-entry period, with only modest loss in market share.

Figure 2 shows Youngstown profits and relative prices over the

Figure 2
Relative Price and Profits for Regular Maxwell House Youngstown Sales District

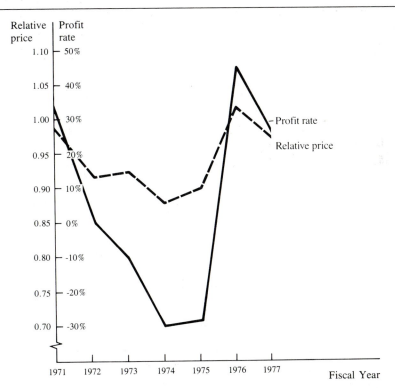

Note: Relative price equals price in Youngstown divided by the national average price.
     Profit equals after-tax return on funds employed.
     Price equals (net sales-promotions)/volume.

Source: CX 897 A-ZZ16, CX987 Z17-Z165

period. Contrary to the presumption stated in the Commission's decision that recoupment could not take place, a return to high profits and high prices is quite evident. Moreover, Youngstown prices and profits returned to the positions predicted by the share-price and share-profits regression lines that characterized the market before Folger entered, suggesting General Foods preserved its share-price premium relationship.[49] If one believed that a more successful Folger entry would have increased competition in the market, then this diagram suggests that there was actual harm to competition, whether or not rivals were forced to exit and whether or not the entrant was a large firm.[50]

Finally, the documents of General Foods make it quite clear that the strategy of selling below cost was intended to deflect Folger's entry and was expected to leave Maxwell House in a dominant position with higher prices and profits than would have been the case had General Foods utilized less aggressive strategies. For example, RX 518 is a General Foods planning document that reports the findings of simulation studies that tested various alternative strategies in a structural model of the coffee industry. As testimony by General Foods' financial expert explained, this document shows that sales below cost were quite intentional and rational.[51] Specifically, this document indicates:

> (1) that General Foods considered alternative responses, some involving above cost sales and others involving below cost sales;[52] (2) that the strategy of selling below cost was more profitable in the long run; and (3) that the higher profits were due to higher long-run prices and lower advertising levels, indicating lower levels of competition in the long run when sales below cost were employed in the short run.

Pricing below cost was just one of several tactics employed by General Foods in the Folger entry areas. General Foods increased advertising several fold, perhaps to reduce consumer responsiveness to Folger advertisements.[53] Similarly, General Foods tried to preempt or bracket Folger consumer coupons to discourage trial or repeat purchasing of Folger. All of these tactics had the effect of muddying Folger's "read" of the effectiveness of its entry effort. Evidence indicates that Folger delayed further entry in part because of these test-market distortion effects. This may have allowed Maxwell House to enjoy higher profits in unentered areas for several additional years, although confounding events, such as a freeze that affected green coffee bean prices, make it hard to determine the extent of this effect.

With respect to pricing in other geographic markets, the record shows a distinct effort by Maxwell House to "signal" Folger to reduce its competitive efforts in the Maxwell House dominated markets. Maxwell House undertook major increases in advertising and below-cost pricing timed explicitly to correspond to changes in Folger activities in two of Folger's largest markets. When Maxwell House felt threatened in Youngstown, it sent a signal to Folger by greatly increasing its selling activities in Kansas City. When Folger entered Pittsburgh and Philadelphia, Maxwell House increased its sales activities in Dallas.[54] When Folger slackened the pace of its efforts in Youngstown, Maxwell House reduced its activities in Kansas City.[55]

These events were not coincidental. Maxwell House documents that discuss the strategy underlying these efforts make it clear that they purposefully targeted Folger's largest markets.[56] Indeed, General Foods measured the success of these ventures, in part, by the costs to Folger of responding to Maxwell House, rather than by the benefits to Maxwell House in these areas.[57] By advancing a counter move into Folger's major markets, Maxwell House was able to reverse the loss relationship and greatly increase the marginal costs to Folger of pursuing its entry efforts.[58]

The third major response by General Foods to Folger was the introduction of Horizon in two sections of the districts entered by Folger. While new product introductions are generally to be applauded, Horizon was apparently introduced chiefly to disrupt the trial and entry efforts of Folger. The brand was originated and evaluated primarily on the basis of its contribution to reducing Folger's share of the market.[59] Given this, its previous failures in distribution,[60] and the precise timing and location of its introduction, it appears to us that Horizon was a fighting brand.

Further Analysis

In *General Foods,* the Federal Trade Commission broke with attempted monopolization precedents that required the weighing of 1) conduct, 2) intent, and 3) dangerous probability of success evidence. Instead, the Commission employed a sequential analysis that requires only an exploration of evidence concerning the dangerous probability of success when that evidence suggests that the accused firm lacks market power. In addition, the Commission narrowed the types of evidence that it is willing to consider when determining whether there is a dangerous probability of success.

What are the effects of these two changes on the efficiency of attempted monopolization law? Specifically, do these adjustments change the law so that guilty firms are now more likely to be found innocent? Are innocent firms now less likely to be found guilty? And, if there is this trade-off between the two types of errors, does the change appear to be in the right direction? In answering these questions, it is helpful to treat the two changes implemented by the Commission separately, since they are somewhat independent changes and the support for each change differs somewhat.

If we turn first to the Commission's adoption of a sequential analysis that requires preliminary evaluation of a firm's market power before conduct and intent evidence is considered, it is immediately apparent that this change streamlines the court proceeding.[61] If the Commission can always correctly determine whether a firm accused of attempted monopolization has market power without considering conduct or intent evidence, then its sequential procedure will not lead to errors that are also avoided using the traditional tripartite approach. However, if the Commission does make mistakes in its analysis of market power that can be offset by an analysis of conduct and intent evidence, then the Commission's sequential analysis may be biased relative to the traditional approach. Specifically, the Commission's test is more likely to find guilty firms to be innocent. Offsetting this bias is the fact that, compared to the traditional approach, which may also err, the Commission's test is less likely to find innocent firms to be guilty.

Despite its bias, does the Commission's procedure improve market efficiency? The answer to this question depends critically on market characteristics and the ability of courts to make correct appraisals of these characteristics. For example, assume that: 1) p is the probability that a firm accused of attempted monopolization is actually guilty; 2) m is the probability that a court correctly evaluates the market power of an accused firm; 3) c is the probability that a court correctly evaluates the conduct (and intent) of an accused firm; and 4) w is the probability that the court chooses to ignore the conduct (and intent) evidence when its interpretation of this evidence contradicts its interpretation of market power evidence. If one also assumes that the only difference between the Commission's attempted monopolization test and the traditional test is the sequential structure of the Commission's test, one can calculate: 1) the probability ($P1$) of correctly identifying firms that attempt to monopolize; 2) the probability ($P2$) of correctly identifying firms that are innocent of attempted monopolization; 3) the probability ($P3$) of incorrectly identifying firms that attempt monopolization as innocent; 4) the probability ($P4$) of incorrectly identifying firms that are innocent as attempted monopolizers.

If one also assumes that $L1$ is the loss that results when a guilty firm is incorrectly found to be innocent of attempted monopolization and $L2$ is the loss that results when an innocent firm is incorrectly found to be an attempted monopolist, one can also calculate the relative social welfare effects of the two standards.[62]

From the resulting probability equations, it is evident that the probability of incorrectly identifying a guilty firm as innocent is higher under the Commission's test by an amount equal to $p(1-m)(c)(1-w)$. Similarly, it is evident that the probability of incorrectly identifying an innocent firm as guilty is higher under the traditional test by $(1-p)(m)$ $(1-c)(1-w)$. This implies that the difference in the welfare loss associated with the two tests depends critically on the size of the probability that collusion actually occurs (p), the probability that the court can correctly determine whether market power is present (m), and the probability that the court can correctly identify whether anticompetitive conduct was employed (c). Specifically, the lower the probability that attempted monopolization actually occurred, the better the Commission's test performs relative to the traditional test. The higher the probability that the court correctly evaluates the presence of market power, the better the Commission's test performs relative to the traditional test.[63] And the worse courts are at appraising conduct (and intent) evidence, the better the Commission's test performs relative to the traditional test.

Table 1 reports the results of some sensitivity tests that illustrate how variations in assumptions about the probabilities of $p,m,c,$ and w can alter the probabilities of courts making the two types of mistakes. In addition, it adds the probability that the court incorrectly finds a guilty firm to be innocent ($P3$) to the probability that the court finds an innocent firm to be guilty ($P4$) to allow a comparison of the welfare effects of the rules under the assumption that the two losses ($L1$ and $L2$) are equal.

Table 1 confirms the relationships derived directly from the equa-

Table 1 Sensitivity of Mistake Probabilities To Underlying Assumptions

| | | | | Probability of Court Mistakes | | | | | |
| | Parameter Values | | | Traditional Rule | | | Commission Rule | | |
p	m	c	w	P3	P4	Sum	P3	P4	Sum
.01	.9	.3	.9	.002	.158	.160	.002	.096	.098
.01	.5	.5	.5	.005	.495	.500	.008	.371	.370*
.01	.9	.9	.5	.001	.099	.100	.001	.054	.056*
.10	.8	.5	.8	.026	.234	.260	.028	.162	.190
.10	.8	.5	.5	.035	.315	.350	.040	.135	.175
.10	.8	.8	.5	.020	.180	.200	.028	.108	.136
.30	.8	.8	.5	.060	.140	.200	.084	.084	.168
.30	.5	.8	.5	.105	.245	.350	.165	.210	.375
.70	.8	.8	.5	.140	.060	.200	.196	.036	.232
.70	.3	.8	.3	.245	.105	.350	.519	.092	.611

*Differs from sum of columns shown due to rounding.

tions. In addition, it shows that if the Commission believed that the probability of predation actually occurring is about 10 percent of all instances of alleged predation (as measured by antitrust cases initiated), that its test for market power is correct around 80 percent of the time, that tests based on conduct evidence are correct only 50 percent of the time, and that courts reject market power findings in favor of conflicting conduct findings about 50 percent of the time, then the Commission's rule is preferable to the traditional rule, since it makes 12 percent fewer mistakes. In contrast, if predation occurs more frequently (e.g., around 70 percent of all cases), if courts' market power and conduct tests are both correct about 80 percent of the time, and if courts rely on conduct and intent findings 50 percent of the time when they conflict with market power findings, then the traditional test is superior. It makes mistakes only 20 percent of the time, compared to the Commission rule's 28.8-percent rate.

Using the Commission's premises that predation is unlikely, that the cost of incorrectly finding predation when it did not occur is high, that the monopoly losses associated with rare cases of predation are small, and that cost-based tests are uncertain identifiers of predation, our calculations suggest that the Commission's test may be superior to the traditional tripartite test. As indicated above, these gains come from the fact that fewer innocent firms will be incorrectly found to be guilty of attempted monopolization.

While our analysis suggests that the Commission's new rule does well if market behavior aligns with Commission expectations, it also indicates the importance of the Commission's expectations. As a result, a complete analysis must consider how accurate these expectations are. In reviewing the empirical literature on attempted monopolization (principally predation) cases, we find that relatively little data have been collected and systematically analyzed. To our knowledge, there have been no quantifications of any of the probabilities that are key to the model we described above, except for the probability (p) that predation actually occurred in cases that were brought to trial.

With respect to these studies, it appears that the Commission view is supported by early studies of predation.[64] For example, Koller (1971) found that relatively few, perhaps less than 15 percent, of a sample of cases alleging predation actually involved true predation.[65] However, more recent studies contradict these earlier studies, suggesting that predation may be more frequent than was thought to be the case. For example, Zerbe and Cooper (1982) suggests that perhaps 68 percent of all predation cases may have involved true predation. Moreover, surveys of predation cases have not consistently performed careful evaluations of predation cases using strategic perspectives, such as raising rivals' costs arguments. As a result, it may be that the probability of predation is substantially higher than the Commission thought it was at the time it wrote the *General Foods* opinion.

The second change in analysis the Commission made in its *General Foods* opinion involved a shift in the evidence it was willing to consider when determining whether a firm has market power. Unlike earlier courts, and many economists,[66] the Commission chose not to consider information about General Foods' conduct and intent when assessing the firm's dangerous probability of success. Not only was substantial evidence of sales below cost disregarded,[67] but the Commission dismissed, with minimal analysis,[68] evidence on variations in prices across areas, the relationship between prices, shares, and profits, the profitability of General Foods' coffee division relative to other manufacturing activities, and the recoupment of losses through subsequent price increases.

The Commission's narrowly focused analysis of evidence regarding the dangerous probability of success not only caused it to ignore substantial empirical evidence that had been introduced into the record, but led it to disregard complaint counsel's strategic arguments. For example, complaint counsel's arguments that were based on the presence of mobility barriers are not considered in the Commission's treatment of barriers to entry. And complaint counsel's discussion of the importance of retailer behavior in the determination of wholesale demand was not considered, leading the Commission to mischaracterize complaint counsel's product differentiation analysis.

By narrowing the type of information that is considered to be evidence of firm market power, the Commission altered the probability that it would correctly find market power when it exists. To the extent the Commission's narrowing of the evidence simply omits misleading information, it has improved the probability that it will correctly assess a firm's dangerous probability of success. However, it appears that the narrowing of the relevant data probably went too far. Valuable information was not treated carefully, and facts that challenged accepted propositions were ignored. As a result, it appears likely that the Commission reduced the probability that it will correctly determine whether market power is present or absent.

A shift in the probability that a court correctly assesses whether market power is present or not is key to the welfare implications of both the traditional and Commission procedures. However, given the sequential nature of the Commission's rule, the Commission's test is particularly sensitive to changes in the size of this probability. As Table 1 indicates, a reduction in this probability will substantially reduce the accuracy of the test by increasing the chance that guilty firms are found to be innocent. For example, if the probability of correctly evaluating market power (m) fell from .8 to .5, the chance of making a mistake may almost double.[69]

Together, the two changes greatly reduce the probability that courts will find accused firms guilty of attempted monopolization. While this means that fewer innocent firms will be found to be guilty, it also means that more firms will be able to monopolize without being found guilty.

Conclusions

The *General Foods* case highlights the strengths and weaknesses of the analytical approach the Commission adopted in trying to adjust attempted monopolization law to some of the changes in the economic understanding of strategic behavior. For those who believe that General Foods did not predate, the Commission's sequential analysis and narrowing of the information it considers appears to have been successful. By streamlining the analysis in these ways, the Commission (and possibly less disciplined courts) steers clear of troublesome behavioral data that might "confuse" matters and lead to incorrect decisions. However, for those who believe that General Foods' response to Folger reduced the procompetitive effects of Folger's entry,[70] the biases in the Commission's test appear to have led it to ignore germane conduct and intent evidence that would have led to a different conclusion.

Our review of the Commission's decision in *General Foods* is mixed. On one hand, we think that the sequential analysis employed by the Commission is attractive. It may be easier to analyze a firm's market power than its conduct and intent (since there is more information), and this approach should reduce litigation costs. However, we have substantial reservations about the Commission's limitation of the information it considers when evaluating market power. Most importantly, we believe an analysis of firm conduct and market performance can be quite helpful in analyzing market power, particularly in monopolization and attempted monopolization cases.

Notes

1. See, e.g., the Supreme Court's decision in *Continental T.V.* v. *GTE Sylvania* 433 U.S. 36 (1977).
2. *General Foods Corp.*, 3 Trade Reg. Rep. (CCH) Par. 22, 142 (April 6, 1984) and *I.T.T. Continental Banking Co.*, 3 Trade Reg. Rep.

(CCH) Par. 22,188 (July 25, 1984). The Supreme Court has not treated these issues directly. However, in *Matsushiita Electric Industrial Co. Ltd., et al* v. *Zenith Radio Corp. et al,* 475 U.S. 574 (1986), the Supreme Court found that predation is only rational if there are "corresponding gains," which emphasizes the importance of market power in predation analysis. And even more recently in *Monfort of Colorado, Inc.* v. *Cargill, Inc.,* 107 S. Ct. 484 (1986), the Supreme Court noted the importance of barriers to entry and market share (key indicia of market power) to finding a likelihood that predation would be successful (note 14).

3. See for example, *E.J. DuPont de Nemours & Co.,* 96 F.T.C. 653 (1980). The Commission's approach, which focuses on the dangerous probability of success element was followed by the staff in designing its remedy, which was limited to areas where the staff felt General Foods had market power. Interestingly, the staff's decision in this area predated an article that presented a formal proposal to approach predatory pricing cases in this way, but was later cited by both the Commission and the staff. See Paul Joskow and Alvin Klevorick (1979).

4. *General Foods Corp.,* 22975–6.

5. Former FTC Chairman Miller who authored the *General Foods* decision wrote: "If the historical literature is to be believed, cases of successful predation are exceedingly rare. And if the theoretical literature is to be believed, this is no accident. Low prices are much more likely to be a reflection of aggressive competition than predation—successful or otherwise. . . . The economic and legal theories of predation are among the most complex in antitrust. One reason is the difficulty of determining whether a specific business practice undermines competition or is part of the competitive process. . . . It is the result of such aggressiveness by competitors that provides the benefits of competition to consumers; lower prices, higher quality options. For obvious reasons, then, it is paramount that enforcement of laws against predation should not be used to stifle normal competitive impulses." Miller and Pautler (1985).

6. See Porter (1976), Caves and Porter (1977), and Porter (1980).

7. Porter (1980, 132). A "strategic group" is composed of those firms that compete most directly with each other, often employing the same types of marketing and production techniques. Firms within a strategic group are to some degree insulated from competition of firms outside the group, but still in the industry, by differences in product attributes, promotional techniques, or other demand or cost characteristics. For example, generic products and store brands may compete in substantially different ways than national branded products, and thus may be in different strategic groups.

8. For theoretical discussion of first mover advantages, see Schmalensee (1982), Folsom and Greer (1980), Whitten (1979), and Bond and Lean (1979).

9. For a discussion of how this can affect analysis of competition at the manufacturing level, see Steiner (1978), Steiner (1984), Lynch (1986), and Nelson and Hilke (1986).

10. The trial staff was aware of Williamson (1968).

11. Harrison (1985). For theoretical support, see Milgrom and Roberts (1982) and Kreps and Wilson (1982).

12. General Foods' Atlanta, Boston, Charlotte, Jacksonville, New York, Philadelphia, Syracuse and Youngstown, sales districts (CX 1072). The areas appear to have been primarily determined by retailer warehousing patterns, so that it basically included all cities served by warehouses that also served Cleveland. Note: In the following discussion, documents submitted into evidence will be cited by their number. CX refers to FTC exhibits and RX refers to respondent's exhibits. In addition, the trial findings will be indicated as follows: CPF (Complaint Counsel's Proposed Findings), RPF (Respondent's Proposed Findings), ALJ (Administrative Law Judge's Decision), and CD (Commission's Majority Decision).

13. Empirical studies support this conclusion. See Huang, Siegfried and Zardoshty (1980).

14. Prehearing conference, Tr. 79–84. Since both parties agreed to this definition, no evidence was organized to support this product market definition. However, public documents suggest there was some basis for this definition. General Foods' pricing documents show that regular Maxwell House focused on the prices of other ground coffees, largely ignoring the price of instant coffee. Indeed, it is rare for instant coffee to be mentioned in documents discussing ground coffee. Furthermore, it is fairly clear that the profit margin on instant coffee exceeded that for ground coffee, perhaps with fewer trade deals, but more consumer promotion (CX 652). Moreover, Huang, Siegfried and Zardoshty (1980) report empirical results that support the treatment of regular and instant coffee as separate markets.

    While the market share position of GF would not change by very much if instant coffee was included in the market, the strategic analysis changes a little. One motive for a predatory response by General Foods is that it might delay entry into instant coffee sales, which makes more sense if instant is a closely related, but not identical, product.

15. Much of this debate is reprinted in Elzinga and Rogowsky (1984).

16. In *United States* v. *Hammermill Paper Co.* 429 F.Supp. 1271 (1977) and *Golden Grain Macaroni Co.* 78 FTC 63 (1971) *aff'd* 472 F.2d 882 (1972), *cert. denied,* 412 U.S. 918 (1973), transportation costs to define geographic markets were approved. In *General Telephone & Electronics Corp.* v. *International Telephone & Telegraph Cor.* 351 F.Supp. 1153, 1174 (1972), *aff'd in pertinent part,* 518 F.2d 913, 937 (1975) and *RSR Corp.,* 88 FTC 800 (1976), the use of shipments data to define markets is approved.

17. The 1982 Department of Justice Merger Guidelines argue that the key question is: Could a monopolist profitably raise prices in one area without such an effort being frustrated by flows of product from other areas? See the Merger Guidelines issued by the Justice Department on June 14, 1982. Also see the Guidelines issued on June 14, 1984.

18. Most notably, complaint counsel looked for evidence of geographic price discrimination, which the Merger Guidelines recognize as

evidence of separate geographic markets. See the Merger Guidelines, p. 14 in the 1982 version and Section 2.32 in the 1984 edition.

19. Elzinga and Hogarty (1973).

20. Transshipment occurs when product sold and delivered to one warehouse (usually at a low price) is reshipped by the retailer to another warehouse for sale to consumers in that second area. Trade flow occurs when a single warehouse serves two areas in which a manufacturer is trying to charge different prices. Goods are purchased by the warehouse at the lower price and sold in both areas.

21. The minority opinion notes that the geographic market may be smaller than the majority opinion contends. See the Concurring Opinion of Commissioner Bailey, pp. 1 and 2, and the Concurring Opinion of Commissioner Pertschuk, footnote 2.

22. For example, one document states: "RMH (Regular Maxwell House) uses case rates (trade deals) tailored to each market to achieve parity shelf pricing" (CPF 10-19). Other documents illustrate this observation in some detail. One tactic that could be used to limit the effect of transshipment was the use of coupons (particularly retailer coupons) to cut the price of coffee in a particular geographic area. Retailer coupons would only be distributed and could only be redeemed in the designated area (CPF 10-253).

23. Where market shares are not evenly distributed, an absolute market share of 50 percent may be enough to establish that a given firm possesses monopoly power. *Broadway Delivery Corp.* v. *United Parcel Service,* 1981-1 Trade Cases Para. 64,068 at 76,469 (1981). An absolute share of 40 percent has been enough to establish the dangerous probability that a firm will acquire monopoly power. E.g., *Times-Picayune Publishing Co.* v. *United States,* 345 U.S. 594 at 612-13 and n. 3 (1953).

24. On the basis of objective blind taste tests conducted by General Foods, there was no evidence that Maxwell House was a superior product. General Foods' witnesses indicated that Maxwell House was, at best, a parity product to Folger (King, Tr. 5620; RLA at 183). Folger actually was preferred in many taste tests (CX 966C). Hills was also preferred over Maxwell House in some taste tests (RX 940Z126; Clinton, Tr. 4917). Even in the most complementary test results on the record, 50 percent of normal Maxwell House users did not prefer Maxwell House to Hills; 32 percent of Maxwell House users did not prefer Maxwell House to Hills; 32 percent of Maxwell House users actually preferred Hills to Maxwell House (RX 953Z9; King, Tr. 5656).

25. According to complaint counsel, grocery stores utilize coffee as a store draw, a signal of the overall price level in the store. In order to use the lower price of coffee to attract customers to their store, retailers frequently will offer a coffee brand at a lower than usual retail price by reducing their margin on that brand. With this background in mind, the product differentiation advantage arises because retailers give more support (accept lower margins) on the brand that had the largest share in previous periods. They are willing to do this because they expect a larger response to reduced prices on the leading brand because more consumers will recognize that a price

reduction has occurred on the brand that most of them have purchased frequently and recently. Again, it is this relationship between historical share levels and retailer support that creates the product differentiation advantage and the mobility barrier. The leading firm in the prior period can obtain a higher wholesale price from the retailer for an equal shelf price to consumers.

26. See, for example, CPF 11-79 through 11-80.

27. CD p. 57.

28. See Nelson and Hilke (1986) for a more complete exposition.

29. Since the Commission decision implicitly recognizes this retailer preference, the decision implicitly recognizes this scenario is possible. See CD p. 55.

30. This cost asymmetry raises barriers to entry because the incumbent can charge prices above its costs, yet entrants would lose money if they charged the same price. For example, if the entry cost was $100 (the cost of differentiating one's product) for the incumbent and is $500 for the potential entrant, the entrant must charge a price that is higher since it must recover $500, while the incumbent must only recover $100 for entry to be profitable. As a result, the incumbent can raise its price above its break-even level.

31. Hills' decline and Folger's growth in Chicago is the only example in the record of a market leader losing its number one position. However, Hills' decline in Chicago may have been due to general problems at the company (Toy, 2190-2191).

32. CX 1072 and CPF 11-13. Chock Full O'Nuts currently advertises that it is the largest brand in New York City. However, this is probably based on its sales through its own restaurants as well as through grocers.

33. In 1971, GF had 46.4 percent in Youngstown. And in 1977, after the entry struggle, it had 55.7 percent. Folger's share was falling in the late 1970s in Youngstown.

34. Procter & Gamble's Folger was thought to be at the head of the queue since it was the largest brand in Western markets and Procter and Gamble had a history of successfully rolling out to national markets. Nestle was thought to be a second possibility, since it produced freeze-dried coffee. In the 1980s Nestle acquired Hills, Chase & Sanborn, and MJB coffees altering the competitive structure. Nestle's decision to acquire leading ground coffee brands, rather than build its own ground business based on its instant franchise, is consistent with the view that ground coffee is a separate market and that product differentiation barriers are significant.

35. Fisher and McGowan (1983). For comments supporting the use of accounting data, see Long and Ravenscraft (1984).

36. General Foods' own documents indicate that it viewed its ground coffee business as a "cash generator" with "few peers in American business" (AB p. 34). In addition, General Foods' documents indicated that 82 percent of the volume, but 92 percent of the profit came from the eastern markets where it had a high relative share (AB p. 34). Thus, the FTC's profit calculations appear to align with General Foods' internal view of its profitability.

37. According to accounting profit calculations performed by Professor

John Dearden, the 1971–1977 average after-tax rate of return on invested funds ranged from 20.5 percent to 39.7 percent in markets where Maxwell House had a total share advantage and did not face Folger's entry (AB p. 31).

38. P. Nelson, 11231–11233.

39. The share data reflect Maxwell House's market share in different sales districts. The profit data report the return on funds invested in the Maxwell House brand for the sales district. And the price data are average prices defined as revenues less all trade and consumer deals, including coupons. Correlation tests based on relative Maxwell House shares produced similar results. General Foods' advertising agency did similar statistical studies in 1972 and 1975 and obtained similar results (CX-1 and CX468). General Foods' executives found the results of this study to be in line with their expectations (CPF 11-32 to 11-33).

40. The trade-dealing principles for regular Maxwell House summarized from respondent's business documents are:
a) If the competitive share is less than 30 percent of Maxwell House's share, the competitor is not a significant factor; b) If the competitive share is between 30 to 50 percent of Maxwell House's share (less than 3-1), Maxwell House's shelf pricing objective is to be within 10 cents per pound higher than the competitor; c) If the competitive share is between 50 and 70 percent of Maxwell House's share (less than 2-1), Maxwell House's shelf pricing objective is to deal to be within the same decile; d) If the competitive share is greater than 70 percent (less than 1.5-1), Maxwell House's shelf pricing objective is to deal for absolute parity [decile parity means that prices would be in the same 10-cent range, e.g., 90–99 cents (CPF 11-42)].

41. "...the information needed to apply simple price-cost predation rules is difficult to obtain and subject to great uncertainty. Where a firm produces many products, the proper allocation of joint or common production costs is difficult, at best. Similarly, the allocation of costs related to advertising and promotion causes problems when expenses cover different markets as when they have a time component due to the investment nature of providing consumer information" Miller and Pautler (1985, at 498).

42. See, for example, Areeda and Turner (1975).

43. Some "colorful cites" from the *General Foods* case do align with economic tests for predation. For example, General Foods documents repeatedly indicate a desire to increase its market share in response to Folger's entry (CPF 3-114), which violates Williamson's (1977) proposed standard for predation that focuses on efforts to increase output in response to entry. And statements like "Provide the dominance (apparently referring to efforts to increase share) necessary to exert leverage, hold dealing down, restore long-term profitability" (CPF 3-114); "Delay Folger expansion" (CPF 3-142); and "Force them (Folger) to carefully consider the financial wisdom of further eastern expansion" (CPF 3-163) all align with the FTC staff's economic theory of the case. Other "colorful cites" employed by the staff have significantly less economic merit. For example, an Ogilvy and Mather executive who participated in General Foods' response

likened its western offensive to the "Bombing of Hanoi" (CPF 5-10) and General Foods documents referred to it as the "eye-for-eye" retaliation (CPF 5-11).

44. While the trial team used various accounting costs in their price-cost comparisons, it is also clear that Maxwell House was sold below "competitive opportunity costs." Since a competitive firm is a price taker, the prices in other eastern markets can be viewed as the "competitive opportunity costs" of selling another unit in a Folger entry area, under the null hypothesis of competitive markets and a competitive response. Since prices in the entry markets were well below prices in other eastern markets, prices were clearly below "competitive opportunity costs." However, we think the more straightforward accounting comparisons are more probative.

45. Although the Commission did not approve of the concept of adjusting its definition of variable costs to fit the duration of the challenged conduct in the *General Foods* case, it did accept this concept in the settlement of the *ReaLemon* (Borden) case. See the "Statement of the Commission on the Proposed Order Modification in Borden, Inc., Docket No. 8978," 1983, p. 2.

46. These sales below cost estimates are conservative because they exclude salesmen's salaries, since General Foods' salesmen sell several coffee brands. Yet, some of these costs probably are variable and these would have been included by Areeda/Turner as variable costs. Similarly, some plant costs and administrative costs that were excluded probably are variable (CPF 3-21 to 3-23).

47. General Foods used sales below "contribution margin less trade deals" as its cost standard. Contribution margin equaled gross revenue less cash discounts, returns and allowances, transportation expenses, warehouse expenses, raw material costs, packaging costs, variable manufacturing labor costs, and variable manufacturing expenses. It excluded all advertising costs, trade deals, consumer coupons, and consumer promotions (CPF 3-43 and 3-44). GF's documents indicate that its trade deals exceeded contribution margin in Pittsburgh and Cleveland (CPF 3-49) (CPRF 1-3).

48. In February and March 1974, Maxwell House dead net price (list price less trade deals and retailer coupons, but excluding consumer coupons) in Pittsburgh averaged $2.095 per three-pound can. The cost of green beans in a three-pound can was $2.10 during this same time period (CRF 1-16).

49. Complaint counsel's chief economic witness, H. Michael Mann, presented graphs of regression lines in which prices or profits were hypothesized to be related to market share. The Youngstown area was initially (pre-entry) located close to the cluster of points representing other areas where Maxwell House had a high relative share. During the entry period, Youngstown's prices and profits dropped out of the cluster. In 1976 and 1977, Youngstown prices and profits were again within the cluster of points representing high-store areas.

50. Some competing firms withdrew from parts of the market following Folger entry and GF's response (CPF 8-20 to 8-45). Others came close to withdrawing (8-46 to 8-53). One regional firm in the

Pittsburgh area went bankrupt. A private antitrust suit stemming from this bankruptcy is still in litigation as of this writing.

51. CPF 3-93 to 3-108.

52. Three options were considered by the Maxwell House Division "Operating Committee" which was framing GF's response to Folger: "not defending," "defending now," and "defending later." GF adopted the "defend now" strategy (CPF 3-85 and 3-86). Under this strategy, GF expected MH to lose money in the short run, (CPF 3-87 and 3-88) but to increase profits in the long run (CPF 3-90.)

53. See Hilke and Nelson (1984).

54. CPF 5-4.

55. CPF 5-13.

56. CPF 5-6.

57. CPF 5-5.

58. This behavior seems particularly notable in light of Maxwell House's staff's comments corresponding to the relative cost of predation arguments advanced by Easterbrook (1981). In disparaging the possibility of predation, he observes that predators may have to spend more to predate than entrants do to respond to predation (since sales below cost occur on more units for dominant incumbent firms).

59. Horizon was packaged to be "as close to them (Folger) as our lawyers would allow us to go" (CPF 4-6.) It was introduced in an effort "to maintain or increase regular Maxwell House's pre-entry share levels," "profits," and "franchise dominance" (CPF 4-19).

60. CPF 4-3. See also Porter (1980).

61. Some analysts have considered three types of error that are associated with antitrust rules: 1) the conviction of innocent parties; 2) the dismissal of cases against guilty parties; and 3) inflating the costs associated with trying a case. See e.g. Fisher and Lande (1983).

62. The following equations are applicable to the traditional rule:

$$P1=[(pmc) + (pm(1-c)w) + (p(1-m)c(1-w))];$$
$$P2=[((1-p)mc) + ((1-p)(1-m)c(1-w)) + ((1-p)m(1-c)w)];$$
$$P3=[(p(1-m)cw) + (pm(1-c)(1-w)) + (p(1-m)(1-c))];$$
$$P4=[(1-p)(1-m)(1-c) + ((1-p)(1-m)cw) + ((1-p)m(1-c)(1-w))].$$

For the Commission's rule, the following equations are applicable:

$$P1=[(pmc) + (pm(1-c)w)];$$
$$P2=[((1-p)m) + ((1-p)(1-m)c(1-w)];$$
$$P3=[(p(1-m)) + (pm(1-c)(1-w))];$$
$$P4=[((1-p)(1-m)(1-c)) + ((1-p)(1-m)cw)]$$

The welfare loss is equal to $(P3*L1)+(P4*L2)$.

63. The effect of changes in w, the probability that the court ignores the intent evidence when it conflicts with monopolization evidence, is straightforward. As w increases, the two tests converge to the same test. That is, if courts ignore all conduct evidence, then the two tests are the same. Similarly, if m and c are equal to one, the two tests are the same.

64. See for example, McGee (1958) and Koller (1971).

65. Koller (1971) found that only three cases out of 36 he reviewed were likely to have involved predation.

66. See articles reprinted in Greer (1980).

67. The authors identified 27 cases out of 68 as involving successful predation. However, in only 7 of these cases were the welfare effects of the predation found to be negative. In 6 cases the welfare effects were found to be neutral.

68. The evidence was typically rejected with a broad claim of it being "unreliable," without reference to numerous sensitivity tests performed by the parties during the trial.

69. From Table 1, if $p=.3$, $c=.8$, and $w=.5$, then the sum of $P3$ and $P4$ increases from .168 to .375 when m changes from .8 to .5 for the Commission's rule. In contrast, the sum for the traditional rule increases from .200 to .350.

70. Two anticompetitive effects of General Foods' actions were identified: 1) entry was slowed so that any post-entry increase in competition was delayed; and 2) post-entry competition was adversely affected because changes in Folger's entry strategy led to a less competitive long-run equilibrium market structure.

References

Areeda, Phillip, and Donald Turner. "Predatory Pricing and Related Practices Under Section 2 of the Sherman Act." *Harvard Law Review* 88 (February 1975): 697–733.

Bond, Ronald, and David Lean. *Sales Promotion, and Product Differentiation in Two Prescription Drug Markets.* In Federal Trade Commission Staff Report. Washington, D.C.: U.S. Government Printing Office, 1979.

Caves, Richard, and Michael Porter. "From Entry Barriers to Mobility Barriers." *Quarterly Journal of Economics* (May 1977): 241–261.

Comanor, William, and H. E. Frech. "Strategic Behavior and Antitrust Analysis." *American Economic Review* 74 (May 1984): 372–376.

Easterbrook, Frank. "Predatory Strategies and Counter-strategies." *University of Chicago Law Review* 48 (Spring 1981): 264–337.

Elzinga, Kenneth, and Thomas Hogarty. "The Problem of Geographic Market Delineation in Antimerger Suits." *Antitrust Bulletin* 18 (Spring 1973): 45–81.

Elzinga, Kenneth, and Robert Rogowsky, eds. "Relevant Antitrust Markets." *Journal of Reprints for Antitrust Law and Economics* 14, no. 2 (1984).

Fisher, A., and R. Lande. "Efficiency Considerations in Merger Enforcement." *California Law Review* 71 (December 1983): 1582–1696.

Fisher, F., and J. McGowan. "On the Misuse of Accounting Rates of Return to Infer Monopoly Profits." *American Economic Review* 73 (March 1983): 82–97.

Folsom, Roger, and Douglas Greer. "Advertising and Brand Loyalty as Barriers to Entry." In *Advertising and the Food System,* edited by John Connor and Ronald Ward, 47–70. Madison, Wisc.: North Central Regional Research Project, 1980.

Greer, Douglas, ed. "Predatory Conduct and Empirical Studies of Collusion." *Journal of Reprints for Antitrust Law and Economics* 10 no. 1 (1980).

Harrison, Glen. "Predatory Pricing in Experiments." Working Paper (March 1985).

Hilke, J., and P. Nelson. "Noisy Advertising and the Predation Rule in Antitrust Analysis." *American Economic Review* 74 (May 1984): 367–371.

Huang, Cliff, John Siegfried, and Farangis Zardoshty. "The Demand for Coffee in the United States, 1963–77." *Quarterly Review of Economics and Business* 20 (Summer 1980): 36–50.

Isaac, M. and V. Smith, "In Search of Predatory Pricing." *Journal of Political Economy* 93 (April 1985): 320–345.

Joskow, Paul, and Alvin Klevorick. "A Framework for Analyzing Predatory Pricing Policy." *Yale Law Journal* 89 (December 1979): 1183–1200.

Koller, Roland. "The Myth of Predatory Pricing—An Empirical Study." *Antitrust Law and Economics Review* 4 (Summer 1971): 105–123.

Kreps, D., and R. Wilson. "Reputation and Imperfect Information." *Journal of Economic Theory* 27 (August 1982): 253–279.

Long, W., and D. Ravenscraft. "The Misuse of Accounting Rates of Return: Comment." *American Economic Review* 74:3 (June 1984): 494–500.

Lynch, M. "The Steiner Effect: A Prediction from a Monopolistically Competitive Model Inconsistent with any Combination of Pure Monopoly or Competition." FTC Working Paper, No. 141, 1986.

McGee, J. "Predatory Price Cutting: The Standard Oil (N.J.) Case." *Journal of Law and Economics* 1 (October 1958): 138–43.

Milgrom, P., and J. Roberts. "Predation, Reputation, and Entry Deterrence." *Journal of Economic Theory* 27 (August 1982): 280–312.

Miller, J., and P. Pautler. "Predation: The Changing View in Economics and the Law." *Journal of Law and Economics* 28 (May 1985): 495–502.

Nelson, P., and J. Hilke. "Retail Featuring as an Entry or Mobility Barrier in Manufacturing." FTC Bureau of Economics Working Paper, No. 144, 1986.

Porter, Michael. *Competitive Strategy.* New York, NY: The Free Press, 1980.

_____. *Interbrand Choice, Strategy and Bilateral Market Power.* Cambridge, Mass.: Harvard University Press, 1976.

Salop, S., and D. Scheffman. "Raising Rivals' Costs." *American Economic Review* 73 (May 1983): 267–271.

Scherer, F. M. et al. "The Validity of Studies with Line of Business Data: Comment." *American Economic Review* 77:1 (March 1987): 205–217.

Schmalensee, Richard. "Product Differentiation Advantages of Pioneering Brands." *American Economic Review* 72 (June 1982): 349–365.

Steiner, Robert. "A Dual Stage Approach to the Effects of Brand Advertising on Competition and Price." In *Marketing And The Public Interest,* edited by J. Cady. Cambridge, Mass.: Marketing Science Institute, 1978.

Steiner, Robert. "Basic Relationships in Consumer Goods Industries." *Research in Marketing* 7 (1984): 165–208.

Whitten, Ira T. "Brand Performance in the Cigarette Industry and the Advantage to Early Entry, 1913–1974." Federal Trade Commission Staff Report. Washington, D.C.: U.S. Government Printing Office, 1979.

Williamson, Oliver. "Wage Rates as a Barrier to Entry: The Pennington Case." *Quarterly Journal of Economics* 85 (February 1968): 85–116.

――――. "Predatory Pricing: A Strategic and Welfare Analysis." *Yale Law Journal* 87 (December 1977): 284–340.

Collusive Predation:
Matsushita v. Zenith

Kenneth G. Elzinga

Introduction

Within a few months of the Supreme Court's 5-4 opinion in *Matsushita* v. *Zenith,*[1] the case had become a widely cited and widely discussed decision of the Court. What the Supreme Court decided in only 17 pages of written text came after millions of pages of documents had been examined and thousands of hours of labor had been expended before the litigation got to the nation's highest court. Even by antitrust standards, *Matsushita* v. *Zenith* was what lawyers call "a big case."

Justice Lewis Powell's Supreme Court opinion recognized that economic analysis merited an important role in the Court's reasoning process. Indeed, it is rare for the Court to place reliance upon economic analysis to the extent it did in this case. But an accurate assessment of the issues would have been difficult without applying economic reasoning to the plaintiffs' charges and the defendants' responses. Indeed it is economic theory that allows one to cut through the mountain of documents and conflicting charges of the attorneys and make sense out of key allegations in the case. Four principles from the economists' toolkit have particular usefulness in assessing this case. They are: the economic theory of predation, the theory of the cartel cheater, the law of one price, and the principle of alternative opportunity cost.

The Background of the Litigation

Some antitrust cases involve allegations of conspiracy. Some entail allegations of predatory pricing. *Matsushita* v. *Zenith* (hereafter *M* v. *Z*) was about *both* conspiracy and predatory pricing. The plaintiffs charged that several companies that were supposed to be independent

Kenneth G. Elzinga served as a consultant for the Japanese television manufacturers in this case. He would like to thank David E. Mills and Kurt R. Schaefer for their assistance.

competitors entered a conspiracy to charge predatory prices in one market while collusively charging supracompetitive prices in another. "Conspiracy" and "predatory pricing" are portmanteau expressions, and they shall be unpacked more fully later in this study. Several laws were said to be violated by the defendants' behavior;[2] but the Sherman Act charges of a conspiracy to restrain trade and a collective attempt to monopolize were the focus of the action.

The Players

Matsushita v. *Zenith* was born in 1970 when National Union Electric Corporation (NUE) brought suit against a number of Japanese firms. NUE was the former Emerson Radio Company, a U.S. pioneer in the manufacture of radios and television receivers. Four years later Zenith Radio Corporation filed a similar lawsuit against the same Japanese firms. The two actions were consolidated. The principal defendants were seven Japanese firms: Matsushita, Toshiba, Hitachi, Sharp, Sanyo, Sony, and Mitsubishi (hereafter the Japanese firms).[3] They are among the largest business corporations in the world. In 1974 the seven firms had combined sales of over $20 billion. Zenith and NUE are not "Mom and Pop" operations either: Zenith had sales of $910 million in 1974, and NUE had sales of $140 million.

The charges in *M* v. *Z* embrace the entire consumer electronics products industry: television receivers, radios, tape players, and stereo equipment. But the case was fought primarily over the relevant market of television receivers (hereafter televisions) in the United States.

Televisions are a consumer durable familiar to virtually everyone. They were originally the product of American and European inventors, and the U.S. industry was the world leader in production volume and quality until the mid-1960s. The birth of the Japanese industry came largely through licensing arrangements and technical assistance from U.S. companies. American firms such as GE, RCA, Westinghouse, Western Electric, and Zenith, along with European firms such as Philips, were prominent exporters of licensed technology to Japan.

The basic charge against the Japanese firms was that they were engaged in a massive global conspiracy lasting more than two decades whose purpose was to destroy the American television industry. The alleged strategy had two prongs: 1) charging monopoly prices in Japan, the defendants' home market, through a price-fixing conspiracy among the defendants there; 2) using the monopoly profits made in Japan to subsidize below-cost, predatory pricing on export sales to the United States. Zenith and NUE claimed that in the short run, U.S.

producers like themselves were economically harmed by the predatory pricing and in the long run, American consumers would end up paying monopoly prices on televisions after domestic competition was eliminated.

Predatory Pricing in the United States

Using monopoly profits made in one market to gain a monopoly position in another is sometimes called war-chesting. In U.S. antitrust annals, it is a strategy often associated with some of the notorious trusts of an earlier industrial era. In *M* v. *Z* the alleged predators were Japanese firms, and their war chest supposedly was derived from a cartelized home market largely shut off from outside competition. This is a tactic commonly believed to be used by foreign firms selling in the U.S. market.

From the perspective of an American consumer, what happened in the Japanese home market is of little economic consequence if predatory pricing did not take place in the United States. So the economic analysis of predatory pricing merits first examination. In a later section, two features of the alleged Japanese home market conspiracy will be assessed. These make up the economic evidence for the joint behavior and the economic rationale of using cartel profits from one market to fund monopolizing activities in another.

The Mechanics of Predatory Pricing in *Matsushita* v. *Zenith*

Two Japanese organizations were said to form the heart of the export portion of the conspiracy: MITI (the Ministry of International Trade and Industry) and the JMEA (Japanese Machinery Exporters Association). Through MITI, an arm of the Japanese government, minimum prices, called "check" (or "reference" or "benchmark") prices, were established governing the sale to the U.S. of consumer electronic products, including televisions. Through the JMEA the defendants allegedly adopted a "Five Company Rule" that limited each Japanese seller to only five wholesale customers in the United States. Under the Sherman Act, it would be illegal for a group of competitors to agree upon minimum prices and to agree not to compete against each other for particular customers.[4]

The plaintiffs contended that not only were agreements made by the Japanese firms on the check prices but that there were additional agreements to *go below* the check price minimums. This disregard of the check prices was done, according to the plaintiffs, through secret rebates and discounts to U.S. customers. Zenith and NUE complained that these prices, or at least some of them, were artificially depressed and predatory. There are, then, two antitrust issues running concurrently here: prices that are predatory in the U.S. television market, and a collusive agreement to put them there. The economic theory of predation sheds light on the first issue; the economic theory of cartels sheds light on the second.

The Economic Theory of Predation and the Evidence

Predatory pricing is a conscious strategy of pricing below cost on a sustained basis to eliminate or discipline one's rivals in order to maintain or establish monopoly power. When this strategy is successful, rivals expire or cede pricing leadership to the predator. The upshot of successful predatory pricing is the monopolization of a market, to the detriment of consumers of that product or service. The topic of predatory pricing has been widely discussed in academic circles during the past decade;[5] and predatory pricing has been a central allegation in several important antitrust cases that did not reach the Supreme Court in the decade prior to *M* v. *Z.*

In many antitrust cases involving predatory pricing, courts typically examine evidence comparing a defendant's prices with its costs. The most common methodology for comparing prices and costs used by courts today is adopted from the economic theory of the firm and was made famous in a 1975 article in the *Harvard Law Review.*[6] This method, now called the Areeda-Turner test, entails comparing an alleged predator's price with its average *variable* cost (as a proxy for marginal cost) and rests on the assumption that no seller normally will produce output if the market price is below the firm's out-of-pocket costs.[7] In the economic theory of the firm, the average variable cost curve is associated with the firm's shut-down point. In a mechanical application of this theory, a price below the shut-down point should cause the firm to cease operations.[8] If the firm chooses not to shut down, the inference is explored (or drawn) that the firm is engaging in predatory pricing.

It is inherent in predatory pricing that the predator must incur a short-run loss in order to impose losses on its prey. Zenith and NUE claimed that the Japanese defendants sold televisions in the United States at prices below cost. Partly because of the difficulty in estimating defendants' variable costs and partly because there was not a full trial on the merits, an Areeda-Turner type test was never used by the court to examine the predation allegation.[9]

Predation as an Investment

In economic analysis, predation can be seen as having an investment-like character. One incurs significant costs, in the form of losses, during the period of predation. These losses are an investment in prospective monopoly profits. Justice Powell recognized this subtle facet of economic analysis when he wrote the following:

> The forgone profits [of predation] may be considered an investment in the future. For the investment to be rational, the conspirators must have a reasonable expectation of recovering, in the form of later monopoly profits, more than the losses suffered.[10]

Figure 1 illustrates and compares a predator's losses during

Figure 1
Predator's Predation Losses and Recoupment Gains

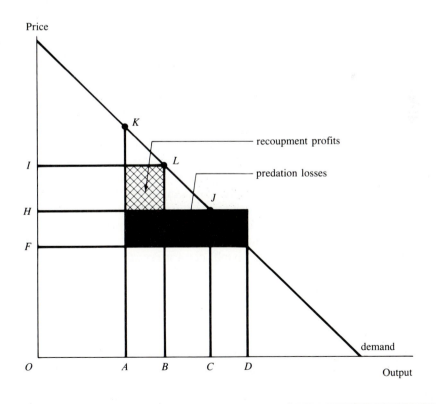

predation and its profits during recoupment. Assume that the competitive, pre-predation price is at a level of 100, and is represented by the distance *OH*. The total quantity sold per year at this price is also 100 and is represented by *OC*. Now suppose the alleged predatory price of the Japanese sellers was equal to the distance *OF,* and assume this unremunerative price caused some U.S. sellers to leave the industry and others to cut back their output such that U.S. sales were only *OA*. Assume further that the demand curve remains unchanged.

The total number of televisions consumers will buy during each year of predation is *OD*. Since U.S. producers have elected to produce only *OA* under the predatory conditions, the Japanese must produce the balance: *AD*. This means the Japanese firms' loss on each unit produced and sold is *FH,* the difference between the average competitive price OH (which is a proxy for long-run average costs, including a normal profit) and the predatory price *OF*. Thus the predators' losses in every year of predation are depicted by the product of *HF* × *AD* (the shaded rectangle).

Figure 1 can be used to assess the prospects for recoupment by the defendants. Assume that when predation is over, the U.S. competition is beaten back and continues to produce only *OA* units. This means the Japanese firms cannot consider the total demand curve as their own. They will raise prices during recoupment to maximize profits over the "residual" demand curve which is that portion of the demand curve southeast of point *K*.[11]

The predators' profit-maximizing (monopolistic) price during recoupment is *OI;* their level of output is *AB* which is the difference between the total demand *OB* at the recoupment price and the output *OA* of their U.S. rivals. The profit on each set is *IH*. The profit during each year of recoupment would be the product of *IH* × *AB* (the cross-hatched area). Based on Figure 1, a predatory pricing strategy would seem rational only if the value to the firm of the recoupment rectangle exceeded the cost to the firm of the loss rectangle. In the example shown, (visually) this does not occur; but the rectangles represent only an annual benefit and cost. The predatory strategy, in its loss stage and recoupment stage, may take several years. Figure 1, therefore, is a heuristic device. A simple comparison of the rectangles, by itself, cannot reveal the full costs and benefits of predation because of the tactic's intertemporal dimension. But Figure 1 does illustrate certain parameters of a predation strategy.

Present Value and Predation

Economic analysis recognizes that a dollar tomorrow is worth less than a dollar today. Consequently a rational predator recognizes that the profit rectangle during recoupment must more than offset the loss rectangle during predation in order to compensate the firm for the time-value of the funds employed. In a more careful analysis of predation, the discounted character of the losses would be compared with the future stream of monopoly profits.[12]

Whether the returns to investment in predation are sufficiently great to warrant the cost depends on how long and how far prices are below costs during the predation period, the rate of return the predator uses in making his investment decisions, the reentry rate of rivals during the recoupment period, and the length of the recoupment period. In addition, the more inelastic is demand in the market, the better the prospects for a predator to be successful.

Using this analysis, Table 1 shows a series of conditions derived from the economic studies submitted by plaintiffs in *M* v. *Z*. The predator price is expressed as a percentage of the prices that plaintiffs alleged would have prevailed, absent predation. For example, in column one, for color televisions, the entry 62 reflects the plaintiffs' contention that the average prices charged by Japanese firms during the period 1968 to 1975 were 62 percent of the but-for-predation price. Column two shows the same calculation for black and white receivers. Both columns reflect the deep discounting allegedly engaged in by the Japanese. Column one adopts plaintiffs' position that the period of predation ran at least from 1965 (when the Japanese first gained 5 percent of the market) to 1975 (the year after the cases were consolidated). Column two indicates that predation in black and white sets purportedly endured for at least 13 years. Given such deep discounting for such a long period, the losses (or magnitude of the investment in predation) would be enormous.

It would be unrealistic for the defendants to expect the output of U.S. television producers to fall immediately to zero under conditions of predatory pricing if only because some consumers may prefer par-

Table 1 Predation in Televisions

	Color Sets	Black and White Sets
Predatory Price	62	58
Years of Predation	10	13
Growth in Demand	5%	−2%
Japanese Beginning Market Share	5%	5%
Japanese Ending Market Share	42%	17%
Recoupment Price Range	119–138	100–106
Years of Recoupment	∞	*

*The alleged predatory pricing cartel could never recoup its predatory losses. Declining demand and increasing levels of non-Japanese imports and stable U.S. production levels would shrink Japanese sales to zero at prices above 100 percent of the open-market level by the tenth year of the recoupment period.

ticular features of U.S. producers, such as cabinet styling, and some retailers who carry a full line of appliances made by a particular U.S. manufacturer may be slow to substitute a Japanese brand of television sets. For these reasons and others, there would be some lag before U.S. firms drastically reduced or ceased their television production because of predatory price levels. But if prices were in fact predatory, predators at a minimum could reasonably expect the output of U.S. firms not to expand during the predation period. If domestically produced output remained constant, as column one of Table 1 assumes, the Japanese would capture all television sales stemming from demand growth. This would have given the defendants 42 percent of the color market by 1975.

The demand for black and white sets was declining during the period under consideration. Column two's calculations ascribe to the Japanese producers their actual share of the black and white segment at the end of the predation period—17 percent. Japanese firms in the manufacturing sector at that time earned an average 12.2-percent rate of return on assets (Holland 1984, Table 1-3, p. 9). If this approximates the alternative opportunity cost for the defendants of an investment in predatory pricing and if 1.2 is a reasonable estimate of the price elasticity of demand for televisions in the United States (Houthakker and Taylor 1966, 130), the size of the putative losses of the Japanese firms can be compared with the prospective returns supposedly available to offset them. From this, one can estimate how long and at what level remunerative recoupment prices would have to be for predation to be worthwhile.

Table 1 shows the range of prices the Japanese could have expected to charge during the recoupment period and the duration of payment to make predation worth the candle. The analysis assumes that the rivals of the Japanese defendants sell the same number of televisions during the years of attempted recoupment as they did at the end of the predatory period. This assumption favors the prospect of the predation strategy's being successful in that it means the rivals of the predators do not expand their output even if monopoly prices were being charged by the Japanese producers. The table suggests that even under this assumption recoupment is impossible for the Japanese firms in either of the television segments. If recoupment could go on for infinity, it would not pay off for the Japanese firms in color televisions because the huge initial losses swamp the modest price enhancement possible during recoupment. In the black and white segment, prospects are even worse. Because of declining demand, charging the best price it can for black and white sets (essentially, the competitive price) shuts the Japanese firms out of the market in ten years.

By the analysis reflected in Table 1, the pricing strategy imputed to the Japanese firms by the plaintiffs in *M* v. *Z* requires that the defendant firms act irrationally. Because the investment characteristics of the market do not support a predation theory, this suggests some other explanation of the events described (such as lower costs for the Japanese firms).

Market Power Prerequisite for Recoupment

Economic theory characterizes successful predation as a two-step sequence. The first step involves below-cost pricing to drive out or discipline rivals; exercise of the second step, recoupment, requires monopoly power. A firm's market share often serves as a proxy for its market power. A seller with a low market share in a market with several sellers cannot dictate market price unilaterally. If it charges a price above the market level, the price will not be sustained because buyers, by assumption, have numerous alternatives. A firm (or group of firms acting collusively) with a large market share may not have significant market power either if customers perceive other products or services as close substitutes, or entry into the market is easy.

The economic study of markets does not offer an exact benchmark for determining when a single firm has substantial market power (or a group of firms acting collusively have such power). In a market with moderate entry barriers, many economists would agree that for a firm to exercise market power unilaterally it must have at least 50 percent of the market under its control. Some economists would put the figure higher; others might go as low as 40 percent. The existence of entry barriers would strongly influence an economist's concern about high seller concentration. In the absence of entry barriers, for example, even high concentration would not enable the exercise of significant market power by firms in an industry.

Notwithstanding the economic devastation supposedly inflicted upon U.S. firms, the Japanese defendants' combined market share (in terms of unit sales) of black and white and of color sets made to U.S. dealers never exceeded fifty percent.[13] Japanese-made color sets exported to the United States went from less than 700,000 units in 1968 to almost 4 million units by 1976. The numbers are impressive but not overwhelming. In 1965, the Japanese defendants supplied only about 10 percent of U.S. purchases of televisions; by 1970, the percentage had grown but was still under 30 percent.[14] If there were no collusion on export sales, *a fortiori,* the low market shares of individual Japanese firms would suggest that the defendants individually had no significant control over price. Indeed, Mitsubishi, in its biggest volume year in the

U.S., sold less than one percent of the black and white and color sets purchased in this country.[15]

While NUE and other U.S. television producers did exit the business, Zenith remained a prominent seller. In 1973, the year before the NUE and Zenith cases were consolidated, Zenith had 23.8 percent of the color television market, selling more sets in the United States than any other seller; Zenith was followed by RCA, another U.S. producer, which at that time had 20.1 percent of the U.S. color market.[16] Plaintiffs had difficulty persuading the court that the Japanese firms, even collectively, ever gained monopoly power or had the prospect of gaining it to accomplish predation's second step. Economic reasoning persuaded the lower court that there was no reason to study or ascertain the height of any entry barriers in the television industry because of the low market shares held by the defendants.

Cheating in a Predatory Cartel

In the economic theory of the cartel, one of the most powerful concepts is that of the cheater. Cartel theory teaches that when a group of rivals collusively establishes prices at the joint profit-maximizing level, it will be economically advantageous for any one seller to operate outside the cartel rather than within. Outside the cartel, a seller—the cheater—can enjoy the high cartel price but not be subject to the output limitation imposed on insiders that makes the high price possible.

Most cartels seek to raise prices. So the cheater typically is the firm that tries to sneak outside, shade prices, and clandestinely sell larger outputs. But in a predatory cartel, the cheater does the reverse. If firms have agreed to charge prices *below* cost, the cheater's incentive is to sell *less* than its share of the jointly mandated amount considered necessary to drive out the rivals. The cheater concept has powerful applicability in analyzing *M* v. *Z*.

Plaintiffs maintained that under the auspices of MITI, Japanese sellers collusively set check prices. The check price minimums were to show the U.S. government that Japan wanted "fair competition" and should not be subject to tariffs and quotas that would be even more restrictive. Then, to circumvent the check prices, the Japanese sellers offered U.S. customers secret price cuts and rebates below the reference prices. Plaintiffs devoted some 2000 pages in their Final Pretrial Statement describing details of this "rebate scheme." The documentation is a powerful showing of the many ways by which buyers can pay transaction prices that are lower than list prices. Zenith and NUE alleged that the prices the Japanese sellers netted after violating the check price minimums were unremunerative.

The factual record surrounding the check price violations actually is powerful evidence that these reference prices were not predatory because sellers sought additional sales at levels below them. It would be irrational (as a matter of economics) to want to sell "more than your share" at prices below cost, especially when such sales involved falsifying purchase orders, shipping documents, export validation forms, and U.S. Customs' invoices, entailed keeping double sets of books, and involved other types of concealment.[17]

It is logical to ask whether the secret rebates and clandestine discounts might not have been part of a concerted effort by the Japanese to move transaction prices down—perhaps without MITI's knowledge—to predatory levels. The fact difficult to reconcile with such a conjecture is the apparent *eagerness* with which Japanese sellers sought to expand their sales at prices below the check price level, a level that allegedly was below production and marketing costs.

For example, an importer told Sharp (one of the seven principal defendants) that Sharp's competitors were rebating off the check prices and that if Sharp wanted any business it must be prepared to lower its prices as well. Sharp obliged. When Matsushita was planning to acquire Motorola, a U.S. firm to which Sharp had sold televisions, Sharp requested Motorola executives not to tell Matsushita of its past rebates and deviations from the check prices.[18]

The only economic rationale for an eagerness to expand one's share of below-cost sales in a truly predatory cartel would be if a seller viewed its product line as being highly differentiated. If there were great customer inertia against switching brands, a cheating member of a predatory cartel might covet additional sales (even during the period of predation) knowing or believing that its new customers will not switch suppliers when prices are raised later to monopolistic levels.

Such a prospect does not square with consumer behavior in the television industry at the time of the alleged predation in *M* v. *Z*. Only Sony, among all the defendants, had significant brand recognition, and it sold at relatively high prices, not low prices. Large-scale buyers of Japanese televisions and other consumer electronics products, such as a K mart or a Woolco, who frequently attach their own "house brand" name to a product, do not become wedded to a particular manufacturer. Moreover Japanese television manufacturers witnessed first hand that American consumers were not locked in to their first television brand. Many consumers switched from U.S. firms like Philco and Admiral to firms like Hitachi and Sanyo when they purchased their second television sets (or replaced their first). Americans may be true to their school but they are not known to be loyal to the manufacturer of their current television receiver, be it of U.S. or Japanese origin, when it comes to shopping for another.

Absent substantial product differentiation, the economic theory of cartels would predict the following type of behavior if there were a predatory export cartel: serious squabbling among the defendants, each seeking to cut back its *own* sales during the predatory period and requiring its rivals to incur more of the per-unit losses associated with each additional television set produced and sold below cost. American importers would be unable to play one Japanese defendant against another trying to get a lower price. If an American buyer tried to whipsaw a Japanese producer by demanding a lower price (or what is the same thing, a larger rebate), the Japanese producer would be eager to decline the offer and graciously allow his co-cartelist to make the sale—if prices were below cost as plaintiffs alleged.[19]

The Economic Literature on Predatory Pricing

Legal opinions usually have many footnotes. But rarely are they references to economists. In *M* v. *Z*, the Supreme Court, to an extent not often seen, relied on economic studies of predation to influence its decision. Justice Powell mentioned the "consensus among commentators that predatory pricing schemes are rarely tried, and even more rarely successful."[20]

The word *consensus* is an apt one; *unanimity* would not have been. Most of the historical studies of alleged episodes of predatory pricing have shown the charges to be unfounded. They tend to support the prediction of economic theory that predatory pricing will be difficult because of the large losses a successful predator must somehow offset. Nonetheless, there are some economists who remain persuaded that predatory pricing is, in particular markets, a matter of serious antitrust concern.

The Law of One Price

Without using the term, the district court addressed the applicability of the economist's "law of one price" to *M* v. *Z*. The law of one price says that in competitive markets, sales of the same product will be at identical prices. Plaintiffs essentially were arguing as follows: If a television set sells for $200 (in yen equivalent) in Japan, and the same set sells for $150 in the United States, sellers should increase supply in Japan and decrease supply in the United States (on the assumption that transportation costs are not substantial). In the process, by competitive arbitrage, only one price will result. If prices do not equilibrate, the argument continues, there must be a reason why Japanese sellers do not expand sales in Japan (the home market conspiracy theory) and reduce sales in the United States (the predation theory). Capping off the argument is the closed Japanese market (for which there is much evidence), which prevents U.S. producers from accomplishing the arbitrage by increasing *their* shipments to Japan. The difficulty of obtaining retail and wholesale distribution appeared to be one of the main barriers to entry.

Plaintiffs offered evidence that compared defendants' home market prices for televisions with prices for U.S. export and argued that Japanese prices exceeded U.S. prices. Defendants claimed that this evidence was marred because the economists' ceteris paribus conditions were not met in making the comparison. The sets were not identical in their engineering specifications, they were sold at different levels of distribution, and they bore different warranty and distribution costs in the two countries. The lower court agreed with the defendants' economic analysis that these differences made the law of one price inapplicable. In fact, Japanese export sales to the United States did not have a lockstep relationship either to their own or to U.S. prices. Some of the defendants, notably Sony, charged relatively high prices in the United States.[21] Some charged relatively low prices. Moreover, relative prices varied among different models among the Japanese defendants themselves and in comparison to their U.S. rivals.

There is still another consideration that argues for the defendants' economic theory. If the price levels in the United States were the result of competition between domestic sellers, a Japanese seller without market power who wishes to sell in the United States must be competitive with U.S. price levels—regardless of prices in Japan or anywhere else in the world. In short, if a television set of a given quality sells for $175 in the United States, and $175 exceeds the marginal cost of Japanese producers, it requires neither a conspiracy hypothesis nor a predation hypothesis to account for sales by any of the Japanese sellers in the United States in the $175 range. Such sales are consistent with each defendants' own independent economic interests and with normal business rivalry.

That Japanese firms often undercut established prices in the United States does not itself prove predation since the Japanese were new entrants in the U.S. market and the market is one where long-term cost reductions led price levels downward over time. In markets where economies of scale and learning-by-doing result in cost reductions, economic theory teaches that prices will trend downward. Frequently such trends are led by the newer firms who are seeking to use low prices to help gain brand recognition, goodwill, and company reputation.[22]

Economists and Inferential Evidence

In the United States, price-fixing conspiracies often do not leave "smoking guns"—direct evidence in the form a written agreement to charge joint profit-maximizing prices or a videotape of the conspiracy. Antitrust enforcement agencies often must use indirect or circumstantial evidence to prove price fixing. But in *M* v. *Z* there was direct evidence that the Japanese firms had signed a document determining minimum export prices on television sales to the United States. Indeed over time there were more than a dozen such agreements covering both black-and-white and color televisions.

This is the language of Article 8 of one such agreement (The Manufacturers' Agreements):

> The parties to this agreement shall not offer for sale, make a contract for sale or deliver to export businessmen goods at prices lower than the prices specified in attached Schedule 2.[23]

Signatories could sell at or above the check prices.

The defendants claimed that these agreements were mandated by the Japanese government through MITI and therefore were immune from U.S. antitrust prosecution by the "act of state" and "sovereign compulsion" doctrines. The plaintiffs contended that MITI did not compel joint action by the Japanese sellers and that MITI at best gave subsequent approval to business strategy initiated by the defendants.

Using economic reasoning, the district court recognized that Zenith and NUE (and other U.S. producers of televisions) could not be harmed by foreign firms setting minimum prices. Zenith, for example, should have been delighted if Hitachi were hamstrung by legal minimums. All Zenith would need to do to compete, on the assumption of comparable quality and other terms, was charge a price less than the minimum to which Hitachi was bound.[24] Moreover, jointly setting minimum prices does not fit gracefully with the theory that prices are predatory.

The Five-Company Rule (see page 243) also was not compelling as evidence of predatory pricing. First, the rule did not always hold— several large American buyers, such as J.C. Penney, Sears, Roebuck, and Western Auto, purchased televisions from more than one of the seven Japanese sellers. Second, the rule was easily circumvented—a defendant could make its American subsidiary one of the five and sell to anyone in the United States through that subsidiary. Moreover, the rule could not have injured Zenith and NUE (or other U.S. producers). Indeed if the five-company rule had constrained Japanese sellers, it should have made it easier for Zenith and NUE to sell to any particular domestic buyer since that buyer allegedly was limited in its Japanese supply alternatives. From an economic perspective, the Five Company Rule runs contrary to the hypothesis of a low price export conspiracy. An organizer of a predatory cartel might have to say, "you *must* sell to these five" but not "you are *limited* to these five."

The Home Market Conspiracy

Price fixing in Japan supposedly was the means by which the Japanese sellers financed the sales of televisions at depressed prices in the United States. As sometimes happens in antitrust cases, as litigation commences from complaint to discovery, legal theories change. The district court noted early in its opinion that the war chest theory, which formed an important part of the plaintiffs' original charge, began to wane as the case progressed. By the time of the summary judgment, the judge wrote: "Little is said at this stage about 'war-chesting,' apparently because plaintiffs finally recognized that there is no evidence of it in the record."[25]

Earlier, in a controversial move, the lower court judge had rejected much of the written opinion of the plaintiffs' economic experts who contended that a home market conspiracy existed. These economists reviewed written materials that persuaded them, circumstantially, that a conspiracy existed. Much of this evidence was held to be untrustworthy and inadmissable. For example, one JMEA document contained this statement:

> Thus, the businessmen involved have decided that, acting as one body, they will strive to maintain export order and, furthermore, to aim for steady expansion of exportation.[26]

Economists for the plaintiffs saw such documents as evidence of conspiratorial intent. But the lower court judge interpreted the document merely as expressing an intent to reduce trade friction between the United States and Japan. Moreover he ruled that making judgments about conspiracy based on circumstantial evidence of this sort is not the task of an expert economist. Judges and juries are supposed to make such decisions. He dismissed much of the work of plaintiffs' economic experts as that of "conspiracyologists" and not the work of economists *qua* economists.[27]

The issue of a home market conspiracy lends itself to economic analysis quite different from conspiracyology. Without trying to interpret the diaries of Japanese managers, without trying to decipher the minutes of meetings between executives, without trying to exegete the notes taken by subordinates, without trying to discern the meaning of business memos, economic analysis can be used to address these two questions: 1) what would be the form of a home market conspiracy? 2) what would be the economic rationale of using the proceeds from a home market conspiracy to support predation? A corollary of this is: To what extent does economic theory teach that evidence of parallel price discrimination between two separate national markets proves conspiracy?

The plaintiffs contended that parallel price discrimination was such strong inference of conspiracy that a trial was merited. The defendants argued that to go from a fact of sustained high prices in Japan and lower prices in the United States to the conclusion of conspiracy is not inference but speculation. The plaintiffs, it should be noted, never submitted any evidence of the rates of return made by Japanese defendants on home market sales. They argued it should be sufficient to show a price difference.[28]

The history as well as the theory of cartels reveals their instability. Cartels require coordination devices and rules of compliance to hold together diverse interests. The interests of this cartel would have been very diverse and complicated to coordinate if only because of the asymmetry of shares between defendants' sales in the home market and the export market. Firms like Sharp and Sanyo had rather small shares of the market for televisions and other consumer electronics products in Japan; they were, however, relatively large sellers in the United States. Without side payments, they would have been unlikely to absorb large losses on many sales in the United States that later would benefit their rivals whose losses were smaller, especially those rivals who, unlike themselves, had large shares of the Japanese market and who therefore should be the firms with the putatively large war chests.

War Chests and Alternative Opportunity Costs

Economic analysis often proceeds from assumption. At this juncture, let us assume that the Japanese firms *had* cartelized their home market and *were* making monopoly prices there. Let us assume too that the Japanese firms are considering a predation strategy in the United States. Plaintiffs in *M* v. *Z* argued that there is a connection or nexus between the circumstances in the two sets of assumptions: a successful television cartel in Japan renders more likely the adoption of a predatory campaign against the television industry in America. The profits from one market subsidize the other. This is the war chest theory of predation.

Economic analysis cautions against a quick adoption of such a theory. War chests, like everything else in the world of economics, do not come free. Their cost is the foregone profits that could have been earned by investing the purported monopoly profits made in Japan in some alternative endeavor. The alternative would include relatively riskless opportunities for the funds such as government bonds. No rational firm would forego a more certain and immediate stream of income for a riskier and more long-term prospect of gain unless the opportunities for the future gains are very attractive.

If predation were an attractive strategy—that is, if it were financially attractive as an investment relative to other risk-adjusted alternatives—then potential predators would adopt this strategy of export pricing independent of their home market position. In other words, if a predatory strategy (involving short-term losses) is a profitable investment because of an expected future monopoly position, it is attractive regardless of whether cartelizing in the home market (or any other market) also has proved profitable.

At most, the plaintiffs posited a "convenience theory" of predatory conspiracy: Since the defendants allegedly were meeting already to set home market prices at high levels, it was convenient jointly to determine predatory prices for the United States. Agatha Christie might have sized up the convenience theory this way: It confuses motive with ability. If enormous profits were in fact being made in the Japanese home market, this may afford the Japanese sellers the ability to finance a costly predatory campaign in the United States, but it does not provide the motive.

The District Court Decision

Judge Edward R. Becker, at the time serving on the U.S. District Court for the Eastern District of Pennsylvania, was the trial judge who in March of 1981 first decided *M* v. *Z*. It was his opinion that eventually was appealed to the Supreme Court. His decision was extraordinarily long, a reflection of the Brobdingnagian number of documents put before him. In 1980 alone, 114 briefs and memoranda were filed in *M* v. *Z*. In reaching his decision, Judge Becker relied heavily upon his own economic analysis and economic arguments placed before him. He ruled that "despite years of discovery, the plaintiffs have failed to uncover any significant probative evidence that the defendants entered into an agreement or acted in concert with respect to exports to the United States in any manner which could in any way have injured plaintiffs."[29] Judge Becker could find no evidence of admissible caliber that "refers or relates to the setting or coordination of export prices. . .or any other aspect of the 'export' component of the 'unitary' conspiracy claimed by plaintiffs."[30]

There were many documents that revealed meetings about home

market conditions. But very few of these even contained reference to exports; those that did were to exports in general, not exports that were U.S.-specific. There was some evidence that a Japanese trade association (the Electronic Industries Association of Japan) gathered and disseminated average prices of televisions sold for export but no record of exchanges of current price information, much less agreement on prices or quantities of export. Absent evidence of this character, the plaintiffs' predation case becomes one requiring proof of predatory pricing by individual defendants. But none of these firms had enough market power, nor even the prospect of sufficient market power, to prey successfully in a unilateral fashion.

Notwithstanding the resources poured into this case, there never was a full trial on the merits. Judge Becker decided the case for the defendants on summary judgment. Summary judgment means the judge read the pleadings in the case, heard oral argument, studied particularly the plaintiffs' Final Pretrial Statement, and determined what evidence of the plaintiffs would have been admissible if a trial were held. He then determined that, even if all of this admissible evidence were accepted as true and unrebutted by the defendants, the plaintiffs did not have a sufficient case and there was no genuine need for a trial.

Conclusion

The U.S. Circuit Court of Appeals was unpersuaded that Zenith and NUE did not merit a trial. Essentially the appellate court, applying different standards of plausibility, would have admitted much of the evidence that Judge Becker held to be inappropriate, including the opinions and studies of economists employed by Zenith and NUE; but upon appeal to the Supreme Court, the highest court in the land thought otherwise, albeit by a narrow majority.

Matsushita v. *Zenith,* from a purely legal perspective, is about the suitability of summary judgment—avoiding a full trial on the merits—in an antitrust case. If the facts about a case, as they are put forward by a plaintiff prior to a full trial on the merits, are not in accord with economic analysis (or "make no economic sense" as the Supreme Court put it bluntly), then a plaintiff's case may be dismissed without a burdensome and costly trial being imposed on the defendant(s). This puts economic theory in the role of a filter, sorting out inappropriate cases from those worthy of a court's full consideration. *M* v. *Z* adds weight to the view that in antitrust, economic analysis matters. Moreover, *M* v. *Z* strengthens the view that vigorous price competition is so desirable and predatory pricing so rare that courts, to ensure more of the former, should set a high standard of proof for allegations of the latter.[31]

Notes

1. The case originally was *Zenith* v. *Matsushita* at the district court: *Zenith Radio Corp. et al.* v. *Matsushita Electric Industrial Corp., Ltd. et al.*, 513 F. Supp. 1100 (1981). Upon the defendants' initial legal victory, the case was appealed by the plaintiffs, *Zenith Radio Corp. et al.* v. *Matsushita Electric Industrial Corp., Ltd. et al.*, 723 F.2d 238 (1983). After Zenith's victory at the initial appellate level, the case went to the Supreme Court, *Matsushita Electric Industrial Corp., Ltd. et al.* v. *Zenith Radio Corp. et al.*, 475 U.S. 574 (1986). Throughout this article the term "plaintiffs" refers to the original plaintiffs in the lawsuit: Zenith and NUE.

2. Sections 1 and 2 of the Sherman Act, Section 73 of the Wilson Tariff Act, Section 7 of the Clayton Act, the Robinson-Patman Act, and the Wilson Antidumping Act. The last law did not involve any conspiracy allegations.

3. There were several other defendants, including subsidiaries of the Japanese firms and some American firms such as Sears, Roebuck. Sony was one of the original principal defendants. It settled with Zenith, but remained a defendant in the NUE half of the case.

4. While both fixing minimum prices and dividing markets are Sherman Act offenses, it is not clear how rivals of firms adopting such behavior would be affected adversely by these practices. In fact, Zenith and NUE should have been the beneficiaries of such tactics, had they been carried out. If fixing minimum prices and dividing markets had constituted the plaintiffs' entire case, the district court would have denied them standing to sue because they would not have been injured parties but rather economic beneficiaries (U.S. District Court, 1981, 1147–1148).

5. The literature on predatory pricing is too large to cite comprehensively here. For a selective introduction to the topic and the ongoing debate, see Areeda (1982, 114–167), Baumol (1979), Beckenstein and Gabel (1986), Brodley and Hay (1981), Calvani and Lynch (1982), Dirlam (1981), Fisher (1987), Isaac and Smith (1985), Joskow and Klevorick (1979), Liebeler (1986), Shepherd (1986), and Williamson (1979) as well as the references to the articles on price predation in footnote 16, *infra*.

6. Areeda and Turner (1975).

7. As Areeda and Turner put it:
   Recognizing that marginal cost data are typically unavailable, we conclude that
   (a) A price at or above reasonably anticipated average variable cost should be conclusively presumed lawful.
   (b) A price below reasonably anticipated average variable cost should be conclusively presumed unlawful. Areeda and Turner (1975, 733).

8. There are benign reasons why a firm may price below average variable cost. The firm may be unloading inventory at distress prices; it may be a new seller engaging in promotional pricing; it may be a new firm whose output does not yet exploit expected lower costs due

to a learning curve phenomenon; and its average variable cost curve may not reflect tax considerations that make pricing below this measure of cost profitable on a post-tax basis.

9. An economic expert for plaintiffs opined that four of the Japanese firms had sold televisions in the United States at prices at least below average cost. The district court judge, for reasons not assessed here, ruled that this price-cost evidence was inadmissible on the grounds that the construction of the cost and price was unreliable.

10. 475 U.S. 574, 588–589 (1986).

11. The profit-maximizing price for the predators will be the midpoint of the segment KJ for a linear demand curve. Any price southeast of J on the demand curve could not be a recoupment option for the Japanese sellers if they were predators since J itself shows the competitive price level. A price higher than K on the demand curve is not an option either. With the U.S. firms supplying OA already, nobody would pay such a price.

12. This approach has been developed in Elzinga and Mills (1987).

13. 513 F. Supp. 1100, 1322 (1981).

14. 513 F. Supp. 1100, 1251 (1981).

15. 513 F. Supp. 1100, 1285 (1981). Mitsubishi owned no manufacturing facilities in Japan, so it is not evident under the plaintiffs' theory of the case how it benefited from a predatory export cartel. It could not use gains from Japanese production to finance losses in the United States. In fact, it is a buyer of televisions (which it resells); it has no incentive to see the Japanese home market monopolized or to drive U.S. manufacturers out of business.

16. 513 F. Supp. 1100, 1255 (1981).

17. The Japanese sellers would secretly rebate to the customer the difference between the nominal price declared for export and import purposes and the actual transaction price quoted to the customer. These activities did not violate the antitrust laws, but they did expose the Japanese producers to other legal action by the U.S. Bureau of Customs and the U.S. Treasury Department.

18. 513 F. Supp. 1100, 1247, 1278 (1981).

19. Cartelization also implies not only concerted behavior but also similar behavior. Rebates were not offered to all customers, and the amount of rebates, when offered, varied as between defendants and between customers of the same defendant. Such disparate behavior balances more with independent rivalry than joint conduct. 513 F. Supp. 1180, 1249 (1981).

20. 475 U.S. 574, 589 (1986). Some of the scholarly articles the Court cited are McGee (1958, 1980); Easterbrook (1981); Koller (1971).

21. Sony was an awkward choice of firms for plaintiffs to group with the others. The prices charged by its profitable American distribution arm, Sonam, were considerably higher than both the check prices and the prices of Zenith and NUE sets. See 513 F. Supp. 1100, 1282 (1981). How Sony's high prices could injure American firms was never specified.

22. The combination of established brand recognition, high combined

market shares, and import protection may explain the higher prices defendants enjoyed in Japan. Together they controlled almost 95 percent of the Japanese market; but there is no credible evidence that transaction prices at the manufacturing level were higher in Japan. Higher prices at retail or wholesale in Japan relative to the United States probably are explained by higher distribution costs in Japan than in the United States.

23. 513 F. Supp. 1100, 1188 (1981).

24. Paradoxically, MITI and the defendants claimed that the rationale behind the minimums was to *limit* the number of televisions exported to the United States and thus the agreements represented a strategy by the Japanese to limit or prevent even more severe U.S.-imposed trade restrictions upon Japanese goods through tariffs and quotas.

25. 513 F. Supp. 1100, 1129 (1981). Indeed, after surveying many of the documents concerning the meetings of Japanese executives about home market prices, Judge Becker concluded that discussions about home market prices were often discussions about how to maintain retailer margins, which may have lowered manufacturers' prices, and conversations about how prices were dropping in Japan to levels too low to enable manufacturers to break even. These were facts Judge Becker found difficult to square with the war chest theory. See 513 F. Supp. 1100, 1203–1204 (1981).

26. 513 F. Supp. 1100, 1231 (1981).

27. 513 F. Supp. 1100, 1138 (1981).

28. 513 F. Supp. 1100, 1205 (1981).

29. 513 F. Supp. 1100, 1117 (1981).

30. 513 F. Supp. 1100, 1209 (1981).

31. It was this concern that provoked the Antitrust Division of the Department of Justice to be a party to this litigation, filing a brief as a friend of the Court. At the request of Zenith and NUE, the Antitrust Division in 1977 and 1978 investigated the plaintiffs' claims and found them without antitrust merit (Brief for the United States as Amicus Curiae Supporting Petitioners 1985, 3). Charles F. Rule, who was then Deputy Assistant Attorney General of the Antitrust Division, appeared before the Supreme Court in *M* v. *Z* and stated the Antitrust Division's fears that if Judge Becker's opinion were not upheld, the case would "offer strong encouragement. . .to beleaguered competitors seeking protection from the rigors of competition, and. . .that's precisely the wrong thing that the antitrust laws should do" (Rule 1986, 21–22).

References

Areeda, Phillip, and Donald F. Turner. "Predatory Pricing and Related Practices under Section 2 of the Sherman Act." *Harvard Law Review* 88 (February 1975): 697–733.

Areeda, Phillip E. *Antitrust Law*. Boston: Little, Brown, 1982 (Supplement).

Baumol, William J. "Quasi-Permanence of Price Reductions: A Policy for Prevention of Predatory Pricing." *Yale Law Journal* 89 (November 1979): 1–26.

Beckenstein, Alan R., and H. Landis Gabel. "Predation Rules: An Economic and Behavioral Analysis." *Antitrust Bulletin* 32 (Spring 1986): 29–49.

Brodley, Joseph F., and George A. Hay. "Predatory Pricing: Competing Theories and the Evolution of Legal Standards." *Cornell Law Review* 66 (April 1981): 738–803.

Calvani, Terry, and James M. Lynch. "Predatory Pricing Under the Robinson-Patman and Sherman Acts: An Introduction." *Antitrust Law Journal* 51 (1982): 375–400.

Dirlam, Joel B. "Marginal Cost Pricing Tests for Predation: Naive Welfare Economics and Public Policy." *Antitrust Bulletin* 26 (Winter 1981): 769–814.

Easterbrook, Frank. "Predatory Strategies and Counter-strategies." *University of Chicago Law Review* 48 (Spring 1981): 263–337.

Elzinga, Kenneth G., and David E. Mills. "Testing for Predation: Is Recoupment Feasible?" Unpublished manuscript (February 1988).

Fisher, Franklin M. "On Predation and Victimless Crime." *Antitrust Bulletin* 32 (Spring 1987): 85–92.

Holland, Daniel M., ed. *Measuring Profitability and Capital Costs.* Lexington, Mass.: Lexington Books, 1984.

Houthakker, H. S., and Lester D. Taylor. *Consumer Demand in the United States.* Cambridge: Harvard University Press, 1966.

Isaac, R. Mark, and Vernon L. Smith. "In Search of Predatory Pricing." *Journal of Political Economy* 93 (April 1985): 320–345.

Joskow, Paul L., and Alvin K. Klevorick. "A Framework for Analyzing Predatory Pricing Policy." *Yale Law Journal* 89 (December 1979): 213–269.

Koller, Roland H. "The Myth of Predatory Pricing: Am Empirical Study." *Antitrust Law and Economic Review* 4 (Summer 1971): 105–123.

Liebeler, Wesley J. "Whither Predatory Pricing? From Areeda and Turner to *Matsushita.*" *Notre Dame Law Review* 61 (1986): 1052–1098.

McGee, John S. "Predatory Price Cutting: The Standard Oil (N.J.) Case." *Journal of Law and Economics* 1 (October 1958): 137–169.

———. "Predatory Pricing Revisited." *Journal of Law and Economics* 23 (October 1980): 289–330.

Rule, Charles F. Oral Argument: Official Transcript Proceedings Before The Supreme Court of the United States, Dkt./Case No. 83-2004, November 12, 1985.

Shepherd, William G. "Assessing 'Predatory' Actions by Market Shares." *Antitrust Bulletin* 31 (Spring 1986): 1–28.

U.S. *Brief For the United States As Amicus Curiae Supporting Petitioners, Matsushita Electric Industrial Co. Ltd. et al.* v. *Zenith Radio Corp., et al.,* June 1985.

Williamson, Oliver E. "Predatory Pricing: A Strategic and Welfare Analysis." *Yale Law Journal* 87 (December 1977): 284–340.

3
Part

Vertical Arrangements

The Economic and Legal Context of Vertical Arrangements

Vertical arrangements—the business relationships between suppliers (sellers) and customers (buyers)—have been a troublesome area for both economics and antitrust law. Incomplete analysis and excessive attention to form over substance has, in the past, marred economic and legal thought in this area, with the consequence that false or minor threats to competition have often been subject to attack, while more valid competitive problems have sometimes been ignored.

In the past twenty-five years, however, there has been a near-revolution in economic and legal thought concerning vertical relationships, and this change has had a substantial effect on antitrust enforcement policy, especially in the 1980s, and on court opinions and the state of antitrust law. The case studies in this section are testaments to these developments.

Economic Theory

For a better understanding of vertical arrangements, a discussion of a few key concepts is warranted. One useful concept is vertical integration—the combining of two or more vertically related production processes under the auspices of one ownership-and-control entity. There is an immediate ambiguity worth noting: any given production process is capable of being divided into narrower, vertically related processes that, in principle, if not in practice, could be handled by separate entities in a supplier-customer relationship to each other.[1] Thus, there is no inherently "natural" level of vertical integration. Instead, various levels of vertical integration (or, conversely, of vertical specialization) are likely to arise according to the efficiency and profitability that firms perceive from various arrangements. In turn, these outcomes are likely to be driven by the state of technology, entrepreneuria, expertise, factor costs, and many legal arrangements (e.g., tax laws), as well as any opportunities for exploiting market power through vertical integration. Vertical integration can, of course, occur through the merging of two previously independent entities or through the *de novo* expansion of an existing firm into vertically related areas.

At the opposite pole from vertical integration is the interaction of buyers and sellers in a spot market, with one-at-a-time transactions. And in between these two extremes is a whole range of vertical arrangements, agreed to by both parties, that limit the behavior of one or both and that thereby, in essence, achieve partial degrees of vertical integration. These arrangements include long-term contracts, franchising, licensing, tying, exclusive dealing, requirements contracts, full-line forcing, territorial restraints, and resale price maintenance.

Prior to the 1960s there had been little rigorous economic analysis and little understanding of these practices or of vertical integration itself. The general attitude toward them was, at best, one of ambivalence: a recognition that they could contribute to efficiency, but also a strong suspicion (sometimes borne of confusion of form and function) that they were frequently the tools for the creation or enhancement of market power.[2]

More recent analyses have shed much better light on these practices of partial or complete vertical integration and have shown that they frequently represent efficient reactions to market imperfections, such as externalities, free riding, informational limitations, and the limitations of formal contract arrangements.[3] Resale price maintenance, for example, may be a way by which a manufacturer can induce point-of-sale services from its retailers, each of whom might otherwise be tempted to free ride on the services of the others. Territorial restraints may be a way that a manufacturer can avoid duplication of selling effort and free riding among its retailers. Exclusive dealing may be a way that manufacturers can achieve focused efforts by their retailers and prevent free riding by other manufacturers. Long-term contracts provide both parties with greater levels of certainty which can be valuable for planning and investment. Franchising and other licensing arrangements can allow the originator of an idea to extend its use and maintain quality control over its use, without the necessity of engaging in the direct production himself (in which he may have little relevant expertise). Vertical integration itself is a way of securing greater control over production processes, internalizing externalities, and overcoming informational deficiencies.

At the same time, however, these practices may be vehicles for the enhancement of market power or the more effective exploitation of that power.[4] Many of the practices can be used to practice price discrimination, which will increase profits (but the social welfare consequences, in terms of creation of deadweight loss, are ambiguous[5]); for example, territorial exclusivity arrangements may make it easier for a manufacturer to charge higher prices in some areas (where demand is perceived to be less elastic) than in others. Other practices may raise barriers to entry or otherwise raise costs to actual or potential rivals. Exclusive dealing arrangements, by allowing a manufacturer to restrict the access of other manufacturers to its retailers, may raise costs to its rivals or may make entry difficult, if the supply of retailing services is an important bottleneck for that line of products. Under certain circumstances, some of these practices may simply be a cover for horizontal collusion among manufacturers or retailers, either to raise prices directly or to raise entry barriers to potential rivals. Resale price maintenance, for example, appears to have acquired a bad image among many economists largely because it was a vehicle for horizontal price fixing among pharmacists and other small retailers during the 1930s. And complete vertical integration itself may raise entry barriers or enhance market power by preventing downstream entities from substituting lower cost alternatives to the upstream entity's product.

In all of these instances, however, the use of these practices for anticompetitive purposes requires the actual or potential presence of market power (individually or collectively), including limitations on or impediments to entry in the areas affected. Accordingly, benign consequences can be presumed in many circumstances in which market power is absent, creating "safe harbors" for policy. If an individual seller's market share is such that its exercise market power is unlikely, and joint exercise of market power with other sellers is unlikely (or none of the other sellers is engaging in the practice), then the partial or complete vertical integration of that seller with its downstream customers (e.g., a manufacturer's resale price maintenance agreement with its retailers, or its own entry into retailing) is unlikely to have anticompetitive consequences. This approach thus calls for closer analysis to be applied only when the entity in question may be able to exercise market power individually or the practice appears among a group of firms who may be able to exercise market power collectively.

Antitrust Law

A broad range of the antitrust laws' provisions has been used to attack vertical arrangements. The Sherman Act's Section 1 language of "contract, combination,. . .or conspiracy in restraint of trade. . . ." has been used to challenge resale price maintenance arrangements and territorial restrictions and other nonprice restraints. The Act's Section 2 language of "monopolize. . . ." has been used to challenge vertical restraints and vertical integration itself. The Clayton Act's Section 3 specifically forbids contracts imposing a restraint whereby the customer "shall not use or deal in the goods. . .supplies, or other commodities of a competitor of the lessor or seller" where the effect "may be substantially to lessen competition or tend to create a monopoly." And Section 7 of the Clayton Act has been used to challenge mergers between vertically related firms.

For the discussion that follows, it is useful to classify the antitrust treatment of vertical relationships into four areas: vertical integration; vertical restraints involving prices; territorial vertical restraints; and other nonprice vertical restraints.

Vertical Integration

Section 2 of the Sherman Act has been used, albeit sparingly, to attack vertical integration that appeared to promote or enhance market power. The 1911 *Standard Oil*[6] decision resulted in vertical dissolution (e.g., oil pipelines being separated from refineries) as well as horizontal dismemberment (refineries in different geographic regions were separated into independent companies). The 1948 *Paramount*[7] case resulted in the separation of movie exhibition (theatres) from distribution and production. The FTC's suit against the integrated petroleum companies,[8] filed in 1973 but dismissed in the early 1980s, was aimed in part at their vertical integration. The Justice Department's *AT&T* case, discussed by Roger Noll and Bruce Owen in this section, was largely based on the theory that AT&T's vertical integration encompassing local exchange service, long-distance service, and equipment manufacturing, when buttressed by local and national economic regulation, created competitive distortions. And the Civil Aeronautics Board's regulatory investigation, framed largely in antitrust terms, of the computerized reservations systems that a few large airlines had developed in the 1970s and 1980s (see the study by Margaret Guerin-Calvert in this section), was an important effort to come to terms with a new technology in a newly deregulated industry.

Section 7 of the Clayton Act has been used to prevent vertical integration through merger. Even before Section 7 was strengthened in 1950, the DOJ was able successfully to challenge a substantial stock ownership position by General Motors in its major supplier of paints and finishes, Du Pont.[9] In the heyday of the antitrust enforcement agencies' merger-prohibition victories of the 1960s, vertical mergers (as well as horizontal mergers) were regularly challenged and stopped.[10] The DOJ's 1968 Merger Guidelines devoted a quarter of that document to vertical mergers, specifying the market shares of the supplier and of the customer in their respective markets that would generate a challenge by the DOJ to the merger.

By the 1980s, however, the new learning of the economics profession was reflected in the enforcement policies of the two antitrust agencies. The DOJ's 1982 and 1984 Merger Guidelines devoted less than a fifth of their lengths to vertical mergers, and their tone was far less hostile than the 1968 version had been. It appears that only one merger in the 1980s has been challenged by the DOJ primarily on vertical grounds.[11] The FTC dismissed the challenge to the integrated petroleum companies. At the same time, however, as the *AT&T* and computer reservations systems cases indicate, the DOJ is prepared to challenge vertical integration under some circumstances.

Resale Price Maintenance

In the 1911 *Dr. Miles Medical Co.*[12] case, the Supreme Court declared that resale price maintenance (RPM) was a per se violation of the Sherman Act's Section 1 prohibition of "every contract, combination,. . .or conspiracy in restraint of trade. . . ." That view has been repeated in a series of decisions, including the important 1984 *Monsanto* decision discussed by Frederick Warren-Boulton in this section.

In 1937 the Congress passed the Miller-Tydings Act, which legalized RPM—"fair trade"—on a state-option basis. It appears that most of the sentiment supporting the legalization of RPM came from small retailers, who saw RPM as a way of checking the spread of larger retailers (since the latter would be forbidden from selling at lower prices than the former); in essence, this was providing a legal cover for horizontal price fixing among the retailers. This exemption from the application of the Sherman Act was repealed by Congress in 1975, however, and *Dr. Miles Medical Co.* still reigns as prevailing law.

The new economics learning, though, has influenced enforcement policy in the 1980s in this area as well, and the two enforcement agencies have not brought any cases challenging unilateral imposition of RPM by an upstream entity on its downstream distributor.[13] The two agencies would likely challenge any RPM arrangement that they believed to be a cover for collusive horizontal price-fixing agreement, however, and private antitrust challenges to perceived RPM arrangements are still a potent enforcement force.

Territorial Restraints

The legal area of territorial vertical restraints represents one of the major turnarounds of the Supreme Court, at least partially in response to the new economics learning.[14] In 1963, in response to the DOJ's challenge to White Motor's imposition of territorial (and customer classification) restraints on its distributors, the Court said, in essence, "We're not sure about these practices," and declined to condemn them as per se violations of Section 1 of the Sherman Act.[15] Four years later, in the DOJ's challenge to similar restraints by Schwinn, the Court had become sure and condemned them as per se offenses.[16] But in 1977 the Court reversed itself and declared in the *GTE Sylvania*[17] case (see the chapter by Lee Preston in this section) that these practices should be judged under the more lenient rule-of-reason approach, in which the relative advantages and disadvantages of the practice need to be weighed. This tolerant view was echoed by the Court in its 1984 *Monsanto*[18] decision, although that decision simultaneously reinforced the Court's hostile view of RPM.

Enforcement policy has embraced this new tolerance. In 1985 the DOJ issued a set of Vertical Restraints Guidelines, which indicated that the DOJ would be unlikely to challenge these arrangements in settings where market power was unlikely to be present. There apparently have been no enforcement agency challenges to these practices, though private challenges are still present.

Other Nonprice Vertical Restraints

Until the mid-1970s, the Supreme Court and the antitrust enforcement agencies showed a general hostility to tying, exclusive dealing, and other nonprice vertical restraints that could be challenged under Section 2 of the Sherman Act and Section 3 of the Clayton Act. Since then, however, the Court has been moving toward greater tolerance and leniency. The Court's rejection of tying claims in a 1984 case[19] is indicative of this new tolerance (which is, at least partly, derived from the new learning in economics), although the Court (by a narrow 5–4 vote) declined to move tying from a per se violation category to a rule-of-reason category.

Enforcement has here also embraced this new tolerance readily, and the DOJ's 1985 Vertical Restraint Guidelines again provide a wide area of forbearance for situations where market power is unlikely to be exercised. Neither enforcement agency has brought any cases in this area, but private antitrust plaintiffs continue to bring challenges.

The Cases

As noted above, the *GTE Sylvania* case represents a milestone in the Supreme Court's absorption of the new economics of vertical arrangements and its adoption of a position of greater tolerance toward these practices. Lee Preston provides the background to this case and illustrates the important economics concepts that influenced the Court's decision.

The 1980s dismemberment of AT&T represents the most substantial antitrust restructuring of an industry since at least the 1940s (when movie exhibition was separated from distribution and production[20]) and possibly since the *Standard Oil*[21] and *American Tobacco*[22] cases of 1911. Roger Noll and Bruce Owen show how the presence of local and national regulation of AT&T was a crucial element in the economics arguments offered by both sides of the case.

The deregulation of the airline industry in the late 1970s and early 1980s was accompanied by an important new technological development—highly sophisticated computerized reservation systems owned by a few large airlines. Margaret Guerin-Calvert discusses the economic principles that were brought to bear by the parties (including the DOJ) in an antitrust-like regulatory proceeding before the Civil Aeronautics Board and in subsequent private antitrust cases.

The 1984 *Monsanto* case gave the Supreme Court an opportunity to re-examine the legal issues surrounding resale price maintenance. Frederick Warren-Boulton provides the details of this case and argues that RPM generally, as well as the specific behavior by Monsanto that was at issue, is pro-competitive and socially beneficial, despite the Court's adverse decision.

These four studies, written by economists who participated in each case, provide illuminating discussions of the useful role that economics arguments played in the four important antitrust cases.

Notes

1. In essence, any production process can be divided into a set of "make or buy" decisions, with the "make" decision implying vertical integration and the "buy" decision indicating otherwise.
2. See, for example, Kaysen and Turner (1959, 120, 126, 133, and 159).
3. See, for example, Telser (1960), Posner (1976), Klein et al. (1978), White (1981), Marvel (1982), Williamson (1983), and Klein and Saft (1985).
4. See, for example, Burstein (1960), Vernon and Graham (1971), Hay (1973), Schmalensee (1973), Warren-Boulton (1974), Salop and Scheffman (1983), Scherer (1983), Comanor (1985), and Comanor and Frech (1985).
5. See Schmalensee (1981) and Kwoka (1984).
6. *United States* v. *Standard Oil Co. of New Jersey et al.,* 221 U.S. 1 (1911).
7. *United States* v. *Paramount Pictures Inc., et al.,* 334 U.S., 131 (1948).

8. *In the matter of Exxon Corporation et al.,* docket no. 8934, complaint filed January 24, 1973.

9. *United States* v. *E. I. Du Pont de Nemours and Co. et al.,* 353 U.S. 586 (1957).

10. See *Brown Shoe Co.* v. *United States,* 370 U.S. 294 (1962); *Reynolds Metals Co.* v. *Federal Trade Commission,* 309 F. 2d. 223 (1962); and *Ford Motor Co.* v. *United States,* 405 U.S. 362 (1972).

11. See White (1985).

12. *Dr. Miles Medical Co.* v. *John D. Park and Sons Co.,* 220 U.S. 373 (1911).

13. Also, the DOJ entered an amicus brief in the *Monsanto* case, urging the Supreme Court to reassess its position on RPM.

14. Indeed, it is this turnaround in the area of territorial restraints that keeps alive the hope by many in the DOJ and FTC that the Supreme Court will eventually reverse its *Dr. Miles Medical Co.* position on RPM.

15. *White Motor Co.* v. *United States,* 372 U.S. 253 (1963).

16. *United States* v. *Arnold, Schwinn and Co. et al.,* 388 U.S. 365 (1967).

17. *Continental T.V.* v. *GTE Sylvania,* 433 U.S. 36 (1977).

18. *Monsanto Co.* v. *Spray-Rite Service Corporation,* 104 S. Ct. 1464 (1984).

19. *Jefferson Parish Hospital District No. 2* v. *Edwin G. Hyde,* 104 S. Ct. 1551 (1984).

20. See *United States* v. *Paramount Pictures, Inc., et al.,* 334 U.S. 131 (1948).

21. *United States* v. *Standard Oil Co. of New Jersey et al.,* 221 U.S. 1 (1911).

22. *United States* v. *American Tobacco Co.,* 221 U.S. 106 (1911).

References

Burstein, Meyer L. "A Theory of Full-Line Forcing." *Northwestern University Law Review* 55 (1960): 62–95.

Comanor, William S. "Vertical Price-Fixing, Vertical Market Restrictions, and the New Antitrust Policy." *Harvard Law Review* 98 (March 1985): 983–1002.

Comanor, William S., and H. E. Frech III. "The Competitive Effects of Vertical Agreements" *American Economic Review* 75 (June 1985): 539–546.

Hay, George A. "An Economic Analysis of Vertical Integration." *Industrial Organization Review* 1 (1973): 188–198.

Klein, Benjamin, Robert A. Crawford, and Armen A. Alchian. "Vertical Integration, Appropriable Rents, and the Competitive Contracting Process." *Journal of Law & Economics* 21 (October 1978): 297–326.

Klein, Benjamin, and Lester F. Saft. "The Law and Economics of Franchise Tying Contracts." *Journal of Law & Economics* 28 (May 1985): 345–361.

Kwoka, John E., Jr. "Output and Allocative Efficiency under Second Degree Price Discriminating." *Economic Inquiry* 22 (April 1984).

Marvel, Howard P. "Exclusive Dealing." *Journal of Law & Economics* 25 (April 1982): 1–25.

Posner, Richard A. *Antitrust Law: An Economic Perspective.* Chicago: University of Chicago Press, 1976.

Salop, Steven C., and David T. Scheffman. "Raising Rivals' Costs." *American Economic Review* 73 (May 1983): 267–271.

Scherer, F. M. "The Economics of Vertical Restraints." *Antitrust Law Journal* 52 (1983): 687–707.

Schmalensee, Richard. "A Note on the Theory of Vertical Integration." *Journal of Political Economy* 81(March/April 1973): 442–449.

Schmalensee, Richard. "Output and Welfare Implications of Monopolistic Third-Degree Price Discrimination." *American Economic Review* 71 (March 1981): 242–247.

Telser, Lester G. "Why Should Manufacturers Want Fair Trade?" *Journal of Law & Economics* 3 (October 1960): 86–105.

Vernon, John M., and Daniel A. Graham. "Profitability of Monopolization by Vertical Integration." *Journal of Political Economy* 79 (July/August 1971): 924–925.

Warren-Boulton, Frederick R. "Vertical Control with Variable Proportions." *Journal of Political Economy* 82 (July/August 1974): 783–802.

White, Lawrence J. "Vertical Restraints in Antitrust Law: A Coherent Model." *Antitrust Bulletin* 26 (Summer 1981): 327–345.

White, Lawrence J. "Antitrust and Video Markets: The Merger of Showtime and The Movie Channel as a Case Study." In *Video Media Competition: Regulation, Economics and Technology,* edited by Eli M. Noam, 338–363. New York: Columbia University Press, 1985.

Williamson, Oliver E. "Credible Commitments: Using Hostages to Support Exchange." *American Economic Review* 73 (September 1983): 519–540.

Territorial Restraints: *GTE Sylvania*

Lee E. Preston

Introduction

The *Sylvania* case,[1] involving restricted distribution of branded television sets, pitted economic concepts and analysis against legalistic formulations and arbitrary rules. This private litigation, involving a nondominant firm and a relatively minor economic activity, ended a long period of controversy and confusion about the legal status of restrictive marketing arrangements and sent ripples into widely scattered sectors of the economy.

The central economic concept in the case is *competition;* and the critical distinction is between *competition in the market,* on one hand, and *freedom of action* by individual firms, on the other. Continental, a small distributor of television sets in northern California, argued that a contractual limitation on its freedom of action—specifically, on the location of the retail outlets from which it might offer Sylvania televisions for sale—constituted "restraint of trade" within the meaning of Section 1 of the Sherman Act. GTE Sylvania, a producer of televisions with an established policy of restricted distribution, countered that the locational restrictions placed on its dealers strengthened the position of the Sylvania brand and enhanced (or at least did not weaken) overall competition in the television market; hence, these restrictions did not restrain trade within the meaning of the antitrust laws. The Supreme Court ultimately accepted Sylvania's position.

The significance of the *Sylvania* case lies in the fact that it essentially returned antitrust policy with respect to vertical restraints (other than those involving price) to the "hospitality tradition" that historically characterized the common law and that had prevailed in U.S. antitrust policy until the mid-1940s.[2] According to this tradition, courts and public policies are "hospitable" to (i.e., tolerant of) restraints on behavior among voluntarily contracting parties as long as no price fixing

---

Lee E. Preston consulted with and testified for GTE Sylvania in this case.

or monopolization is involved. In the opposing "inhospitality" tradition, all restraints on any firm's freedom of competitive action are at least suspect, if not per se illegal.

Restraints on the distribution of branded merchandise have been commonplace in contractual marketing arrangements and franchise agreements since the mid-nineteenth century. Their legality was upheld in private litigation both before and after the passage of the Sherman Act.[3] The "hospitality tradition" was even extended to vertical price restraints in the McGuire-Tydings Act (1937), which legalized resale price maintenance wherever it was authorized by the states.

The "inhospitality tradition" can be traced to the *Bausch & Lomb* decision,[4] in which the Supreme Court affirmed the view that vertical territorial restrictions were illegal per se when they were integral elements of a vertical price maintenance system. Based upon this ruling, the Antitrust Division of the U.S. Department of Justice took the position that distributive restrictions that totally prevent intrabrand competition were presumed to be illegal without specific scrutiny of their price maintenance aspects, and obtained a number of consent decrees on this basis.[5] The high points of the "inhospitality tradition" were the *Schwinn* decision,[6] further discussed later, and the repeal of the McGuire-Tydings Act (1975). The Supreme Court decision in *Sylvania* explicitly reversed *Schwinn,* reestablished the sharp distinction between price and nonprice restraints that had characterized both the common law and earlier antitrust policy, and set the stage for continuing policy developments such as the Soft Drink Inter-Brand Competition Act of 1980 and the Department of Justice's Vertical Restraints Guidelines of 1985.

Vertical Market Relationships and Restraints

Vertical integration in all of its forms has played a major role in the evolution and growth of firms, industries, and markets in the U.S. for more than a century (Chandler 1977, Parts III & IV). Although ownership integration has been predominant in basic industries and producer goods, contractual integration has characterized consumer goods industries, particularly wholesale and retail distribution of branded merchandise. In contractual integration, otherwise independent buyers and sellers mutually agree to accept some limitations on their normal freedom of action in order to accomplish common goals. In the extreme form, distributive or service franchisees adopt total business plans provided by parent franchisors. Less extreme forms limit reseller-buyers (and often sellers as well) with respect to price, product lines, service offerings and methods, choice of customers and/or locations, and so forth. Williamson (1985) refers to all of these arrangements as "nonstandard contracts," since they depart from the "standard" transaction in which both merchandise and title are simultaneously transferred from sellers to buyers (and reciprocal payment made from buyers to sellers) with no further restriction on the actions of either party.[7] (The transfer of title is particularly significant, since if title does not pass, a formal *agency* arrangement is established and the title-holder retains decision-making authority.)

Why do "nonstandard" vertical arrangements ever arise?; why are all manufacturer-distributor transfers *not* simply arm's length, discrete transactions? This is a highly significant question, since the policy evolution analyzed in this chapter was strongly affected by changing views about its answer. Complete vertical integration (a sequence of related activities under a single ownership and control) offers many advantages—elimination of transactions costs, coordination of operations, avoidance of suboptimization, etc. However, particularly with regard to distribution of manufactured products, there are notable disadvantages as well: capital and management requirements; incongruency in the "mix" of products efficiently produced, on one hand, and distributed or sold, on the other; and the forgone value of profit incentives and flexible adaptation to local market conditions at the distributive level.[8]

Nonstandard contracts between manufacturer/branders and distributor/dealers establish a middle ground between the extremes of vertical integration and unrestricted merchandise/title transfer. Vertical restraints are often preferred to formal agency arrangements because they are less burdensome to operate and much more flexible. Specific purposes of nonprice vertical restraints include the following:

1. standardizing sales and service practices among dealers, including product line availability and display, conformance with manufacturer's return and repair policies, supply of authorized parts, personnel training;
2. avoiding "free riding" on advertising and other promotional efforts by either the manufacturer or other dealers;
3. encouraging dealers to exploit their own market situation—location, customer contacts, etc.—to the fullest, rather than struggle with each other over the most attractive accounts while neglecting the rest of the market; and
4. establishing common cost structures, and an awareness of both costs and marketing possibilities, that will discourage undesirable dealer pricing practices, even when no overt price restrictions are involved.

Both the common law and the antitrust tradition have historically made sharp distinctions between nonstandard contracts involving price and those involving other aspects of business operations. Attempts by sellers (manufacturers and branders) to restrict the pricing options of their reseller customers (wholesalers and retailers) have typically been regarded as the equivalent of price-fixing conspiracies. That is, by adhering to a common price policy ostensibly established by a manufacturer, dealers effectively suppress price competition among themselves. Moreover, it is widely believed that vertical restraints on wholesale/retail prices, which reduce dealer-initiated price diversity and greatly facilitate comparisons of prices and price differences, may also facilitate conspiracies or informal understandings about prices among manufacturers and branders as well. In the light of these considerations, supplier control of reseller prices, absent formal agency arrangements in which title does not pass, has been traditionally regarded as a per se violation of Section 1 of the Sherman Act—i.e., a "combination or conspiracy in restraint of trade." (It is true, however, that during the period 1937 to 1975 while the McGuire-Tydings Act was in force, such otherwise illegal restraints were exempted from federal antitrust challenge wherever they were specifically authorized by state law.)

By contrast, nonstandard contracts involving aspects of business operations other than price have traditionally been tolerated by both the courts and the Congress (although not always by the Antitrust Division), unless obvious anticompetitive effects could be demonstrated. For example, the Clayton Act's Section 3 prohibition of tying arrangements and exclusive dealing—both obviously forms of restraint on product choice—extends only to those that tend "substantially to lessen competition," and even the lessening of competition has been permitted by the courts in an "infant industry."[9] In short, the "hospitality tradition" with respect to nonprice restraints generally holds that voluntary agreements between buyers and sellers that limit the freedom of action of one or both parties can properly be left to the business judgment of the entities themselves and the competitive reaction of the marketplace. If the parties involved are willing to make the agreement, and subsequent customers are willing to pay any costs (or take advantage of any savings) that may arise, then—absent demonstrable tendencies to lessen competition—the nonstandard contracts in themselves are not considered to be undesirable restraints upon trade.

This policy position is entirely in accord with conventional economic analysis, which has long held that vertical integration between firms operating at successive, fully competitive stages of the production-distribution process need not in itself alter competitive conditions at any market level. Two caveats to this analytical conclusion are in order, however.

1. If either party to the integration possesses monopoly power at *its own* market level, then integration may expand that power to other levels, with potentially significant anticompetitive consequences.
2. If vertical integration alters the condition of entry in favor of integrated firms through economies of scope, increased capital requirements for competitive entrants, or foreclosure effects, then a reduction in the strength of competition may occur.[10]

Earlier Legal Challenges

White Motor

The Antitrust Division initiated its attack on the "hospitality tradition" with a series of complaints that led to consent decrees, so that the matters at issue were subject to neither adjudication nor economic analysis. The first litigated case was *White Motor*,[11] which brought into sharp focus conflicting viewpoints that were not resolved until the *Sylvania* decision, more than a decade later.

The White Motor Company, a manufacturer of trucks, had organized a two-tiered system of distribution, involving both "distributors" operating at a regional wholesale level and "dealers" who sold to final customers. Both of these groups of franchisees were restrained by contract with White as to their sales areas, selection of customers, and resale prices. The entire arrangement was challenged by the Antitrust Division as a *per se* violation of the Sherman Act, and the District Court granted summary judgment on the basis of White's formal pleadings and documents.[12] White appealed to the Supreme Court, which upheld the summary judgment with respect to price restraints but remanded the other charges for complete trial on the merits. The Court declared:

> [T]his is the first case involving territorial restriction in a *vertical* arrangement; and we know too little of both that restriction and the one respecting customers to reach a conclusion on the bare bones of the documentary evidence before us. . . .We do not know enough of the economic and business stuff out of which these arrangements emerge to be certain [about their legal status].[13]

In contrast with this agnostic position, Justice Tom Clark found White's distributive system "one of the most brazen violations of the Sherman Act that I have experienced in a quarter of a century."[14] According to Clark, all of White's justifications involved "*economic* arguments or business necessities none of which have any bearing on the *legal* issue."[15] The conflict between a "rule-of-reason" approach, in which economic and business considerations would receive serious attention, and a legalistic approach based upon per se rules could not be more clearly stated. This conflict was not resolved at the time, since White chose to abandon its distribution arrangements rather than engage in further litigation.

Schwinn and Its Consequences

The issue of nonprice vertical restraints reached the Court again in 1967 in *Schwinn,* which became the high-water mark of the "inhospitality" doctrine. Schwinn was a long-established bicycle manufacturer with sales amounting to almost one-fourth of the domestic market in 1951. By 1961 that share had fallen to 12.8 percent, and market leadership had shifted to mass merchandisers (e.g., Sears, Montgomery Ward, discount houses) and their foreign and domestic suppliers. As part of its effort to maintain a strong position in the higher price end of the bicycle market, Schwinn developed a complex system of distribution involving both 1) wholesale distributors and order takers, who operated within exclusive territories and served only authorized (i.e., franchised) retailer customers, and 2) franchised retailers who both purchased bicycles outright and received them for resale as agents or consignees of Schwinn. This system of practices and modes of operation, which appeared to include some potential for resale price maintenance as well, was challenged by the Antitrust Division as a congeries of per se violations.

The District Court attempted to sort out the legal and illegal aspects of this complex system.[16] It rejected the charge of price fixing, but held that the territorial and customer restrictions on both wholesale distributors and retailers were illegal per se. When the case reached the Supreme Court, this judgment was upheld and even strengthened.

Both the argument and the opinion focused entirely on *intrabrand* competition—the limitation on Schwinn's *wholesale* distributors in their choice of retail customers, along with any limitation on *retail* competition in Schwinn bicycles that might result as a consequence. No lessening of *interbrand* competition was alleged. In fact, the Court held that the Schwinn marketing program's "net effect is to preserve and not to damage competition."[17] However, in the words of Justice Fortas:

> [W]here a manufacturer *sells* products to his distributor subject to territorial restrictions upon resale, a *per se* violation of the Sherman Act results. . .Such restraints are so obviously destructive of competition that their mere existence is enough.[18]

Thus, in spite of Schwinn's declining market share, and in spite of the fact that "competition made necessary the challenged program [which] was justified by, and went no further than required by, competitive pressures,"[19] Schwinn's distribution arrangements constituted illegal restraints upon trade *in its own products alone.*

The role of economic analysis in this milestone decision has been a matter of dispute. Richard A. Posner, who "briefed and argued" the case for the Antitrust Division subsequently contended that his position "reflected the then prevailing thinking of the economics profession."[20] The only economic study cited in the Government Brief is Preston (1965), which assumes without analysis that the *intrabrand* effects of vertical restraints are anticompetitive, but demonstrates the virtues of distributive restraints as elements of *interbrand* competitive strategy in situations such as that involved in *Schwinn.* Shepherd (1985, 305) seems to believe that the critical element in the decision was market share, with a 12 percent share being considered too large to permit any departure from standard contracting. There is, however, no indication in the Supreme Court's opinion that market share was a critical consideration. Williamson faults the *Schwinn* decision for "defective economic reasoning."[21] However, a more accurate statement would be that the very limited economic analysis developed was simply ignored in the final ruling. The truth is that *Schwinn* is a simple—one might even say simplistic—application of pure legal doctrine, without regard to economic considerations. Although the record states that Justice Clark took no part in these proceedings, Fortas' opinion perfectly follows the reasoning set forth in Clark's *White Motor* dissent.

The *Schwinn* decision appeared straightforward, and a *per se* rule for vertical restraints was clearly enunciated; however, the consequence was confusion rather than clarification in this area of antitrust policy. The Court explicitly declared that its ruling did *not* "prohibit all vertical restrictions of territory and all franchising,"[22] and legal scholars and lawyers debated the implications of individual phrases in the opinion in detail.[23] One commentator described the "usual pattern for these cases" over the next decade as "one day, one court—the rule of reason; next day, different court—the per se doctrine. The following day, all courts switch doctrines."[24]

One major development in the aftermath of *Schwinn* was the FTC's attack on one of the oldest and strongest systems of vertical restraints in the economy: territorial franchises in the soft drink industry. Although lacking direct Sherman Act jurisdiction, the FTC filed complaints in 1971 and 1972 against eight large soft-drink manufacturers charging that geographic restrictions on their licensed bottlers constituted "unfair methods of competition" within the meaning of FTC Section 5.

Further discussion of this proceeding will follow the details of *Sylvania*.

Continental-Sylvania: Facts and Analysis

Although the critical antitrust decisions involving restrictive practices typically arise from cases brought by the Antitrust Division and the FTC, a host of private suits challenging some aspect of a specific contractual marketing arrangement routinely passes through the courts. These contracts cases are generally handled under the "hospitality tradition." That is, it is assumed that manufacturers ordinarily have the right to establish whatever contract terms they wish, which dealers can either reject (withdrawing from the contract) or accept and comply with; litigation arises about just what the contract terms really mean and whether or not all parties have complied. It is, however, true that private litigants (especially plaintiffs) in such cases tend to invoke antitrust claims wherever possible in order to create a basis for treble damage computations, which may be even more significant in settlement discussions than in the courtroom. In the *Sylvania* case, the *Schwinn* rule that vertical restrictions on a manufacturer's independent reseller-customers constitute illegal restraints upon trade within the meaning of the Sherman Act was invoked by a private litigant.

GTE Sylvania was one of the early manufacturers and marketers of television sets in the United States. Like other such firms, during the 1950s it sold finished products through both independent and company-owned wholesale outlets, which in turn sold to a diverse group of retailers. By the early 1960s the dynamics of the marketplace had brought RCA into the leading market position, with 60 to 70 percent of nationwide sales. Sylvania's share had fallen to less than 2 percent. In an attempt to recover a small but stable position in the market, Sylvania phased out all independent wholesalers and began to sell directly to retailers. Moreover, Sylvania chose to pursue a policy of "selective" rather than "saturation" distribution, limiting the number of dealers in each market area and specifying the precise location of each dealer. These policies were intended to strengthen each dealer's ties with Sylvania and to concentrate dealer attention on Sylvania products, on the grounds that each relatively isolated dealer would reap the sales benefit of its own promotion and service efforts rather than lose customers to nearby "free riders." However, exclusive dealing (i.e., restricting dealers to Sylvania products only) was not required, nor were retailers restricted in any way in their choice of customers. Under this new system of distribution, Sylvania's nationwide market share rose to approximately 5 percent by 1965.

Continental T.V., Inc., was the collective name for a group of retail television outlets in the San Francisco area, all owned in large part by one individual. Continental was a franchised Sylvania dealer and apparently a successful firm, although Sylvania appeared to feel some dissatisfaction about the relationship and wanted to obtain additional outlets in the San Francisco area. (Sylvania's market share in the San Francisco area was only 2.5 percent, half of its national level.) In the course of its San Francisco expansion, Sylvania franchised an additional dealer with an outlet approximately one mile from one of Continental's outlets. Continental protested, but to no avail, and ultimately cancelled a large Sylvania order. At the same time, Continental wished to open an outlet in Sacramento, where Sylvania already had successful dealerships established and enjoyed a 15 percent market share. Sylvania, citing the restricted location clause in its franchise contracts, denied Continental's request to become a Sylvania dealer in Sacramento; but Continental nevertheless moved some Sylvania merchandise to its Sacramento outlet. In response to this series of developments, Sylvania reduced Continental's line of credit; Continental for its part began to withhold payment on obligations due Sylvania. Sylvania terminated Continental's franchises and filed suit for payments due and recovery of remaining unsold merchandise. Continental filed a counterclaim, charging that Sylvania's location clause violated Section 1 of the Sherman Act as interpreted in the *Schwinn* decision and demanding treble damages for sales allegedly lost due to its inability to market Sylvania sets in Sacramento.

The case came to trial in San Francisco before retired Justice Tom Clark, the dissenter in *White Motor,* who was now sitting as a District Judge.[25] In response to Continental's charges of restraint of trade, Sylvania's economic expert pointed out that there were 12 significant domestic brands of television sets on the U.S. market in 1965, the date of the original complaint, with RCA overwhelmingly the most popular, and that imports were already beginning to become established as well. At the nationwide market level, Sylvania's strategies appeared to be attempts to survive, not to monopolize. With respect to the local retail level, the expert pointed out that there were some 50 to 60 retail television outlets in the City of Sacramento and about twice that number in the three-county Sacramento SMSA. All of these outlets carried multiple brands and about a dozen carried Sylvania. The expert's analytical conclusion was that, under these circumstances, the presence or absence of the Sylvania brand in a single outlet (i.e., Continental) could not conceivably affect the state of competition in the market for television sets, either in general or in the Sacramento area in particular.

Cross-examination by Continental's attorney stressed the point that selective distribution would ordinarily be expected to reduce the number of dealers from what it otherwise would be, and in fact the number of Sylvania dealers in Sacramento had fallen somewhat over time. There was no suggestion, however, that any such decline, either in general or in this case, would actually affect the strength of market competition; and, indeed, it is quite possible that without the selective distribution policy there would have been fewer Sylvania dealers, or even none at all. Cross-examination also stressed the point that the location clause reduced the freedom of action of all dealers covered by it, which is obviously true. The cross-examiner's only suggestion that specific restrictions on Continental might have any effect on local market competition was based on a contention that Continental utilized unusually aggressive advertising and merchandising policies, which might have marketwide impact. Without exploring the likelihood of such effects, Sylvania's expert pointed out that the challenged restriction involved only the Sylvania brand and that Continental was free to operate—and, in fact, did operate—as a TV set retailer in Sacramento. The specter of monopoly was introduced, in the possibility that Sylvania might eventually permit only *one* Sylvania retailer in Sacramento; the expert pointed out the availability of alternative brands and outlets, and of Sylvania sets in many nearby locations, plus the convenience of price comparison through newspaper ads, including those from the San Francisco metropolitan area. No economic expert testified for Continental.

Sylvania's ultimate position was that if a Sherman Act violation of "restraint of trade" required any significant reduction in *economic* competition, either in the Sacramento market or elsewhere, then there was no evidence supporting Continental's charges. This economic argument became moot, however, because Clark instructed the jury that Sylvania's location clause was itself a per se Sherman Act violation. Since the clause was indisputably present in Sylvania's dealer contracts and implemented through its practices, the jury found Sylvania guilty, and treble damages of $1.8 million were assessed on the basis of Continental's estimate of its lost sales and profits.

This decision was appealed to the Ninth Circuit, which first affirmed and then, sitting *en banc* (i.e., all judges on the circuit, rather than the usual three-judge appellate panel), reversed the lower court in a divided vote. Continental appealed to the Supreme Court, where the *en banc* decision was affirmed and the *Schwinn* decision explicitly reversed.

What factors account for the final decision in the *Sylvania* case and the explicit reversal of *Schwinn?* At the outset there had to be some recognition that the acceptability/unacceptability of particular contractual arrangements depended to some extent upon their purposes and effects—i.e., that economic analysis is relevant. The *Sylvania* Court found *Schwinn* to be "an abrupt and largely unexplained departure" from prior doctrine and invoked the earlier standard that only arrangements with "pernicious effect on competition and lack of any redeeming virtue" ran afoul of the law.[26]

The *Sylvania* Court insisted that attention be shifted from legal distinctions based upon the passage of title to economic criteria based on the concept of *competition in the market*. Neglect of this distinction was held to be the fatal error in *Schwinn*. Justice Powell's analysis proceeded as follows:

> The *market impact* of vertical restrictions is complex because of their potential for a simultaneous reduction of intrabrand competition and stimulation of interbrand competition. . . . Vertical restrictions reduce intrabrand competition by limiting the number of sellers of a particular product competing for the business of a given group of buyers. Location restrictions have this effect. . . [but] the ability of retailers to exploit the resulting market may be limited both by the ability of consumers to travel to other franchised locations and, perhaps more importantly, to purchase the competing products of other manufacturers. . . [Moreover], [v]ertical restrictions promote interbrand competition by allowing the manufacturer to achieve certain efficiencies in the distribution of his products. . . . Economists have identified a number of ways in which manufacturers can use such restrictions to compete more effectively against other manufacturers.[27]

The core of the Court's judgment derives from the conventional economic conclusion, summarized above, that if the overall marketplace itself is competitive, nonprice restrictions placed by a single manufacturer on the resale of its products do not, in and of themselves, constitute restraints on *competition in the market,* although they certainly do (and are intended to!) constrain the *freedom of action* of individual dealers. Thus, after more than a decade of uncertainty and litigation, public policy with respect to nonprice vertical restrictions returned to the legal standard of the "rule of reason" and to the congruence with conventional economic analysis represented by the "hospitality doctrine."

The *Sylvania* decision has been subjected to numerous interpretations, not all of them fully consistent with the record. As noted above, Shepherd (1985, 305) appears to believe that the distinction between *Sylvania* and *Schwinn* is based on market share; however, nothing in the text of the decision supports this view. If market share had been the critical factor, Sylvania's distribution arrangements could have been permitted without reversing *Schwinn*, since even after a period of decline

Schwinn still held a much larger share of the bicycle market than Sylvania did of the television market.[28]

Advocates of "transactions cost" or "efficiencies" approaches to antitrust policy have argued that *Sylvania* represents a triumph for their position.[29] This claim, however, is overdrawn. It is true that Powell's text states that there may be "certain efficiencies" that are implicitly recognized as "'redeeming virtues' in every decision sustaining vertical restrictions under the rule of reason."[30] However, there is no attempt anywhere in the record—including the expert's testimony—to document such efficiencies in detail; and the opinion clearly states that private economies do not always result in social benefits in any event.

Analysis of efficiencies in antitrust cases, particularly in mergers, was originally suggested by Williamson as a check to see if there were any social gains that might *offset* social losses resulting from departures from unrestricted competition (Williamson 1968). It was argued that if some trade restraints or mergers might lead to welfare losses due to increases in monopoly power, the presence of efficiencies might be considered as an offsetting factor in their defense. However, since no monopoly or price-fixing effects, and hence no social welfare losses, were shown to be associated with Sylvania's challenged practices, there was no need to adduce evidence of offsetting economic efficiency gains. It is also true that an efficiencies analysis might reveal something about the *purpose* of a particular practice or arrangement; in this sense, Sylvania's marketwide recovery following the adoption of selective distribution might serve as evidence of an efficiency—or, more accurately, an "effectiveness"—purpose, rather than a monopolization attempt.

In spite of these varied interpretations, the real truth is that the *Sylvania* decision is not a triumph for new and more sophisticated approaches to antitrust analysis, but rather for the simple but powerful idea that the appropriate determinant of the legality/illegality of specific business arrangements voluntarily adopted by independent competitive firms is their overall impact on competition in the market, not their consistency with arbitrary and simplistic legal doctrines.

Related Developments

In the wake of the *Schwinn* decision, the FTC had launched an attack on the soft drink industry's long-standing system of geographically restricted sales territories. There is a slight, but arguably irrelevant, distinction between the two situations: soft drink bottling is considered "manufacturing," because bottlers mix purchased syrup with carbonated water to produce the finished product, which they then distribute. (They may, however, also purchase the finished product—particularly canned beverages—from authorized suppliers for subsequent distribution as well.) Territorial restrictions were originally related to transportation convenience from individual bottling plants; their continuing purpose was to provide complete market coverage for the parent soft drink franchisors and to stimulate each bottler to exploit fully the sales potential of his own territory.

The FTC cited these restrictions in the contracts of eight major soft drink syrup manufacturers as "unfair methods of competition" in complaints filed in 1971 and 1972.[31] These complaints, following the *Schwinn* rule and the Antitrust Division's interpretation of *Bausch & Lomb,* were initially phrased in terms of per se violations; however, while the proceeding evolved, this position was modified and a "rule-of-reason" analysis was substituted. It was essentially argued that the vertical restraints adopted by all the major brand suppliers unduly limited *retail* price competition on soft drinks. The FTC issued cease and desist orders against Coca-Cola and PepsiCo in 1978,[32] and Coca-Cola, as the lead company in the litigation, appealed to the courts.

The FTC proceeding not only challenged the established distribution arrangements of all the leading soft drink companies but threatened the existence of the great majority of local soft drink bottlers throughout the country. There were more than two thousand such firms in operation at the time, and although some were large publicly traded companies, most were small firms owned by local entrepreneurs. The combination of a broad-based constituency, a well-organized trade association, and the financial resources and sophistication of very large corporations (including the largest bottlers, as well as Coca-Cola and PepsiCo) permitted an attempt to bypass the court system and turn directly to the Congress for relief. In the early 1970s, the soft drink industry began an effort to obtain a legislative exemption that would protect its manufacturing-distribution system from antitrust attack. The ultimate result was the Soft Drink Interbrand Competition Act of 1980 (94 Stat. 939), passed while the FTC order was still on appeal in the courts, which rendered the appeal moot. This legislation declared the use of exclusive geographic territories for any soft drink product to be immune from antitrust attack wherever "such product is in substantial and effective competition with other products of the same general class in the relevant market or markets." This phraseology introduces a rather weak "market share" criterion, since a firm with a very large market share might not be thought subject to "substantial and effective competition." The main effect, however, is a strong endorsement of the "hospitality" doctrine in this specific industry.

A number of other industries, particularly the beer industry, attempted to gain similar specific exemptions covering their distribution practices, but none of these efforts was successful. Further efforts along this line are probably unnecessary, since aggressive governmental challenge of long-established nonprice vertical restrictions now seems unlikely.

In 1985 the Antitrust Division issued its Vertical Restraints Guidelines, spelling out the full text and implications of the "hospitality doctrine" as it now prevails. According to this document, "the legality of a vertical restraint in each case depends on its economic effect, assessed under a 'rule of reason' standard." Two analytical steps are involved:

1. a market share test, which "provides a safe harbor for the use of vertical restraints by any firm having ten percent or less of the market at its level of distribution," and also attempts to exclude other "situations in which neither collusion nor anticompetitive exclusion is plausible"; and
2. a subsequent "structured rule of reason" test, applicable to situations not already eliminated, which "focuses exclusively on effects on competition," primarily the condition of entry.

The clear implication of the Guidelines is that, after application of these tests, very few vertical restraints will merit antitrust challenge. Indeed, a number of classic restraints, including location clauses, are listed under the rubric "Vertical Restraints that are Always Legal" (Guidelines, 12). Serious antitrust scrutiny is to be limited to "airtight" territorial and customer restraints and exclusive dealing arrangements, and even here there is a strong emphasis on the likelihood of procompetitive effects.

There have been some recent developments on the purely analytical side as well. White (1981) notes that many, although not all, analytical possibilities indicate some tendency for vertical restraints to improve the allocation of resources at the *retail* level. A series of papers by Mathewson and Winter (1983a, 1983b, 1984, 1986) examines various vertical restraints within a rigorous microeconomic model and shows, among other things, that positive welfare effects (increases in both consumer and producer surplus) may arise even when the analysis is restricted to *intrabrand* aspects (i.e., a single manufacturing firm and its own dealer network) with no consideration of *interbrand* competition. This result modifies Preston's original assumption—adopted by the court in both *Schwinn* and *Sylvania*—that *intrabrand* effects are always anticompetitive. Rey and Tirole (1986), however, emphasize that all privately desirable restraints may not be socially desirable.

The long legal trail from *Bausch & Lomb* (1944), through *Schwinn* and *Sylvania,* to the 1985 Guidelines, and the corresponding evolution in economic analysis from Preston (1965), to the spate of highly sophisticated current papers cited above, lead to conclusions that are both simple and complicated. The simple point—and one on which a full-circle revolution has surely occurred—is that, apart from price fixing and obvious forms of horizontal collusion, the legal status of vertical restraints depends primarily upon their economic effects. The complicated point is that the effects of vertical restraints on both intrabrand and interbrand competition, both short-term and long-term, vary greatly according to the assumed characteristics of the markets under analysis and are extremely difficult to observe and measure in actual market situations. A quarter century of "new learning" has strengthened the need for careful and comprehensive analyses of "the economic and business stuff out of which these arrangements emerge," as originally called for by Justice Douglas in *White Motor.*

Notes

1. *Continental T.V.* v. *GTE Sylvania,* 433 U.S. 36 (1977).
2. The contrast between "hospitality" and "inhospitality" traditions with respect to vertical restraints has been developed by Williamson, based on a remark of Donald Turner: "I approach customer and territorial restrictions not hospitably in the common law tradition, but inhospitably in the tradition of antitrust." Quoted in Williamson (1985, 19).
3. See American Bar Association Antitrust Section (1977), p. 7, n. 14, for relevant citations.
4. *United States* v. *Bausch & Lomb Optical Co.,* U.S. 707 (1944).
5. These decrees are listed in American Bar Association Antitrust Section 1977, p. 7, n. 17.
6. *United States* v. *Arnold, Schwinn and Co., et al.,* 388 U.S. 365 (1967).
7. An influential collection of papers dealing with the antitrust aspects of such arrangements is *Law and Contemporary Problems,* v. 30, no. 3 (Summer 1965); see particular papers by Preston and Telser. More recent surveys are Blair and Kaserman (1983) and Caves (1984).
8. For a comprehensive analysis of these and related issues, see Blair and Kaserman (1983).
9. *United States* v. *Jerrold Electronics Corp.,* 187 F. Supp. 545, (1960); *affirmed per curiam,* 365 U.S. 567, (1961).
10. For the conventional wisdom on these issues, see Blair and Kaserman (1983); Scherer (1980, Ch. 10).
11. *White Motor Co.* v. *United States,* 372 U.S. 253.
12. *United States* v. *White Motor Co.,* 194 F. Supp. 562 (1961).
13. 372 U.S. 253, 261, 263.
14. 372 U.S. 253, 276.
15. 372 U.S. 253, 279.
16. *United States* v. *Arnold, Schwinn and Co., et al.,* 237 F. Supp. 323 (1965).
17. 388 U.S. 365, 382.
18. 388 U.S. 365, 379.

19. 388 U.S. 365, 382.
20. Quoted in Williamson (1980, 75, note 101).
21. Williamson (1980, 45) and Williamson (1985, 183–189).
22. 388 U.S. 365, 379.
23. This debate is summarized in American Bar Association Antitrust Section (1977), pp. 8–16.
24. Quoted in Howard (1983, 171).
25. When Ramsey Clark was appointed Attorney General of the United States by President Jimmy Carter, Justice Tom Clark (Ramsey Clark's father) retired from the Supreme Court and accepted ad hoc assignments at lower levels.
26. *Northern Pacific Railroad Co.* v. *United States,* 356 U.S. 1, 5 (1956).
27. 433 U.S. 36, selected phrases from pages 51–55, emphasis added. The text cites Preston (1965) in support of the last statement; the entire quotation is, of course, a paraphrase of his testimony as Sylvania's economic expert.
28. Shepherd's interpretation is, however, consistent with *current* Antitrust Division policy, as embodied in the 1985 Guidelines.
29. Williamson (1980, 51) also quoting Bork; and Williamson (1985) making reference to Posner and Turner.
30. 433 U.S. 36, 54.
31. FTC Docket Nos. 8853–8859 and 8877.
32. 91 FTC 517; 91 FTC 680.

References

American Bar Association Antitrust Section. *Vertical Restrictions Limiting Intrabrand Competition,* 1977.

Blair, R.D., and D.L. Kaserman. *Law and Economics of Vertical Integration and Control.* New York: Academic Press, 1983.

Caves, R.E. "Vertical Restraints as Integration by Contract: Evidence and Policy Implications." In *Impact Evaluations of Federal Trade Commission Vertical Restraints Cases,* edited by R.N. Lafferty, R.H. Lande, and J.B. Kirkwood, 430–466. Washington: Bureau of Competition, Bureau of Economies, Federal Trade Commission.

Chandler, A.D. *The Visible Hand: The Managerial Revolution in American Business.* Cambridge, Mass.: Harvard University Press, 1977.

Howard, M.C. *Antitrust and Trade Regulation.* Englewood Cliffs, N.J., 1983.

Mathewson, G.F., and R.A. Winter. "Vertical Integration by Contractual Restraints in Spatial Markets." *Journal of Business* 56 (October 1983a): 497–518.

———. "The Incentives for Resale Price Maintenance Under Imperfect Information." *Economic Inquiry* 21 (July 1983b): 337–348.

———. "An Economic Theory of Vertical Restraints." *Rand Journal of Economics* 15 (Spring 1984): 27–38.

_____. "The Economics of Vertical Restraints in Distribution." In *New Developments in the Analysis of Market Structure,* edited by J.E. Stiglitz and G.F. Mathewson, 211–236. Cambridge, Mass.: MIT Press, 1986.

Preston, L.E. "Restrictive Distribution Arrangements: Economic Analysis and Public Policy Standards." *Law and Contemporary Problems* 30 (Summer 1965): 506–534.

Rey, P., and J. Tirole. "The Logic of Vertical Restraints," *American Economic Review* 76 (December 1986): 921–939.

Scherer, F.M. *Industrial Market Structure and Economic Performance.* Chicago: Rand McNally, 1980.

Shepherd, W.G. *Public Policies Toward Business.* Homewood, Ill.: Irwin, 1985.

Telser, L.G. "Abusive Trade Practices: An Economic Analysis." *Law and Contemporary Problems* 30 (Summer 1965): 488–505.

U.S. Department of Justice, Antitrust Division. 1985. Vertical Restraints Guidelines.

White, L.J. "Vertical Restraints in Antitrust Law: A Coherent Model." *Antitrust Bulletin* 26 (Summer 1981): 327–345.

Williamson, O.E. "Economies as an Antitrust Defense: The Welfare Tradeoffs." *American Economic Review* 58 (March 1968): 18–35.

Williamson, O.E. "Assessing Vertical Market Restrictions: Antitrust Ramifications of the Transaction Cost Approach." In *Antitrust Law and Economics,* edited by O.E. Williamson, 44–85. Houston, Texas: Dame Publications, 1980.

Williamson, O.E. *The Economic Institutions of Capitalism.* New York: Free Press, 1985.

The Anticompetitive Uses of Regulation: *United States* v. *AT&T*

Roger G. Noll and Bruce M. Owen

Introduction

On January 1, 1984, the largest telecommunications enterprise in the world, the American Telephone and Telegraph Company, was divided into eight pieces in the largest antitrust settlement in history. The divestiture from the Bell System of seven regional local service telephone companies came more with a whimper than a bang, for two years earlier the defendants had essentially capitulated. In the middle of the trial, the defendants agreed to a settlement that gave the United States government virtually everything it had sought when it filed its antitrust complaint in 1974.

The importance of the *AT&T* case rests on more than the fact that over one-hundred-billion dollars in assets were involved in the divestiture. From the perspective of national economic policy, it set the American economy on a course that has never been explored. In nearly all countries the telephone company is a government-owned monopoly. The *AT&T* case committed the United States to open entry and at least oligopolistic rivalry, if not competition, in equipment manufacturing, long-distance telephone calls, and numerous other services. As a matter of antitrust policy, it also charted new waters by further defining the role of antitrust in regulated industries.

This chapter lays out the major elements of the economic analysis behind both sides of this historic case.[1] Because the case was settled after eleven months of trial (approximately three weeks before the trial was scheduled to end), the record of evidence and legal arguments is in-

Roger G. Noll and Bruce M. Owen were both deeply involved in the development of the government's antitrust case against AT&T; Owen testified at trial for the government. While objectivity in presenting the primary economic arguments of both sides was of utmost concern, their views were no doubt influenced by this experience. The authors are grateful to Peter Greenhalgh, John Kwoka, David Sappington, and Lawrence White for useful comments and advice in preparing this chapter. Part of the costs of preparing this manuscript was supported by a grant to Roger Noll from the John and Mary Markle Foundation, to which the authors express their gratitude.

complete. The Bell System[2] did not complete its defense, no post-trial briefs were filed by either side, and a hearing on relief issues, to be held if the Bell System lost the case, did not occur. Nevertheless, the essential elements of the two economic cases are clear from the documentary record of the litigation. In this study, we adopt the convention of referring to our summation of this work as either the government's or the Bell System's economic case. The reader should bear in mind, however, that the relative emphasis given here to the key economic arguments is not necessarily the same as either side would have given in its final arguments and briefs.

Historical Background

When the government filed its 1974 antitrust suit against the Bell System, the telecommunications industry had been a monopoly for nearly all of its 140-year history. The telegraph was the technology of the industry from the 1830s until the 1870s. Initially, telegraphy was competitive, but due to a combination of key patents, mergers, and cutthroat practices, Western Union soon emerged as a virtual monopolist. Its position was not seriously challenged until the late 1870s when Alexander Graham Bell's telephone came on the scene. After a brief period of competition between Bell's technology and an alternative developed by Western Union, the two companies reached an accommodation which, retrospectively, surely was one of the most one-sided deals ever struck. Western Union agreed to stay out of telephones, and Bell Telephone agreed to forswear the telegraph.[3]

By the 1890s, Bell had grown into a highly successful company. Owing to its patents, it had a virtual monopoly in both the manufacture of telephone equipment and the provision of service. Meanwhile, Western Union faced shrinking markets and experienced financial difficulties. Telegraphy had proved to be a weak competitor indeed for the telephone. But the Bell patents were expiring, and in the late 1890s numerous entrants entered the field in competition with Bell. Not only did the companies fight vigorously for equipment sales and new areas to be wired for service, they even competed in the same geographic area. Customers in large cities often faced rival telephone companies, allowing a choice of which local service to buy. Soon after the turn of the century, Bell's share of local telephone customers had dipped below fifty percent, and prices of service had fallen precipitously.

In the first decade of the twentieth century, Bell Telephone learned two important lessons that would eventually play a major role in *United States v. AT&T.* One was the importance of interconnection as a competitive weapon. The value of telephone service to a subscriber is directly related to the number of other subscribers to the system; the more subscribers a system has, the greater the number that any given customer can call. As calls are the source of consumer demand for service, the number of people with whom one can talk determines the value of service.[4] The Bell System was the largest and hence could offer the greatest number of people with whom a prospective subscriber could talk. By denying its competitors interconnection—that is, a link between two telephone systems that would allow each system's customers to talk to subscribers of the other system—Bell could use its absolute size as a competitive edge.

Denial of interconnection, however, was by itself insufficient to give the Bell System a clear victory in the telephone wars of the early twentieth century. The companies that composed the other half of the industry had an effective response: they formed an alliance by interconnecting with each other. Hence, the industry was growing in the direction of two competing systems of roughly equal size, each unable to communicate with the other.

Victory for the Bell System came in connection with Bell's second big lesson: the importance of rapid technological progress. Soon after the turn of the century, Bell acquired the patents on the first (and, for years, only) really effective long distance telephone technology. The key to this technology was electronics for repeating and amplifying telephone calls that significantly reduced static as the calls were transmitted along cables. For the first time, people could carry on comprehensible telephone conversations over hundreds and later thousands of miles. Exclusive control over this technology greatly increased the significance of Bell's interconnection policy. A customer of an independent telephone company had access to roughly as many *local* subscribers as a Bell customer, but only very poor quality access to people *in other cities,* even subscribers to other independent systems. Hence, when Bell constructed its long-distance system, it possessed a quality advantage that its competitors could not muster.

The long-distance patent monopoly quickly reestablished a virtual Bell monopoly in the rest of the industry. Through acquisitions and bankruptcies of competitors, Bell again began to push up its national share of the telephone subscribers to nearly ninety percent. But unlike its acquisition of a monopoly in the 1880s, this was not achieved without considerable public controversy and government attention. As Bell acquired an increasing number of local monopolies, local and state governments responded by imposing economic regulation. In 1913, as Bell's share of telephone subscribers passed sixty percent, federal antitrust authorities became concerned. Theodore Vail, the brilliant entrepreneur who had engineered the successful reestablishment of the Bell monopoly, recognized that a permanent accommodation with government was necessary. What emerged, in 1913, was the Kingsbury Commitment between Bell and the United States Department of Justice. Bell agreed to stop acquiring competing companies, not to fight against the imposition of regulation, and to divest Western Union, acquired in 1908. It also agreed to interconnect its system with the remaining independent companies. In return, it was not required to give up either the acquisitions of local service companies or its monopoly in long distance. Local monopolies in basic service and the national monopoly in long distance were to be contained by economic regulation, not by competition. Acquisitions of local telephone companies proceeded apace, and by 1930 Bell served over eighty percent of telephone subscribers.

The system created by the Kingsbury Commitment remained in place for nearly half a century. The only major changes were in the identity, power, and legislative policy objectives of the federal regulators. Originally the job of regulating long-distance telephone calls fell upon the Interstate Commerce Commission, but eventually it achieved stability with the passage of the Communications Act of 1934, which created the Federal Communications Commission. The sections of the Act dealing with telecommunications remained essentially unchanged for fifty years thereafter, even as the industry's dominant firm, the Bell System, underwent divestiture.

The Bell System performed well and prospered under the regime of regulated monopoly. It rapidly provided local telephone service to all urban areas in its service territories,[5] and it extended its long-distance service to every local exchange in the country. The extent, quality, and price of American telephone service were unsurpassed in the world and superior to most of the government-owned telephone systems in other societies. Nevertheless, the federal government persistently revealed its ambivalence, if not downright regret, at what the Kingsbury Commitment had wrought. Two continuing sources of controversy were Bell's policy of purchasing virtually all of its telecommunications equipment from its manufacturing affiliate, Western Electric, and the Bell monopoly in long-distance service.

Because Bell's long-distance monopoly rested on its superior technology, that monopoly was persistently threatened by further technological progress. After each important technological innovation, the government permitted some degree of competition. For example, when transoceanic coaxial cables became technically and economically feasible, the government permitted several firms to own them in addition to AT&T. Microwave technology, which was developed for the government during World War II, provided an alternative to coaxial cable for domestic long-distance telecommunications. After a decade of indecision, the FCC permitted large corporations to use microwave to build their own private telephone networks (1958) and then allowed firms to go into direct competition with AT&T in providing certain categories of services (1969).[6] Finally, when communications satellites became available for international and domestic long-distance telecommunications services, use of the technology was given first to other firms; indeed, for approximately a decade the Bell System was not permitted to own satellites for any purpose.[7] For reasons elaborated in the following discussion of the government's case against AT&T, the policies that enabled competitors to nibble at the fringes of Bell's long-distance monopoly played a key role in *United States* v. *AT&T.*

Bell's vertical integration into manufacturing was controversial because it increased the difficulty of regulating local and long-distance services. Soon after the FCC was created, it began to question whether the prices paid by AT&T's service companies for Western Electric equipment were reasonable. Eventually, the controversy led to the filing of an antitrust suit by the federal government, *United States* v. *Western Electric,* in 1949. The government claimed that the practice by Bell operating companies of buying only from Western Electric was an illegal exclusionary act. The relief the government sought was the divestiture of Western Electric. But the Eisenhower administration was unsympathetic to the case, and in 1956 agreed to a settlement that appeared to be a total victory for AT&T. No divestiture was required, and AT&T was forced to agree only to enter into licensing agreements for its various equipment patents (including transistors) and not to sell equipment to others than its own subsidiaries. At the time, these restrictions appeared unimportant because they were already the general policy of Bell. Within a few years their significance increased as Bell was thereby prohibited from entering the computer industry. With its leadership in semiconductor technology, Bell was positioned to be a very effective early competitor in computers; indeed, one can speculate that AT&T might well have been better off giving up the telephone but retaining its rights in transistors and computers.[8]

The 1956 settlement only temporarily resolved the manufacturing issue. The FCC almost immediately became embroiled in attempts by manufacturers to circumvent the Bell System's prohibition against "foreign attachments," Bell's term for non-Bell equipment. This reopened the issue of the wisdom of Bell's exclusive reliance on its own equipment and led after a decade to a series of FCC decisions that permitted competition in terminal equipment.

The government filed its second major antitrust suit against AT&T in November 1974. The new complaint restated the claim that AT&T's relations with its manufacturing affiliate were an antitrust violation; however, because of the settlement of the previous case, the government focused on developments after 1956 to back up its complaint. In addition, the government claimed that Bell had illegally monopolized long-distance telephone service. The government sought separation of both manufacturing and long distance from the provision of local telephone service.

The case was scheduled to go to trial early in 1981, which raised the prospect of a reversal of the government's position as had occurred when the Eisenhower administration inherited the 1949 case from Truman's Department of Justice. Fears that the Reagan administration would repeat history were immediately dispelled when Reagan's Assistant Attorney General for Antitrust, William Baxter, announced within weeks of taking office his intention to "litigate to the eyeballs" the government's case.

A few months later, when the government completed its liability case, AT&T moved for dismissal. The judge, Harold Greene, responded with an unusually detailed denial of what is normally a perfunctory step in the litigation of an antitrust case. In his denial of AT&T's motion, Judge Greene revealed that he had been strongly impressed by the government's case, and that the Bell System faced a mammoth challenge to escape unscathed. Settlement discussions, which had begun in the Carter administration and which had been suspended when Baxter took office, were renewed in the fall of 1981.

The Government's Case

The essence of the government's case against the Bell System was that it had used its status as a regulated monopoly in most of its markets to erect anticompetitive barriers to entry in potentially competitive markets.[9] The novel feature of this line of argument was that much of the Bell System's anticompetitive behavior was economically rewarding to the company only because it was regulated and, consequently, that one arena of public policy, economic regulation, was a cause of illegal acts in another area, antitrust.

Because most of the government's case hinged on its view of regulation, it is useful to lay out that view in some detail. The essence of the government's conception of regulation was that regulators did constrain the behavior of the Bell System, but not perfectly. As a result, the Bell companies had an important degree of flexibility in setting prices and deciding which services to provide, and they succeeded in earning profits that, while substantially below the monopoly returns that might be earned in an unregulated market, were nonetheless greater than a firm in a competitive industry could expect.

In taking this view, the government was not indicting the integrity or competence of regulators. Indeed, it used several former FCC officials as witnesses about the ineffectiveness of regulation.[10] Rather, the government's view was that regulators possessed insufficient information, staff, and legal authority to be able to regulate the Bell System effectively, a problem that was made worse by the fragmentation of regulation among the states and the federal government. In exercising discretion within the range of flexibility created by the imperfection of regulation, the government asserted that a regulated firm was obliged to obey the antitrust laws.

The importance of the government's perception of how regulation works is very great. If regulation is perfect, in that a firm can never earn more than the competitive rate of return and never incur unnecessary expenditures that benefit managers, or if regulation is completely ineffective so that a firm can evade its constraints without limit, then it is doubtful that the regulated firm would have any financial incentive to engage in the anticompetitive practices that Bell was alleged to employ.[11] But partially effective regulation creates an entering wedge for attempted evasion of regulatory constraints and for financially lucrative anticompetitive actions. Moreover, as we shall discuss, the methods used by regulators to control profits, costs, and prices actually increase the financial return to some anticompetitive practices.

Market Definition

The telecommunications industry offers a dazzling array of products and services. The system is used primarily for telephone calls, but it is also used extensively for computer interconnection and the distribution of radio and television programs. In the 1970s it began to be used for a variety of other services, ranging from burglar and fire alarm systems to automatic teller machines and electronic funds transfer. Each service is provided through many distinct devices, including the growing number of customer telephone instruments that can differ aesthetically or in function.

The government approached the problem of market definition by vastly simplifying it.[12] It viewed the telephone system as selling basically one relatively homogeneous technical product: electronic communications capacity of given technical characteristics. Moreover, the method of provision had essentially two forms: local service (in essence, communications passing through only a single local switch to connect customers in the same community), and long-distance service (communications between communities that require routing through more than a single switch). Hence, regarding services, the key distinction was simply whether a service was local or long distance.

Lumping the various local or long-distance communications services into common categories was justified in part by the fact that the capacity of the telephone network was fungible: in general, the Bell System could supply various services (business versus residential, voice versus data, private line versus public message service) in any proportions it chose using the same equipment. Indeed, for the most part the distinctions among these services were designed to facilitate price discrimination rather than to distinguish services that required unique supply arrangements. Another major factor entering into this market definition was that it corresponded roughly to the separation between state and federal regulatory jurisdictions. The government did not seek to impose competition in areas traditionally regulated by the states; however, it did seek to facilitate the federal policies that had been developing at the FCC to make the long-distance market more competitive. Hence, the government proposed to define a local service market, which it recognized was and would probably continue to be a monopoly regulated by the states, and a long-distance market, which was regulated by the FCC and was potentially competitive.

Equipment markets also had to be defined. Here, again, the government made a distinction, this time between equipment sold to customers of telephone companies, called Customer Premises Equipment (CPE), and equipment sold to telephone companies. Not only the Bell System, but other large United States telephone companies (e.g., General Telephone and Continental Telephone) were vertically integrated into both types of equipment manufacturing. In the 1970s, the FCC had adopted policies designed to introduce competition into CPE; however, no serious attempt had been made to interfere with vertical ties between telephone companies and manufacturers of telephone company equipment. Despite the fact that there are dozens of different kinds of telephone equipment in each of these categories, most of them not substitutes for each other, the broader categories were regarded as antitrust markets because suppliers (especially Western Electric) could generally produce all types and because each company dealt almost exclusively only with its own manufacturing affiliate. Hence, narrower, more accurate market definitions would only have led to a repetitive account of essentially the same facts regarding market shares and procurement practices.

An important feature of all of the market definitions was that they were geographically constrained to Bell System services. That is, the Bell System was accused of monopolizing access to long distance, CPE, and telephone company equipment in the service territories of the Bell System's local operating companies. Again, the rationale was largely institutional. Local telephone service was a franchised monopoly, protected by state regulatory policies against competitive entry. Customers of a local telephone company were its captives. Access to these customers, either directly in the sale of long-distance service and CPE[13] or indirectly by selling the telephone company equipment that they used for local calls, of necessity had to be through the local telephone company. A customer in Bell territory, for example, could not substitute General Telephone service or equipment for that offered by Bell, nor could General Telephone enter Bell territory in order to compete.

One test for the validity of market definitions is whether a firm with a very large share of the hypothesized market can, in fact, raise prices and extract monopoly profits. As applied in this case, two separate issues need to be addressed. In principle, the fact that local service companies possess legally enforceable monopoly franchises meant that customers did face a monopoly. The demand for telephone services was obviously not perfectly elastic; indeed, the economics literature showed that for a variety of services demand was almost perfectly inelastic.[14] Hence, if prices increased for long-distance service from the Bell System or for CPE sold by the Bell System prior to the FCC's actions to break this monopoly, customers had no alternative but to pay the increase or give up service. And, if the Bell System's equipment manufacturing branch raised prices, its practices, all but prohibiting its local operating companies from buying equipment from other sources, would assure that Bell companies would continue to buy Bell equipment and pass along the price increase to their customers. Thus, the first step of the analysis is easy and supports this approach to market definition: the Bell System's customers had no alternatives, had less than perfectly elastic demand, and hence were vulnerable to monopolistic pricing.

The difficulty arises in the second step. Most of these practices and pricing decisions were regulated. The "in principle" argument was vulnerable to the "in practice" possibility that the monopoly could not be exploited. Indeed, the inelasticity of demand for local service was evidence that regulation worked, preventing local telephone companies from extracting the full benefits of their market power. An unconstrained monopoly would set marginal revenue equal to marginal cost. Marginal cost is obviously some positive number; hence marginal revenue has to be positive as well. But positive marginal revenue implies that demand is elastic (greater than unity), not inelastic with values of 0.02 to 0.10, as econometric investigations typically find for local telephone service. Hence, local telephone companies must be charging prices well below the levels that an unregulated monopolist would charge.

The government's analysis of this problem started with the observation that the issue is not whether monopoly prices are charged, but whether some prices are higher than competitive levels. Even if regulation holds a regulated firm to competitive profits overall, prices can be higher than they would be with competition. To understand this requires an understanding of the details of utility regulation.

The Role of Regulation

Although each regulatory agency proceeds to regulate a utility in its own way, all take essentially the same fundamental steps.[15] First, the regulators determine the "rate base"—that is, the stock of capital facilities that the company uses to provide regulated services. The key test is whether a given piece of equipment is "used and useful." This means not only that the equipment is in service, but that it makes sense for the company to be using that equipment, rather than something else. The idea is to force the company to use the right technology for providing services. Once the capital facilities satisfying this test are identified, they enter the rate base at their current book value. Usually, this is their original cost to the utility, less depreciation.

The second step in the process is to determine the firm's cost of capital. The question addressed here is what interest rate on debt and returns on equity investment must the company pay in order to attract the funds necessary to make its investments, and in what ratio of debt to equity? The point of this phase is to guarantee a firm sufficiently high returns to attract investors, but no more.

The first two steps of the regulatory process are intended to make a trade-off between policy objectives. The first is to prevent monopolists from making substantial excess profits. But some profit is necessary and even socially desirable. The United States Constitution protects private investors from expropriation of their investments by government without adequate compensation. Courts have long held that to deny a regulated firm an adequate return on investment is, in fact, to expropriate its capital. Moreover, if a firm is denied a reasonable return, it will not be able to expand its capital investment to serve new customers, nor will it be able to invest in new technologies that provide new or better quality services. Hence, steps one and two are designed to produce a sufficient profit on the appropriate investment for providing the monopoly service to attract adequate capital investment.

The third step of the process is to add depreciation and operating costs to the product of the rate base and the allowed rate of return. This sum is the "revenue requirement" of the firm, which it is permitted to recover from its customers.

The last step of the process is to set prices. The pricing policy followed by regulators in the telephone industry for several decades has been "residual pricing." Regulators closely scrutinize what they regard as the socially significant (or politically expedient) prices: installation charges and basic monthly service charges for residential customers, and pay-telephone prices.[16] These have been permitted to grow only very slowly, substantially less rapidly than the overall rate of inflation. The regulated firm is then free to set prices for other services (e.g., business local service, toll calls, CPE other than ordinary telephones), subject to the limitation that it must not exceed its overall revenue requirement. Although regulators can control these prices as well, in practice they generally did not. Regulatory agencies rarely even bothered to articulate a policy regarding the price structure for other than the three services regarded as most important.

A key point in the government's arguments about market definition and, subsequently, monopolization was that this process of price regulation did not preclude anticompetitive price increases for customers of telephone companies. Hence, the captive nature of customers to local telephone companies also held the danger that they would face anticompetitive prices. The government argued that this could occur in two important ways. First, state regulators had no way of knowing whether the prices paid for equipment (both CPE and telephone company equipment) were too high. For almost all large local telephone companies and for the Bell System's long-distance carrier, equipment was not acquired through competitive bidding, but from a corporate affiliate at posted prices. In the absence of a benchmark of competitive procurement outside of a vertical relationship, regulators had no basis for assessing the reasonableness of equipment prices. If manufacturing affiliates earned excess profits or simply were inefficient, telephone companies would pay too much for equipment. This would translate into a bloated rate base and bloated profits on that rate base. This in turn would raise the firm's revenue requirements and hence prices charged to at least some customers for some services. A similar argument applied to long-distance services, where the affiliate of the local telephone company that provided long distance did not have to do so efficiently, at lowest possible price, to retain all long-distance business in its service territory. Indeed, in both instances regulation had a certain perverse character. If demand is inelastic, a firm can actually earn *greater* total profits from excessive investments in capital equipment. This increases the size of the rate base and, hence, revenue requirements; as long as demand is inelastic, total revenues can be increased by raising prices, so that the higher costs of inefficient production can be recovered.

The second way in which customers of a regulated monopoly could face prices above the competitive level is through cross-subsidization, which occurs when one group of customers pays part of the cost of providing service to another group.[17] Once again, regulation causes the problem by creating an incentive to use price increases for some monopoly customers to offset losses elsewhere. Suppose that at all feasible prices one market has elastic demand, while another has inelastic demand. If a regulated firm lowers the price in the former, it will increase sales by a relatively large amount, requiring that it commit substantially more capital to that market. But if it increases prices in the latter market, it will suffer a relatively small reduction in sales, and hence a small reduction in capital requirements. Thus, changing both prices simultaneously in this way increases the total required capital that is "used and useful" by the firm. This, in turn, increases the firm's allowed profits. Because regulators do not exercise very close control over most prices, such behavior, within bounds at least, is seldom effectively controlled by regulation.

It is important to emphasize that these strategies become financially rewarding only if regulation is otherwise effectively holding down prices in a market in which the firm could otherwise profitably increase its prices. The best possible strategy for a firm is *always* to raise prices without paying higher costs or lowering prices elsewhere; however, regulation presumably prevents such a straightforward monopolistic practice. If so, inflated equipment prices and cross-subsidization are profitable, if imperfect, substitutes.[18]

Thus, the government concluded that focusing on customers served by the Bell System local companies was valid as a relevant market. Both in principle and in practice, such customers could be vulnerable to supercompetitive prices, even if the firm made only normal, competitive profits across all its lines of business.

In most antitrust cases it is important to demonstrate the market share of the defendant, because market share is often taken as one of the indices of market power. In *United States* v. *AT&T,* market share was not a major issue for two reasons. First, for any reasonable market definition, the Bell System had a huge market share. Indeed, AT&T did not seriously contest the government's definitions. Second, both parties contended that it was regulation rather than market share that determined the market power of the Bell System. The government contended that it was regulatory barriers to entry and regulation-induced incentives to cross-subsidize, confirmed with imperfect regulation of profits and prices, that gave the Bell System market power. The Bell System contended that regulators constrained and directed its behavior, preventing it from exercising whatever market power it might have if it were not regulated.

Monopolistic Abuses

The government argued that the Bell System retained its virtual monopoly not by superior efficiency, for there was no assurance that the Bell System had settled on the most efficient technology or the least costly means of providing service, but through a series of anticompetitive practices against firms that were willing and able to compete in virtually all of the Bell System's lines of business except local service. The specific charges were: 1) refusals to deal—denial of interconnection to competing services and CPE; 2) discriminatory practices that raised the costs of competitors; 3) abuse of the regulatory process—failures to provide complete information to regulators that sought to promote competition, and the use of regulatory process as a means of retarding entry and raising competitors' costs; and 4) setting prices in a manner designed to exclude competitors and that did not preclude predatory pricing.

Refusals to deal. A major component of the government's equipment case at trial was a set of "horror stories" from competitors to the Bell System about the company's persistent refusal either to buy their products or to permit the Bell System's customers to buy them. In addition, the Bell System refused to permit its customers to own nearly all types of CPE, instead insisting that CPE be leased from the telephone company. Similarly, in the case of competing long-distance services, there was evidence that Bell systematically refused to provide rivals with interconnection, or comparable interconnection, with its local facilities.

Prior to divestiture, the Bell System owned either all or a controlling interest in 23 local telephone companies. In all but a few cases, the Bell operating companies purchased essentially all of their equipment from Western Electric, the Bell System's manufacturing arm. The Bell System's policy in this regard was hardly unique, for large telecommunications companies the world over tend to be vertically integrated, including Bell Canada, which buys almost exclusively from Northern Telecommunications, and General Telephone, which purchased almost all of its equipment from its manufacturing divisions. The key point regarding the Bell System, however, was that other manufacturers, notably Northern Telecom and International Telephone and Telegraph (ITT), were regarded as significant potential competitors to Western Electric. Indeed, in a few cases, with prodding from state regulators, Bell operating companies had bought some non-AT&T equipment with favorable cost and performance characteristics. Hence, the government contended that the Bell System's vertical relationships prevented other manufacturers that produced good equipment at lower prices from taking away the business of Western Electric. The effect was greater sales and higher profits at both ends of the Bell System's business—unregulated equipment manufacture, and regulated telephone service (because higher costs and inelastic demand meant higher allowed profits).

In CPE, the government's case turned on the practices of the Bell System prior to the FCC's decisions in the early 1970s that forced the

Bell System to permit its customers to buy equipment from competitors.[19] The Bell System had insisted that CPE posed a serious threat to the integrity of the telephone system and the safety of its employees. Bad CPE, it argued, could emit electrical charges into the network, disrupting the quality of service. Moreover, these charges might be sufficiently powerful that they could electrocute workers attempting to repair the system. Thus, in order to maintain the integrity of the system, the Bell System first insisted that it be permitted to own all CPE, thereby taking responsibility for its quality. This placed the decision about the source of such equipment in the hands of the local Bell operating company, which in turn purchased exclusively Western Electric devices.

The Bell System's motives for undertaking such a policy, according to the government's argument, were another by-product of regulation. If local telephone companies owned CPE, the Bell System could earn profits on their sale twice: once at the manufacturing level, and then again as part of the rate base of the local telephone company. Either procurement from a competitor or customer ownership of Bell System CPE caused one of these sources of profit to disappear, and customer ownership of competitive equipment eliminated the profits entirely. In the absence of regulation, the Bell System could have charged monopoly prices for basic telephone service. It would have had no incentive to insist on owning and leasing CPE unless to do so would reduce the customer's cost of service or improve the quality of service (and thereby cause customers to be willing to pay prices that yielded a higher profit). Nor would an unregulated monopoly want to stay in the business of manufacturing CPE if others could do so more cheaply, for expensive CPE would simply reduce the profits it could extract from its telephone monopoly. But once regulation is imposed on telephone services, profits become dependent on costs, and as long as demand is inelastic, higher costs mean greater revenues and greater allowed profits.

The most amazing aspect of the Bell System's policies was that they were accepted for so long by federal and state regulators. Each major telecommunications company pursued the same policy, buying only its own CPE and leasing it rather than selling it, for alleged reasons of system integrity and worker protection. This raises obvious questions: Why were GTE phones safe in GTE service areas, but not in the Bell System service areas, and vice versa? Why could independent telephone companies with no manufacturing affiliate safely purchase CPE from multiple suppliers, but not the vertically integrated companies?

Eventually, the FCC required that the Bell System allow its customers to own CPE and to buy it from whomever they pleased. Initially, at the urging of the Bell System and other telephone companies, the local telephone company insisted that it be permitted to require that customers who owned their CPE purchase a "protective" interface device that would prevent dangerous electrical feedback to the network. Indeed, the process by which this policy came about became another example of Bell's anticompetitive actions, as will be discussed subsequently. Eventually, the FCC adopted its own testing procedures whereby CPE could be licensed for interconnection to the nation's telecommunications system without the protective device, and the Commission simultaneously insisted that the Bell System separate its CPE leasing business from other activities. By the time the case came to trial, these policies had opened the doors to a competitive CPE market, and by the time divestiture actually took place, most lines of CPE were highly competitive. Nevertheless, the government used CPE as an illustration of the Bell System's generally anticompetitive corporate policy.[20]

The final example of refusals to deal was the Bell System's actions regarding private telecommunications systems and competitive long-distance companies. Again, once the FCC had permitted corporations to own their internal telecommunications systems and to interconnect corporate offices with private, long-distance links, the Bell System effectively thwarted this policy for several years by refusing to permit these systems to be connected to its national network.[21] The Bell System's long-distance competitors initially entered the business by providing private networks. Then, after a favorable FCC decision in 1969, MCI, Inc. began to offer "private line" competition, providing long-distance lines that connected a company's office in one city to the local telephone network in another. Shortly thereafter, Datran also entered to provide high quality, high-speed long-distance service mainly for computer interconnections. Refusing to permit these systems to connect with local networks meant that relatively few companies would find it useful to have a private system. Without interconnection, the large fixed costs of private networks were useful only for intercity intracorporate communications, and not for communications between the same two cities that were directed at people outside the company. Only companies with large corporate facilities in several cities would find a noninterconnected system worthwhile.

As with the CPE issue, by the time the case came to trial, refusals to interconnect were no longer a live issue. The Bell System had lost numerous battles in courts and regulatory agencies over its interconnection policies, and by the late 1970s it could no longer deny interconnection without facing the possibility of stiff fines. Nonetheless, it persisted in denying interconnection that had the best technical properties. Basically, two kinds of lines are connected to a local switch. One kind is used for connecting local customers to the central office ("line side") and the other is for connecting the central office to other switches in the long-distance network ("trunk side"). The Bell System eventually allowed competing long-distance companies to have line-side connections, but not trunk side. Line-side connections to the local switches imposed substantial costs on the Bell System's competitors that were not imposed on the Bell System, which supplied long-distance service through its trunk side connections. At the time of trial, the issue of access quality was being litigated at the FCC, and undoubtedly some requirement to provide trunk side connections (e.g., an "equal access" requirement) would have emerged from the agency. Yet it remained for the settlement of the antitrust case, not a regulatory decision, to deal with this issue. At trial, the inability of long-distance competitors to obtain trunk-side connections was used as an example of several antitrust violations, one of which was refusal to deal.

Raising costs of competitors. The Bell System's practices in both CPE and long-distance interconnection were also cited as discriminatory practices designed to preserve the company's monopoly in these areas. The protective device that the Bell System required for all "foreign attachments"—that is, CPE manufactured by someone other than the Bell System—was expensive, yet, as the FCC's tests proved, totally unnecessary. Some of the government's most devastating evidence was testimony from AT&T employees that, indeed, during the periods in which the Bell System forbade foreign attachments altogether, and then insisted on the protective interface device, the company's own technicians were reporting that the policy was unnecessary. Hence, the requirement to use an expensive interface device amounted to nothing more than a means to make more expensive the use of competitive CPE relative to the Bell System's products. By imposing costs on users of competitive CPE, the Bell System guaranteed that it could retain most of the market even if its prices were higher (but by less than the cost of the interface device), thereby earning supracompetitive profits for products it produced efficiently and lower but positive profits on products that it produced less efficiently than its rivals.

Again, at the time of trial the CPE issues were largely moot, because Bell's share of CPE sales had begun a precipitous decline. The principal purpose of raising them was to support the fundamental contentions of the government that the Bell System practiced a corporate policy of monopolization and that regulation was not an effective means of preventing the policy from working. Even though CPE had eventually been made relatively competitive through changes in regulatory policies, the process had taken literally decades, and in the intervening period the Bell System's customers had been effectively denied the right to use CPE that they wanted to have and that there was no good reason to deny them. Moreover, there was no reason to suppose that the Bell System, perhaps taking advantage of changing technology, would not find new and equally effective policies to recreate a dominant position in the future.

The provision of unequal access to competitive long-distance carriers was also used as an example of a discriminatory practice designed to raise the costs of Bell's potential competitors. The effects of line-side connections were that customers had more difficulty using competitive long-distance companies, and that those companies had to make unnecessarily duplicative capital investments. Customers of competitive long-distance companies had to dial the local telephone number of their long-distance carrier before placing a long-distance call. Then, because information regarding the source of a call was not transmitted, the customer had to dial an account number so that the call could be billed. Only then could the customer dial the long-distance number to be reached.

This method of interconnection had numerous undesirable consequences. Most obviously, it forced customers to dial many more digits than they would have to dial if they used the Bell System's long-distance service. In addition, the quality of the connection was worse. The local lines create most of the distortion in the telephone system, and competitors' calls had to travel over four local lines rather than two. Thus, the denial of equal access simultaneously reduced the quality and raised the costs of competitive companies.

In some ways, inferior interconnection was an advantage to Bell's competitors. Because of the pricing methods used in telecommunications, the Bell System's long-distance prices contained a substantial implicit tax, the purpose of which was to pay some of the cost of local service lines for residential customers, especially in rural areas.[22] Initially, competitive long-distance carriers avoided this tax. Eventually, regulators partially closed this loophole by imposing additional fees on long-distance carriers, but, in recognition of the inferior connection, these fees were far lower than the amount of tax that was avoided. For example, the FCC in 1980 set the long-distance surcharge on the type of interconnection that was used by competitors at approximately 60 percent of the amount paid to local exchange companies by AT&T for its trunk-side connections.

Nonetheless, the competitive carriers, despite the pricing advantages of inferior access, preferred equal access. The insistence that inferior access be used, therefore, was alleged to be a discriminatory act that limited the success of Bell's competitors and thereby denied customers the full benefits of competition in long distance. By undermining the quality and raising the costs of competitive services to levels that the competitors regarded as more than offsetting the pricing advantages, the Bell System protected itself against the extent of price and quality competition that would otherwise have emerged. In so doing it harmed both its competitors and its customers.

Abuse of process.   In presenting its case, the government had to deal with a pervasive problem. Politically legitimate regulatory agencies could in principle have put an end to the Bell System's anticompetitive activities by making appropriate decisions and enforcing them through legal action and franchising decisions. That the agencies had either not done so, or had done so only slowly and cautiously, was attributed in part to the behavior of the Bell System. The essential points were that the Bell System had strategically withheld information that was harmful to its self-interested claims, had purposely entangled its competitors in numerous regulatory and judicial proceedings to inhibit their ability to compete, and had refused to comply with procompetitive regulatory policies that were clearly enunciated by the agencies.

Two examples of refusals to supply relevant information were with regard to the alleged dangers of foreign attachments and the costs of providing competitive services. Throughout the 1950s and 1960s, the Bell System claimed that it had to have control of CPE to protect the network and its employees, yet it also knew these claims to be false for a wide variety of competitive manufacturers. Moreover, the Bell System also claimed that to build an effective interface device to protect the network was technically infeasible. Yet, the Bell System's Bell Laboratories had in fact invented such a device, and when the FCC finally ordered that competitive CPE be permitted with an effective interface, the Bell System was ready to provide it.

The Bell System was also charged with failing to supply regulators with proper cost information for the purpose of determining whether prices proposed in competitive markets were reasonable. The issue first became important when the FCC decided to permit companies to build their own private telecommunications networks. The Bell System responded in 1960 by substantially lowering the price of service for very large customers, essentially offering huge quantity discounts. These prices were controversial, and some charged that they were below cost. The FCC then embarked on an investigation to determine the actual costs of service, but the proceeding dragged on for nearly two decades and was never resolved. The FCC repeatedly found that the Bell System had provided insufficient information to permit the government to determine whether the prices were justified. The Bell System never did provide the kinds of cost information that would permit the question to be answered with any certainty.

The conclusion that this represented a strategic decision to withhold information was clearly incorrect at a superficial level. The Bell System could not have withheld this information, because, as the government learned in the discovery phase of the case, the Bell System did not possess decent cost information itself. Estimates of the costs of components of the Bell System were calculated using computational algorithms developed within the Bell System. The estimates were based on hypothetical configurations of components of the long-distance network, with average prices of inputs, rather than with the actual design of real components of the network and the prices actually paid. The estimates were also "bottom up" engineering cost estimates, rather than estimates derived from actual experience in constructing and operating the network. The result was cost estimates that were only loosely related to actual costs of providing service, or even to the actual book costs of the Bell System's local and long-distance companies. As a result Bell companies never could answer questions such as "What is the cost of providing local telephone service to households in Cambridge, Massachusetts?" or "What is the cost of a peak-period long-distance telephone call from Cambridge, Massachusetts, to Palo Alto, California?" Instead, Bell could only provide hypothetical answers from engineering cost analysis, or average book costs for broad categories of services over large geographic areas.[23]

To claim that this constitutes abuse of process requires arguing not that the Bell System willfully withheld information that its own managers possessed, but that it designed an accounting system that obscured the actual sources of costs within the company. Here the government offered no evidence that Bell consciously adopted a policy of not gathering such information for anticompetitive reasons, but relied instead on arguing that such a policy could serve no other purpose than the anticompetitive benefit it provided. The benefit was that it made the regulator's job of preventing anticompetitive pricing next to impossible. Specifically, if regulators were to impose a price structure on the Bell System that was based on principles of cost-causation (e.g., that prices for each service ought to be related to the cost of providing it), they would have to sustain a burden of proof in subsequent court appeals. Without reliable cost data, the best that regulators could do was to require that the company abandon its proposed price structure until it could be supported by data. The company, in turn, could then submit a new proposed set of prices, which under the regulatory statute would go into effect until an evidentiary hearing in support of them was completed. Thus, by failing to collect relevant information, the Bell System prevented regulators from regulating the price structure effectively.

Regulatory agencies were helpless to prevent anticompetitive pricing. Their procedures had been designed with the problem of overcharges in mind. If an FCC investigation of overcharges was underway, the company could be forced by an "accounting order" to keep track of the money received, so that it might later be refunded. But in an investigation of possible below-cost or predatory pricing, these procedures were useless. Nothing could deter the Bell System from continuing to charge the questionable prices until the investigation finally ended, and if the Bell System continually failed to supply necessary information, the investigation could never end.

The final allegation regarding abuse of process was that the Bell System purposely entangled its competitors in needless regulatory and judicial processes before the latter could compete effectively.[24] A principal example was the company's stonewalling tactics regarding interconnection with long-distance companies. After the FCC required interconnection, the Bell System continued to deny it on the grounds that state regulatory policy precluded it. This required the competitors to fight the battle in other forums. First, they had to deal with state agencies to attempt to induce them to order interconnection as well, but regardless of the outcome, the issue eventually then ended up in the courts.

The government had to deal with a highly significant problem in this part of the case. The United States Constitution protects the right of citizens (and hence corporations) to plead their cases to government officials and before the courts. A key question, then, is when simple exercise of constitutional rights becomes abuse of process.[25] The government did not argue that the Bell System had no right to appeal FCC decisions, nor to try to get state regulators to undo what the FCC had done. The argument was that the Bell System persisted in using this tactic long after the outcomes were completely predictable. By litigating the issue in a large number of states, the Bell System's use of process was argued to have become abusive after the first few court decisions had ruled (in favor of the competitors) that, indeed, the FCC had the jurisdictional authority to require interconnection and that its rulings had to be obeyed. At this point, further pursuit of relief in state regulatory agencies and before additional courts constituted nothing more than a tactic for raising the entry costs of competitors and delaying the date of effective entry, to the short-run anticompetitive benefit of the Bell System.

Pricing without regard to cost.   When the government filed its 1974 case, a recurring complaint from the Bell System's competitors was that it was engaged in predatory pricing. Yet, as discovery proceeded, it became apparent that such a charge could not be sustained in court for exactly the same reason that regulators could not effectively regulate the Bell System's price structure. Specifically, because the Bell System did not itself possess reasonably accurate information about the costs of its individual services, one could not prove that it had engaged in predatory pricing, which requires a demonstration that prices are set below some measure of costs. Thus, closely in step with the allegations regarding abuse of process, the government proposed a new variant of an exclusionary pricing claim: "pricing without regard to cost." The central argument was that, as implied by the absence of reasonable cost data, the Bell System set prices for competitive services purely on the basis of competitive market conditions, or more specifically on the basis of an objective to exclude competitors, paying no attention at all to whether prices bore any relation to costs. Thus, Bell's sole pricing goal in competitive markets was to retain a monopoly, regardless of the costs of doing so.

The pricing allegations were made in the context of private line services during the period when the Bell System faced competition on a very limited range of its services. Such pricing behavior clearly would be irrational for an ordinary, unregulated firm. But the Bell System could readily have assumed that losses in these services, even from prices that were a small fraction of cost, would be negligible compared to the Bell System's total revenues and so could readily be made up by increasing regulated monopoly prices by a very small amount. Thus, pricing competitive services without regard to cost was not irrational for the Bell System as long as regulators held its prices and overall return below the level that it would achieve as an unconstrained monopolist. In addition, there was documentary and other evidence that the prices in question were established by Bell System officials who did not consult, or even possess, cost information.

This theory of Bell System pricing differs from predatory pricing[26] in a number of significant ways, all of which ultimately relate to the set of incentives and opportunities that are accorded to a regulated firm. In an unregulated market, predatory pricing has two distinctive aspects. The first is that, in response to entry or price competition, a dominant firm lowers its prices below its own costs of production. Several cost tests for predatory pricing have been proposed, but the key idea is that a price is predatory if it simultaneously causes the firm to lose money by staying in the market *and* it has the effect of driving out efficient competitors. For example, if a price falls below the marginal cost of production, the firm is losing money by selling the last units of output. Or, in a multiproduct firm, if the price of one product falls below its average incremental cost, the firm would be better off withdrawing from the market than continuing to offer the product at that price. Normally, the relevant costs here are short-run production costs; however, if a firm persistently invests in excess capacity so that it is always prepared to drop price to short-run marginal cost and to increase output should a competitor emerge, then this, too, can be predatory.[27]

The second important element of predatory pricing is its purpose, which is to achieve a temporary, anticompetitive advantage. An unregulated firm has no interest in permanently selling its product below cost, although in some circumstances it may quite legitimately want to do so temporarily. Grocery and department stores often offer "loss leaders"—products that are advertised at a very low price to attract customers—or sell off excess inventories at prices below acquisition costs in order to avoid storing them any longer or even throwing them away. For a price to be predatory, ordinarily it must be below cost for the purpose of harming competitors so that, later on, prices can be raised to anticompetitive levels, either because the competitor has left the market, or because the competitor has learned a lesson and will henceforth follow a more cooperative pricing policy. This may be rational if there are substantial barriers to entry to protect the monopolist later, when prices are increased. The key point is that a period of low prices is followed by—and is designed to create—a subsequent period in which prices exceed the long-run competitive level. Thus, prices are predatory if their long-run effect is to create supercompetitive profits later that more than balance the losses in the period of predation.

The government did not contend that the Bell System's prices were predatory for two reasons. First, it could not prove that any price was below some reasonable definition of costs because the data on costs were so poor. Second, even if adequate data existed, the government saw no reason to believe that the prices could satisfy the second test— that they were temporary, for the purposes of creating short-term losses that would be made up later when competition abated. The latter was due to the pernicious influence of rate-of-return regulation combined with residual pricing. The existing system of pricing and regulation made it perfectly reasonable for the Bell System, if permitted to engage in competitive as well as regulated monopoly markets, to use cross-subsidization as a way to set *permanent* exclusionary prices in some competitive markets.

The essence of the cross-subsidization argument is the one that was addressed in the discussion of market definition. There we explained how a regulated firm has an incentive to charge prices below costs in markets with elastic demand and then raise prices in markets with inelastic demand. Precisely the same argument applies here. Competitive entry—or the threat of effective entry—has the effect of making a monopolist's demand curve more elastic. Hence, it increases the chance that the monopolist will find it profitable to engage in cross-subsidization of the competitive service. This maximizes sales (and, hence, required capacity and allowed profits), even as a permanent, long-run pricing policy.

Pricing without regard to cost implements such a plan. The regulated monopoly will match or beat whatever price a competitor sets in order to preserve the rate base that serves the competitive market. Costs are irrelevant beyond the contribution they make to revenue requirements. Hence, for setting individual prices, they can be ignored as long as there are other markets in which demand is more inelastic and competition is not a threat and as long as regulators have been effective in keeping prices and profits below monopoly levels in the other markets.

This perspective casts a new light on the FCC's multiyear, and ultimately unsuccessful, effort to measure service-specific costs in order to assure that the Bell System prices for competitive services were not below costs.[28] The Bell System price response to competitive entry in long distance was simply to lower prices to whatever level was necessary to keep the market. Not asking whether these prices recovered even marginal costs was consistent with the incentives facing the company. As long as the revenue requirement remained the same, and some services could have their prices profitably raised, it did not matter whether the competitive services were profitable in their own right, and it was reasonable for the Bell System not to worry even about meeting these conditions as long as the competitive sector was a small part of the business.

The implication of this allegation for regulated monopolies is profound. It implicitly confers on regulated firms a positive antitrust obligation to know their costs and to be sure that their prices are not anticompetitive, even if the regulators approve their price structure and do not care whether prices are anticompetitive. The Bell System was not charged with actually setting competitive prices below any cost standard; it was charged with *not knowing or caring* whether such a cost standard was satisfied and hence introducing the *possibility* that its prices would fail the cost test for predation.

The reason that the government's argument makes sense as antitrust policy is that if pricing without regard to cost is permitted, it retards all entry, whether warranted or not. In a sense, the issue was not whether any entry to date had been warranted or any price to date had fallen below a reasonable cost standard. It was that a potential competitor with lower costs than the Bell System would be unlikely to enter because of the certainty that no matter how low its costs might be as compared to the Bell System, the Bell System's prices would be set to preserve its monopoly.

Relief

Although the government did not present a detailed relief proposal until the settlement agreement, the principles of the case dictated divestiture. The cornerstone of all aspects of the case was the perniciousness of combining economic regulation with competition. Hence, the regulated parts of the business had to be separated from the unregulated or competitive parts. In theory, this could have meant even more divestiture than that which took place. Because local telephone service was likely to remain a regulated monopoly for the foreseeable future, it had to be quarantined from competitive markets. In addition, at the time of divestiture, long-distance service, although subject to some competition, was still dominated by AT&T and regulated by both the FCC (interstate) and the states (for long-distance calls within individual states). Hence, an argument could be made for separating AT&T Long Lines, the regulated long-distance carrier, from Western Electric, the unregulated equipment manufacturer.

Nevertheless, the government decided not to pursue total dissolution. For one thing, it could not establish that vertical integration between manufacturing and service did not provide some efficiency benefits. Second, with several competitors busily constructing national networks at the time of divestiture, the durability of AT&T's ability to use its remaining vertical connections to damage competition was dubious. The FCC had removed entry restrictions for services subject to its jurisdiction, leaving few, if any, long distance services free of potential competitive discipline. Moreover, a practice of inefficient production and an irrational price structure in a regime of open entry would simply hasten the entry and growth of competitors. Thus, the government was willing to rely on the FCC's decision not to let AT&T have any remaining protected regulated monopolies as sufficient to prevent regulation-induced anticompetitive behavior.

The second aspect of the relief proposal was to decide how many local operating companies to create. Permitting the Bell operating companies to remain a single entity was potentially damaging to the equipment market, for the companies would have considerable monopsony power. In addition, creating multiple operating companies could also assist state regulators. Over the years, differences in the performances of the companies could form the base of more realistic and accurate tests of the efficiency of operations, including the "used and useful" tests for capital investments. Finally, if the quarantine on competitive activities by local service companies were relaxed, one could expect local telephone companies to have some incentive to begin competing with each other in services that had no geographic tie to their franchise area. Examples are Yellow Pages directories and radio telephone systems, where in fact, after divestiture, the local operating companies have invaded each other's territories to offer competition.

Given that multiple operating companies made sense, the next step was to determine how many there should be. One possibility was to make all the 23 Bell operating companies separate. Another approach was simply to allow combination up to the point at which the market shares would begin to raise competitive questions. The government opted for the latter, ultimately settling on seven regional companies, each of which operates in several states. This line of argument does not support seven companies, rather than eight or six, and so the final con-figuration of the divestiture must be regarded as somewhat arbitrary, at least from the perspective of antitrust analysis.

The next issue was to decide where to draw the boundary between the local companies and long distance. The government case at trial im-plied that the place to divest the local companies was at the local service switch. All calling from one local service area to another would be re-garded as long distance and open to competition. In practice, during settlement negotiations AT&T convinced government officials that this was impractical. Within metropolitan areas, adjacent local switches often had dedicated trunks connecting them. To allocate these trunks to AT&T rather than the local companies would give it a large number of stand-alone trunks that really were a part of a somewhat ex-panded local network.

Once the dedicated trunks were assigned to local companies, it was difficult to determine precisely where to draw the line between local and long distance. Whether a pair of switches was connected by a dedicated trunk became a question of the level of demand and hence could be ex-pected to change over time with changes in population, commuting pat-terns, and the structure of local economies. From this discussion emerged what amounts to a new political jurisdiction: "Local Access and Transport Areas" (LATA), of which there are 160. In each state, the Bell operating company was subdivided into one or more LATAs. The center of a LATA is normally a Consolidated Metropolitan Statistical Area. Smaller towns do not have their own LATA, but instead are adjoined to a larger city somewhere else in the state—not necessarily on the basis of economic integration or even propinquity. Within the LATAs, Bell oper-ating companies can provide long-distance service. Between the LATAs, they cannot provide service, whether interstate or intrastate.

The effect of creating such large LATAs is that about 25 percent of long-distance calling takes place within the LATAs and is provided by Bell Operating Companies. This is, of course, inconsistent with the gov-ernment's basic argument, for it leaves a large chunk of prospectively competitive services rooted in regulated monopoly and subject to the same incentives for abuse that motivated *United States* v. *AT&T* in the first place. For the most part, state regulators have forbidden competi-tion in the business of providing long-distance service within LATAs.

The most interesting feature of the government's relief is that with one exception it was not designed to create structurally competitive mar-kets. The exception is the creation of seven separate operating companies to counteract monopsony problems and to encourage competition among these companies at the fringes of their operations. But in long dis-tance service, where AT&T possessed over 90 percent of the market, and in equipment, where AT&T enjoyed smaller but still dominant market shares, no horizontal divestiture was sought. The government relied on its theory that regulation had preserved these market shares, so that by simply severing the ties of AT&T to local service and its regulation by the states, competition would have a reasonable chance.

The government did not pursue further divestiture in part because to do so would have required an additional affirmative burden of proof that would have been very difficult to bear. Specifically, the government would have had to show that AT&T, divested of the local companies, somehow could continue to forestall warranted entry by erecting barriers against its competitors. The government's case contained no absolute barriers because of the FCC's policy after 1976 of permitting entry in every area; the actions to harm competitors that the government did cite were all rooted in the incentives and practices of regulation, which was gradually receding in the federal jurisdiction. No one would argue that entry into long-distance was quick and easy even after divestiture and deregulation, and the possibility remained, especially with respect to long-distance service, that the most efficient (cost-minimizing) structure for the telephone industry might be a monopoly or near-monopoly. Breaking up the Bell long-distance network could prove costly if this were so. The actual relief therefore preserved the possibility that Bell could maintain its monopoly by legitimate competitive means.

In addition to structural relief, the government sought injunctive remedies to forestall possible future anticompetitive practices by local service companies. The government sought to require the local operating companies to provide equal interconnection arrangements ("equal access") to all long-distance companies, and it sought to keep the local operating companies out of all lines of business that were likely to prove to be competitive. For example, the government wanted to give Yellow Pages directories to AT&T, not the local operating companies. The position of the government was relatively purist: local service companies should be given no opportunities to operate in competitive markets lest they repeat the practices that gave rise to the case.

The Bell System's Defense

Defendants contend that modern Bell management accurately perceived the fact that the elimination of competition was an essential element of the creation of an efficient industry structure and necessary for the provision of efficient telephone service.

—*A&T proposed stipulation 127, Episode 5/57A.*

The government's case ended in the summer of 1981, after about five months of trial. The Bell System stood accused of monopolizing markets for intercity telephone service and telephone equipment used by telephone companies and consumers through an anticompetitive course of conduct motivated in part by incentives and opportunities inherent in its structure and regulation. AT&T responded by moving to dismiss the case on a number of grounds, including assertions that the government had not established a *prima facia* case that the antitrust laws had been broken or that the laws even applied to a firm that was regulated by a federal agency. In September, United States District Court Judge Harold H. Greene not only denied AT&T's motion, but filed a strongly worded opinion that supported the government's principal contentions.[29] The burden thereupon shifted to the Bell System to rebut the government's case.

In broadbrush terms, the Bell System's defenses were as follows:

1. The Bell System lacked market power because its businesses were subject to regulation by state and federal commissions. These regulators controlled both prices and entry in the telephone business. Hence the Bell System did not meet the legal standard for possession of market power, which courts had held to be "the power to control prices and exclude competitors."

2. The Bell System had not earned monopoly profits and hence had not exercised monopoly power.

3. The court had no legal jurisdiction over the issues in the case because only regulators could exercise such jurisdiction.

4. The specific acts that the government alleged were denied. For example, the Bell System denied that it had abused the regulatory process and denied that it had priced its intercity services below or without regard to cost.

5. To the extent the Bell System engaged in any anticompetitive behavior it was inadvertent and excusable in light of the massive and sudden changes taking place in the industry. The telephone industry had been run as a monopoly for many years with the active encouragement of state and federal regulators; the change in policy designed to encourage competition was very recent; and signals from the regulators to the Bell System were ambiguous or contradictory, leaving Bell System employees in great doubt not only as to the permissible nature and extent of competition, but also as to the proper course of behavior for the Bell System in response to entry.

6. To the extent the Bell System had acted to eliminate competition, its behavior was justified by the natural monopoly characteristics of the telephone industry. The telephone business had economies

of scale, scope, and vertical integration that only a monopolist could exploit fully. Dismemberment of the Bell System was an inappropriate and unnecessary remedy, on account of the economies that would be lost.[30]

Several of these defenses are concerned with legal rather than economic issues, and we will not discuss them further except to say that Judge Greene generally rejected these arguments in the course of denying the Bell System's motion to dismiss at the close of the government's case.

The bulk of the economic evidence offered by the Bell System focused on two areas: the pricing of intercity services and the natural monopoly characteristics and historical economic performance of the Bell System. The pricing evidence was designed to show that the Bell System's difficulties in satisfying the FCC's criticisms of its pricing practices did not amount to an antitrust violation because the FCC had adopted the wrong pricing standard. Other evidence was introduced to show that if the correct pricing standard were considered, the Bell System had priced its competitive services above cost. Experts testified that AT&T personnel had carefully and accurately measured costs, so that the company had not priced without regard to cost. The natural monopoly evidence was designed to show that the Bell System's actions in excluding competitors were economically justified and that the Bell System's dissolution would be harmful to consumers. AT&T offered the testimony of numerous academic and consulting economists, as well as former regulators, in support of its arguments.

Pricing

The Bell System's defense against the government's charge of "pricing without regard to cost" contained two basic points. First, because the danger of pricing without regard to cost was that the firm would engage in predatory pricing, the government was required to show that some Bell System prices were, indeed, predatory according to a legally acceptable standard. The Bell System then went on to argue that, using the Areeda-Turner standard for predatory pricing (prices below average variable cost), Bell prices were not predatory. Second, Bell challenged the government's assertion that it did not systematically collect relevant cost information.

The practical problems of determining whether a multiproduct firm, such as the Bell System, is engaged in predatory pricing are often quite severe. The core of the problem is the appropriate method for estimating and incorporating "common costs" into the analysis. A firm has some costs that are "attributable" to—that is, caused by—the production of a specific service. Its remaining costs are common costs; the costs of inputs that are used to provide several different services. Examples are administrative overhead, marketing, the fixed costs of a firm enjoying economies of scale, and equipment that is used simultaneously for multiple purposes. In telecommunications, regulated firms typically argue that common costs are quite significant; however, the first practical problem of common cost analysis arises at this stage. The amount of common costs is to some degree a choice variable of the firm. A firm selects its technology of production and hence itself controls the extent to which it adopts common facilities or production methods that exhibit scale economies. In a regulated world, firms do not necessarily minimize costs, and so there is no reason to believe that the relative amounts of common and attributable costs are optimal.

Even accepting a firm's choice of technology, the extent to which a cost is attributable or common depends in part on the effort of the firm in attributing costs. For example, time allocation studies of administrative and marketing personnel can be used to attribute at least some of their costs, so that the amount classified as common depends on the firm's effort in performing such studies. Similarly, costs of engaging in regulatory and legal processes are typically regarded as common; however, some litigation arises from practices of the firm with respect to a particular service.

The cost standard adopted by the FCC for evaluating Bell System prices was "fully distributed costs." According to this procedure, the common costs of the firm are allocated to all of its services, typically in proportion either to attributable costs or to the quantity of output. The FCC's rationale for this policy was twofold. As a matter of equity, the FCC believed that each service should cover its "fair share" of common costs. But beyond this, the FCC was not convinced that Bell's estimation of common versus attributable costs was valid. Fully distributed costs minimize the importance of these errors and eliminate some of the incentive of the firm to overestimate the fraction of costs that are common or to adopt technologies that exhibit greater common costs relative to attributable ones.

In investigating Bell System pricing, the FCC had often found that some prices did not satisfy its fully distributed cost standard and on this basis had rejected some tariffs as illegally unremunerative. The Department of Justice did not adopt the position that this constituted evidence of predatory pricing, nor did it embrace the FCC's pricing policy. Nevertheless, several of the economists who testified on the government's behalf had previously advocated the FCC's fully distributed cost standard. Hence, the Bell System attacked FCC pricing policy as inappropriate and went on to propose its own, superior alternative.

The Bell System argued that the purpose of a predatory pricing standard is to separate legitimate from illegitimate responses to competitive entry by an incumbent firm. The criterion it proposed for determining the legitimacy of a pricing response was economic efficiency. In this case, economic efficiency has two components: serving as many customers as possible who are willing to pay at least as much as the cost of providing service to them, and producing the amount of service demanded by these customers at minimum cost. Fully distributed cost pricing fails both tests.[31]

The logic of the argument against fully distributed costs leads to the conclusion that the proper test for the legitimacy of a price response is whether price is below marginal or incremental cost.[32] Marginal cost refers to the additional costs to produce the last unit of any given service. Incremental cost refers to the average cost of a service arising from making the service available, i.e., the change in the firm's total costs arising from offering the service divided by the quantity of service provided. As long as a price exceeds both standards, the service is contributing to the coverage of the firm's common costs, and so any business retained by the firm is in the interests of *all* of the firm's customers (as well as in the interests of the firm).[33] Bell's argument was that to be found guilty of predatory pricing, the government should be required to show that the Bell System did not satisfy the incremental or marginal cost standard for predation. The difficulty with this argument was that it simply ignored the issues raised by the government.

The Areeda-Turner test is based exclusively on considerations of cost. It assumes that the firm operates so as to minimize production costs and that the firm does not engage in strategic investments to evade some of the bite of regulation or to deter entry. Many economists, including some who testified for the Bell System,[34] have expressed reservations about the sufficiency of the Areeda-Turner test, even in an unregulated environment. For example, a firm may find it profitable to make commitments to certain unnecessary costs (e.g., in excess capacity or in research and development beyond the amount required for optimal technological progress) in order to be better positioned to respond effectively to entry—and thereby deter entry even when an entrant has superior efficiency.

In a regulated environment, where firms do not necessarily seek to minimize costs, such tactics are more likely to be profitable. The reason is that a regulated firm can recover the costs of strategic entry deterrence if it can convince the regulators that these expenditures are "used and useful" in providing service. Hence, as long as a firm is not detected in so doing, it can respond to an Areeda-Turner standard by adopting otherwise inefficient technologies that minimize measured marginal incremental cost and thereby provide maximum pricing flexibility in response to entry.

The Bell System's attack on pricing without regard to cost went beyond its positive affirmation that the appropriate standard was the Areeda-Turner test. In addition, Bell argued that a pricing-without-regard-to-cost standard provided no useful guidance as to whether a price is predatory.[35] Obviously, a monopolist with very low costs and facing a very inelastic demand curve might well find that estimating marginal costs was not worth the trouble. Such a firm could earn very close to the maximum monopoly profit simply by setting prices to maximize revenues. Such a policy of "pricing without regard to cost" would clearly not be predatory. Again, as with the discussion of the proper cost standard, Bell's arguments simply ignored the *strategic* aspects of pricing policy. If a firm credibly commits to price without regard to costs, all entry is deterred, whether efficient or not, out of the expectation that the incumbent monopolist will always undercut the entrant's price.

Finally, the Bell System contended that pricing without regard to cost rested on an incorrect factual premise, the absence of reliable cost data within the company. Bell's case here was not merely to present detailed cost studies to prove that such data existed, but to offer testimonials from several economists and former regulators that they had, indeed, seen such studies and were convinced that Bell knew its costs in great detail. The essence of this testimony was that the analysts within Bell who undertook cost studies did so prudently and conservatively, doing their best to come up with reasonable estimates of service-specific costs in a practically challenging and difficult circumstance. Bell contended that it was inconceivable that these analysts were monkeying with the data to arrive at figures favorable to the company because to do so would involve a conspiracy among a large number of professionals throughout the Bell System.[36]

Once again, Bell's rebuttal simply did not address the issues about cost estimation that were raised by the government. One issue was the source of the basic data in the cost studies, which the government contended was not actual cost experience. Another was that the process of cost estimation was completely independent of the process of price setting within the Bell hierarchy. People who set prices for competitive services did not consult with cost estimators or have access to basic information about costs. Another was the dependence of cost estimates on choices regarding technology and accounting practices for estimating common costs. The thrust of Bell's defense was that there were numbers called costs floating around the company, but not that these numbers were actually used by corporate decision makers or that they were based on economically sensible accounting principles.

Natural Monopoly

In support of its claim that the Bell System was justified in eliminating competitors, and to prove that dismemberment of the Bell System was an inappropriate remedy to the antitrust problem, the Bell System submitted expert testimony by a number of distinguished academic and consulting economists who had studied economies of scale in the United States telephone industry and in Canada and the growth of factor productivity in the United States telephone industry. In addition, experts introduced engineering cost studies of economies of scale in the Bell system.

On the basis of a review of the studies, the Bell System contended that the telecommunications system had economies of scale and scope.[37] Economies of scale refer to a circumstance in which an increase in a firm's output causes a lower percentage change in its total costs. Economies of scope arise when a single firm can produce a group of two or more products more economically than separate firms, each of which produces only some of the products.[38]

Scale and scope economies in telecommunications come from several sources. The first is switching or networking economies. Bell argued that the same networking economies that lead economists to believe that local service is a natural monopoly also apply to intercity service. Second, intercity transmission trunks have static scale economies: larger capacity facilities have lower unit costs if they are fully utilized. Third, dynamic scale economies exist. In markets where demand is growing and where there are static scale economies, it may make sense to install facilities ahead of demand in order to achieve the lower unit costs of larger facilities. Thus, the faster demand is growing, the larger the facility it makes sense to install since demand will catch up to capacity more quickly. The faster a firm grows, the more it can take advantage of scale economies. Dynamic scale economies may lead to duplicate facilities. When demand is growing, it will generally make sense to build duplicate facilities at different points in time. So, even if a company has in place three alternative routes between a city pair (as Bell often did have) there may still be economies of scale to be exploited when adding a fourth route. The existence of duplicate facilities therefore does not disprove the existence of scale economies.

The point of introducing this evidence was to show that the FCC's policies of permitting competition in long-distance service were misguided and that Bell was justified from a public interest perspective in taking measures to delay entry and to drive new entrants out of the market. If dynamic scale economies exist, it does not make sense to split demand growth among alternative suppliers. To do so would raise costs by requiring simultaneous construction of smaller, higher cost facilities.

Economies of scope in intercity telephone service, according to Bell's economic witnesses, were largely due to scale economies in transmission. If so, only one company should provide both ordinary telephone service and private line service, since by doing so it can justify building larger capacity transmission facilities. (As noted above, most of the exclusionary pricing allegations against the Bell System involved private line service during the period prior to 1976 when the Bell System faced no competition in ordinary long-distance service.) Bell's arguments regarding economies of scale and scope were based on a review of the pertinent literature, including engineering cost studies, econometric studies, and factor productivity studies. It is useful to summarize briefly the nature of these studies.

Engineering studies proceed by making a detailed examination of the production process, asking exactly what facilities in what combinations can produce various output levels most efficiently, given the prices and performance characteristics of all relevant facilities. For a particular production configuration, one examines the range of output the facilities could produce, obtaining cost estimates for these facilities. How much do they cost to build, and how much do the labor and other inputs necessary for operation cost? Having done that, one can trace out an average cost curve for the particular mix of facilities examined. By reproducing the exercise for other mixes of facilities, one can trace out average cost curves for those facilities as well. Plotting the curves all together, if one can trace out an envelope curve that is generally downward sloping, the technology exhibits static scale economies. At trial, the Bell System introduced two engineering studies that found both static and dynamic scale economies for telecommunications. According to those studies, for the patterns of demand growth experience in United States telecommunications and the unit cost savings associated with larger capacity facilities, it pays to build capacity ahead of demand.

The Bell System pointed out that engineering cost studies do not measure scale economies actually realized. They measure the economies that are potentially achievable from large-scale physical facilities. Diseconomies of size in other areas—e.g., management—could in principle cancel them out. Thus, engineering studies, even if well done, should be supplemented by other forms of empirical analysis. Econometric studies of scale economies can provide a measure of the extent to which scale economies have in fact been achieved. Thus, econometric findings reinforce the findings from the engineering studies.

The Bell System argued that, despite various weaknesses, taken as a whole the econometric studies strongly support the hypothesis that scale economies exist.[39] Because of the (probably inherent) weakness of econometric studies of telecommunications scale economies, Bell witnesses did not claim that any individual study was important to their conclusion. Rather, the uniformity of the finding of scale economies over a number of studies using different statistical methods and applied to different data bases convinced them that disagreements over econometric practice do not bring the basic finding of scale economies into dispute.

Econometric studies of scale economies in this industry face at least two serious problems. First, it is difficult to separate the effects of scale and technological change.[40] As the phone system has grown, it has adopted new technologies. Thus the data will tend to show a strong correlation between lower costs and large size. To separate the effects of technological change and economies of scale, some measure of technological change must be included in the study. It is far from obvious that there is a good way to do this. The actual studies usually do something fairly crude, such as including percentage of households with direct distance dialing, to measure technological change. In some studies, whether scale economies were found actually depended on which crude measure of technological change was employed.[41]

A second problem with the econometric studies is separating the effects of scale from the effects of fill.[42] Any system will have lower unit costs if used at closer to full capacity. One might therefore conclude scale economies exist when in fact all that is being observed is an increase in capacity utilization. Given the tendency toward more intensive use of telephone plant over the period typically studied, the fear of misinterpreting scale economies from the effects of greater fill is not an idle concern. Only one of the econometric studies attempted to separate out the effects of scale and fill.

The problems of controlling for technological change and fill are not nearly so severe in engineering cost studies as they are in econometric studies, for the former explicitly enables an analyst to examine the relationship between fill and average cost. This is one way in which the econometric and engineering studies reinforce each other.

The final class of studies that served as a basis for the economic conclusion that the Bell System had economies of scale and scope was factor productivity studies. These studies measure changes in output from given amounts of inputs over time. When, as here, factor productivity increases, one knows either that there are scale economies or that technological change has occurred. It is not clear why factor productivity studies were offered in evidence. Because technology and scale cannot be separated, a finding of increased factor productivity does not shed light on the scale economies question. And these factor studies add little to the econometric results, for both use the same data. However, these studies do show that growth in factor productivity has been considerably greater in telecommunications than in the economy at large, although not greater than in technically similar industries, such as computers and microelectronics.

The government was prepared to respond to Bell's evidence regarding economies of scale and scope and the efficiency of the Bell System;[43] however, the larger question is what significance these arguments had in relation to the government's case. Specifically, if the Bell System could produce all products and services at lower costs than its rivals, why did it need to engage in various anticompetitive practices to preserve its monopoly? The government had expected that Bell would argue that its monopoly was unsustainable, relying on the theoretical work of economists at Bell Labs that demonstrated that a natural monopoly could not always set prices that precluded inefficient competitive entry.[44] But the Bell System did not in fact make this claim. The cost and demand conditions that cause a natural monopoly to be unsustainable are complex and rather special, and they normally imply that the scale of the entrant needs to be quite large.[45]

If sustainability theory does not apply to the Bell System, as is implied by Bell's failure to make use of it at trial, we are left with something of a puzzle regarding the relevance of Bell's efficiency arguments. The government did not propose competition in local exchange service, nor did it propose breaking up either Long Lines or Western Electric. Hence, any economies of scale in each of the three components of the Bell System were not threatened. Economies of scope across large numbers of local exchanges were threatened only to the extent that there are significant economies of combining local exchanges across the entire nation into one corporation—and indeed into a corporation that had already seen fit to decentralize local exchange operations into 23 separate local exchange companies. Economies of scope between long-distance and manufacturing also were not sacrificed. Hence, the only remaining plausible loss of economies of scope was between local service and either long-distance or manufacturing. Yet Bell's evidence did not focus on this aspect of the system. Much of it related to the economies of scale in transmission and the economies of scope in the long-distance network, neither of which was threatened by the government's proposed relief.

Research and Development

The Bell System has long operated industrial research facilities of the highest quality, organized as Bell Telephone Laboratories. Bell Labs has been a national leader in all phases of communications R&D, from basic research in physical sciences and mathematics to developmental work in equipment and network architecture. A key element of Bell's defense was that divestiture threatened the continuing excellence of Bell Labs research.

Bell's basic contentions regarding R&D were as follows.[46] First, the ultimate uses of much of Bell's R&D could not easily be predicted in advance. One could not predict whether local service, long distance, or manufacturing would be the principal beneficiary of a given line of research. Divested portions of the company, then, would no longer be able to benefit from some of the products of its research. Hence, facing lower expected benefits, the divested company would undertake less R&D, thereby slowing productivity advances in the industry. This appropriability problem is used to explain the general empirical finding in the economics literature that the private sector tends to invest too little in R&D.[47] Economic theory predicts that a profit-seeking enterprise will invest in R&D up to the point where the marginal cost of further research effort equals the marginal benefit *to the firm* of the results of that effort. If the benefits to the firm are only a fraction of the larger social benefits of R&D, the firm will spend too little on R&D. Applied to a divested AT&T, Bell's argument was that after divestiture Bell Labs would produce some research output that was valuable primarily to its divested operating companies. AT&T would not benefit from these applications and so would have no incentive to invest in producing them.

Second, Bell argued that intra-organizational methods of communication are better suited to designing research projects than inter-organizational relationships.[48] Hence, dissolving the Bell System would reduce the ability of Bell Labs to identify the most promising lines of research from the perspective of the national telecommunications network. The basis of this argument is that, after divestiture, conflicts of interest were likely to emerge between AT&T and its divested operating companies. As a result, each was likely to withhold some potentially important information from the other. Consequently, even if AT&T ignored the appropriability problem arising from research that benefited the operating companies, it would still be less favorably positioned to undertake the most desirable research projects.

Bell's arguments amount to a defense of the proposition that a monopoly will do more and better R&D than a competitive firm. While both arguments have merit, they are incomplete as an analysis of the economics of R&D in a regulated industry. Empirical economics research provides no factual support for the proposition that monopolists do more or better R&D. As a theoretical matter, the appropriability argument must be augmented by two additional considerations. One is that the optimal R&D by a firm depends on its expectations regarding R&D by its rivals. In an industry with rapidly evolving technology, incomplete appropriability must be balanced against the likely consequences of doing significantly less R&D than a rival, and thereby facing the loss of the entire business. The other is the effect of regulation, which by setting prices on the basis of costs tends to pass the gains from R&D on to customers, though with a lag. Even if the technology, costs, and demand conditions of an industry suggest that a monopoly has a greater incentive to pursue R&D than a competitive firm, it may still be the case that a *regulated* monopolist has less incentive to invest in R&D than an *unregulated* competitor. Because the government's case foresaw competition as a means to relax if not eliminate regulation of long-distance services, the latter comparison was the appropriate one.

Moreover, the regulated status of the Bell System could have provided an incentive to invest too much in R&D as a means of preserving monopoly. Like investment in excess capacity, expenditures on R&D constitute a commitment to lower costs and higher quality in the future. Investing too much in R&D—that is, expenditures beyond the point at which a dollar of R&D can be justified on the basis of its expected long-term effects on cost and quality of service—can retard warranted entry. If regulators do not, or for informational reasons cannot, force the regulated firm to be efficient in its R&D intensity, the costs of excessive R&D are simply passed on in regulated prices, thereby imposing little cost on the firm. The benefit, however, is to deter entry, even by firms that are more efficient. Entrants will expect that the incumbent's excessive R&D will eventually erode the entrant's ability to compete.

Which of these arguments is most applicable to the telecommunications industry is a matter of considerable uncertainty. Indeed, probably the least predictable ultimate effect of divestiture is what it will do to R&D in the industry.

The Outcome

In January 1982, the government and the Bell System announced that they had reached an agreement to settle the case. When the proposed settlement was made public, it was clear that the government had achieved virtually total victory. The Bell System agreed to divest its operating companies and to do so in a way that created seven regional companies. It agreed to spin off part of Bell Laboratories to become a research arm for the operating companies. And it agreed that the local operating companies should be prevented from engaging in any competitive activities.

While the Bell System did not admit that it had violated the law, that conclusion was, according to Judge Greene, "implicit" in the nature of the consent agreement.[49] In a 1987 review of progress under the consent decree, Judge Greene wrote:[50]

Although it may be difficult to recall this now, the fact is that for thirty years prior to 1984, the Congress, the courts, the Federal Communications Commission, and state regulators wrestled with the problem of what to do about the Bell System monopoly, its arrogance in dealing with competitors and consumers, and its power to shut out competition. . . . [Courtroom proceedings were protracted and]. . .regulators issued edicts that were largely ignored. . . In the meantime, competitors languished and the American ideal of free and fair competition remained absent from the telecommunications industry. When ultimately the decree. . .was negotiated between the parties and approved by the Court, it resolved the problem of claimed monopolistic conduct in telecommunications by going to its root.

That root was the control of the Bell System of the local telephone switches—in which it had a monopoly—and its simultaneous presence in several other markets (long distance, telecommunications manufacturing, and information services)—in which it had competitors. The competitors in each of these markets were suffering from an insuperable disadvantage: they could reach their ultimate customers only by connecting their circuits and products to the Bell System's local switches, the only technologically available avenue to the homes, offices and factories of America where the individual telephone instruments are located. It followed that these competitors were at the mercy of the Bell System's managers, who could with ease discriminate against them by such practices as delaying interconnections, providing inferior connections, charging exorbitant prices, or refusing to attach competitors' products altogether. The Bell System was also able to subsidize its competitive products with funds syphoned off from monies paid in by the ratepayers, thus to undercut the prices charged by independent firms and drive them out of business.

The quite predictable result was that no independent long distance, manufacturing, or information company ever really got off the ground: for practical purposes, the Bell monopoly remained just that. Since exhortations, regulations, and orders requiring a cessation of the Bell System's activities had proved fruitless, the remedy adopted in the decree, as simple as the problem itself, had but two basic aspects: first, the divestiture from AT&T of its local monopoly affiliates (thus forcing AT&T's other enterprises, all competitive, to stand or fall on their own); and second, an order prohibiting the new owners of the local bottlenecks—the Regional [local Bell operating] Companies—from engaging in the competitive long-distance, manufacturing, and information services markets (so as to make it impossible for them to duplicate the Bell practices, now that *they* controlled the bottleneck.)

These simple yet drastic measures have already begun to bear fruit for the benefit of competition and of the users of the telephone. Contrary to popular belief, the overall trend with respect to telephone rates is down, and the cost of telephone instruments is down dramatically. More importantly, competition has brought about innovations in telephone features on a scale and variety unknown before divestiture. While complaints about that divestiture and the ensuing inconveniences have by no means ceased, an understanding is beginning to emerge that these temporary dislocations are a necessary price for what the newly competitive marketplace can achieve.

The settlement agreement proposed by the parties was not the final outcome. Citing the Tunney Act requirements to assure that antitrust settlements protect the public interest, Judge Harold H. Greene held further hearings on the details of the plan, and ultimately changed it in several ways.[51] Most notably, he gave Yellow Pages to the local operating companies and instituted an ongoing waiver process whereby the local operating companies could be granted permission to enter competitive businesses by demonstrating to the court that they could do so efficiently and without competitive harm.

The concern that motivated these changes was the somewhat surprising one that the local operating companies were likely to be in difficult financial straits after divestiture. The foundation of the case had been that regulation does not fully succeed in preventing a monopoly from extracting some of its monopoly returns, yet the ultimate relief was based partly on the premise that the remaining regulated monopoly portion of the industry was potentially unviable. Another possible concern was that the relief proposed by the parties would lead to price increases for local service, causing a political backlash against divestiture. Giving the local exchange companies more lines of business might be thought to forestall this possibility. Hence, giving local companies access to some competitive markets was seen as a potential avenue to keep the companies both financially successful and politically acceptable.

Just why and how profits in competition could be expected to subsidize monopoly was never explained, and it seems likely that Judge Greene may now recognize this as an error.[52]

Another important aspect of the ultimate agreement was the process by which the local operating companies would provide equal access to all long-distance companies. The Bell System had never produced a switch that was designed for equal access; hence, the local operating companies faced a mammoth task in providing it—one that they could not reasonably be expected to undertake quickly. The question then was the rate and sequencing of equal access provision. One possibility was to proceed on the basis of LATAs. That is, a local company would provide equal access in one LATA, then move on to the next. The advantage of this approach was that at some specific date, all customers in a given area would, at the same time, be given the opportunity to choose a long-distance telephone company. This would have enabled the competitors to design their investment and marketing strategies to parallel the development of equal access, thereby making them more equal competitors to AT&T.

The approach that was instead taken was to sequence equal access on a switch-by-switch basis. The costs of converting a switch to equal access depend on its technology and vintage. Modern electronic switches need merely to be reprogrammed. Older technologies often need to be replaced entirely. From the local operating companies' standpoint, the sensible sequencing arrangement was to minimize costs. This means undertaking, first, to reprogram electronic switches and to replace the oldest remaining switches, which were nearing replacement anyway, and then to move on to the others. In fact, this was the policy that was adopted. Local operating companies were asked to propose their own strategies for providing equal access and to implement them by 1986 in the areas that were most desired by the long-distance competitors. The result was a patchwork that advantaged AT&T in the first round of competition for long-distance customers. Under patchwork equal access, it does not pay competitors to make market-wide investments in marketing or network design until most switches in a LATA have been converted.

At the end of his examination of the proposed settlement, Judge Greene issued a final order. It was entered as a modification of the 1956 settlement of the government's 1949 case against Western Electric, and so is called the Modified Final Judgment or MFJ. The divestiture plan went into effect in January 1984. Events since divestiture are broadly consistent with the government's economic theory.[53]

AT&T's market share in telephone equipment has declined dramatically since divestiture; it is now generally well below 50 percent in most categories.[54] In long distance, the competitive carriers have substantially improved their position, but AT&T remains the dominant firm, with over 80 percent of the market. However, by 1986 equal access had still not yet been provided in most of the country and was unlikely to be complete until 1988 or 1989. In expectation of this, the competitors have built substantial capacity, and their share of industry capacity is more than double their share of sales. Thus, a definitive test of whether structural competition will emerge in this industry awaits developments in the early 1990s.

Perhaps the most significant development in long distance occurred in 1987 when the FCC proposed to reduce its regulatory oversight of AT&T. It proposed to abandon traditional rate-of-return regulation and instead apply a ceiling price based on past prices plus inflation. This is the first logical step toward total deregulation and is in line with the government's operating premise in the antitrust case that long distance could eventually be deregulated and competitive.

The conclusion to be drawn from these trends is that the government's and Judge Greene's expectations concerning the industry are largely fulfilled. After three years, and with no horizontal dissolution on the supply side in any market, monopoly has been replaced either by rivalrous oligopoly or by a dominant firm with a growing competitive fringe. This strongly supports the government's contentions that AT&T's practices prior to divestiture did effectively weaken competition, that regulation was not only ineffective in preventing abuses but actually encouraged them, and that AT&T's success in monopolizing long-distance and equipment markets was largely owing to the vertical integration of AT&T into the regulated monopoly of local service.

The economic analysis that played a role on both sides of *United States* v. *AT&T* is by no means unique in its application to that case. The decree that ended the case provided for a triennial review of the status of competition in the telephone industry in order to assess the necessity to continue the various restrictions on the local Bell operating companies. The restrictions prevent the local companies from providing long-distance service, from manufacturing equipment, and from various other lines of business. The first triennial review, in 1987, led to the filing with Judge Greene of more than 300 briefs totalling some 6000 pages, many containing economic analyses bearing on the same issues that were litigated in the trial. At the conclusion of the review, Judge Greene once again upheld the validity of the original economic theory put forward by the Department of Justice at trial.[55] It seems likely that these economic theories will remain relevant in future controversies involving telecommunications and other regulated industries.

Notes

1. For general treatments of the telecommunications industry, histories of the events leading to the case, and retrospectives on the divestiture itself, see: Brock (1981), Shooshan (1984), Evans (1983), von Auw (1983), W. Tunstall (1985), J. Tunstall (1986), and Faulhaber (1987).

2. In order to avoid confusion with the present, truncated AT&T, the predivestiture organization known as AT&T will generally be referred to herein as the Bell System.

3. The "telegraph" in AT&T's name reflects the fact that twice the Bell System has been in the telegraph business. The first was early in its history, when it competed with Western Union in all services. The second occurred when AT&T acquired control of the faltering Western Union in 1908, an acquisition it was subsequently required to divest.

4. Discussions of the structure of telecommunications networks may be found in Huber (1987) and Bolling (1983).

5. For the most part, service to rural areas was and is provided by heavily subsidized small local companies, often cooperatives. The federal government has supplied loan subsidies and technical assistance through the Rural Electricification Administration, and regulators adopt pricing policies that tax urban customers to subsidize rural ones. See Noll (1985).

6. For a history of the development of communications competition using microwave technology, see President's Task Force Staff Papers (1969).

7. Bell developed the first successful communications satellite, Telstar, but the superior technology proved to be the geosynchronous system developed shortly thereafter by Hughes Aircraft. In 1963, Congress passed the Communications Satellite Act, which created the Communications Satellite Corporation (COMSAT) and gave it exclusive control over international satellite investments. COMSAT immediately contracted not only with AT&T, but also with RCA and Hughes, for further development of the technology. Initially AT&T was permitted to own a minority (25 percent) of COMSAT, but a few years later, after it had lost the technological competition to Hughes, it divested this interest. On the domestic side, the FCC in 1971 adopted an "open skies" policy whereby it initially forbade AT&T from using domestic telecommunications satellites to serve any but ordinary telephone uses and simultaneously declared that it would authorize satellites in a manner that would create a competitive satellite industry.

8. For discussion of the 1956 case and the circumstances surrounding its settlement, see House Committee on the Judiciary (1959); *United States* v. *AT&T,* 552 F. Supp. at 131, 135–138 (1982). The 1956 consent decree was long thought to have retarded competition in the computer industry by keeping AT&T out. Experience since the dissolution of AT&T in 1984 has provided little support for this supposition, however.

9. The Government case is described in the Department of Justice pretrial brief filed in December 1980, in its Memorandum in reply to AT&T's brief on the motion to dismiss, filed August 16, 1981, in its Competitive Impact Statement in the Tunney Act proceeding that followed the announcement of the settlement, *United States* v. *Western*

Electric, 47 Fed. Reg. 7170 (Feb. 17, 1982), and in its response to the public comments in that proceeding, 47 Fed. Reg. 23,320 (May 27, 1982).

10. Cornell (1981), Melody (1981), and Hinchman (1981).

11. The point of anticompetitive practices is generally assumed to be enhanced profits. Both the unfettered monopolist and the perfectly regulated firm have no opportunities for increased profits through such means as Bell employed, and hence no incentive to pursue them. Accordingly, an antitrust offense in either case would have to be based on some other motive, such as the maximization of the size of the company.

12. Modern principles of market definition in antitrust cases are set out in the 1984 Merger Guidelines published by the U.S. Department of Justice and are analyzed in American Bar Association (1986).

13. At the time the case was filed, the local telephone company's monopoly on CPE was still largely intact, but it was about to crumble. By the time the case came to trial, several lines of CPE—most notably, ordinary telephone instruments—had become relatively competitive as a result of FCC policies discussed below.

14. Telephone demand studies are summarized in Taylor (1980) and Wenders (1986).

15. For more details, see Kahn (1971, vol. 2).

16. See Noll (1986).

17. Averch and Johnson (1962) probably provided the first formal statement of the incentive of a regulated firm to cross-subsidize its activities in competitive markets. A very large literature dealing with the issue of cross-subsidization has since developed. See for example Posner (1969), Grawe (1983), Williamson (1975), Warren-Boulton (1978), and Brennan (1986).

18. The second-best strategy for a regulated firm is to substitute capital investment (on which it can earn a profit) for operating costs (on which it cannot earn a profit), as demonstrated by W. Brock (1983). In the telephone business, possible examples are the design of excessively durable equipment that substitutes for maintenance, or the replacement of human service assistance by automated alternatives (e.g., directory assistance through computers instead of operators). Thus, a regulated monopolist would exhaust all substitutions of capital for other costs that regulators will allow before turning to excessive equipment prices or cross-subsidization.

19. For a brief history of the FCC's regulatory treatment of CPE, and citations to the leading cases, see *United States* v. *AT&T,* 524 F. Supp. 1336, 1348–1352 (1981).

20. The fact that the FCC had, after a decade's struggle, finally succeeded before the settlement in preventing Bell from maintaining a near-absolute monopoly of CPE does not mean, however, that there was not still an antitrust problem. Unless cross-subsidization and similar abuses can be stopped by near-perfect regulation, the market share of the regulated firm that is permitted to compete in unregulated markets will in general be too high. The higher it is relative to what would be the competitive outcome, the greater the social cost due to price and cost distortions. Thus, the mere fact that AT&T did not maintain a

monopoly share of CPE does not mean that the CPE story was irrelevant to any antitrust concern. See *United States* v. *Western Electric,*—F. Supp.—(1987), slip opinion at 84.

21. For a discussion of the history of the FCC's program to permit entry into the long-distance business, first by large customers building their own networks, later by specialized private line carriers, and finally by public message carriers, see *United States* v. *AT&T,* 524 F. Supp. 1336, 1352–1357 (1981).

22. For a discussion of this tax, see Temin and Peters (1985).

23. For more details on how the Bell System estimated costs, see Cornell and Noll (1986).

24. For a discussion of the use of the regulatory process to discourage or retard competition, see Noll and Owen (1983) and Owen and Braeutigam (1978).

25. The classic antitrust cases involving use or abuse of the regulatory process are *Eastern Railroad Presidents Conference* v. *Noerr Motor Freight,* 365 U.S. 127 (1961) and *United Mine Workers* v. *Pennington,* 381 U.S. 657 (1965).

26. Definitions of and proposed standards for treating predatory pricing are numerous. Two of the leading articles are Areeda and Turner (1975) and Joskow and Klevorick (1979).

27. See Dixit (1982) and references therein.

28. For a general discussion of cost allocation problems in the public utility context, see Young (1985).

29. *United States* v. *AT&T,* 524 F. Supp. 1336 (1981).

30. See generally, AT&T (1980).

31. Arrow (1981).

32. Arrow (1981).

33. The Areeda-Turner standard, average variable cost, is intended to be a practicable approximation of marginal cost.

34. Baumol (1979).

35. Baumol (1981).

36. Baumol (1981).

37. Rosse (1981).

38. Technically, the conditions for economies of scale and scope are somewhat more complicated than this. If $C(\cdot)$ is a firm's cost function, and $X_1, \ldots, X_n$ are the quantities of each of the firm's n outputs, then the respective definitions are as follows:
    Global economies of *scale*: for all $\alpha > 1$,
    $C(\alpha X_1, \ldots, \alpha X_n) < \alpha C(X_1, \ldots, X_n)$.
    Global economies of *scope*: for all $0 < \beta < 1$ and all $1 < k < n$:
    $C(X_1, \ldots, X_n) < C(X_1, \ldots, X_{k-1}, \beta X_k, \ldots, \beta X_n) + C(0, \ldots, 0, (1-\beta) X_k, \ldots, (1-\beta) X_n)$.

39. For a summary of the various studies that AT&T relied upon, see Rosse (1981).

40. Fuss and Waverman (1981).

41. See Evans (1983) for discussion of the econometric evidence presented by AT&T witness Rosse.

42. Evans and Heckman (1983).
43. Evans (1983) contains much of the background research for the government's rebuttal.
44. Baumol, Panzar, and Willig (1982).
45. Baseman (1981).
46. For a summary of Bell's expert testimony on the economics of Bell Labs, see Mowery (1987). Bell was in the middle of developing its R&D arguments when settlement was announced, and one of its primary economic witnesses on R&D was scheduled to testify when the trial was stopped. Hence, this discussion is based in part on what Bell witnesses would have said had the trial gone to completion.
47. Mansfield *et al.* (1977).
48. Harris and Teece (1987).
49. *United States* v. *Western Electric Company,*—F. Supp.—(1987) slip opinion at 117–118, nn. 191–193.
50. Footnotes omitted; emphasis in original. *United States* v. *Western Electric Company,*—F. Supp.—(1987) slip opinion at 211–215.
51. See *United States* v. *AT&T,* 552 F. Supp. 131 (1982), aff'd by the U.S. Supreme Court sub nom. *Maryland* v. *United States* 460 U.S. 1001 (1983).
52. *United States* v. *Western Electric,*—F. Supp.—(1987), slip opinion at 112–113.
53. For details, see Noll and Owen (1987).
54. For a survey of competitive conditions in telephone equipment and long-distance markets as of 1986, see Huber (1987).
55. Curiously, in the first triennial review the Department of Justice itself abandoned several of its positions in the trial, a fact that caused Judge Greene to be quite critical of the Department. A little less curiously, AT&T offset this development by wholeheartedly adopting the original rationale of the case, against which it had fought so hard only six years before.

References

American Bar Association, Section of Antitrust Law. Monograph 12: Horizontal Mergers: Law and Policy. ABA, Chicago, 1986: 62–161.

Areeda, Philip, and Donald Turner. "Predatory Pricing and Related Practices Under Section 2 of the Sherman Act." *Harvard Law Review* 88 (February 1975): 697–733.

Arrow, Kenneth. Testimony in *United States* v. *AT&T* (1981).

AT&T. Defendants' Pretrial Brief, filed December 10, 1980, in *United States* v. *AT&T.*

Averch, Harvey, and Leland Johnson. "Behavior of the Firm under Regulatory Constraint." *American Economic Review* 52 (December 1962): 1053–1069.

Baseman, Kenneth. "Open Entry and Cross-Subsidization in Regulated Markets." In *Studies in Public Regulation,* edited by Gary Fromm. Cambridge: MIT Press, 1981.

Baumol, William J. Testimony in *United States* v. *AT&T* (1981).

Baumol, William J. "Quasi-Permanence of Price Reductions: A Policy for Prevention of Predatory Pricing." *Yale Law Journal* 89 (November 1979): 1–26.

Baumol, William, John Panzar, and Robert Willig. *Contestable Markets and the Theory of Industry Structure.* San Diego: Harcourt, Brace, Jovanovich, 1982.

Bolling, George H. *AT&T: Aftermath of Antitrust.* Washington, GPO, 1983.

Brennan, Timothy. *Regulated Firms in Unregulated Markets: Understanding the Divestiture in* United States *v.* AT&T, United States Dept. of Justice, EAG Discussion Paper 86–5 (1986).

Brock, Gerald W. *The Telecommunications Industry: The Dynamics of Market Structure.* Cambridge: Harvard University Press, 1981.

Brock, William. "Pricing, Predation, and Entry Barriers in Regulated Industries." In *Breaking Up Bell*, edited by David S. Evans. New York: North-Holland, 1983.

Cornell, Nina W. Testimony in *United States* v. *AT&T.* (1981).

Cornell, Nina, and Roger G. Noll. "Local Telephone Prices and the Subsidy Question." Department of Economics, Stanford University, 1986.

Dixit, Avinash. "Recent Developments on Oligoloply Theory." *American Economic Review* 72 (May 1982): 12–17.

Evans, David S., ed. *Breaking Up Bell: Essays on Industrial Organization and Regulation.* New York: North Holland, 1983.

Evans, David S., and James J. Heckman. "Natural Monopoly." In *Breaking Up Bell,* edited by David S. Evans. New York: North Holland, 1983.

Faulhaber, Gerald R. *Telecommunications in Turmoil: Technology and Public Policy.* Cambridge: Ballinger, 1987.

Fuss, Melvyn, and Leonard Waverman. *The Regulation of Telecommunications in Canada.* Ottawa: Economic Council of Canada, 1981.

Grawe, Oliver. *IntraFirm Subsidization and Regulation,* FTC Bureau of Economics Working Paper No. 91 (1983).

Harris, Robert G., and David J. Teece. "Structure, Strategy and Politics in Telecommunications: Implications for Research, Development and Innovation by the Regional Bell Operating Companies." Processed. Berkeley: University of California, 1987.

Hinchman, Walter. Testimony in *United States* v. *AT&T.* (1981).

House Committee on the Judiciary. Report of the Antitrust Subcommittee on the Consent Decree Program of the Department of Justice, 86th Cong., 1st Sess., Jan. 30, 1959 (Committee Print).

Huber, Joel. *The Geodesic Network.* Washington, United States Department of Justice, 1987.

Joskow, Paul and Alvin Klevorick. "A Framework for Analyzing Predatory Pricing." *Yale Law Review* 89 (December 1979): 213–269.

Kahn, Alfred. *The Economics of Regulation.* 2 vols. New York: Wiley, 1971.

Mansfield, Edwin, et al. "Social and Private Rates of Return from Industrial Innovation." *Quarterly Journal of Economics* 91 (May 1977): 221–240.

Melody, William. *Testimony in United States* v. *AT&T.* (1981).

Mowery, David C. "Forecasts of the Impact of Divestiture on Bell Telephone Laboratories: An Assessment." Pittsburgh: Carnegie Mellon University, 1987.

Noll, Roger G. "State Regulatory Responses to Competition and Divestiture in the Telecommunications Industry." In *Antitrust and Regulation,* edited by Ronald E. Grieson, 165–200. Lexington, Massachusetts: Lexington Books, 1986.

Noll, Roger G. "'Let Them Make Toll Calls': A State Regulator's Lament." *American Economic Review* 75 (May 1985): 52–56.

Noll, Roger, and Bruce Owen. *The Political Economy of Deregulation: Interest Groups in the Regulatory Process.* Washington: AEI, 1983.

Noll, Roger G., and Bruce M. Owen. *"United States* v. *AT&T:* An Interim Assessment." Studies in Industry Economies No. 139. Stanford, Calif. Department of Economics, 1987.

Owen, Bruce, and Ronald Braeutigam. *The Regulation Game: Strategic Use of the Administrative Process.* Cambridge: Ballinger, 1978.

Posner, Richard. "Natural Monopoly and Its Regulation." *Stanford Law Review* 21 (February 1969): 615–643.

President's Task Force on Communications Policy. Staff Papers. Staff Paper Five: The Domestic Telecommunications Carrier Industry. NTIS Accession Numbers PB 184 417,416. Washington, D.C.: National Technical Information Service, 1969.

Rosse, James N. Testimony in *United States* v. *AT&T* (1981).

Shooshan, Harry M., ed. *Disconnecting Bell: The Impact of the AT&T Divestiture.* New York: Pergamon, 1984.

Taylor, Lester. *Telecommunications Demand: A Survey and Critique.* Cambridge: Ballinger, 1980.

Temin, Peter, and Geoffrey Peters. "Is History Stranger than Theory?: The Origin of Telephone Separations." *American Economic Review* 75 (May 1985): 324–327.

Tunstall, Jeremy. *Communications Deregulation: The Unleashing of America's Communications Industry.* New York: Basil Blackwell, 1986.

Tunstall, W. Brooke. *Disconnecting Parties: Managing the Bell System Break-Up: An Inside View.* New York: McGraw Hill, 1985.

United States Department of Justice. 1984 Merger Guidelines. Washington, GPO, 1984.

United States Department of Justice. Competitive Impact Statement in *United States* v. *AT&T* and *United States.* v. *Western Electric* 47 Fed. Reg. 7170 (Feb. 17, 1982)

United States Department of Justice. Memorandum in reply to AT&T's brief on the motion to dismiss in *United States* v. *AT&T* (August 1981).

United States Department of Justice. Pretrial brief in *United States* v. *AT&T* (December 1980).

United States Department of Justice. Response to public comments. *United States* v. *Western Electric* 47 Feb. Reg. 23,320 (May 27, 1982).

von Auw, Alvin. *Heritage & Destiny: Reflections on the Bell System in Transition.* New York: Praeger, 1983.

Warren-Boulton, Frederick R. *Vertical Control of Markets: Business and Labor Practices.* Cambridge, Mass.: Ballinger, 1978.

Wenders, John T. *The Economics of Telecommunications: Theory and Policy.* Cambridge: Ballinger, 1986.

Williamson, Oliver. *Markets and Hierarchies.* New York: Free Press, 1975, 113–115.

Young, H. Peyton, ed., *Cost Allocation: Methods, Principles, Applications.* New York: North Holland, 1985.

Vertical Integration as a Threat to Competition: Airline Computer Reservations Systems

Margaret E. Guerin-Calvert

Introduction

On November 14, 1984, the Civil Aeronautics Board (CAB) implemented regulations governing access, pricing, and bias in the computer reservations systems ("CRSs") owned and operated by major airlines in the United States. The final CRS rules adopted by the CAB were the result of a lengthy proceeding at the Board inquiring into the Carrier-Owned Computer Reservations Systems.[1] Participants in the proceeding included all of the major players in the industry—the major CRS vendors, independent airlines, major travel agent groups—as well as the Department of Justice, which intervened as part of its competitive advocacy program to provide the essential economic and legal framework for evaluating the markets involved in the CRS industry. The proceeding and the resulting CRS rules followed several years of complaints by Congress, some airlines, the government, and consumer groups that the ownership of CRSs by certain airlines affected competition in the CRS industry as well as in the newly deregulated airline industry.

Prior to the CAB proceeding, the Department of Justice had begun two investigations into the pricing and access policies of the two major CRS vendors. These investigations followed complaints from independent airlines and travel agent groups that the dominance of American Airline's SABRE system and United Airline's Apollo system was affecting the ability of airlines to compete with United and American and to provide information on their prices and schedules to consumers. The focus of attention switched from the Department of Justice to the CAB when, in late 1982, Congress requested that the CAB write a re-

Margaret E. Guerin-Calvert co-authored the 1985 Department of Justice *Report to Congress on Competition in the CRS Industry* and has been involved in a number of Justice Department reviews of CRS issues. She would especially like to thank Roger Fones, Andrew Joskow, and Craig Conreth for insightful comments on the issues discussed in this chapter.

port on the state of competition in the CRS industry.[2] This report, which was released in June 1983, raised sufficient concerns about the effect of CRS market power on competition in airline markets that the Board initiated its rulemaking proceeding in September 1983. The Department of Justice chose to participate actively in the rulemaking and thereby—at least temporarily—switched the focus of its possible relief options for CRS problems from structural relief, such as the divestiture of the CRSs from their airline owners, to behavioral relief. Thus, the ultimate outcome of three years of extensive antitrust investigations into the competitive problems raised by the vertical integration of major airlines into the distribution and ticketing of air travel through CRSs was decided in a regulatory context rather than in a district court. On July 27, 1984, just over a year after the report to Congress, the CAB issued its *Final Rule on Carrier-Owned Computer Reservations Systems.*

The CRS rules were an important development for a number of reasons. First, they represented an outcome where behavioral rules were chosen over structural relief as a mechanism for dealing with competitive issues raised by the vertical integration of a firm with market power into a second and otherwise competitive level of an industry. Prior to participation in the CAB proceeding, the Department of Justice had been considering both structural and behavioral relief as possible solutions to CRS problems. Indeed, some of the airlines that petitioned the CAB for action on the CRS industry requested that the CAB seek divestiture of the CRSs, believing that only separation of a CRS from its airline parent would solve the competitive problems raised by CRS dominance. In setting the stage for issues to be considered in the proceeding, however, the CAB indicated that its primary focus was on the development of sound and enforceable behavioral rules rather than on structural relief.[3]

Second, the proceeding at the CAB was important because both it and subsequent developments provided dramatic empirical evidence that competitive problems at one level of an industry can have significant effects on performance at other levels. Specifically, in a newly deregulated airline industry that held out the promise of substantial gains to consumers from the entry and expansion of new low-cost carriers into a wide array of markets, there were numerous instances of carriers' not getting their product to consumers because incumbent airlines dominated the CRS market. Any airline that attempted to expand its operations beyond a very few city-pairs was dependent on travel agents to market and distribute its product and thus on the CRS used by those travel agents. Moreover, because the major CRS vendor-airlines were dominant in different regions of the country, the airline had to be listed on each of the major CRSs in order to have its flight information available in each region. In most cases, the airline was therefore dependent on one of its major competitors for an essential input into its distribution of airline transportation services. Indeed, CRSs may have many of the attributes of an essential facility; that is, the facility is one not easily replicated or likely to be replicated in the market and is an essential input into the production of a related product.[4]

Finally, the CAB proceeding demonstrated the important policy role of thorough economic analysis. The behavioral rules that were ultimately implemented were chosen after a long process of evaluation of the structure of the CRS industry, the role played by CRS in the marketing and distribution of air transportation, and the application of antitrust principles of market definition and evaluation of entry to a complex and changing industry. The CAB intended that the rules implemented in 1984 would, subject to enforcement procedures, limit the majority of possible competitive abuses in the CRS industry.

Since 1984, there have been a number of follow-up reports on the state of competition in the CRS industry, as well as continued complaints and private litigation by certain airlines and travel agents. Thus, an issue still open in the industry is whether the 1984 rules are the best possible rules—that is, whether they are sufficient or whether they should be changed to deal with new situations—or whether the only long-term policy for eliminating competitive abuses is the divestiture of the major CRSs from their owner-carriers. The Department of Transportation has taken over the responsibility for responding to complaints alleging violations of the CRS rules and is currently seeking additional information on competition in the CRS industry. In addition, the CAB *Final Rule*—anticipating that changes may affect performance in the industry—requires that a mandatory review of the CRS industry be conducted in 1990.

The purpose of this study is to set out the economic analysis that was presented by both sides involved in the CRS rulemaking at the CAB. Roughly, the parties divided along the following lines: the government, travel agent associations, and independent airlines advocated regulation of the airline-owned CRSs; and the major CRS vendor carriers—specifically, American Airlines (SABRE) and United Airlines (Apollo)—argued for either no regulation or limited regulation of the CRSs. While there were a number of events leading up to the CAB rulemaking and numerous developments in the industry since the 1983–84 rulemaking proceeding, the filings made by the parties to the CAB proceeding represent the first major public record and the most thorough record of economic analysis of the CRS industry.

The record in the CAB proceeding has also set the basis for evaluating complaints that have arisen since the rules were issued, as well as other CRS issues. Important among these latter were the joint venture of the TWA PARS system with Northwest Airlines and private litigation that has arisen between independent carriers and the major vendors and between the CRS vendors over the conversion of travel agents from one system to another.[5] The continued usefulness of the economic thinking laid out in the CAB rulemaking highlights the important role that sound economic analysis of markets and entry conditions can have, even in an industry that continues to change and to raise new issues. The careful definition of the CRS market and its relation to the airline market, including the complex issues raised by the ownership by airlines of CRSs, has enabled analysts to analyze effectively a far broader range of issues than was ever considered when the initial rulemaking started.

Background

When complaints started to surface about CRS performance, the CRS industry had been in existence for less than ten years. Nonetheless, the marketing and distribution of air transportation had been revolutionized by the placement of an extensive network of computer terminals in 15,000 of the over 20,000 travel agent locations in the United States. These terminals were connected to massive mainframe computers with thousands of pieces of information on flights, fares, schedules, and passenger ticket records. The development of several large CRSs in less than ten years was attributable to the ability of airlines to adapt existing technology to marketing needs and to expand the capabilities of information processing systems—often by internal development of software and hardware when the computer industry did not keep pace with the airlines' requirements.

A CRS has several basic components. First and foremost, it is a computerized database of information relevant to the making of reservations (referred to as "bookings").[6] In general, the CRS database includes information on all flights and fares on which airlines have provided information to the CRS vendor.[7] In addition to the information provided on airlines, CRS databases also store substantial information on hotels, car rentals, tours, and other travel-related services. The CRS database can be accessed whenever a travel agent or airline using the terminal of the CRS vendor submits a request for information concerning travel between two or more points. The request is initiated through the use of CRTs (cathode ray terminals) linked to the main database through a complex set of telecommunications facilities.[8] The response to the travel agent request is in the form of a "display" on the agent's CRT screen. A display represents an array of flights for the specific origin and destination requested. The ordering of the display information depends on a number of factors that are embodied in the CRS algorithm.[9]

There were three main types of CRSs when the CAB considered regulation of the industry: proprietary (or single-access) systems, direct-access, and multi-access systems. A proprietary system is a CRS in which the user has direct access to the database of the CRS, which is basically an extension of the CRS's airline owner's internal reservations systems. All the information provided by carriers that have chosen to participate in a specific CRS is added to the complete data on all the flights and fares of the airline owner.[10] In 1983, the majority of CRSs in the United States were proprietary systems. These included American Airline's SABRE system, United Airline's Apollo, Delta's Datas II, and TWA's PARS. All of these systems started out as the internal reservations systems of the airlines and were subsequently enhanced and expanded for sale and distribution to travel agents. A direct-access system is a CRS in which the travel agent first accesses an expanded internal database and then can access separately and directly other participating carriers' inventories. An example was Eastern Airline's SODA system.[11]

The third type of system—a multi-access system—involves a central switch that processes the users' requests and directs them to the internal inventories of each of the participating carriers. Thus, in the case of a multi-access system, there is no central database that combines information on all carriers or any one carrier, but rather a link to a set of individual databases. Tymshare's Mars Plus was the only multi-access system existent in the early 1980s.[12]

Terminals and related software were typically leased or sold to travel agents, who used one system as their primary system in part because of the costs associated with having more than one system and the types of contracts that CRS vendors signed with agents.[13] While travel agents paid lease fees for use of the terminals, the booking fees for all reservations and ticketing through CRSs were paid by the airlines on whom the travel was booked. Generally, the CRS booking fees were on a per-segment basis, such that a connecting flight with one stop would be counted as a two-segment booking. While each carrier was charged a single price per segment, carriers were typically charged different booking fees depending on a number of factors. Prior to the CAB rules, newer carriers were charged somewhat higher fees than carriers that had been with the system for a longer time, and some airlines paid additional fees for enhancements, such as boarding passes and preferential listings in the display.

Between their initial development in 1976 and the beginning of the CAB proceeding in 1983, the CRSs came to be the most important means by which airlines made available to the traveling public information on flights and fares. This occurred for two reasons: first, during the same period travel agents were becoming the predominant means of distribution and marketing of air transportation. Travel agents' bookings accounted for well over 70 percent of all airline tickets sold in the United States.[14] Particularly with the proliferation of new service and new fares that followed the deregulation of airlines in 1978, the public increasingly came to rely on travel agents to provide accurate and timely information on the availability of service and low fares. This phenomenon of vastly expanded service and fare offerings accompanying deregulation taxed the ability of agents to handle requests and bookings through direct phone calls to numerous carriers and to write tickets manually. Thus, a second factor that facilitated the rapid expansion of the new computerized reservations systems was that they provided a convenient and simple way to collect in one source most of the relevant information that agents would need on endless possibilities of flights and fares, with the additional capability of making direct bookings for clients.

As the travel agent network became more critical to the carriers, and as the CRS became an increasingly important tool for the travel agent to serve the public, access to and the cost of access to the major CRSs became an important factor in the airlines' ability to market and distribute their product in the United States. This set the stage for the issues raised before the Department of Justice and involved in the CAB proceeding—claims that the major CRS vendors had market power in CRS and that they had, indeed, used that market power to exclude rivals from markets and to raise substantially their rivals' costs of marketing and providing air transportation services. The government and several carriers entered the CAB proceeding on one side, and the major CRS vendors on the other.

The Government's and Independent Airlines' Case

Numerous parties to the CAB proceeding filed comments on the advance notice of proposed rulemaking in the CRS industry. By far the most extensive and analytically complete of these filings was the comprehensive review of the industry presented by the Department of Justice.[15] The Department's filings represented the culmination of over two years of investigation into the CRS industry, participation in an advisory capacity to the CAB in its 1983 report to Congress on CRS competition, and extensive interviews of the major participants in the industry. The Department also relied heavily on the information gathered by the CAB from the major CRS vendors. The Department applied the principles of product and geographic market definition to the CRS industry and developed basic market share and concentration measures for the major CRS markets. They also analyzed the competitive issues raised when airlines that have vertically integrated into the CRS industry have market power over the distribution of information and bookings, which are important inputs into their competitors' provision of air transportation services. The theoretical and empirical analysis of the Department of Justice set the framework for the entire CAB proceeding.

Market Definition in the CRS Industry

The product market.   The Department found that the product offered by the CRSs was the provision, in computerized form, of extensive and organized information on flights, schedules, and fares on airlines, as well as other travel-related services. The first stage in the Department's definition of the relevant product market was to consider possible substitutes for these CRS services and to determine whether these were alternatives to which CRS users would turn if the price of CRS services were to be raised substantially above competitive levels. In considering this issue the Department identified two main groups of users of CRS services: travel agents (and, thus, indirectly the traveling public) and airlines.

Based on the Department's interviews in the industry and examination of data on travel-agent use of CRS services, the Department concluded that travel agents had few alternatives to CRS. Travel agents that were not automated had to call carriers directly to obtain information on the availability of seats, flight schedules, and fares. Moreover, these agents had to rely on less accurate and timely hard copy schedules such as the Official Airline Guide ("OAG"), which might not include all the relevant flight information. Without access to a CRS, the agent had to write tickets manually. The Department found that these operations entailed substantially higher costs than the costs of using a CRS. Evidence of this was that over 60 percent of travel agents had chosen to have automated facilities by 1983. All of the major travel agents with substantial volumes of bookings were automated. As a result, the Department concluded that for travel agents CRSs were a relevant product market. The Department then considered whether individual CRSs could have market power over travel agents; that is, whether travel agents could switch easily among the several CRSs if any one system was to raise prices.

In considering this question, the Department found that many travel agents could not easily switch among systems. Due to the costs of leasing or buying a CRS and the advantages of using one system for booking and accounting purposes, most agencies either used one system or had one system as their primary system. As a result, there was limited ability on the part of a travel agent to switch among CRSs within the travel agency. While the terms and conditions of the various CRS vendors' contracts varied, most were long-term contracts that committed the travel agent to staying with one vendor for substantial periods of time.

More importantly, travel agents often chose as their primary system the CRS that was offered by the airline with the greatest share of the traffic in the metropolitan area in which the travel agent was located. This was related to the fact that such an airline's CRS was most likely to have the most accurate and timely information on the carrier on which the travel agent was booking the majority of its business. In 1983, the travel agent could get last seat availability and boarding passes only on the CRS vendor's airline.[16] Because the reliability of the agent's bookings depended in part on last seat availability, this provided an additional incentive to use the CRS of the dominant air carrier in a city.[17] From this evidence, the Department concluded that it was not likely that a sufficient number of travel agents would be likely to switch to other CRSs if the dominant CRS were to raise lease fees. Moreover, it did not seem likely in the Department's view that travel agents could switch from the dominant CRS vendor if it raised one or more carriers' booking fees or biased the displays in favor of the vendor's flights.

While travel agents in practice chose only one system, the Department found that airlines needed to participate in all of the major CRSs. The product provided to airlines by the CRS was the dissemination of information on carriers' prices and services and a mechanism for booking and ticketing passengers by the travel agent. The alternatives to the CRS that were available to the airlines were to expand significantly their in-house operations by adding more airline ticket agents and more telephone lines or to expand ticketing by mail and the other distribution facilities controlled by carriers. These were found to be substantially higher cost means of distributing information than listing in a CRS. Indeed, in 1983, only two carriers (Southwest and People Express) had elected not to use CRSs for the distribution of tickets.[18] The Department, therefore, concluded that CRS was a relevant product market for airlines. Because the CRSs often had a concentration of travel agent locations near cities where their airline owners were dominant, and because the Department found that these airline owners were important in different regions of the country, no individual CRS served all parts of the country adequately. As a result, if airlines wanted to market their services through CRSs nationwide, they had to be listed in all the major CRSs. Thus, for airlines, CRSs were not substitutes for each other. One CRS could raise booking fees without causing carriers to shift substantially to the others.

The geographic market.   The relevant geographic market for the CRS product was found to be a local market. The Department used Metropolitan Statistical Areas (MSAs) and consolidated MSAs (CMSAs) as the geographic markets in which CRS vendors competed for travel agent locations. Since the travel agents were the point of distribution for the CRS and since the travel agents often chose the CRS of the airline with the greatest share of traffic originating in the immediate metropolitan area, they delimited the boundaries of the relevant market. That is, travel agents served the needs of a local community's passengers with information on the availability and price of air transportation to and from the local community, as well as to other points beyond the local community. Passengers in a given local community could not, and typically did not, turn to travel agents elsewhere. Moreover, carriers were competing to offer service to customers who used travel agents. Thus, even if the relevant air transportation service included some segment that did not include the local community as an endpoint, the customers were accessing the system through locally limited travel agents.

The local nature of the market was not significantly affected by the expansion of carriers. The major carriers, which were expanding to serve in most of the major markets in the United States, found that they had to participate in all the major CRSs in order to insure that information on their flights was provided to all the markets they intended to serve. The need to be listed in more than one system was related to the CRS's domination of the local markets in which their vendor-owners were major carriers. For example, United's Apollo had the majority of travel agent locations in Denver, and Eastern had a large share in Atlanta. As a result, an airline such as Continental, which served Denver markets and also markets on the East Coast, had to be listed on both Apollo and SODA.

Market Shares

Using this basic construct of the relevant product and geographic markets, the Department relied on an extensive survey of travel-agent use of CRSs to develop measures of market shares and concentration. Three types of market shares were developed: the number of CRTs, the number of travel agent locations with CRTs, and a weighted average number of locations. The weighted average measure, considered to be the best indicator of market power, adjusted the number of travel agent locations with CRTs by the volume of business (bookings) of the travel agency. Based on these measures, it was determined that the two main systems—Apollo and SABRE—had market power in a large number of major metropolitan markets. As shown in Table 1, American was found to have more than 40 percent of the travel agent locations in 17 urban markets with more than $100 million in air transportation revenues. Based on similar measures, Apollo was the dominant system in 10 markets and PARS in 4 urban markets. Table 2 shows Apollo's and SABRE's combined control of about 45 percent of all travel agent locations on a nationwide basis, which was responsible for 70 percent of revenues. Of automated agencies, the two CRSs accounted for 69 percent of locations and 80 percent of revenues. Whether or not these market shares were predictive of the ability of American and United to exercise market power in the CRS industry, depended, however, on whether other CRSs could enter and compete. Thus, the government undertook an extensive analysis of the prospects for entry in the CRS industry.

Table 1 CRS Shares of Travel Agencies in $100-Million Urban Markets (CMSA)
(18 Months Ended June 1983)

SABRE (American)		Apollo (United)		PARS (TWA)	
Anchorage	92%	Denver	72%	Kansas City	71%
Dallas-Ft. Worth	88	Portland	66	St. Louis	57
Cincinnati	84	Cleveland	64	Columbus	51
Phoenix	69	Milwaukee	57	Pittsburgh	41
Boston	69	Sacramento	52		
Rochester	69	Salt Lake City	52		
Houston	68	Seattle	48		
San Diego	54	Honolulu	47		
Detroit	53	Buffalo	44		
Wash., D.C.	51	Chicago	42		
New York	50				
Miami	49				
Minn.-St. Paul	49				
Hartford	44				
Los Angeles	43				
Salt Lake City	42				
Chicago	41				

Source: U.S. Department of Justice Comments, November 17, 1983 (Appendix).

Table 2   CRS National Shares of All Travel Agencies,
(18 Months Ended June 1983)

CRS	Number of Travel Agencies	Percent of Total	Percent Automated	Domestic Revenues ($ millions)	Percent of Total	Percent Automated
SABRE (American)	5692	27	41	6376.3	43	49
Apollo (United)	3865	18	28	4040.9	27	31
PARS (TWA)	2159	10	16	1561.1	10	12
SODA (Eastern)	1074	5	8	605.3	4	5
Datas II (Delta)	688	3	5	259.8	2	2
Mars Plus						
(Tymshare)	344	2	2	281.9	2	2
Unautomated	7546	35	—	1822.5	12	—
TOTAL	21,368	100	100	14,947.8	100	100

Source: U.S. Department of Justice Comments, November 17, 1983 (Appendix).

Entry into CRS

The Department reviewed a substantial body of evidence gathered from the CRS vendors in considering the entry issue. In the eight years between 1976 and the CAB proceeding, five CRSs had been developed and marketed by airlines, and one additional system had been advanced by a nonairline vendor (Tymshare). In these brief eight years, however, substantial modifications had been put into place by the two major systems. In large part, these modifications entailed the airlines' adapting state-of-the-art computers to the complex task of organizing and using vast databases—far larger in scale than had been ever considered in other computer applications. Such adaptation resulted in the modification of software initially developed for electronic funds transfer among banking organizations for use in the CRS context. Within the eight-year period, the incumbent airlines had proceeded well along the learning curve in the industry.[19] Moreover, much of the technology and software was specific to each CRS and could not simply be purchased "off-the-shelf" in the form of a mainframe and standard software.

In addition to the rapid advances in technology, the CRSs had greatly expanded their networks. American Airlines had over 8000 travel agent locations, and United was not far behind with about 6000 locations. A new entrant with a new CRS would have to be able to convince carriers that it was a viable competitor at a point when the entrant had no locations. The long-term, and sometimes exclusive contracts for travel agents reduced the likelihood that new entrants could easily and at low cost convert travel agents to their systems.

Thus, in 1983, the Department of Justice concluded that the prospects for new entry were not heartening. The CRS investment appeared to entail very substantial sunk costs, the scale of entry required for entry appeared to be high, and any entrant was likely to have substantially higher costs than those of an incumbent for a long period of time.

The Department also evaluated the extent of entry and expansion by existing CRSs into each others' markets in evaluating the market definition and entry issues. Here, it concluded that long-term contracts and the dominance of certain carriers in markets with control over their own airline's data and last seat availability made it unlikely that such entry could constrain the market power of the dominant CRS vendor.

Most of the entry analysis focused on the prospects for entry by another airline's CRS. This focus was due in part to the limited success of the few nonairline vendors in the CRS industry. While some of this differential success could have been due to differences in the ability of industry participants to respond to industry needs better than could an outsider, much of the relatively poor performance of the nonairline CRSs was due to their inability to reap benefits in airline revenues from CRS market power. The nature and effects of exercise of this CRS market power was the next and most intriguing part of the government's analysis of the CRS problem.

Exercise of CRS Market Power: Problems and Effects

Numerous carriers and travel agent parties filed petitions with the CAB and submitted information in interviews and filings at the CAB about the problems associated with CRS dominance by a few carriers. The problems fell into several general categories: access to the CRS, bias in the CRS display, monopolistic or discriminatory pricing of booking fees, and exclusive arrangements with travel agents that limited entry and competition with other vendors. The net effects of these practices were gains to CRS vendors labeled "incremental revenues." Incremental revenues were the additional revenues that a CRS airline obtained when travelers were diverted to its airline because of anticompetitive practices. Thus, for example, when a CRS was biased in favor of its owner-carrier, the CRS airline's flight would show up on the top of the display—even if its flight was not the best suited to meet the traveler's needs. Moreover, by excluding certain carriers from CRS access in certain markets, CRS airlines could limit erosion of their dominant market share by new entry.

The issue of incremental revenues was troubling in itself, but was heightened by concerns that incumbents from the formerly regulated airline industry were using CRS market power to harm the prospects for the many new carriers that developed immediately after deregulation. The Department believed that the decision to enter new markets by an existing carrier or by a new one depended on the load factor—the percentage of seats that are filled when the plane takes off—that the carrier could expect for a given price in the market. Load factor was found to be a critical determinant of the cost per passenger of a flight; the greater the load factor, holding constant other factors, the lower the average per passenger cost. Swings in load factor, and particularly differences between expected and actual load factor, could be critical determinants of the profitability of entry—and thus, the likelihood of entry. Bias or pricing problems in the CRS industry, thus, could dramatically affect the incentive and ability of carriers to enter new markets. Moreover, to the extent the CRS vendor was successful in deterring or limiting entry into its airline markets, it earned substantial incremental revenues from diverted passengers that it could use to subsidize its CRS operations. This, in turn, made less likely the successful entry of smaller carriers or nonairline vendors into the CRS industry.

The government's extensive interviews of industry participants identified a number of practices that CRS vendors used to earn incremental revenues. The most important of these were bias in the CRS displays (and the underlying algorithms that created the displays) and discriminatory access and pricing.

Bias.   The two major CRS vendors were found to have developed algorithms that ordered the display of information in ways that were biased in favor of the owner-airline or its co-hosts. The displays were ordered by using carrier-specific factors as the means for ranking flights, rather than, say, the best elapsed time or the most convenient departure time. In many cases, the result was that other carriers' nonstop service would often show up on the display well after all of the connecting service of the owner was listed. Such bias in the display had dramatic effects, because interviews revealed that travel agents tended to book over 80 percent of tickets off the first screen, and the majority of tickets off the first line. American Airlines for example, was found to have systematically biased its displays against New York Air by adding the equivalent of 40 minutes of delay to all New York Air flights.[20] Furthermore, American failed to show some of Continental's lower fares in its listings.[21]

Pricing.   The Department found that the CRS vendors had engaged in a variety of pricing practices—charging different carriers different prices for booking services. The government and several airlines alleged that these prices were not related to the costs of the services purchased, but rather varied depending on the extent of competition presented by the carrier. Thus, it was alleged that the discriminatory pricing was a means to raise the CRS vendor's airline competitors' costs. In particular, the Department found that American had raised prices for booking services to its new competitors—Air Florida, New York Air, and Midway Airlines.[22]

Other anticompetitive practices.   In addition to bias and pricing, airlines raised a variety of allegations about practices of the CRS vendors. These included substantial delays in loading a carrier's fare and schedule data into the system—such that the vendor carrier could respond to market conditions more quickly than other airlines—and claims that the CRS vendor had the ability to use the CRS to get immediate access to information on all carriers' prices and bookings in any market. This latter claim was among the most controversial raised by the airlines and was one of the few allegations for which the Department of Justice found little empirical support.

Conclusions Reached by the Government and Other Parties

Based on its findings that at least the two major CRS vendors had market power and had indeed exercised that market power in an industry where there were limited prospects for new entry, the Department of Justice and other parties urged the CAB to adopt strong rules regulating CRS behavior. The Department favored a few simple, but enforceable rules designed to limit existing anticompetitive abuses of market power and to improve the prospects for new entry and expansion by smaller CRS vendors. The hope was that behavioral relief would result in sufficient structural change in the industry in the long run to preclude the necessity of seeking divestiture of the airline-owned CRSs.

The Department's proposed rules fell into three general types: bias, pricing, and control of information and contracts. With respect to bias, they recommended that the CAB prohibit the use of any carrier-specific factor as the basis for a CRS algorithm. While there was concern that some subtler forms of bias would remain, the Department concluded that this simple rule would eliminate most of the bias. The Department also warned the CAB to write the bias rule in a way that the regulation could not be evaded through the development of secondary screens that were biased. With respect to pricing, the Department initially opposed any form of pricing regulation, indicating that the costs of such regulation probably exceeded its benefits. The Department eventually supported the CAB's final rule of nondiscriminatory pricing, indicating that smaller carriers might benefit from the countervailing bargaining power of the large carriers. Finally, the Department supported rules that would prohibit exclusive contracts with travel agents and did not object to the CAB's limit on the length of such contracts to five years.

The Response Of United and American Airlines

While United and American Airlines, as the two dominant CRS vendors, had roughly the same share of travel agent locations, the two airlines took dramatically different positions concerning the need for and type of rules that the CAB should implement for CRSs. Throughout the CRS proceeding, United Airlines consistently held the position that no regulation was required because United's Apollo system did not have market power and, therefore, could not affect competition adversely in any of the three areas of concern to the CAB—service to air passengers, service to travel agents, and competition among carriers.[23] By contrast, American Airlines took the position that any problems of bias and pricing stemmed from the historical origins of the CRSs in the internal reservations systems of individual carriers and their application as a means of distributing the carriers' products. American conceded that bias and selective application of enhancements could result in incremental revenues for the CRS vendor and did not oppose many of the proposed rules. Rather, American took the position that any rules concerning bias and pricing should be general and should be applied uniformly to all CRS vendors.[24]

Both United and American submitted studies by economics experts in their filings to the CAB. United Airlines' two experts provided reports aimed at refuting directly the contentions of the Department of Justice and the CAB that the Apollo system had market power and that such market power enabled United to gain substantial incremental revenues in airline markets. American Airlines submitted an expert report by an economics consulting firm, which addressed issues of competition and economies of scale in the CRS industry. The main arguments addressed in each of these three reports are considered in the following sections.

Economic Analysis by United Airlines

In considering the competition issues raised by the CAB in the notice of proposed rulemaking, United found there was "no justification for the imposition of direct overall regulatory control" by the CAB.[25] Indeed, to impose any such regulation on the newly developing CRS industry would result in the loss of the substantial efficiencies and benefits that all airlines and consumers gained from the risks that carriers such as United undertook in developing the sophisticated software and hardware embodied in the CRSs.[26] The foundation of this position—and perhaps the most controversial—was the analysis and conclusion that the CRS represented a multiproduct industry that was "contestable." The theory of contestability, developed by William Baumol, Robert Willig, and John Panzar, holds that in the absence of "sunk costs" (i.e., costs that are not recoverable when a firm exits a market or an industry) and of entry barriers, and with some lag in the ability of incumbents to react to the pricing initiatives of entrants, even markets with a lone incumbent will behave as if they were perfectly competitive. The essential concept in contestability is that entrants can engage in "hit-and-run" entry in response to profit opportunities; the constant prospect that such entry could occur forces incumbents to price competitively or risk losing their entire market to an entrant.[27] United concluded that airline markets and travel agents' markets were definitely contestable. They then used this conclusion of contestability to refute the claims made by the Department of Justice and the CAB that United and other CRS vendors had market power and that this market power was likely to persist because entry into the CRS industry was difficult.

This analysis began with the description of CRS as a multiproduct firm. Each CRS could simultaneously provide three separate products: service to airline passengers in the form of information on routings; information processing, booking, and ticketing services (as well as accounting services) for travel agents; and a means of marketing and distributing air transportation services for the CRS airline owner.[28] United also argued that the CRS exhibited "economies of scope"—that is, that overall costs were lower if all three functions were performed within one CRS than if three separate entities each performed them singly. The analogy was made to the simultaneous provision of three travel-related services and the broadcaster that provides news as well as advertising. Moreover, it was argued that Apollo essentially served as a mode of advertising or marketing for United and asserted that any incremental revenues that accrued to United derived from Apollo's superior marketing performance. Thus, United opposed regulation generally and also opposed any specific rules against bias, claiming they would eliminate one of three important sources of revenue for the CRS. With the loss of incremental revenues, the costs to travel agents and carriers would increase, and the result would be a more costly and less efficient production of CRS services than in the absence of rules.

United directly attacked the Department of Justice's findings on market power—and thus, indirectly on contestability—in the CRS industry by criticizing the Department's market definition and market share analysis. They indicated that any market shares for the CRSs on a national basis were vastly overstated and misstated the possibilities of entry, because the Department had failed to consider that there were numerous alternatives to the sale and distribution of airline tickets through CRSs. Direct marketing of tickets and increased advertising were alternatives readily available to carriers. People Express, for example, had decided not to participate in any of the CRSs. In addition, the sophistication of many travelers, especially business travelers, and competition among travel agents would be useful means to limit any harmful effects from bias that might arise in a CRS. As a result, United concluded that CRS was not a relevant product market and that market shares based only on CRS data were meaningless.

Assuming that the CAB rejected this view, United also critiqued the approach taken by the Department of Justice in calculating market shares, indicating that the relevant geographic market was not a regional or metropolitan market but rather the individual city-pair routing from each hub. The basis for this geographic market analysis was that the city-pair was the relevant air transportation market in which the passenger was traveling and that the CRS market should be consistent with this market. With this market definition, United's Apollo actually accounted for only a small portion of all tickets sold on routings, such as Denver-Chicago where United offered service and where tickets might be booked through Apollo. Other sources of ticketing that were alternatives to Apollo's services in that specific city-pair included United's internal reservations system, American's SABRE, TWA's PARS, Eastern's SODA, and sales through unautomated agents.[29] Based on calculations of this type, United's Apollo did not have a high market share in any city-pair routing, and its national market share was significantly below the over 30 percent alleged by the Department of Justice.[30]

Even if it were found that the relevant product and geographic markets were those advanced by the Department, United argued that they could still not exercise market power because the CRS industry was contestable. First, CRS did not have natural monopoly characteristics.[31] There were several CRSs in operation, and, generally, all seemed to be financially healthy operations. While there were substantial economies of scope inherent in CRS operations, much of the economies came from the marketing function that the CRS performed for its airline-owner. As a result, there was no reason to expect that only one CRS would exist in the long run in any relevant market.

A second argument advanced in support of the contestability of CRS markets was one challenging CRS as a relevant market—the notion that airlines did not need access to CRSs in order to market air transportation effectively. Finally, United argued that the long-term contracts in the CRS industry actually promoted entry rather than deterred entry into CRS markets. At a minimum, existing CRSs would find it relatively easy to enter each other's markets. Accordingly, United concluded that CRS rules were not only unnecessary, but actually harmful to the efficiency with which CRS services were provided to consumers.

United also submitted three reports that, respectively, disputed the contention of the CAB that CRSs had been used to increase the load factors of the CRS airline at the expense of its competitors,[32] examined the profitability of Apollo as a stand-alone CRS, and quantified the amount of incremental revenues earned by United from its Apollo ownership. The conclusion drawn from these three analyses was that United was not gaining unduly from its investment in CRS.

The CAB in its initial report to Congress and in the notice of proposed rulemaking advanced the view that bias in a CRS could affect entry into airline markets because an entrant's expected load factor would depend not only on its price, its costs, and the level of service, but also on the extent to which the incumbent carrier with a CRS biased the display against the entrant. Thus, all else equal, an entrant would have a lower load factor when faced with a biased display or the refusal of a CRS to list its flights and fares. United attempted to refute this contention by examining the relationship between average load factors on 572 United flight segments with the percentage of bookings on those segments that were made on Apollo. Thus, it was hypothesized, if bias affected entry, then one should see a correlation between load factor and the share booked on Apollo. No such relationship was found, leading to the conclusion that United had responded to changes in market conditions by increasing capacity on a route rather than by flying with higher load factors.[33]

The two other reports provided empirical estimates of the profits earned by Apollo and the level of incremental revenues, based on actual cost and revenue data. These reports were an important addition to the record in the CRS proceeding, because some of the major issues were whether the CRSs were actually earning monopoly profits from bias and access limitations in the CRS. The first evaluated the profit to United of Apollo, regarding Apollo as a stand-alone entity. This meant that the return to United's investment in Apollo was calculated as if the investment had been made by an independent company. The costs of a stand-alone entity used estimates of replacement costs of the hardware and software associated with Apollo. On the revenue side, revenues from other bookings were included, as well as an estimate of United's willingness to pay for a host position in an independent Apollo. The report concluded that, as a stand-alone entity, Apollo actually operated at a small loss. This study was subsequently critiqued because it had attributed to Apollo's costs all of the costs associated with the CRS for its CRS functions as well as the internal reservations functions that it performed for United. While it is difficult to apportion these costs correctly, their inclusion would overstate the costs of a stand-alone CRS that would not provide internal reservations services.

In assessing the revenue side of the balance sheet, the report on incremental revenues estimated the value to United of owning Apollo. It set up the following hypothetical: what proportion of its booking revenues would United be willing to pay for a position as host in a stand-alone CRS? The report evaluated this by considering what happened to United's bookings when agents switched from Apollo to SABRE or from SABRE to Apollo for a period of two quarters before actual changes and two quarters after such changes. Based on actual data, it concluded that United revenues that could be attributed to its host status in Apollo were 13 percent of United's revenues. The report concluded, however, that the 13 percent was not a true measure of incremental revenues because the figure reflected switching between two airline-owned CRSs and not from Apollo to a truly unbiased system.

Economic Analysis by American Airlines

Throughout the CRS proceeding, American Airlines took the position that the CAB should intervene in the CRS industry only to a very limited extent and that any rules that the Board might impose on the CRS vendors should be the minimum possible and should be applied uniformly across all vendors. Thus, American's concern appeared to be that the Board might choose to regulate only American's SABRE and United's Apollo and thereby handicap them relative to the other CRSs. It was American's view that bias and variable pricing did exist in the CRS industry, but that these were not unexpected given the origins of the CRSs as an extension of individual carriers' marketing and ticket distribution programs and because the contracts and hosting arrangements made by carriers were of different vintages. In support of these points and to aid the Board in its economic analysis of regulations, American submitted an expert report by an economics consulting firm.[34]

The report provided an overview of the CRS industry that found that CRSs exhibited definite economies of scale and scope. Furthermore, and in direct contrast to United's position, the American report found that the CRS and its production of information had high fixed (and sunk costs) and low variable costs. CRS was different from other applications of computer technology, such as automated supermarket scanners, because the CRS performed not only information processing but also marketing functions for its owner. As a result, an airline CRS owner would have the incentive to price the initial CRS services at a very low price in order to gain acceptance, because it would gain revenues from both fees charged for CRS services and airline tickets booked on the owner. Consequently, CRS services were not likely to be priced on a stand-alone basis. The initial low start-up prices and the varying vintages of CRS contracts with carriers, in turn, meant that an array of different booking fees would prevail in the industry. Thus, the American report contended that the varying prices noticed by the CAB were not intended to be discriminatory or aimed at harming certain competitors, but were an historic accident.

In discussing bias, the report concluded that the fact that the many major carriers were competing with each other for distribution by the development of competing CRSs had naturally led to bias in the systems. Moreover, the report found that this bias had resulted in incremental revenues, which in turn had effectively subsidized travel agents' use of CRSs.

Based on this finding that there was substantial competition among CRSs and that such competition and the history of CRS development explained prices and bias, the report cautioned the Board to apply only minimal regulation on the industry. Any specific standards, it was argued, would inhibit the flexibility of the different vendors to compete with each other and respond to new needs. Furthermore, to preserve a level playing field for the different airline CRSs, any standards on bias should be applied uniformly and simultaneously for all CRSs.

In addition to the recommendations made in the report, American argued against any specific pricing regulation that would set booking fees. Instead, American preferred a rule for nondiscriminatory fees. With respect to the other rules proposed by the CAB and recommended by other parties, American attempted to limit the bias regulation to only the primary display, and favored letting CRS vendors charge each other lower or different reciprocal booking fees than each would charge to independent airlines. Finally, American wanted to maintain pricing control over any sales data generated from SABRE that it would be required to make available to any other airline.[35]

The CAB Decision and Final CRS Rules

In its initial report to Congress in June 1983, the Civil Aeronautics Board indicated substantial concern with the current and prospective effects of CRS competition both on the distribution (marketing) of air transportation and on air transportation markets themselves. The Board viewed both of these areas—distribution and provision of air transportation—as its two fundamental areas of responsibility as a regulatory agency.

With respect to distribution—or air travel marketing—the Board's concern was not a new one. It had recently completed a two-year oral evidentiary hearing process in the Competitive Marketing Investigation, which had examined the importance of an extensive and experienced network of impartial air transportation retailers. The Board had concluded there that the deregulation of airline markets and the proliferation of fares and flights had dramatically increased the reliance of air travelers on the travel agent network. Moreover, in removing antitrust immunity for certain air carrier agreements concerning travel agents, the Board highlighted the important economic benefits that accrued to passengers from open entry into distribution and competition among air transportation retailers. In its CRS report to Congress, the CAB had also stressed its concern that market power on the part of certain CRS vendors could significantly impair the operation of the travel-agent network and limit the ability of travel agents and other retailers to provide fair and impartial service to passengers.

The CAB was even more alarmed, however, about the prospect of CRS market power's undermining the substantial gains that had been won for consumers with the deregulation of airlines in 1978. If CRS market power meant that certain airlines could either disadvantage entrants or completely preclude their entry in certain markets, then the dramatically lower fares and improved frequency of service that consumers had gained in many city-pair markets would be challenged.[36] Thus, in publishing its advance notice of proposed rulemaking in September 1983, the Board set out clear guidelines of the issues that it wanted considered by participants in the proceeding. The goal advanced by the CAB was to gather specific information and to develop sound economic analysis on the theoretical and empirical effects of vertical integration by airlines into the distribution of tickets and information through CRSs.

The notice of proposed rulemaking that the CAB issued on March 27, 1984, condensed and analyzed the submissions and comments of over 25 participants who had responded to the Board's advance notice in September of 1983. The March 1984 document from the CAB accomplished two things: first, it provided the CAB's assessment of the nature and effect of CRS competition. Second, it set out proposed rules governing bias, pricing, and access for comment by the parties before final rules were issued. Both of these accomplishments derived from the CAB's independent evaluation of the extensive economic and legal analysis provided in the record by the major participants—the Department of Justice and the two major CRS vendors.

In evaluating the competitive effects of vertical integration by airlines into CRS, the Board accepted the Department of Justice's analytical and empirical evidence on market definition and market power in CRS. That is, the Board found that the relevant antitrust market in which to evaluate market power was the regional market as delineated by metropolitan areas. The Board rejected United's expert's view that the relevant market was the city-pair market. Moreover, the Board concluded that there was overwhelming evidence that distribution through modes other than the CRS (e.g., direct marketing, increased advertising) were poor alternatives and substantially more costly means than distribution through CRSs. The Board expressly rejected United's argument that carriers could follow People Express' example and not use CRSs. The Board distinguished People Express from most other carriers by pointing out that the airline provided non-stop service in only a few city-pairs of high density on a frequent and regular basis; this implied less reliance on the kinds of service that would be provided by travel agents and by a CRS. The CAB also agreed with the Department's findings that airlines generally had to be listed on all CRSs. Thus, in analyzing the extent of market power in CRS markets, the Board used the Department's extensive market tables detailing market shares for each of the major metropolitan markets in the United States and concluded that in many of these markets either United or American were dominant systems.

In order to evaluate whether these market shares reflected market power, the CAB then examined the evidence on entry into the CRS industry. The Board pointed to a number of factors that suggested that new entry was very unlikely and that entry by existing CRSs into each other's markets was adversely affected by the long-term contracts with high penalties that some of the CRS vendors had signed with travel agents. Moreover, the Board found evidence of CRS market power in the fact that vendors such as United could force travel agents to sign contracts that required agents to use Apollo virtually to the exclusion of other systems. Complicating the picture even further was the fact that enhancements such as boarding passes and the last-seat availability access meant that many travel agents would tend to remain with the dominant airline's CRS, even if that system were biased.[37]

In reaching these conclusions on the costs of entry and the prospects for entry and expansion, the CAB adopted most of the analysis and evidence presented by the Department of Justice and addressed by American's expert report. By contrast, the Board completely rejected United's notion that CRS markets were contestable and that long-term contracts were facilitating entry into the CRS industry.

Having established that the two dominant CRS vendors had market power in a number of markets, and that the remaining vendors might have market power in some, but fewer markets, and that such market power was unlikely to be undermined by entry, the Board turned to a review of industry performance. Indeed, a major portion of the Board's March 1984 opinion is devoted to detailed descriptions of the many ways in which the dominant CRSs had exercised their market power, thereby harming airline competitors and earning incremental revenues. By way of summary, the CAB found that there was evidence of persistent discrimination, that the CRSs had restricted the output of CRS services, and that they tended to earn very high rates of return on their CRS investments, due mostly to the incremental revenues earned from bias.

The Board's opinion lists the examples of Frontier, which had experienced substantial problems with loading of data, and those of newer carriers such as New York Air and Air Florida, which alleged that they were forced to pay far higher prices than major carriers for access to CRS services. The Board pointed out that booking fees ranged from about $.30 to well over $3, and that such fees seemed to be clearly related to the extent to which carriers competed with the dominant CRS vendors.[38] The Board concluded that these fees substantially raised new airlines' costs of serving airline markets. For example, the threat that CRS vendors would charge an airline a fee as high as $3 for all of its bookings, when the average profit per segment in 1978 was $2.50, seemed to have deterred a number of carriers from entering markets dominated by the major CRS vendors' airlines.[39] The Board also found a disturbing trend of some carriers making commitments to United that they would not compete aggressively in some of United's markets. In some cases, these commitments were made because carriers feared that United would raise booking fees or refuse to load the carriers' data into the CRSs.[40] Finally, the Board said that United and American were able to use marketing data from the CRSs to target commissions to travel agents, which would tend to enhance further their share of CRS markets.

To limit the exercise of market power the CAB issued proposed rules in its opinion of March 1, 1984. In large part, these rules governing bias, access, agency contracts, and pricing were those recommended and supported by the Department of Justice and other airline parties. The only major difference was that the CAB proposed nondiscriminatory pricing as its preferred method of limiting competitive abuses related to CRS pricing. In comments filed on April 26, 1984, the Department of Justice signaled that it did not oppose this form of pricing regulation.

After a lengthy comment period, the CAB issued final rules to be effective as of November 14, 1984. The final CRS rules prohibited the use of any carrier-specific factor for ordering displays; limited agency contracts to five years and prohibited exclusive agent contracts; required that all carriers be charged the same booking fees; required that once a service enhancement was offered to any other carrier than the CRS airline it must be offered to all airlines on a nondiscriminatory basis; and required that if a CRS vendor developed and sold marketing data for one carrier, it must make it available to all at a reasonable price.

Some of the CAB rules—those concerning bias, price discrimination, and deletion of certain connecting flight information—were challenged by United Airlines and British Airways on the basis that the Board did not have the authority to issue such rules to enforce prohibitions in Section 411 of the Federal Aviation Act against unfair and deceptive practices. The U.S. Court of Appeals, in hearing this case, upheld the CAB rules.[41]

With these rules, the CAB expressed its hope—echoed by the Department of Justice—that behavioral relief, subject if necessary to enforcement proceedings at the CAB, would both limit current abuses and alter eventually the structure of the industry.

Epilogue: The State of the CRS Industry

Three years after the implementation of the rules, allegations of substantial abuses of market power by CRS vendors continue, but some positive changes have occurred in the industry as well. On balance, CRS continues to present a difficult and complex policy problem of the costs and benefits associated with vertical integration where market power in one market can affect other markets in irreversible ways. Indeed, many of the current problems in the CRS industry follow the very unexpected (and unanticipated at the time the CRS rulemaking was initiated) demise of most small carriers and the substantial reduction in the number of existing carriers through mergers and bankruptcy. Thus, while there was substantial concern that abuse of market power could limit the ability of new carriers to enter markets in 1983, there was little realization that three years later the prospects for entry by new carriers would be remote. Now, it appears that the exercise of CRS market power against smaller carriers would have even more dramatic effects on the long-term structure of the airline industry.

In early 1985, in response to complaints that the CRS vendors were evading the spirit of the CRS rules by developing secondary and biased screens that were easier to use than the primary unbiased screen and had raised prices for booking fees to "monopoly levels," Congress held a series of hearings on the need for divestiture of the CRSs. The result of the hearings was twofold. First, the Department of Transportation, which had taken over the CAB's oversight of the CRS industry after the legislatively-mandated demise of the CAB, negotiated agreements with American, United, and TWA to eliminate the biased secondary screens. Second, the Department of Justice and the General Accounting Office were asked to prepare reports considering the current state of competition in the CRS industry and the level of profits earned by the CRSs, respectively.

The Department of Justice filed its report in December 1985, indicating that while the rules appeared to have eliminated all but the most subtle forms of bias, there was still evidence that the incumbents had market power.[42] Moreover, they expressed concern that the likelihood of entry appeared limited despite the potential for a new and neutral CRS considered by a joint venture of carriers. Finally, the report indicated concern over the possibility that the removal of bias may have resulted in CRS vendors' exercising market power by charging monopoly prices, but indicated there was no simple way to test for the existence of monopoly pricing.

The GAO, in considering the issue of profitability, evaluated three studies by United, American, and a group of airlines reviewing the profits and investments in the SABRE and Apollo systems. The GAO indicated there was some chance that the profits earned were in excess of competitive levels.[43] While these studies and hearings were continuing in the public arena, a group of major carriers filed a private lawsuit against American and United charging them with monopolization of the CRS market. That suit, which employs much of the same market definition and entry analysis in the original 1983 filings, is still ongoing at the time of writing.

Some major changes have occurred in the industry since the 1984 rules. After its merger with Republic, Northwest Airlines became a joint-venture owner of the TWA PARS system. Continental Airlines and the Texas Air Corporation, through its acquisition of Eastern Airlines, gained control of the SODA system, now called System One. These developments have vastly increased the amount of traffic accounted for by the airline owners of the two systems and has thereby improved their ability to attract travel agents. In particular, the Texas Air acquisition appears to have put pressure on both American and United. Other technological enhancements have occurred, some possibly due to the rules and developments in the industry. Most of the major CRSs now offer direct access to all carriers, and many are testing new enhancements such as low-fare features and the use of personal computers and software for travel agents.

Airlines and travel agents, however, continue to file complaints at the Department of Transportation alleging anticompetitive practices on the part of the major vendors. Delta Airlines accused American Airlines of manipulating the elapsed time of its flights so as to bias the display in favor of American. Travel agents have filed a major petition seeking relief from new provisions in CRS contracts called liquidated damages clauses. These clauses force travel agents to pay the CRS vendors for all the lost bookings that would have accrued if the agent had not converted to a different CRS system. Agents also oppose the ability of carriers to circumvent the five-year limit on contracts by rollover provisions that start a new contract whenever an agent makes any change in the services he/she buys from the CRS vendor. This latter problem was recently corrected through negotiations between the Department of Transportation and the major vendors. Finally, the Department of Transportation initiated a major fact-gathering investigation into the industry to determine the extent of problems after the rules.

Underlying these allegations and counterclaims is the same fundamental issue that provoked the first CAB rulemaking proceeding: when does the operation of a business such as a CRS cross the line from a set of efficiency-enhancing arrangements designed to recoup for the owner a reasonable (but competitive) rate of return, to a set of practices that while profitable to the CRS vendor are, on balance, harmful and costly to competition and thus to consumers? Defining that line in the CRS industry was, and still is, an extraordinarily complex task. The basic economic analysis in the CAB proceeding set the context for evaluating the problems in 1983 and for continued evaluation now. The same troubling question remains, however. Is behavioral relief—in the form of the 1984 CAB rules, or some modification of those rules—sufficient to push the CRS vendors back over the line into the generally competitive arena? Or is the dramatic and final relief of divestiture of the CRS from the airline the only means to achieve the benefits of the CRS industry without the costs?

Notes

1. The CAB proceeding on Carrier-Owned Computer Reservations Systems, (EDR-466) was initiated on September 14, 1983, when the CAB consolidated requests from a number of carriers and travel agent associations for an investigation into CRSs and for consideration of rules governing the carrier-owned CRSs. These requests were filed as early as March 16, 1983, while the CAB was in the midst of compiling a report to Congress on the state of competition in the CRS industry based on interviews of industry participants and assisted by the Department of Justice.

2. The request from Congress was in the Conference Report with P.L. 97-369, which contained the Civil Aeronautics Board's 1983

Appropriations Act. The report was issued to Congress on June 1, 1983 *(Report To Congress on Airline Computer Reservations Systems)*, and was written with assistance from the Department of Justice. The Department, during early 1983, was engaged in two investigations of the major CRS vendors and had, as a result, a substantial amount of expertise to provide to the Board. To assist in their analysis and report, the CAB opened Docket 41207, which provided for information on CRS vendors and industry practices; the CAB also interviewed industry participants in the course of writing the report.

3. In part, this was due to the array of legal remedies that were directly available to the CAB under its statutory authority concerning the marketing and distribution of air transportation services. The CAB would have had to make recommendations to Congress concerning divestiture, while it could directly regulate CRS operations under existing authority. For a legal discussion of this authority, see Notice of Proposed Rulemaking, March 1, 1984, 5–7.

4. In *United Airlines, Inc.* v. *Civil Aeronautics Board,* 766 F. 2d 1107 (1985), the U.S. Court of Appeals, Seventh Circuit, in an opinion by Judge Posner found that the CRS was an essential facility. That is, the CRS could either bias the display or charge monopoly prices and competitor airlines did not have a practical alternative means to the CRS for distributing and marketing air transportation.

5. In 1985, many of the non-CRS airlines, including Continental Airlines, filed suit in San Francisco charging American and United with antitrust violations concerning CRS ownership and operation. That lawsuit is still pending. In addition, Texas Air Corporation, now owner of Eastern's CRS by its acquisition of Eastern Airlines, has sued American over American's alleged attempts to exclude Texas Air from entering SABRE's markets and converting agents. See *Aviation Daily,* November 25, 1987, 300. Finally, American Airlines has alleged that European airlines have denied American's SABRE access to European travelers by refusing to let SABRE print tickets on certain European carriers. *Aviation Daily,* November 30, 1987, 307.

6. Individual airlines provide data on flights, including the flight number, flight schedules, classes of service offered, fares, and restrictions on the flight. This information is provided to the CRS vendor in the form of tapes, hard copy transmissions from the carrier to the CRS, or by electronic links between the carrier and the CRS. A second important type of information that is stored in the CRS is the "passenger name record" or PNR. A PNR contains all the relevant information on the passenger or group of passengers booked on a specific flight.

7. This information is typically subject to some additional processing to determine, for example, the elapsed time of the flight (the difference between the departure and arrival times). In addition, most CRSs use the Official Airline Guide (OAG) database to obtain other relevant information on the flights and schedules of carriers that may have chosen not to participate in a particular CRS. In general, the OAG is regarded as less complete than the information that a carrier maintains on itself, as well as the tapes that are provided to the CRS vendors. An additional linkage among CRSs and airline inventories is

ARINC, an electronic switch that connects the airlines' and CRSs' databases.

8. Essentially, the mainframe acts as a mechanism for processing requests from the travel agent, by searching through the database for all the relevant information responsive to the requests organizing those data in a form that displays on the screen of the travel agent all the flight schedules, fares, and times that are relevant to the travel agent's requests. Clearly, the greater the number of fares, routes, passenger name records, hotel rooms, car rentals, and tour reservations that are stored in the database, the greater must be the capability of the main computer to process that information on a timely basis.

9. An algorithm is simply the method by which the CRS is told to rank order information. For example, a simple algorithm would be to list all the flights between two cities in alphabetical order based on the carriers' names. Thus, American Airlines flights would tend to be at the top of the list and United's near the bottom. In general, CRS algorithms use a combination of elapsed time of the flight and the closeness of a flight's scheduled departure time to the time requested by the traveler to order the display. In addition, nonstop flights tend to be listed first, followed by connecting flights. To account for the time required for connections at hubs, a CRS will usually use average connecting times that the carriers have provided to the OAG. In general, because the gates of one carrier tend to be located near each other, the connecting time for an on-line connection (on the same carrier) tends to be lower than for an off-line connection.

10. There are a number of categories of participating carriers. A "host" carrier is the airline that owns the CRS. The information on this carrier tends to be very complete because it is transmitted directly from the host's internal reservation system to the CRS. A "co-host" is a carrier that may have paid a premium to have timely information on its flights and schedules stored on a CRS and may as a result have access to features called enhancements, such as boarding passes and last-seat availability. A third category of airlines is participating carriers—those that provide data to the CRS vendor and thus participate in the CRS. A final category is nonparticipating carriers—those that do not provide data but on whom the CRS vendor gets data from other sources such as the Official Airline Guide (OAG).

11. A related type of CRS, which has developed more extensively since the CAB rules, is a CRS using direct links. A system with a direct link is a proprietary system with the additional enhancement that the user can subsequently access the inventories of other carriers directly after it has accessed the main database. For a review of current CRS practices and the types of systems, see Lyle (1987).

12. Mars Plus was developed by ITT and sold to Tymshare in 1979.

13. Some vendors required that the agents use a system exclusively or for a majority of their bookings. Some of the systems also provided accounting and bookkeeping software for travel agents. Travel agents paid fees for the terminals and related equipment subject to contracts of duration from one to over 20 years.

14. Until December 1984, travel agent accreditation and appointment was controlled by a set of collective agreements among domestic and international carriers with antitrust immunity for the agreements granted by the CAB. The result of these agreements was that travel agents who met certain restrictive standards were the only nonairline retailers who were allowed to distribute and ticket air transportation in the United States. Moreover, until the early 1980s the commissions paid to travel agents were fixed by the carriers. As the result of the Competitive Marketing Investigation at the CAB, which commenced in 1979, the CAB removed antitrust immunity for these agreements as of December 1984, thus potentially opening up the retailing of transportation to any type of agent (e.g., a business travel department or firms such as Ticketron) that an individual carrier might want to appoint. In the course of the investigation, the CAB found that travel agents had become the single most important source of distribution for carriers, but that the exclusive appointment of travel agents limited innovation and competition in the travel marketing industry.

15. The government's case is presented in the many filings of the Department of Justice in response to the CAB's proposed rulemaking on CRS. The several filings span initial comments, comments proposing rules, and comments on the preliminary rules proposed by the CAB. Among the several filings, the November 17, 1983, Comments of the Department of Justice provided a thorough analysis of the product and geographic markets involved in CRS, developed the concept of how market power in CRS affected competition in airline markets and the notion of incremental revenues, and provided a solid empirical summary of the markets in which the different CRSs had market power with market share and concentration tables. The November 17, 1983, filing contains most of the government's case as it is set out in this section. In addition to the Department of Justice, a number of other participants in the CAB rulemaking alleged that the dominant CRS vendors had market power and had exercised that market power to harm other carriers. Among these other parties who recommended some form of regulation of the industry were: the Association of Retail Travel Agents (ARTA), Continental Airlines, Delta Airlines, Frontier Airlines, Golden Pacific Airlines, Muse Air, Air Cal, Jet America, Pan American, TWA, Western Airlines, Omega World Travel, Republic Airlines, and Tymshare, Inc. The last three parties argued for divestiture of the major CRSs from their owner-carriers.

16. Last-seat availability refers to the ability of a travel agent to get confirmation that the seat booked is actually available at the specific fare and that the client has been booked for the seat. Essentially, last-seat availability involves a communications link between the CRS and the inventory of the airline (called the real-time inventory because it is the inventory that the airline is using and contains the most current information), which enables the CRS to transmit and receive immediate confirmation on a booking. When this link between a carrier's inventory and the CRS does not exist, carriers are reluctant to signal travel agents that all of the seats on a flight are actually open. Carriers may hold a few seats out of the CRS

inventory, because communications lags can mean that several travel agents could simultaneously request and get apparent confirmation on seats, when in fact the flight would be over booked. Thus, last-seat availability gives the travel agent access to the most complete information on a carrier's offerings and also provides immediate confirmation of bookings, which improves a travel agent's quality of service to clients.

17. Some parties alleged there was a "halo" effect surrounding the dominant airline carrier's CRS. The halo effect seemed to include all of the service factors such as last-seat availability and timely information, as well as the desire of travel agents to use the system of the carrier on which they earned the greatest amount of commission revenues.

18. Both of these carriers eventually chose to list their services in CRSs and to pay booking fees for travel booked through CRSs.

19. For a review of the learning curve literature and the relevance of learning as a possible cost associated with entry, whereby the entrant may have higher initial costs than the current costs of the incumbent, see, e.g., Spence (1981).

20. Department of Justice Comments, at p. 90.

21. Ibid, at p. 145.

22. Ibid, at pp. 108–115.

23. United Airlines' position in the CAB rulemaking is set out in: Comments of United Airlines, November 17, 1983; Reply Comments of United Airlines, December 16, 1983; Comments of United Airlines, April 26, 1984, and Reply Comments of United Airlines, May 11, 1984.

24. For the position and analysis of American Airlines, see, Comments of American Airlines, November 17, 1983; Reply Comments of American Airlines, December 16, 1983; Comments of American Airlines, April 26, 1984; and Reply Comments of American Airlines, May 11, 1984.

25. "Testimony of William J. Baumol: The Apollo Reservations System and the Public Interest (hereafter, Baumol Testimony), filed with Comments of United Airlines on November 17, 1983.

26. "Comments by William J. Baumol on the CRS Rules Proposed by the Department of Justice" (hereafter, Baumol Reply Comments)," filed with Reply Comments of United Airlines on December 16, 1983, at p. 2.

27. The principles of the contestability theory are set out in Baumol, Panzar, and Willig (1982). The contestability theory has been critiqued both for its theoretical validity (Schwartz and Reynolds 1983; Schwartz 1986), and its empirical applicability, see, e.g., Hurdle, et.al., (1987). For a review of the contestability literature and its critics, see Spence (1983).

28. Baumol Testimony at p. 2.

29. Interestingly, United's own numbers in this example show the importance of the different CRSs in regional markets. Of the CRSs providing bookings for the particular United flight used in this example, the majority were made by SABRE and Apollo or by

United's internal reservations system. This is consistent with the Department of Justice's finding that United and American both have a substantial share of the CRS market in Chicago. By contrast, SODA and PARS combined had less than 6 percent of the tickets sold on this segment, and over 80 percent of tickets were sold by automated means.

30. In its filings at the CAB, United used this analysis to contest the CAB's authority to impose rules in the CRS industry, indicating that market shares would have to be far higher than they are in the CRS industry before the CAB could take action. See, Comments of United Airlines, April 26, 1984, 20–21.

31. Natural monopoly refers to a situation where, due to substantial economies of scale or scope, one firm can serve an entire market at lower long-run average cost than could two or more firms. For a thorough review, see Sharkey (1982).

32. "Comments of William E. Wecker on the CAB's Notice of Proposed Rulemaking," filed with Reply Comments of United Airlines, December 16, 1983; Report A, "Profit of Apollo on a Stand-Alone Replacement Cost Basis" 1–8; and Report B, "The Amount of Additional Air Transportation Revenue United Receives Because of Apollo," submitted November 17, 1983, 1–6.

33. One critique of this analysis is that it fails to capture whether United's load factor is higher than it would have been in the complete absence of bias or CRS ownership. Furthermore, it does not capture whether entry failed to occur or whether new entrants were forced to exit despite lower fare offerings.

34. National Economic Research Associates, Inc. (NERA) prepared a report on the "Economic Aspects of Airline Computerized Reservations Systems" submitted with the Comments of American Airlines, November 17, 1983.

35. Comments of American Airlines, April 26, 1984.

36. A very extensive literature has developed on the gains to consumers from the deregulation of pricing and entry of airlines in 1978. These include: Bailey et al. (1985), Miller and Douglas (1974), and especially, Morrison and Winston (1986), which found that consumers saved $6 billion in 1977 dollars relative to what they would have spent if airlines had not been deregulated. In addition to this literature, there is a substantial literature analyzing the nature and effects of competition in the deregulated airline industry. A very thorough summary is found in Levine (1987); specific studies include Strassman (1986), Moore (1986), Hurdle, et.al. (1987a and b); and Call and Keeler (1985).

37. The Board noted that the "no rec" problem—that is, the loss of any record of a booking due to communications problems between the CRS and the individual carriers through an industry-wide link called ARINC—meant that most travel agents would always prefer to book directly into the inventory of the carrier, rather than rely on this link. The ability to get the last seats available by booking directly into the inventory was only available on the CRS vendor's airline in 1983. Notice of Proposed Rulemaking, March 1984, p. 18.

38. Notice of Proposed Rulemaking March 1984, p. 15.

39. Notice of Proposed Rulemaking March 1984, p. 28.

40. The Board, referring to interviews conducted by the Department of Justice, noted that Air Florida, Pan American, and Jet America had all made such promises to United. Notice of Proposed Rulemaking, March 1984, p. 29.

41. See *United Airlines, Inc.* v. *Civil Aeronautics Board,* 766 F. 2d 1107 (1985).

42. Department of Justice Report, 1985.

43. GAO Report, 1985.

References

American Airlines. *Comments on the Advance Notice of Proposed Rulemaking—Airline Computer Reservations Systems (EDR-466) Docket 41686 before the Civil Aeronautics Board,* November 17, 1983.

_____. *Reply Comments of American Airlines,* December 16, 1983.

_____. *Comments of American Airlines,* April 26, 1984.

Bailey, E.E., D.R. Graham, and D.P. Kaplan, *Deregulating the Airlines.* Cambridge, Mass.: The MIT Press, 1985.

Baumol, William J. "Contestability: An Uprising in the Theory of Industrial Structure." *American Economic Review* 72 (March 1982): 1–15.

_____. "Contestability: An Uprising in the Theory of Industry Structure: Reply." *American Economic Review* 73 (June 1983): 491–496.

Baumol, William J., John C. Panzar, Jr., and Robert D. Willig. *Contestable Markets and the Theory of Industry Structure.* San Diego: Harcourt Brace Jovanovich, 1982.

Bittlingmayer, G., "The Economics of a Simple Airline Network." Manuscript, 1985.

Call, G.D., and T.E. Keeler. "Airline Deregulation, Fares and Market Behavior: Some Empirical Evidence." in *Analytical Studies in Airline Transportation,* edited by Andrew F. Daugherty, 221–247. Cambridge: Cambridge University Press, 1985.

Civil Aeronautics Board. *Report to Congress on Airline Computer Reservations Systems,* June 13, 1983.

_____. *Advance Notice of Proposed Rulemaking—Airline Computer Reservation Systems,* EDR-466, Docket 41686, September 13, 1983.

_____. *Notice of Proposed Rulemaking,* March 1, 1984.

_____. *Final Rule,* EDR-466. Adopted July 27, 1984.

_____. *Information Directives Concerning Computer Reservations Systems.* Docket 44643, February 2, 1987.

Douglas, G.W., and J.C. Miller III. *Economic Regulation of Domestic Air Transport: Theory and Policy.* Washington, D.C.: Brookings Institution, 1974.

Graham, D.R., D.P. Kaplan, and D.S. Sibley. "Efficiency and Competition in the Airline Industry." *Bell Journal of Economics* 14 (Spring 1983): 118–138.

Hurdle, Gloria, R. Johnson, A. Joskow, G. Werden, and M. Williams. "Concentration, Potential Entry, and Performance in the Airline Industry," Paper presented at the 57th Annual Conference of the Southern Economic Association, November 24, 1987 in Washington, D.C.

Levine, Michael E. "Airline Competition in Deregulated Markets: Theory, Firm Strategy, and Public Policy." *Yale Journal on Regulation* 4 (Spring 1987): 393–494.

Lyle, C. B. "ICAO Looks into Possible Abuses in Computer Reservations System Services." *ICAO Bulletin* 42 (January 1987): 25–31.

Moore, Thomas G. "U.S. Airline Deregulation: Its Effects on Passengers, Capital, and Labor." *Journal of Law and Economics* 29 (January 1986): 1–28.

Morrison, S.A., and C. Winston. *The Economic Effects of Airline Deregulation.* Washington D.C.: The Brookings Institution, 1986.

Schwartz, Marius. "The Nature and Scope of Contestability Theory." *Oxford Economic Papers* 38 (Supp. 1986): 37–57.

Schwartz, Marius and Robert J. Reynolds. "Contestability: An Uprising in the Theory of Industry Structure: Comment." *American Economic Review* 73 (June 1983): 488–490.

Sharkey, W.W. *The Theory of Natural Monopoly.* Cambridge: Cambridge University Press, 1982.

Spence, A. Michael. "Contestable Markets and the Theory of Industry Structure: A Review Article." *Journal of Economic Literature* 21 (September 1983): 981–990.

——. "The Learning Curve and Competition." *Bell Journal of Economics* 12 (Spring 1981): 49–70.

Strassman, Diana L. "Contestable Markets and Dynamic Limit Pricing in the Deregulated Airline Industry: An Empirical Test. Unpublished Rice University working paper, 1986.

United Airlines. *Comments and Proposed Rules on Computer Reservations Systems,* EDR-466, Docket 41686, before the Civil Aeronautics Board. November 17, 1983.

——. *Reply Comments of United Airlines,* December 16, 1983.

——. *Comments of United Airlines,* April 26, 1984.

U.S. Department of Justice. *Comments and Proposed Rules on Computer Reservations Systems,* EDR-466, Docket 41686, before the Civil Aeronautics Board, November 17, 1983.

——. *Reply Comments of U. S. Department of Justice,* December 16, 1983.

——. *Comments of U.S. Department of Justice,* April 26, 1984.

——. *1985 Report of the Department of Justice to Congress on the Airline Computer Reservation System Industry,* December 20, 1985.

U.S. General Accounting Office. *Airline Competition: Impact of Computerized Reservation Systems.* Report to Congressional Requesters, Report No. GAO/RCED-B6-74, May 1986.

Williams, Michael A., Andrew S. Joskow, Richard L. Johnson, and Gloria J. Hurdle. "Explaining and Predicting Airline Yields with Non-Parametric Regression Trees." *Economics Letters* 24 (1987): 99–105.

13
case

Resale Price Maintenance Reexamined: *Monsanto* v. *Spray-Rite*

Frederick R. Warren-Boulton

Introduction

On August 31, 1986, the Monsanto Company, a major U.S. manufacturer of chemical products, declined to renew its distributorship with the Spray-Rite Service Corporation, a small Iowa herbicide distributor whose net revenue from sales of Monsanto herbicides in 1968 had been about $16,000. Some sixteen years and millions of dollars in legal costs later, the Supreme Court upheld a Federal District Court's award of $10.5 million to Spray-Rite.[1]

Monsanto Co. v. *Spray-Rite Service Corp.* is really two stories. The first is a legal saga that exemplifies many of the worst characteristics of private antitrust cases. In brief, in this author's opinion the wrong side won an astonishingly large amount. But the *Monsanto* case is also the story of the ongoing attempt to transform antitrust into rational public policy. In this broader context, *Monsanto* was a limited but significant tactical victory; though the patient died, the operation was a success.

We begin with the broader story—the evolution of the tension between the legal and economic analysis of resale price maintenance (RPM). We then turn to our particular story to determine what happened and how. Finally, we examine the legacy of *Monsanto* for current and future antitrust law and policy.

Frederick R. Warren-Boulton was a consultant for Monsanto at the District Court stage of this case. The views expressed in this study are strictly those of the author and do not represent those of the U.S. Department of Justice, and no resources of the Justice Department were used in its research, writing, or production.

The Economics of RPM

Resale price maintenance (RPM), or "fair trade," is the practice whereby an upstream entity (e.g., a manufacturer) specifies a minimum price (or sometimes a maximum price) to which a downstream entity (e.g., a retailer) is required to adhere in its sales efforts. Note immediately that the manufacturer is not the direct beneficiary of this action, since RPM specifies the retail price, whereas the manufacturer's profits are determined by its wholesale price. In essence, once the wholesale price is given, RPM specifies a retail margin.

How might RPM be anticompetitive? Two possible explanations hinge on RPM's being a cover or facilitating device for horizontal price fixing or a horizontal cartel. One possibility is a cartel among manufacturers that cannot observe each others' wholesale prices but that can observe retail prices. They may collectively fear that "price wars" among their retailers may tempt individual manufacturers among them to cut wholesale prices surreptitiously, thereby undermining the cartel. RPM would prevent these price wars.

Alternatively, RPM might be motivated by a dealer cartel (among a group of dealers that collectively have market power, if they could succeed in colluding) that find they cannot collude without external help. Accordingly, they ask one or more manufacturers to enforce their cartel by establishing RPM.

These cartel-motivated views of RPM, supplemented by a general notion that RPM had to be anticonsumer because it meant higher prices, were prevalent until the 1960s. It was reinforced by the experience of the 1930s, in which political pressures by small retailers (especially druggists) led to individual states' passing of fair trade laws for intrastate commerce and to the Congress' passing of the Miller-Tydings Act of 1937, which permitted RPM on a state-option basis for goods involved in interstate trade that were sold in the relevant state.

This general view of RPM as anticompetitive and harmful to consumers began a slow process of reversal when Telser (1960) laid out the first of the "free-rider" efficiency explanations for RPM. Telser began by pointing out what would now seem to be obvious—that a manufacturer would appear only to lose from a higher retail margin. Any supranormal return to the retailer acts as a tax on the product, appropriating revenue that could have gone to the manufacturer. Using RPM to impose a higher retail margin could be in the manufacturer's interest only if the higher retail margin were somehow necessary to induce retailers to provide services that were worth more to consumers than they cost the retailers.

One example of this phenomenon, suggested by Telser, is the provision of information or other services at the point of sale, for which the retailer cannot charge a separate fee. Suppose the following: A manufacturer of a complicated item—e.g., a stereo receiver—believes that its product is best sold if the retailer provides a great deal of point-of-sale service, such as information, demonstration models, the opportunity to hook up the receiver with many other combinations of stereo components, etc., even if this high level of retailing services is costly and means that the receiver will carry a higher retail price than in the absence of these services. But retailers usually find it difficult to charge a separate fee for these services. Under these circumstances, some retailers would be tempted to establish the equivalent of catalog stores, urging their customers to obtain the necessary information and demonstrations at a neighboring full-service retailer and then to return to the catalog store, which could sell the product for less (because the catalog store did not have the extra costs of providing the information and the demonstrations). In essence, the catalog retailer would "free ride" off the full-service retailer; however, the full-service retailers would then lose sales, no one would want to be a full-service retailer of that product, and the manufacturer's sales would suffer.

One solution for the manufacturer would be for it to insist that all of its retailers provide a full range of services; but policing their provision of service may be difficult. An alternative would be to establish a system of RPM. By insisting that all retailers sell at the same minimum retail price, the manufacturer would eliminate the price advantage of the catalog retailer, thereby reducing the free-riding problem. In essence, by restricting price competition among its retailers, the manufacturer would be virtually forcing its retailers to compete among themselves on the basis of service (since, with prices uniform among the retailers, improved service would presumably be the means by which the retailer would attract and retain customers). And, if it is easier for the manufacturer to police the RPM scheme than to police a direct insistence on the provision of retailer service, then RPM could be the manufacturer's preferred method.[2]

As Klein and Murphy (1984) have pointed out, however, the "free riding on special services" argument for RPM poses two major difficulties. First, why should a wider nominal retail margin induce retailers to provide special services? Why not just take the additional money and continue to free ride? Even better, even if RPM prevents the free-riding retailer from reducing the nominal retail price, why not indirectly cut the real price by providing some other unrelated service (a free gift, for example) that is contingent upon purchase from that retailer? Second, RPM has been imposed on many products that do not obviously require free-ridable special services: Litigated examples include Russell Stover candies, Levis blue jeans, and Coors beer.

Klein and Murphy argue that in such cases the manufacturer may be using RPM to reduce the cost of enforcing an implicit or explicit contract with retailers. Manufacturers often want retailers to provide particular inputs or services that, in the absence of some special incentive, retailers would underprovide or even not provide at all, but the desired retailer behavior cannot cheaply be contractually specified and enforced. A manufacturer could reduce policing costs and still deter contract violations if it could increase the penalty imposed when a violation was detected;[3] but where is that higher penalty to come from?

Following earlier work by Klein and Leffler (1981), Klein and Murphy argue that a manufacturer can use RPM to offer a retailer a margin that is intentionally higher than the retailer's costs. This creates a potential stream of future rents that the retailer would lose if the manufacturer responded to a contract violation by terminating the retailer. A profit-maximizing retailer would then be deterred from any act that would lead to termination as long as the potential gain from that act, G, is less than the expected value of the loss: i.e., the probability of detection, π, times the capitalized value of the stream of future rents, V. Deterrence thus requires $G < \pi V$ or, equivalently, $\pi > G/V$. A wider retail margin increases V, thereby lowering the minimum probability of detection required to achieve deterrence and allowing the manufacturer to spend less on monitoring and policing the agreement.

This strategy is particularly attractive to the manufacturer because this reduction in enforcement costs can be achieved at little or no cost to the manufacturer. As long as the manufacturer's commitment to maintain RPM is credible, potential retailers will be willing to pay an amount up to V as a franchise fee to the manufacturer.

At first glance even the unilateral imposition of RPM by a manufacturer may appear to be anticompetitive. After all, the manufacturer is restraining price competition among its retailers. But if the manufacturer is correct in its judgment that a high level of retail service is best for selling the product, this outcome should generally mean enhanced satisfaction for consumers.[4] As another way of seeing this point, consider that the manufacturer could vertically integrate, establish its own retail outlets, specify the retail price of the product sold by these outlets, and instruct its own retail employees to provide a high level of retail service in conjunction with the sales of the product. Would this latter situation generally be considered anticompetitive? RPM, in essence, achieves the same outcome.

The Legal Treatment of RPM

In contrast with the changed economics perception of RPM, the legal treatment of RPM has remained harsh. In the 1911 *Dr. Miles Medical* case[5] the Supreme Court declared RPM to be a per se violation of Section 1 of the Sherman Act; i.e., this form of vertical restraint was placed in the same category of condemned practices as horizontal price fixing among competitors (and, indeed, RPM is frequently characterized as "vertical price fixing"). Eight years later, in the 1919 *Colgate* case, the Supreme Court appeared to open a major loophole for RPM, declaring, "In the absence of any purpose to create or maintain a monopoly, the act does not restrict the long recognized right of a trader or manufacturer engaged in an entirely private business, freely to exercise his own independent discretion as to parties with whom he will deal. And, of course, he may announce in advance the circumstances under which he will refuse to sell."[6] Thus, it appeared that a manufacturer could legally enforce an RPM program by simply announcing the expected retail prices in advance and refusing to deal with any retailer who did not adhere to those prices. But the Court quickly closed the loophole, consistently finding in subsequent cases in 1920, 1921, and 1922[7] that manufacturers' efforts to enforce RPM among their dealers constituted agreements between the manufacturer and the dealers and hence were violations of the Sherman Act, consistent with *Dr. Miles Medical.* And in a long line of cases since then, the Court has repeatedly reaffirmed its condemnation of RPM as a per se violation.[8] The Court has even condemned RPM in a situation in which a newspaper attempted to impose *maximum* resale prices on its distributors.[9]

As was noted above, in 1937 the Congress overrode the Court and exempted RPM from the reach of the Sherman Act (at the option of the individual states). But the Consumer Goods Pricing Act of 1975 repealed the Miller-Tydings Act and returned the legal position of RPM to where the Supreme Court decisions had left it.

It is worth noting that the Supreme Court has not been nearly as consistently harsh with respect to nonprice vertical restraints—e.g., a manufacturer's instructions to retailers of its products as to where they may locate or in which geographic areas they may sell. Here, after condemning these practices as a per se violation in 1967,[10] the Court in 1977 reversed itself and declared them instead to be subject to the rule of reason.[11] This disparity in legal treatment is striking, since the economic logic underlying the two forms of vertical restraint is fundamentally similar, and both (since they restrain competition among the retailers of a manufacturer's product) are likely to cause retail prices of the relevant product to be higher than in the absence of the practice.[12]

Monsanto Co. v. Spray-Rite Service Corporation

Background

Monsanto is a major American manufacturer of chemical products, including agricultural herbicides.[13] During the 1960s, several companies, including Monsanto, Geigy, Stauffer, Eli Lilly, Dupont, and Rohrer AmChem, developed a new generation of weed killers for use on corn and soybeans. Previous herbicides were sprayed on weeds after the weeds were grown and had already injured the crops. The new "pre-emergent" herbicides prevented this damage by killing weed seeds before they germinated.

By 1968, the leading producer of corn herbicides was Geigy, whose Atrazine brand held a 70 percent market share, while Monsanto's Randox (introduced in 1956) and Ramrod (introduced in 1966) brands accounted for 15 percent of the corn herbicide market. In soybean herbicides, where the two leading firms held market shares of 37 percent and 33 percent, Monsanto's market share was only 3 percent.

Monsanto marketed its herbicides primarily through about 100 independent distributors who resold to retail dealers, including feed stores and farm implement dealers, who in turn resold to farmers. Each distributor was assigned a geographic "area of primary responsibility," but that assignment was nonexclusive: authorized distributors could sell herbicides of other manufacturers; distributors could sell outside their assigned area of primary responsibility; and Monsanto assigned approximately ten to twenty distributors to each area.

Between 1957 and 1968, one of those distributors was the Spray-Rite Service Corporation. Spray-Rite was a small family business whose owner and president was also its sole salaried salesman. Spray-Rite bought herbicides from Monsanto and other manufacturers and resold them to retail dealers and farmers in northern Illinois and adjacent areas. In 1968, 90 percent of Spray-Rite's sales volume came from herbicide sales. Spray-Rite was the tenth largest of the approximately 100 distributors of Monsanto's primary corn herbicide. Monsanto's products, however, accounted for only about 16 percent ($551,217) of Spray-Rite's $3,380,947 in total sales in 1968; Geigy's Atrazine corn herbicide accounted for 73 percent of Spray-Rite's herbicide sales. Spray-Rite was a low-margin, high-volume operation that even characterized itself as a "brokerage house." Spray-Rite sold primarily to large seed-corn companies, large sprayers, and large dealers; 30 percent of its 1968 sales were made to one large seed-corn company, De Kalb, and only six customers combined accounted for nearly 75 percent of its total sales of Monsanto products.

In 1967, faced with a flat market share in corn herbicides and a declining market share in soybean herbicides, Monsanto decided to change its marketing strategy to stress dealer education. Herbicide application is technically complex and risky. The optimal application depends on location, soil, weather, and weed type, and selecting an inappropriate herbicide or misapplying an appropriate one can result in an ineffective application or even serious crop damage. Monsanto relied upon its distributors to educate the dealers, who in turn would provide individual farmers with specific technical advice on the optimal selection and application of its herbicides.

In September 1967, Monsanto informed each of its distributors, including Spray-Rite, that for the upcoming 1967-1968 season it would appoint distributors for only one-year terms and that authorized distributorships would expire automatically unless renewed by Monsanto. Renewal would depend on compliance with six criteria, including the following:

> Is the Distributor's primary activity the solicitation and distribution of agricultural chemical products to dealers? ...
>
> Is the Distributor willing and capable of carrying out Monsanto's technical programs at both the Dealer and Farmer levels with properly trained personnel? ...
>
> Can the Distributor be expected to "exploit fully" the potential markets for the Goods in the Distributor's area of primary responsibility?[14]

In October 1968, Monsanto declined to renew its contract with Spray-Rite and four other distributors. After its termination by Monsanto, Spray-Rite continued to purchase some Monsanto products from other distributors. In 1969 its total sales increased by 52 percent to $5,151,450, although its sales of Monsanto products declined from $551,217 (16.3 percent of its total sales in 1968) to $133, 869 (2.6 percent of its total sales) in 1969. Spray-Rite also reported its first net loss on herbicide operations since 1965. In 1970, total sales fell to $2,421,057 and net losses rose to $91,513. While sales recovered and losses fell in 1971, by 1972, with sales down to $1,359,400 and losses up to $75,469, Spray-Rite went out of business.

In the meantime, jolted by a 30 percent fall in sales in 1968, Monsanto had taken several other marketing actions. First, it tried to push dealer education directly; it hired additional salesmen to work with dealers, established herbicide training schools for dealers and for distributor personnel, offered cash bonus payments to distributors that sent salesmen to training classes, and offered distributors price discounts on herbicides resold to dealers who attended Monsanto's technical programs. Second, it changed its shipping policies to encourage distributors to develop the market in their areas of primary responsibility. Beginning in 1968, it permitted distributors to pick up products only at Monsanto warehouses within each distributor's area and provided free deliveries of products to the distributor or its customers only within that area. A distributor that resold the product outside its primary area had to pay the additional shipping costs. Third, it reduced the prices charged to its distributors as well as the suggested resale prices. While this reduced the suggested distributor profit margin from 11 percent to 7 percent, Monsanto also offered price discounts, rebated to the distributor at the end of the season, on orders purchased early in the season. Fourth, in 1969 it introduced its "third-generation" corn and soybean herbicide, LASSO.

The combined effect was dramatic. Monsanto's share of the corn herbicide market went from 15 percent in 1968 to 28 percent in 1972; its market share in soybean herbicides went from 3 percent in 1968 to 19 percent in 1972. These increases came largely at the expense of the firms with the largest market shares. In corn herbicides, Geigy's share fell from 70 percent in 1968 to 52 percent in 1972. In soybean herbicides, the combined share of the two leading firms (Eli Lilly and AmChem) fell from 70 percent in 1968 to 55 percent in 1972. During the same period, total use of corn and soybean herbicides grew by approximately 15 percent and 75 percent respectively.

While most of this growth probably was due to the demand curve for herbicides shifting out, some of the quantity increase appears to be due to lower relative prices. Evidence was introduced at trial indicating that Monsanto's suggested prices declined. Even Spray-Rite's expert characterized the herbicide market as "highly competitive."

The District Court

In 1972, Spray-Rite sued Monsanto for violating Section 1 of the Sherman Act, alleging that it had been terminated as part of a conspiracy to fix the resale price of Monsanto herbicides and that the termination, combined with a post-termination boycott by Monsanto and its distributors and the use of Monsanto of such nonprice vertical restraints as areas of primary responsibility and dealer compensation and shipping programs, had eventually forced Spray-Rite out of business. Spray-Rite's case thus consisted of three separable factual allegations: 1) its termination was pursuant to an RPM conspiracy among Monsanto and some of its distributors; 2) Monsanto's nonprice policies were pursuant to that conspiracy; and 3) Monsanto and some of its distributors conspired to boycott Spray-Rite after the termination.

On the first and most important allegation, Monsanto denied ever engaging in RPM and contended that it had decided unilaterally not to renew Spray-Rite's distributorship because of the latter's failure to satisfy Monsanto's announced criteria for renewal. Monsanto also argued that Spray-Rite failed to prove the existence of an agreement among Monsanto and any of its distributors to terminate Spray-Rite because of its price-cutting and pointed out that price-cutting by other, nonterminated distributors was widespread. But Spray-Rite was able to show that Monsanto was concerned about the resale prices of its herbicides, that Monsanto had agreed that its company-owned outlets would not undercut its suggested retail prices, that Monsanto had received price complaints about Spray-Rite from other distributors, that Monsanto representatives had informed Spray-Rite of those complaints and requested that prices be maintained, and that Monsanto terminated Spray-Rite subsequent to those complaints but without ever having discussed with Spray-Rite the distributorship criteria that were the alleged basis for the action. In addition, evidence was introduced that, subsequent to Spray-Rite's termination, Monsanto had advised price-cutting distributors that if they did not maintain the suggested resale price they would not receive adequate supplies of Monsanto's new herbicide, LASSO.

On the boycott allegation, Spray-Rite was able to deliver testimony from Monsanto employees and from distributors that Monsanto had threatened to terminate distributors who sold to Spray-Rite. Finally, with respect to Monsanto's nonprice policies, Spray-Rite did not argue that Monsanto's promotional programs and distribution policies were illegal under the *Sylvania* rule-of-reason standard. Indeed, it agreed that Monsanto had become a more effective competitor after their introduction. Spray-Rite did argue, however, as the court eventually instructed the jury, that it was *per se* unlawful for a manufacturer to utilize customer or territorial restrictions as part of a comprehensive price-fixing plan or boycott and that the jury could consider the effect of Monsanto's distributor compensation programs as circumstantial evidence of the conspiracy to boycott.

These three allegations were reformulated by the court and given to the jury as three special interrogatories:

1. Was the decision by Monsanto not to offer a new contract to plaintiff for 1969 made by Monsanto pursuant to a conspiracy or

combination with one or more of its distributors to fix, maintain, or stabilize resale prices of Monsanto herbicides?

2. Were the compensation programs and/or areas of primary responsibility and/or shipping policy created by Monsanto pursuant to a conspiracy to fix, maintain, or stabilize resale prices on Monsanto herbicides?

3. Did Monsanto conspire or combine with one or more of its distributors so that one or more of those distributors would limit plaintiff's access to Monsanto herbicides after 1968?

The jury responded "yes" to each interrogatory and returned a general verdict against Monsanto, awarding Spray-Rite $3,500,000 in damages. The court trebled the jury's damage award, ordering Monsanto to pay Spray-Rite $10,500,000 plus interest from the time of final judgment, as well as $895,747.80 in attorney's fees and $16,875.79 in court costs.

Damages.   The story of how a jury could decide that Monsanto had inflicted $3,500,000 in damages on Spray-Rite is an interesting one. Spray-Rite's damage estimate came from its expert witness, a professor of marketing. He testified that even though Monsanto's products accounted for only 21 percent of Spray-Rite's total sales in 1967 and 16 percent in 1968, a herbicide distributor needed to carry a "full line" of different products because dealers and farmers wanted to buy all their herbicides from one seller. Access to Monsanto's products was thus essential for survival. The combination of Monsanto's 1968 termination of Spray-Rite, the post-termination boycott, and Monsanto's post-termination compensation programs, delivery policies, and territorial restrictions forced Spray-Rite out of business in 1972. Further, the conspiracy to impose RPM and boycott Spray-Rite was the only event of substance that would have affected Spray-Rite's actual or potential business after 1968. It would thus be reasonable to expect that, in the absence of the alleged conspiracy, the relationship from 1969 to 1978 between Spray-Rite's total sales and the total corn and soybean herbicide sales in the region would have been the same as it had been from 1963 to 1968. The expert therefore regressed Spray-Rite net sales for 1963 to 1968 on total expenditures on corn and soybean herbicides in Regions 3 and 5 for 1963 to 1968, and reported the result to be: Spray-Rite Net Sales = $-\$314{,}702.17 + 0.01792439 \times$ (Total corn and soybean expenditures in Regions 3 and 5).

Applying this formula to the observed total herbicide sales in the two regions from 1969 to 1978, the expert forecasted that Spray-Rite's sales in the absence of the conspiracy would have continued to increase each year from 1969 to 1978, reaching $15,223,861 by 1978. The 1963 to 1968 relationships between total revenue and some twenty cost components were then used to predict a net profit margin that could be applied to these sales forecasts to estimate Spray-Rite's potential profits over the ten-year period from 1969 to 1978. He concluded that, in the absence of the conspiracy, Spray-Rite would have made $522,863 in profits between 1969 and 1972 instead of losing $230,812 and would have made an additional $2,573,913 between 1973 and 1978. The jury took the grand total of $3,327,587, apparently rounded it off to the nearest half million, and awarded Spray-Rite $3,500,000 in damages.

There were at least two other procedures for estimating damages that could have provided a check on this amount. First, one could have estimated how much extra Spray-Rite would have had to have paid after 1968 to acquire as much of Monsanto's products as it had before it was terminated. This would have involved adding up all the discounts, bonuses, shipping allowances, etc., that Spray-Rite would have received as an authorized distributor. The result would have been an overestimate of actual damages since, if Spray-Rite could have purchased Monsanto's products without such discounts but chose not to do so, then the value of such potential discounts must exceed the loss from termination. Even if such estimates were not available, a maximum value for the total of such discounts could have been arrived at by looking at Spray-Rite's expected profit margins and sales of Monsanto products. For example, in 1967, the year when Spray-Rite's sales of Monsanto products peaked at $638,736, Spray-Rite's gross profit margin was 6.8 percent and its net profit margin was 3.6 percent. This implies that, if the unavailability of Monsanto products would not have affected other sales, the maximum damage from being cut off from Monsanto products would have been 3.6 percent of its sales of Monsanto products, or about $23,000 per year. If Monsanto products were an essential part of a "full line," then the maximum damage would have been the income foregone from purchasing Monsanto products at the retail price, i.e., 6.8 percent of Spray-Rite's sales of Monsanto products, or about $43,000 per year. Note that actual damages could reach that amount only if Spray-Rite incurred no costs in distributing Monsanto's products—i.e., provided no services at all. Cumulated over ten years, under whatever rationale, this would imply a ceiling for damages of either about $230,000, or about $430,000, depending on whether the "full-line" assumption was accepted—only a fraction of the $3,500,000 awarded by the jury.[15]

A second method would have been to estimate the value of Spray-Rite as a going concern in 1968. For accounting purposes, Spray-Rite valued itself at $70,000 in 1968. Alternatively, Spray-Rite could have been valued at some multiple of net income. Between 1963 and 1968,

Spray-Rite's net income ranged from a loss of $20,404 in 1964 to a profit of $106,585 in 1967, averaging $34,547 per year over those six years. A multiple of eight times net income (i.e., the use of a discount rate of 12.5 percent) would thus imply damages of about $275,000 under the "full-line" assumption or about $55,000 if a full line were not required. A third alternative would have been to examine what similar distributorships were valued at or had been sold for recently.

One might be concerned about, or even appalled by, the arbitrariness of a process that can produce "reasonable" damage estimates that range from $40,000 to $3,500,000. But the important point is the irrelevance of any such estimate. After all, if Monsanto's purpose and effect was a more efficient distribution system that would increase its sales and benefit its consumers, no antitrust injury had been suffered by anyone, regardless of whether that distribution system relied on price or nonprice restraints. The only "damage" suffered by Spray-Rite would have been the foregone profits from no longer being allowed to free ride on the efforts of other dealers, and Spray-Rite should no more have had standing to sue than would a burglar who found that a homeowner had put a lock on his front door.

Alternatively, if Monsanto's purpose and effect were to facilitate a manufacturer's cartel, then all consumers of all herbicides, not just Monsanto's, were harmed. But such a conspiracy could not be expected to harm distributors significantly, including Spray-Rite, since virtually all of any increase in the wholesale price would have been passed through to the next stage.[16] In any event, the amount of such damages to consumers would bear no relationship to the value of one distributorship.

As a third alternative, if Monsanto had terminated Spray-Rite under pressure from a distributor cartel attempting to raise distributor margins on Monsanto's and/or all herbicides, then the victims of that conspiracy would have been both the consumers and the manufacturers of herbicides, including Monsanto. Spray-Rite's role would then be similar to that of a member of a gang of burglars who missed out on the Monsanto burglary because he had been thrown out of the gang for excessive greed, but now hopes to use the antitrust laws to extract an additional payment from the victim equal to three times the loss from the first burglary.[17]

Strategy.   The jury can hardly be blamed, however, for this decision. *Monsanto* was argued as a per se case; the jury was not to wonder if Monsanto's actions benefited either its customers or society in general. As the Supreme Court later noted, Monsanto's lawyers never argued that a rule-of-reason standard should apply to RPM, nor did they dispute Spray-Rite's contention that any nonprice practices instituted as part of an RPM conspiracy should also be subject to per se treatment.

Monsanto's trial strategy was to argue the case on as narrow grounds as possible. The appropriateness of a per se standard for RPM was never disputed, and herein lay the fundamental conflict between the legal staff and any potential economic witness. For an economist, *Monsanto* offered a golden opportunity to argue RPM as a rule-of-reason case. The facts of the case provided strong support for an efficiency explanation for RPM and no support for any inference that RPM had been part of a price-fixing conspiracy by either dealers or manufacturers.

For a litigator, however, that same evidence of the social desirability of RPM carried several dangers. First, to the extent that RPM is a rational, profit-maximizing, appropriate, efficient, and effective response to free riding by distributors, it is also a more likely response. Spray-Rite's factual allegations thus become more plausible, and it becomes harder to convince the jury that RPM never occurred. Second, the attorney's goal is to win, while the goal for many expert economists is to win for the right reasons.[18] A trial attorney could reasonably be suspicious that an expert might have his own agenda and that his client's interests may be only one of a number of potentially conflicting items on that agenda. A natural response by a trial attorney might be to overcompensate, a response that also prevents any possible future allegation that a truly hard-bitten trial attorney who put the interests of his client first and ignored the social or precedential impact of the case might not have lost.

Third, any trial attorney has limited resources, and any jury has a limited ability to absorb information; putting on a rule-of-reason case could distract attention or resources away from other lines of defense. Finally, it can be difficult for an attorney to evaluate the potential for a defense that removes him from strictly legal and evidentiary issues where he is sure of his competence and places him in the unknown, speculative, uncertain, and uncontrollable world of economics.

Balanced against these dangers from a rule-of-reason strategy were only limited benefits. The jury might have been persuaded that any use of RPM by Monsanto was in the public as well as the private interest, and this might have countered some of the natural sympathy for a small local businessman and his extensive family (all of whom appeared regularly at trial) in their battle against a huge corporation. But even after the recent decision in *Sylvania,*[19] the probability that *Monsanto* would be the case in which the Supreme Court would finally reverse its long-standing position on the per se illegality of RPM must have seemed de minimus. The social gain from using *Monsanto* as a vehicle for such a reversal was an externality appropriately ignored by Monsanto's legal staff. It was thus left to the Department of Justice, whose friend-of-the-court (amicus brief) program was designed precisely to respond to the social externalities that private attorneys general would ignore, to use *Monsanto* to argue for an end to the per se treatment of RPM.

In retrospect, however, the decision to forgo a rule of reason defense at the district court level may have been expensive for both Monsanto and for society. The use of a per se strategy meant that the full evidentiary record that was needed to support a rule-of-reason argument before the Supreme Court case was never developed. In addition, the Supreme Court was able to argue that the failure to raise the issue at the district court level meant that the court was not required to reach the broader issue in *Monsanto.*

The Court of Appeals

Monsanto appealed, arguing that there were errors in the district court judge's charge to the jury, that there was insufficient evidence to support the verdict, and that the district court made several erroneous evidentiary rulings. The United States Court of Appeals for the Seventh Circuit found none of these arguments persuasive and affirmed the judgment of the district court.[20]

The principal nonfactual issue was evidentiary: Monsanto argued that evidence of price complaints coupled with evidence of termination in response to those complaints should be insufficient to prove the existence of a RPM agreement. The Court of Appeals disagreed, stating, "We believe . . . that proof of termination following (subsequently rephrased as "in response to") competitor complaints is sufficient to support an inference of concerted action."[21]

Monsanto also argued that its promotion and distribution policies should be tested under the *Sylvania* rule-of-reason standard. The Court of Appeals held, however, that *Sylvania* did not limit the Supreme Court's earlier holding in *Sealy*[22] that otherwise lawful vertical restrictions imposed as part of an unlawful scheme to fix prices are per se illegal and that *Sylvania* applies only if there is no allegation that the territorial restrictions are part of a conspiracy to fix prices.

The Supreme Court

On petition from both Monsanto and the Department of Justice as amicus curiae, the Supreme Court granted certiorari. The petitioners presented three central questions to the Supreme Court. The first two were evidentiary: What evidence is sufficient to infer that nonprice restraints are so connected to an RPM scheme that they should be treated under a per se rather than a rule-of-reason standard, and what evidence is sufficient to infer that a dealer has been terminated as part of a conspiracy to impose RPM? The third question was presented only by the Department of Justice: Should RPM be per se illegal?

On the first question, both Monsanto and the DOJ seized on the perhaps unfortunate statement by the Court of Appeals that *Sylvania* applies to nonprice restraints only if there is no "allegation" that those restraints are part of an RPM conspiracy. Both Monsanto and the DOJ argued that, given the potentially procompetitive benefits from nonprice restraints that the Supreme Court had recognized in *Sylvania,* a "mere allegation" that such restraints were part of an RPM scheme should be insufficient for per se treatment. Even evidence that nonprice restraints have had an effect on price should not be sufficient. As the DOJ's amicus brief pointed out, nonprice restrictions that prevent free riding and encourage dealers to provide more or higher-quality point-of-sale services can be expected to result in higher retail prices. If the value of those additional services to consumers is greater than the increase in the retail price, however, consumers will be better off and will respond to the increase in both price and quality by buying more of the product. Thus the critical evidentiary distinction between a procompetitive vertical restraint and an anticompetitive increase in either the manufacturer's wholesale price or the dealer's margin is its effect on quality: The former results in an increase in the quantity sold, the latter in a decrease.

The Supreme Court disposed of this question in a footnote, stating that the District Court's language could be read to say that a plaintiff must prove, as well as allege, that the nonprice restrictions were in fact part of a price conspiracy. Monsanto had conceded that if the nonprice practices were proved to have been instituted as part of a price-fixing conspiracy, they would be subject to per se treatment. Since the jury had found that the nonprice practices were created by Monsanto pursuant to a conspiracy to fix resale prices, Monsanto's argument was reduced to the proposition that the jury did not have sufficient evidence to support this finding. Monsanto had failed to make that argument at the Court of Appeals and, since that court did not address the point, the Supreme Court declined to reach it, stating only that "nothing in our discussion today undercuts the holding of *Sylvania* that non-price restrictions are to be judged under the rule of reason."[23]

The question that did interest the Supreme Court was whether a per se unlawful vertical price-fixing conspiracy could be inferred solely from evidence that a manufacturer had received price complaints from a distributor's competitors and later did not renew the distributor's contract. Monsanto and the DOJ argued that the District Court's holding that "termination following competitor complaints is sufficient to support an inference of concerted action" was incorrect for two reasons. First, it undermined the Sherman Act's crucial distinction between collective and unilateral conduct by permitting a jury to infer conspiracy from normal marketplace behavior that was fully consistent with unilateral conduct. Manufacturers routinely terminate distributors unilaterally for being unwilling or unable to promote or service their product in the way desired by the manufacturer. Indeed, one indicator of that failure may be the distributor's pricing strategy. In a decision cited by both Monsanto and the DOJ, the Seventh Circuit had observed that "if a supplier wants his distributors to emphasize non-price rather than price competition, . . . he will be hostile to price cutters because they will make it harder for his other distributors to re-coup the expenditures that he wants them to make on presale services to consumers and on other forms of non-price competition, and of course the undersold distributors will be equally or more hostile."[24] Thus, even a manufacturer that is making no effort to control the resale price may have good reasons for closely monitoring the operations of price-cutting dealers. In doing so, he is likely to be helped by complaints from rival dealers, especially if those dealers believe that they are losing sales because the price-cutting dealer is free riding on their efforts. Neither parallel desires nor evidence of communication, by themselves or in combination, provide sufficient evidence to infer collusion between a manufacturer and one or more dealers. Further, the practical effect of a "termination that follows complaints" standard for inferring collusion could be virtually to immunize dealers from terminations once a competitor had complained. The DOJ thus argued that in the absence of direct evidence of collusion, an inference of concerted action should require a showing that the conduct is not in the individual self-interest of the participants, acting independently, and is in their collective self-interest only when they coordinate their actions.

This overriding concern with the distinction between concerted and independent action—i.e., whether a conspiracy exists—may seem odd to the nonlawyer. After all, we do not insist that murder or burglary be committed by a group for such actions to be considered a crime. Yet Section 1 of the Sherman Act requires that there be a "contract, combination . . . or conspiracy" in order to establish a violation; independent action is not proscribed.

Two reasons can be offered for requiring proof of an agreement. The first is that an agreement is essential to achieve the antisocial end. This neatly distinguishes between murder and horizontal price fixing: one can murder alone, but one cannot fix prices with oneself.[25] But it appears to break down for "vertical price fixing," since RPM can be imposed unilaterally by the manufacturer.

There is a good reason, however, why the presence or absence of an agreement fails to distinguish between procompetitive and anticompetitive RPM. Agreements among firms with market power can be either pro- or anticompetitive; the critical characteristic is whether the agreeing firms are supplying substitutes or complements. If the firms are supplying substitutes, agreement is necessary for antisocial effects; one firm will agree to raise its prices and lower its output only if its rivals (i.e., producers of substitutes) agree to do the same. Similarly, if the parties individually are supplying complements, agreement *may* be essential for socially beneficial effects. Thus a hypothetical bread monopolist might agree to increase bread output and reduce bread prices only if a hypothetical butter monopolist increased butter output and reduced butter prices. Most observed examples of complementarities, however, are vertical. Except under unusual conditions, the inputs supplied at successive vertical stages will be "gross complements" to each other.[26] Firms at different vertical stages, such as manufacturing and distribution, are generally not competitors but rather members of the same team. As the National Association of Manufacturers' amicus brief put it, ". . . a manufacturer and its distributors are essentially joint venturers in marketing the manufacturer's product." Attempts by one or more firms at any one level to restrict output and raise prices—or even simple incompetence—will harm both consumers and firms at other vertically related levels. Thus agreements between firms at vertically related levels may be essential to prevent the exercise of unilateral market power at one level or to control other actions that may generate externalities across stages.

It can thus be argued that an agreement between firms that supply complementary products cannot violate the Sherman Act because any such agreement, whether on price, quantity, or quality, would not be "in restraint of trade." Since firms at different vertical stages nearly always supply complementary products, this implies that RPM agreements between a single manufacturer and its dealers should not create a violation of the Sherman Act. In contrast, an RPM agreement among manufacturers of the same or similar products, or an RPM agreement among distributors of one product or of a group of substitute products is clearly an agreement in restraint of trade.

The second reason for the emphasis on agreement in the Sherman Act is its effect on "false positives." Again, this makes excellent sense in the context of horizontal price fixing. There are a large number of reasons why manufacturers may unilaterally raise or lower their prices, increase or decrease quality or quantity, or make any of a host of decisions that affect consumers. The low probability that any one of those decisions, chosen at random, would be an anticompetitive act that society would wish to prevent and the inability in practice to distinguish such instances from pro-competitive actions mean that any sanction against unilateral conduct is likely to suffer from a very high false positive rate. In other words, one can monopolize alone, just as one can burglarize alone; the problem is comparable to that of not being able to differentiate burglars from innocent homeowners who are climbing in the window because they have lost their keys. In contrast, there are very few good reasons why a group of competitors would otherwise need to meet to discuss price. The chance of a false positive from a covert horizontal price-fixing conspiracy is so small that a per se standard for such actions seems entirely appropriate.

The Supreme Court began its approach to the evidentiary standard in *Monsanto* by reiterating the two central themes of the legal approach to vertical restraints—the distinction between concerted and independent action, and the distinction between concerted action to set prices and concerted action on nonprice restrictions. The Court acknowledged that the economic effects of vertical arrangements, whether concerted or unilateral, price or nonprice, are often similar or identical. The Court did not, however, proceed from this observation to conclude that these distinctions were invalid as the basis for choosing between a rule-of-reason or a per se standard. The Court seems to have been more concerned that the same conduct is likely to be observed whether the vertical arrangement is unilateral or concerted, price or nonprice, and thus evidence of such conduct is insufficient to diagnose accurately a concerted agreement on prices. The Court cited, in particular, evidence of constant communications about prices and marketing strategies between a manufacturer and its distributors. The Court also noted that a correct diagnosis of concerted price fixing is important because the latter is subject to per se treatment and treble damages and that this differential treatment creates the potential for significant harm from allowing such agreements to be inferred from highly ambiguous evidence.

The Court concluded that "something more than evidence of complaints is needed. There must be evidence that tends to exclude the possibility that the manufacturer and non-terminated distributors were acting independently .... The antitrust plaintiff should present direct or circumstantial evidence that reasonably tends to prove that the manufacturer and others 'had a conscious commitment to a common scheme designed to achieve an unlawful objective, ... a unity of purpose or a common design and understanding, or a meeting of minds in an unlawful arrangement.'"[27]

The Court thus rejected the Court of Appeal's evidentiary standard of termination following complaints. The new standard, however, was not enough to save Monsanto. Applying the new standard to the facts of this case, the Court concluded that "there was sufficient evidence for a jury to have concluded that Monsanto and some of its distributors were party to an 'agreement' or 'conspiracy' to maintain resale prices and terminate price cutters" and affirmed the judgment of the lower court.[28]

The third question presented to the Court in the DOJ's amicus brief was potentially the most important: Should RPM be per se illegal? The amicus brief argued that the Court should take this opportunity to do what it had never done—analyze RPM in terms of its actual economic effects. It pointed out that a manufacturer who wished only to raise the resale price could and would do so simply by raising its own price to the distributor and that preserving or increasing the downstream margin may be a more efficient way to achieve procompetitive effects than various nonprice restraints judged under a rule of reason. The brief went on to cite control of the free-rider problem as a major beneficial effect of RPM and argued that the evidence in *Monsanto* pointed to this as the explanation for Monsanto's conduct. Finally, the brief argued that the conditions under which any adverse competitive effects (i.e., a manufacturer or dealer horizontal cartel) from RPM might occur are readily ascertainable. (Necessary conditions for RPM to facilitate manufacturers' collusion include high concentration, barriers to entry, and industrywide use of the practice. Necessary conditions for RPM to be a disguised dealer cartel include market power by dealers in the resale market and some price inelasticity for the product of the manufacturer or group of manufacturers coerced by dealer pressure). While some of the justices showed a keen interest in the question during oral argument, the Supreme Court's opinion ducked the question, stating only in a footnote that

> Certainly in this case we have no occasion to consider the merits of this argument. This case was tried on *per se* instructions to the jury. Neither party argued in the District Court that the rule of reason should apply to a vertical price-fixing conspiracy, nor raised the point on appeal. In fact, neither party before this Court presses the argument advanced by *amici*. We therefore decline to reach the question, and we decide the case in the context in which it was decided below and argued here.[29]

Justice Brennan, in a concurring decision, did, however, provide one explanation by stating that

> As the Court notes, the Solicitor General has filed a brief in this Court as *amicus curiae* urging us to overrule the Court's decision in *Dr. Miles Medical Co.* v. *John D. Park & Sons Co.,* 220 U.S. 373 (1911). That decision has stood for 73 years, and Con-

gress has certainly been aware of its existence throughout that time. Yet Congress has never enacted legislation to overrule the interpretation of the Act. Because the Court adheres to that rule and, in my view, properly applies *Dr. Miles* to this case, I join the opinion and judgment of the Court.[30]

The history of Congress' views of RPM is a long and complex one. The amicus brief for the United States argued that Congress' views on RPM had varied over the years, that in repealing the broad per se legality afforded by the Fair Trade Laws (the Miller-Tidings and McGuire Acts) in 1975 Congress did not specify that RPM be treated as per se illegal, and that that determination could properly be assumed by the Court.

But Congress had made its recent views extremely clear in resolutions, committee hearings, and, most strikingly, in passing a statute to prohibit the Justice Department from urging in its oral argument before the Court in *Monsanto* that the *per se* treatment of RPM be altered.[31] The Court was surely aware of these views.

An Economic Analysis of *Monsanto*

Turning now to economic diagnostics, can we discern from the available evidence the "true" reason and effects of Monsanto's actions? For all practical purposes, the answer is yes. But the ability of the Court or any observer to diagnose this case correctly is severely hindered by the legal structure under which it was brought.

First, Monsanto was not appropriately an antitrust case at all: If anything, this was a contract dispute between a manufacturer and a distributor that was transformed into an antitrust case by the combination of a per se standard and the prospect of treble damages. In general, the ability of courts to resolve such contract disputes efficiently requires that the parties provide information on explicit or implicit contracts and address any violations directly. Costuming such disputes as antitrust claims leaves some valid contract claims unaddressed while other efficient contracts are heavily penalized, thus reducing the incentives of firms to enter into efficient contracts.

To this author's knowledge, Spray-Rite never asserted that Monsanto had violated an explicit or implicit contract. In general, however, distributors' legal claims of violations of implicit contracts by a manufacturer may be economically defensible. For example, Spray-Rite could have reversed the free-rider argument against Monsanto by asserting that it (Spray-Rite) had invested a considerable effort over ten years in building up an understanding and acceptance of Monsanto's products among a group, however small, of major customers; that as a result, sales of Monsanto products to these customers had become a highly profitable business; and that Monsanto's decision to terminate Spray-Rite was simply a naked seizure of Spray-Rite's investment. Termination would allow Monsanto to appropriate that investment directly by making those sales through its vertically integrated sales system. Alternatively, Monsanto could assign such highly profitable customers to its other distributors, extracting in return either additional distributor services or a lower average distributor margin. Thus, instead of Spray-Rite's free riding on the efforts of Monsanto or of other distributors, Monsanto was attempting to free ride on Spray Rite.[32]

Second, even if this were appropriately an antitrust case, the application of the per se rule meant that only by accident would the court discover the cause and effects of Monsanto's decision to terminate Spray-Rite. If *Monsanto* had been judged under a rule-of-reason standard, it would not have been sufficient to show that Monsanto had agreed with other distributors to impose a minimum distributor margin and had terminated Spray-Rite for price cutting. Under the *Sylvania* standard, Spray-Rite would have had to have shown that RPM by Monsanto had an anticompetitive effect. Under a per se standard, however, all that mattered was whether Monsanto had done the deed, not why or with what effect.

The absence of any incentive for Spray-Rite to establish the cause or effect of RPM by Monsanto placed Monsanto in a dilemma. Monsanto, of course, vigorously denied ever engaging in RPM—a response that could only be expected but one which may also have prevented much valuable information from ever appearing. As the DOJ's amicus brief later put it,

> It is true that Monsanto has denied engaging in resale price maintenance; but the per se unlawful status of that practice has been universally assumed by courts for so long and the consequences of being adjudged to have engaged in the practice are so severe—treble damages and possible felony prosecution—that few antitrust defendants can be expected to concede participating in such an agreement, a concession that is necessary as a matter of litigation strategy if they wish to argue that the practice was procompetitive. For 70 years, then, it has been unlikely that the per se status of resale price maintenance would be placed directly in issue by an antitrust defendant.

Monsanto did, of course, go to some efforts to argue that their real goal was to improve dealer education and increase customer services. The strategy, however, appears to have been more to provide an explanation for Monsanto's behavior that might be taken by the jury to be an alternative to—or even perhaps mutually exclusive with—RPM, rather than an attempt to justify RPM.

The per se treatment of RPM thus forced both parties to adopt litigation strategies under which a number of important factual questions were neither asked nor answered. Nevertheless, a great deal is clear beyond a reasonable doubt. First, both of the standard anticompetitive scenarios—dealer collusion and manufacturer collusion—can be ruled out. With respect to dealer collusion, there was evidence that other distributors complained to Monsanto about price cutting by Spray-Rite. As noted, however, such dealer complaints are both routine and explicable on other grounds. There was no evidence of any concerted effort by a group of distributors to force Monsanto to raise the retail margin against its will. It might be argued that an explicit agreement among distributors would not be essential if a few large distributors each accounted for a large proportion of the sales of one or more relatively small and powerless manufacturers. But the large number of actual or potential distributors, the absence of any entry barriers into distribution, and the enormous size discrepancy between manufacturers and distributors of herbicides would render incredible any scenario of unilateral threats by dealers against an unwilling manufacturer. The evidence from both structure and conduct show clearly that any RPM in this case was inspired and enforced by the manufacturer.

It is also clear that any RPM was imposed unilaterally by Monsanto. Again, no evidence was introduced, nor any allegation made, that Monsanto imposed RPM as part of an agreement among manufacturers aimed at facilitating oligopolistic price coordination. Collusion among herbicide manufacturers would not be implausible. The available data showed that in 1968 both the corn and soybean herbicide markets were highly concentrated.[33] But there was no evidence of the kind of pricing behavior that RPM is alleged to prevent—retail price shading that induces retaliatory wholesale price cuts by manufacturers. Most important, there was no evidence or allegation that RPM was being imposed industry-wide or even by a group of firms with a sizable share of the market.[34] Moreover, Monsanto would appear to have probably been the least likely instigator of any attempt at collusion. In 1968 Geigy dominated the corn herbicide market, while in soybean herbicides Monsanto's 3 percent market share made it a fringe firm in that market. RPM seems to have appealed more to small fringe firms than to the large firms that might be expected to have had an interest in "stabilized prices."

The ease with which the only two anticompetitive scenarios can be dismissed allows us to rule out any potential for an anticompetitive effect from the use of RPM by Monsanto and would have been enough to dismiss the case under a rule-of-reason analysis. But both Monsanto and the DOJ argued that the available facts in *Monsanto* not only demonstrate the absence of the necessary conditions for an anticompetitive effort but also provide considerable positive evidence that Monsanto's vertical practices were procompetitive and beneficial to consumers.

The most dramatic evidence is the very large increase in Monsanto's share of the market between 1968 and 1972, from 15 percent to 28 percent in corn herbicide and from 3 percent to 19 percent in soybean herbicide. With much of those increases coming at the expense of the leading firms, concentration fell significantly in both markets.[35] Unfortunately, we do not know how much of the increase in Monsanto's market shares to ascribe to Monsanto's introduction of its "third-generation" herbicide, LASSO, in 1969.

Monsanto could also point to a significant fall in the relative prices of its products. Between 1967 and 1979, while an index of Monsanto herbicide prices rose by 23 percent, prices of all agricultural chemicals increased by 53 percent, the CPI rose by 119 percent, and the overall indexes of prices received and paid by American farmers rose by 147 percent and 149 percent, respectively. Again, however, little if any of this fall in Monsanto's relative prices could be ascribed to Monsanto's new distribution policies. A number of critical patents expired after 1975—notably Geigy's Atrazine patent in 1976 and AmChem's Amibem patent in 1978—and some price cutting to deter postexpiration entry was expected by 1972.[36] Moreover, if the goal of RPM had been to increase services provided to customers, Monsanto's prices could be expected to increase as a result. Thus, even if reliable evidence on the effects of changes in Monsanto's distribution system on retail prices had been available, it could not be used to distinguish between the horizontal conspiracy scenarios and the "free riding on special services" scenario.

Both Monsanto and the DOJ as amicus argued that the relevant model was Telser's "free riding on a special services" model. Indeed, *Monsanto* appeared to provide almost a textbook example of the free-rider scenario: a complex product, where the provision of complete and accurate presale information is crucial, sold by a discounting broker. Curiously, however, to this author's knowledge no evidence was ever presented of even one uninformed farmer or dealer who had been educated in the benefits of Monsanto's product by a full service distributor and who then purchased Monsanto herbicides from Spray-Rite at discount prices. Perhaps there were instances of such postservice but presale switching, but Monsanto decided not to introduce them at trial for fear of emphasizing the pricing aspects. It might also be argued that no switching might have been observed because the potential for switching deterred other dealers from ever providing those presale services. This explanation can be ruled out, however, by the fact that Monsanto was itself vertically integrated into distribution. Indeed, Spray-Rite introduced a document from another distributor stating that Monsanto had agreed to maintain margins and not discount at its wholly owned distribution centers. Thus, while the standard free-riding story cannot be entirely dismissed because we cannot be certain that no significant postservice/presale switching occurred, it seems dubious at best.

What does emerge clearly is Monsanto's concern that Spray-Rite was selling too little rather than too much and in particular was refusing to attract new, smaller customers in its area of primary responsibility. Monsanto's criteria for renewal, its partial vertical integration into distribution, its shipping policies, and its complex pricing and payment system for distributors all point to a concern with the intensive margin and a concerted effort to increase Monsanto's market share by pushing distributors to develop new customers and expand purchases by past customers.

Why was this necessary? Why could not Monsanto simply establish a wholesale price and sell to anyone interested in buying? Why could Monsanto not rely on competitive downstream distributors and dealers to make the same decisions as Monsanto would have if it were vertically integrated and controlled those decisions directly? In other words, why did the price system fail? The usual reason given is Telser's free-riding story. But, as many authors have commented, the free-riding story, while elegant, internally consistent, and capable of explaining a number of anecdotes, does not seem to fit this particular set of facts very well.

The concern with and attempts to influence decisions by competitive downstream firms appears almost ubiquitous among manufacturers who have "market power" or even just a differentiated product, even if presale services are not priced separately or are easily free-ridable. This points to a much broader market failure than free riding. Simply put, whenever an input or intermediate product is sold at a price above marginal cost, an inefficiency can arise because socially incorrect information and commands are being provided to the downstream market. There is a considerable literature on the effects of upstream pricing above marginal cost when market power is also exercised independently downstream. Such "successive monopoly" conditions give rise to incentives for vertical integration or for partial forms of vertical control such as setting maximum resale prices. The result is an increase in joint profits and a decrease in prices to consumers. Thus vertical control under successive monopoly conditions is unambiguously socially beneficial.[37] In addition, even when the downstream stage is competitive, if the monopolized input can be used in variable proportions with competitively supplied inputs, the upstream firm has an incentive to integrate vertically (or use other vertical practices such as tying arrangements) to control the input proportions decision.[38] In these models, the competitively supplied inputs and the monopolized inputs are net substitutes, and the upstream firm's problem is that when it sets its price above its marginal cost, independent downstream firms are induced to use too much of the competitive inputs relative to monopolized inputs. While vertical control by the upstream monopolist results in each unit of the product's being produced at a lower social cost, the impact of vertical control on consumers and on total welfare depends on the values of a set of critical parameters that will seldom (if ever) be known in practice.

In the manufacturer-distributor context, however, inputs provided at successive stages appear to be net complements. When the manufacturer of a differentiated good sets the wholesale price above marginal cost, the independent distributor or retailer will "underprovide" complementary downstream services, whether those services are shelf space for breakfast cereal or blue jeans, or complete inventories and presale information to customers in the case of agricultural herbicides.

As a simple numerical example, suppose that the marginal cost (MC) of a differentiated product is $4, that the manufacturer sells the product at a wholesale price of $P_w = \$10$ to a number of competitive retailers, resulting in an equilibrium retail price of $P_r = \$15$. If free riding on other dealers is impossible, that competitive retail margin of $5 will be the margin that equates the marginal cost of an additional unit of dealer services, S, with the marginal benefit of those services to consumers. Given a wholesale price of $10, the retailers' decisions maximize the joint welfare of retailers and consumers. If the social marginal cost of production had been $10, the competitive retailer would also have produced the level of retail services that would have maximized total welfare.

Unfortunately for the manufacturer, however, its pricing above marginal cost has distorted the information provided by the pricing system, and the retailers' independent decisions will no longer be optimal for the manufacturer. In our example, suppose that a retailer could sell one more unit of the product if it spent $6 more on services (shelf space for blue jeans, salesperson time for herbicides). That extra sale would generate only $5 in additional revenue for the retailer, so the provision of those services will be unprofitable for the independent retailer. But because the manufacturer has set a wholesale price above marginal cost, that extra sale would also have resulted in an increase in profits to the manufacturer of $6. The combined gain to manufacturer and dealer of $11 exceeds the $6 cost of the additional retail services.

But the effect on the manufacturer's profits is an "externality" to the retailer. The retailer's profits are given by $\pi_r = [P_r - P_w] Q(P_r,S) - C_s S$ (where Q is the quantity of goods; P_r and P_w are the retail and wholesale price, respectively; S is the level of services provided by the retailer; and C_s is the marginal [equals average] cost of retail services) which is maximized by providing the level of services where

$$\frac{\delta\pi_r}{\delta S} = [P_r - P_w] \frac{\delta Q}{\delta S} - C_s = 0.$$

In Figure 1, which illustrates the decision in input space, the independent retailer sets $C_s = [P_r - P_w]\frac{\delta Q}{\delta S}$, choosing S_r^* level of services. In Figure 2, which illustrates the decision in output space, the retailer sets $[P_r - P_w] = C_s/[\delta Q/\delta S]$ resulting in sales of Q^*_r. Total profits by retailer and manufacturer, however, are given by

Figure 1
Input Space

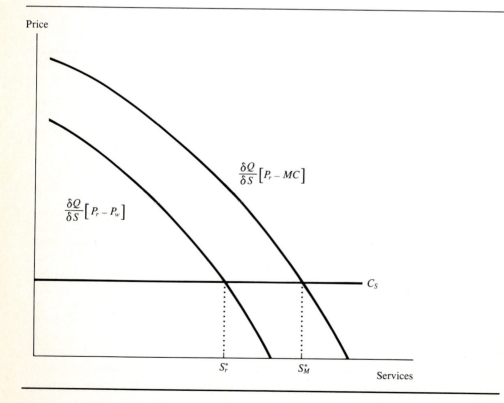

396   Frederick R. Warren-Boulton

$$\pi_r + \pi_m = [P_r - P_w] \, Q(P_r, S) - C_s S + [P_w - MC] \, Q(P_r, S)$$

which are maximized by increasing S to the level where

$$\frac{\delta(\pi_r + \pi_m)}{\delta S} = [P_r - MC] \frac{\delta Q}{\delta S} - C_s = 0,$$

that is, to S_M^* in Figure 1, resulting in Q_M^* units of the product in Figure 2.

The manufacturer has several alternatives. First, it can vertically integrate downstream into retailing and provide those enhanced services directly. Second, it can establish complex nonlinear pricing and subsidy schedules that raise the return to the dealer at the margin without raising the average dealer return (i.e., lower the inframarginal return and raise the marginal return). Third, it can force dealers off their parametric response functions entirely by making an all-or-

Figure 2
Output Space

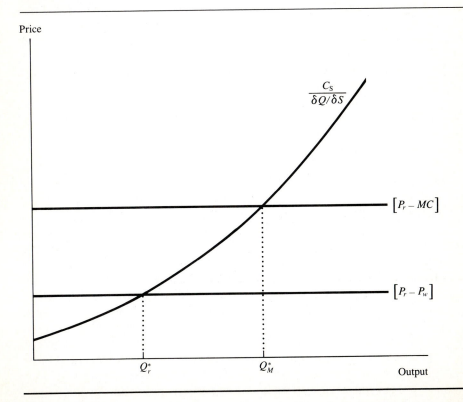

nothing offer. Either the dealer provides specific services (e.g., to small herbicide customers in its area of primary responsibility) that would not be profitable by themselves to the dealer, or the dealer is terminated. Of course, the threat to terminate is only meaningful if termination would preclude profitable sales to other customers—perhaps that dealer's share of large and well-informed herbicide users in his area of primary responsibility, to whom large sales can be made at relatively low cost and at resale margins protected by the manufacturer through threats of dealer termination. All three strategies have the same effect, and Monsanto appears to have tried all three, searching for the most effective and least-cost combination.

Whichever form or combination of forms of vertical control is used to achieve the manufacturer's goal, both consumer and total welfare from such an expansion of downstream services would appear to be substantially greater. Even in the short run, the manufacturer and marginal consumers clearly gain, while, given the endogeneity of the wholesale prices, inframarginal consumers—the large and well-informed purchasers—may gain or lose. The effects seem to be analogous to first-degree price discrimination. In the long run, given the ex ante competitive conditions that are likely to prevail at the research and development stage, any increase in potential manufacturer profits will be dissipated ex ante in the form of additional expenditure on research and development, leading to a large number and variety of such products.

This is a far cry from a practice that invariably has a pernicious effect on competition and lacks any redeeming competitive virtue for which the rule of per se illegality was intended. Clearly, in the history of antitrust cases brought against anticompetitive practices, *Monsanto,* and, almost without exception, all cases involving resale price restraints unilaterally imposed by a manufacturer, are false positives.

Unfortunately, while the first and the second strategies are generally legal by themselves, under legal current doctrine attempting the third can expose a manufacturer to the possibility of very large penalties. This is a triumph of form over function.

The uncertainty and arbitrariness of such a legalistic distinction between price and nonprice forms of vertical control have imposed large transaction costs on society, including the legal costs of the many manufacturer-dealer contract disputes transformed into RPM cases. But the major cost must be the cost of acts committed and the forgone benefits of acts not undertaken by those threatened by such sanctions. In the former category is a bias toward nonprice forms of vertical control, such as vertical integration—surely a paradoxical result of a legal standard apparently motivated in part by a political desire to protect small business. In the latter category are the downstream services not provided and the output not produced and sold or perhaps not even developed.

The Legacy of *Monsanto*

In *Monsanto* a jury found sufficient evidence to conclude that Monsanto had been conducting an illegal RPM program, and the Court of Appeals and then the Supreme Court both affirmed. The plaintiff won, and RPM continued to be condemned as a per se violation of Section 1 of the Sherman Act. Yet, ironically, *Monsanto* has come to be considered a substantial victory for the defendant's bar.

This paradoxical outcome stems from the standard of proof that the Supreme Court enunciated in its opinion: "Permitting an agreement to be inferred merely from the existence of complaints, or even from the fact that termination came about 'in response to' complaints, could deter or penalize perfectly legitimate conduct. . . . Thus, something more than evidence of complaints is needed."[39] The Court found enough "more" in *Monsanto* to affirm the jury's conclusion, but the standard itself tightened the criteria that had been used by the Court of Appeals. And, subsequent to the decision, a number of dealer termination cases, in which RPM allegations were based largely or solely on evidence of complaints followed by termination, were dropped by the plaintiffs.

Political evidence of this perception of a defendant's victory can be found in the following: as this is written in 1988, the 100th Congress is considered likely by many observers to enact H.R. 585, a bill that would specifically overrule the evidentiary standard enunciated in *Monsanto* and permit evidence of only complaints followed by termination to be sufficient for a conviction.

This Congressional sentiment indicates that the per se treatment is likely to continue for the indefinite future. Even if the Supreme Court would reconsider its position in some future RPM case and substitute the rule of reason as the proper legal standard (as it did in the nonprice vertical restraint area), the Congress—at least in the current political climate—would likely overrule the decision and enact the per se principle into law. Thus, microeconomists still have a heavy educational burden before them.

Notes

1. *Monsanto Co. v. Spray-Rite Service Corp.,* 465 U.S. 752 (1984).
2. This could be true if it was easier for the manufacturer to verify instances of off-price sales—perhaps in response to other retailers' complaints—than to verify instances of the lack of adequate service.
3. See Becker (1968).
4. For arguments that even unilateral RPM may not be in the interest of

most consumers, see Scherer (1983), Comanor (1985), and Comanor and Kirkwood (1985). For a criticism of these arguments, see White (1985).

5. *Dr. Miles Medical Co.* v. *John D. Park & Sons Co.,* 220 U.S. 373 (1911).

6. *United States* v. *Colgate Co.,* 250 U.S. 300, 307.

7. See *United States* v. *Schrader's Son, Inc.,* 252 U.S. 85 (1920); *Frey & Sons, Inc.* v. *Cudahy Packing Co.* 256 U.S. 208 (1920); and *FTC* v. *Beech-Nut Packing Co.,* 257 U.S. 441 (1922).

8. See *United States* v. *Bausch & Lomb Optical Co.,* 321 U.S. 707 (1944); *United States* v. *Parke, Davis & Co.,* 362 U.S. 29 (1960); *Simpson* v. *Union Oil Co.,* 377 U.S. 13 (1964); and *Albrecht* v. *Herald Co.,* 390 U.S. 145 (1968).

9. *Albrecht* v. *Herald Co.,* 390 U.S. 145 (1968).

10. *United States* v. *Arnold, Schwinn and Co.,* 388 U.S. 365 (1967).

11. *Continental T.V.* v. *GTE Sylvania,* 433 U.S. 36 (1977).

12. See White (1981)

13. Monsanto's sales in 1974 were about $3.5 billion, with about 10 percent of those sales accounted for by its agricultural chemical products group.

14. Plaintiff's exhibit #196.

15. If sales were expected to increase at the same percentage rate as the discount rate used for valuing future profits, then the simple cumulation over ten years achieves the correct present value.

16. Under current law (i.e., since *Illinois Brick*), however, even if the distributor would pass on almost all of any increase in the wholesale price, the immediate purchaser has the exclusive right to sue for the entire conspiracy overcharge. See *Illinois Brick Co.* v. *Illinois,* 431 U.S. 720 (1977). Such a rule, while it completely ignores victim compensation as a possible goal of the antitrust laws, is fully consistent with deterrence as the preeminant goal of antitrust law and is thus probably both efficient and desirable. For an evaluation of the *Illinois Brick* rule, see Landes and Posner (1979), Werden and Schwartz (1983), Snyder (1985), and Joyce and McGuckin (1986).

17. Oddly enough, this latter "dealer cartel" scenario is the only one consistent with the level of damages accepted at trial. There are no significant barriers to entry into the distribution of herbicides. The only important qualification appears to be accreditation by the major herbicide manufacturers, who have a clear interest in avoiding paying supranormal rents to their distributors. A valuation of $3,500,000 for such a business with a book value of $70,000 implies the presence of supranormal profits that probably could only come from an effective (and presumably criminal) horizontal price-fixing conspiracy among herbicide distributors, enforced perhaps by threats of boycott against hapless manufacturers who did not penalize cheaters.

18. This difference stems partly from a difference in professional ethics. The attorney ethic is premised on the belief that if each side presents its most favorable arguments, the truth will emerge as biases cancel each other out in the adversarial process. In contrast, the expert economist is cast as the unbiased scientist who presents the "truth" to

the best of his or her ability. Any nonprofessional behavior by an expert is deterred in two ways. First, all expert testimony is a matter of record, and any inconsistency with any past testimony or publications can be very damaging. Second, most economists care deeply about their reputation among their peers. While some lenience may be allowed, peer pressure can provide a powerful force to ensure that the expert's opinions are both consistent over time and not too far out of line from what the profession could credibly believe to be that expert's true position. The deterrent capability of peer-group sanctions, however, depends on the human capital at risk on the stand: while a winner of the Nobel Prize in economics may not be wiser or purer than the average expert, his credibility on the stand is enhanced by the reasonable belief that, with so much to lose, it would be irrational for him deliberately to deceive a jury if it was likely that this could be detected by his peers.

19. *Continental T.V.* v. *GTE Sylvania,* 433 U.S. 36 (1977).

20. See *Spray-Rite Service Corp.* v. *Monsanto Co.,* 684 F. 2d. 1226 (1982). The Court of Appeals did, however, decide that the jury had gone too far in awarding Spray-Rite $3,500,000 when Spray-Rite's expert had testified that Spray-Rite's damages were only $3,327,588. The Court agreed with Monsanto that $172,412 of the verdict was excessive and offered Spray-Rite a choice between accepting a remittitur of $172,412 or having the case remanded for a new trial on the question of the amount of damages. Spray-Rite chose the $3,327,588.

21. 684 F. 2d 1226, 1238 (1982). One paragraph later in the decision the court rephrased the word "following" to "in response to," 684 F. 2d 1226, 1239 (1982).

22. *United States* v. *Sealy,* 388 U.S. 350 (1967).

23. 465 U.S. 752, 761, n. 6 (1984).

24. *Valley Liquor, Inc.* v. *Renfield Importers, Ltd.,* 678 F. 2d, 742, 744 (1982).

25. Although the courts have come close to concluding otherwise. Concerted action between a firm and one of its wholly owned subsidiaries was only recently ruled not to be an "agreement" that violated the Sherman Act. See *Copperweld Corp.* v. *Independence Tube Corp.,* 104 S.Ct. 2731 (1984).

26. Two inputs are gross complements if the elasticity of demand for the final product is greater than the elasticity of substitution between the two inputs. For a discussion of the conditions under which a merger or agreement between input suppliers, or the use of various practices by one input supplier to control other input suppliers, is in the interest of consumers of the final product or society as a whole, see Warren-Boulton (1978).

27. 465 U.S. 752, 764 (1984).

28. 465 U.S. 752, 765 (1984).

29. 465 U.S. 752, 762, n. 7 (1984).

30. 465 U.S. 752, 769 (1984).

31. "None of the funds appropriated ... may be used for any activity the purposes of which is to overturn or alter the *per se* prohibition against resale price maintenance in effect under Federal antitrust laws." Pub.

L. No. 98–166 (1983), sec. 510. This law was passed after the DOJ had submitted its written amicus brief but before the DOJ's oral argument before the Supreme Court in *Monsanto*. The reason for this hostility is unclear: An individual state's preference for making RPM per se illegal within its boundaries might perhaps be explained by the desire to free ride on other states (see Marvel and McCafferty 1986), but this cannot explain hostility at the federal level. Economists usually fall back on the proposition that the public is economically illiterate. But economists have been successful in eventually persuading the political process that what had previously been touted as beneficial was actually harmful—airline regulation is a recent example. Despite twenty years of proselytizing, the hidden features of RPM appear only to be discernible by the cognoscenti of the Chicago School. Even more difficult to explain is the continual per se ban on a manufacturer's setting *maximum* resale prices, a practice that is unambiguously beneficial both to consumers and society as a whole. One intriguing possibility is that the problem may be language—that the "sway of the price-fixing metaphor is too powerful to allow rational debate (see Boudin, 1986). If the per se treatment of RPM is ever changed, the pressure would be from the top down—by the fiat of a judiciary persuaded by intellectual argument, rather than as a response to some widespread public pressure through the political system.

32. Even if this scenario were factually correct, however, the difficulty of proof as compared with a *per se* standard, and the comparatively minor damages available under contract law even if Spray-Rite were successful, would argue for Spray-Rite's strategy of bringing such a contract claim as an antitrust complaint.

33. All indications are that corn and soybean herbicides are separate product markets. The standard measure of concentration is the Herfindahl-Hirshman Index, or HHI, which equals the sum of the squares of the individual market shares of all the firms in the market, a measure that reflects both the number of firms in the market and the dispersion of their market shares. The Department of Justice Merger Guidelines (1984) describes markets where the HHI is below 1000 as "unconcentrated," markets where the HHI is between 1000 and 1800 as "moderately concentrated," and markets where the HHI is above 1800 as "highly concentrated." Even using only the available market share data, the HHI was over 5125 in corn herbicides and over 2822 in soybean herbicides.

34. One Monsanto document reported that "Stauffer, DuPont, and Elanco have sold on a Fair Trade policy. Elanco [the division of Eli Lilly that produced Treflan] dropped Fair Trade in about 1968." (Monsanto's Corn/Soybean Product Area Business Plan 1970–1975. Plaintiff's Exhibit 13a.) Of these three, only Treflan accounted for a sizable market share.

35. The HHI fell from over 5125 to over 3488 in corn herbicides, and from over 2822 to over 1886 in soybean herbicides.

36. See Monsanto's Corn/Soybean Product Area Business Plan 1970–1975, Plaintiff Exhibit 139.

37. For a review of that literature, see Warren-Boulton, (1978).

38. See Vernon and Graham (1971), Schmalensee (1973),

Warren-Boulton (1974; 1977; 1978), Mallela and Nahato (1980), and Westfield (1981).

39. 465 U.S. 752, 763, 764 (1984).

References

Becker, Gary S. "Crime and Punishment: An Economic Approach." *Journal of Political Economy* 76 (March/April 1968): 169–217.

Boudin, Michael. "Antitrust Doctrine and the Sway of Metaphor." *Georgetown Law Journal* 75 (December 1986): 395–422.

Comanor, William S. "Vertical Price-Fixing, Vertical Market Restrictions, and the New Antitrust Policy." *Harvard Law Review* 98 (March 1985): 983–1002.

Comanor, William S., and John B. Kirkwood. "Resale Price Maintenance and Antitrust Policy." *Contemporary Policy Issues* 3 (Spring 1985): 9–16.

Hay, George A. "An Economic Analysis of Vertical Integration." *Industrial Organization Review* 1 (1973): 188–198.

Joyce, Jon, and Robert H. McGuckin. "Assignment of Rights to Sue Under *Illinois Brick:* An Empirical Assessment." *Antitrust Bulletin* 31 (Spring 1986): 235–259.

Klein, Benjamin, and Keith Leffler. "Non-Governmental Enforcement of Contracts: The Role of Market Forces in Assuring Contractual Performance." *The Journal of Political Economy* 89 (August 1981): 615–641.

Klein, Benjamin, and Kevin M. Murphy. "The Economics of Resale Price Maintenance." UCLA Dept. of Economics Working Paper #332, July 1984, and *Journal of Law & Economics,* forthcoming.

Landes, William M., and Richard A. Posner. "Should Indirect Purchasers Have Standing to Sue Under the Antitrust Laws? An Economic Analysis of the Rule of *Illinois Brick.*" *University of Chicago Law Review* 46 (Spring 1979): 602–635.

Mallela, P., and B. Nahala. "Theory of Vertical Control with Variable Proportions." *Journal of Political Economy* 88 (October 1980): 1009–1025.

Scherer, F. M. "The Economics of Vertical Restraints." *Antitrust Law Journal* 52 (1983): 687–707.

Schmalensee, Richard. "A Note on the Theory of Vertical Integration." *Journal of Political Economy* 81 (March/April 1973): 442–449.

Snyder, Edward A. "Efficient Assignment of Rights to Sue for Antitrust Damages." *Journal of Law & Economics* 28 (May 1985): 469–482.

Telser, Lester G. "Why Should Manufacturers Want Fair Trade?" *Journal of Law & Economics* 3 (October 1960): 86–105.

Vernon, J. M., and D. A. Graham. "Profitability of Monopolization by Vertical Integration." *Journal of Political Economy* 79 (July/August 1971): 924–925.

Warren-Boulton, Frederick R. *Vertical Control of Markets: Business and Labor Practices.* Cambridge, Mass.: Ballinger, 1978.

_____. "Vertical Control with Variable Proportions." *Journal of Political Economy* 82 (August 1974): 783–802.

———. "Vertical Control by Labor Unions." *American Economic Review* 67 (June 1977): 309–322.

Werden, Gregory, and Marius Schwartz. "Illinois Brick and The Deterrence of Antitrust Violations." Department of Justice Economic Policy Office Working Paper, EPO83-10, July 1983.

Westfield, F. M. "Vertical Integration: Does Product Price Rise or Fall?" *American Economic Review* 71 (June 1981): 334–346.

White, Lawrence J. "Vertical Restraints in Antitrust Law: A Coherent Model." *Antitrust Bulletin* 26 (Summer 1981): 327–345.

———. "Resale Price Maintenance and the Problem of Marginal and Inframarginal Customers." *Contemporary Policy Issues* 3 (Spring 1985): 17–22.